Self-Inference Processes:
The Ontario Symposium, Volume 6

ONTARIO SYMPOSIUM ON PERSONALITY AND SOCIAL PSYCHOLOGY

E. T. HIGGINS, C. P. HERMAN, M. P. ZANNA, EDS.
Social Cognition: The Ontario Symposium, Volume 1

M. P. ZANNA, E. T. HIGGINS, C. P. HERMAN, EDS.
Consistency in Social Behavior: The Ontario Symposium, Volume 2

C. P. HERMAN, M. P. ZANNA, E. T. HIGGINS, EDS.
Physical Appearance, Stigma, and Social Behavior: The Ontario Symposium, Volume 3

J. M. OLSON, C. P. HERMAN, M. P. ZANNA, EDS.
Relative Deprivation and Social Comparison: The Ontario Symposium, Volume 4

M. P. ZANNA, J. M. OLSON, C. P. HERMAN, EDS.
Social Influence: The Ontario Symposium, Volume 5

J. M. OLSON, M. P. ZANNA, EDS.
Self-Inference Processes: The Ontario Symposium, Volume 6

SELF-INFERENCE PROCESSES:

The Ontario Symposium, Volume 6

Edited by

JAMES M. OLSON
University of Western Ontario

MARK P. ZANNA
University of Waterloo

LEA LAWRENCE ERLBAUM ASSOCIATES, PUBLISHERS
1990 Hillsdale, New Jersey   Hove and London

Lawrence Erlbaum Associates, Inc., Publishers
365 Broadway
Hillsdale, New Jersey 07642

Library of Congress Cataloging–in–Publication Data

Self–inference processes / edited by James M. Olson, Mark P. Zanna.
    p.   cm. — (Ontario symposium : v. 6)
    Revised papers presented at the Sixth Ontario Symposium on
Personality and Social Psychology, held at the University of Western
Ontario, June 4–5, 1988.
    Includes bibliographical references.
    ISBN 0-8058-0551-6
    1. Self-perception—Congresses. I. Olson, James M., 1953– .
II. Zanna, Mark P. III. Ontario Symposium on Personality and Social
Psychology (6th : 1988 : University of Western Ontario) IV. Series.
BF697.5.S43S44   1990
155.2—dc20   90-32629
                                                                    CIP

Printed in the United States of America
10   9   8   7   6   5   4   3   2   1

Contents

Preface

The Sixth Ontario Symposium on Personality and Social Psychology was held at the University of Western Ontario, June 4–5, 1988. The topic of the symposium was self-inference processes, and the presentations covered a wide variety of issues in this area. As has become the fortunate custom of the Ontario Symposium series, the conference generated many spirited discussions among participants, as well as many productive interchanges with audience members.

The current volume consists of the expanded versions of papers originally presented at the conference. The time lag between the conference and the book reflects that the authors were given the opportunity to revise their papers based, among other things, on feedback obtained at the conference. Contributors also provided comments on preliminary drafts of other participants' chapters—an undertaking for which we, as editors, are grateful.

The chapters in this volume are loosely organized in a sequence going from personal (Chapters 1 to 5) to interpersonal aspects of self-inference processes (Chapters 6 to 10) to alternative perspectives on self-inference (Chapters 11 and 12) and ending with a look ahead to future research (Chapter 13). Specifically, in Chapter 1, Sande addresses how people make inferences about their own personality traits. In Chapter 2, Olson considers the relevance of self-inference processes to the experience of emotion. In Chapter 3, Wilson describes his research showing that self-persuasion can result from analyzing the reasons for one's behavior. In Chapter 4, Jones identifies some of the conditions under which changes in self-concept can occur following externally-induced behavior. In Chapter 5, Polivy, Herman, and Pliner review the literature on self-perceptions of body image. In Chapter 6, Turnbull, Miller, and McFarland discuss the relation between the frequency of an attribute in a population and the centrality of that attribute in individuals' self-images. In Chapter 7, Ross and Holmberg propose that gender differences may exist in memory for information about relationships. In Chapter 8, Higgins, Tykocinski, and Vookles discuss the role of social interactions in the development of self-guides and describe the consequences of discrepancies between these self-guides and the actual self. In Chapter 9, McCann identifies some of the interpersonal effects of the self-concept and self-inference processes. In Chapter 10, Lepper, Aspinwall, Mumme, and Chabay describe techniques used by expert tutors to produce desired self-inferences in students. In Chapter 11, Sorrentino and Roney address individual differences in the self-inference process. In Chapter 12, Baumeister considers some of the conditions under which self-awareness and self-inference will be avoided. Finally, in Chapter 13, Olson and Hafer review past contributions to the study of self-inferences and identify some emerging trends in the area.

We believe that these chapters illustrate both the diversity and vitality of research on self-inference processes. Our hope is that the volume will create a more readily identifiable self-inference "literature" (self-inferences have traditionally been a component of several, distinct research areas) and will stimulate additional research on this topic.

Five previous Ontario Symposia on Personality and Social Psychology have been held. The series is designed to bring together scholars from across North America who work in the same substantive area, with the goals of identifying common concerns and integrating research findings. Participation by Canadian faculty and graduate students in the conferences has been gratifying. We hope that the symposia have contributed to (and will continue to stimulate) the growth of personality and social psychology in Ontario and Canada. The first Ontario Symposium, held at the University of Western Ontario in August 1978, dealt with social cognition (see Higgins, E. T., Herman, C. P., and Zanna, M. P. (Eds.) (1981). *Social cognition: The Ontario Symposium*. Vol. 1. Hillsdale, NJ: Lawrence Erlbaum Associates); the second, held at the University of Waterloo in October 1979, had the theme of variability and consistency in social behavior (see Zanna, M. P., Higgins, E. T., and Herman, C. P. (Eds.) (1982). *Consistency in social behavior: The Ontario Symposium*. Vol. 2. Hillsdale, NJ: Lawrence Erlbaum Associates); the third, held at the University of Toronto in May 1981, addressed the social psychology of physical appearance (see Herman, C. P., Zanna, M. P., and Higgins, E. T. (Eds.) (1985). *Physical appearance, stigma, and social behavior: The Ontario Symposium*. Vol. 3. Hillsdale, NJ: Lawrence Erlbaum Associates); the fourth, held at the University of Western Ontario in October 1983, was concerned with relative deprivation and social comparison processes (see Olson, J. M., Herman, C. P., and Zanna, M. P. (Eds.) (1986). *Relative deprivation and social comparison: The Ontario Symposium*. Vol. 4. Hillsdale, NJ: Lawrence Erlbaum Associates); and the fifth, held at the University of Waterloo in August 1984, dealt with social influence (see Zanna, M. P., Olson, J. M., and Herman, C. P. (Eds.) (1987). *Social influence: The Ontario Symposium*. Vol. 5. Hillsdale, NJ: Lawrence Erlbaum Associates).

Once again, primary financial support for the Sixth Ontario Symposium was provided by the Social Sciences and Humanities Research Council of Canada, whose continuing support has been the backbone of the series. We are also deeply indebted to the Department of Psychology and the Faculty of Social Science of the University of Western Ontario for their financial and administrative support of the symposium. We are also grateful to Carolyn L. Hafer for helping to coordinate the conference, which was attended by approximately 75 persons from more than 20 universities. Finally, Mary Olson and Betsy Zanna provided assistance during the conference and encouragement throughout the project.

James M. Olson
Mark P. Zanna

1 The Multifaceted Self

Gerald N. Sande
University of Manitoba, Winnipeg, Canada

INTRODUCTION

The research program described in this chapter investigated the manner in which people attribute traits to themselves and to others. More specifically, it examined the notion that people see themselves as being multifaceted, as possessing a rich and varied set of personal characteristics. Furthermore, it tested the proposition that people would see themselves as being more multifaceted than others, as possessing *more* traits than other people possess.

Jones and Nisbett's (1971) chapter on actor–observer differences in attributions offered a different hypothesis about self and social trait inferences. Their analyses of Heider's (1958) writings led them to propose that actors will tend to attribute their own behavior to external or situational causes, whereas observers will attribute the actor's behavior to internal or dispositional causes. Jones and Nisbett argued that one of the consequences of this actor–observer effect is that "each individual may view every other individual as possessing more personality traits than he himself possesses" (p. 160).

One of the rationales Jones and Nisbett (1971) offered for their hypothesis pertains to differences in the kinds of information that are available to people about their own and others' traits. First, people have greater exposure to the variability of their own past conduct than they have to the behavior of others. According to Jones and Nisbett, knowledge of behavioral variability leads to the conclusion that one's own behavior is responsive to and caused by the demands of the circumstances one has faced. Thus, "The actor's knowledge about the variability of his previous conduct—associated, in his mind, with different situational requirements—often preempts the possibility of a dispositional attribution" (p. 85). According to this argument, because we have not witnessed as great a range of others' actions, we are more likely to attribute their behavior to stable, underlying dispositions.

The second actor–observer informational discrepancy involves differences in the availability of evidence about internal states such as motives, intentions, and emotions. For example, an actor who insults someone may be aware that he or she did not mean to be insulting, intending instead to be taken in jest. Or the actor may see the insult as a result of the frustration at the behavior of the target of the insult. Because of this "internal" evidence, the actor would be unwilling to make a dispositional inference for his or her behavior (to see himself or herself as an "insulting" or sarcastic person). The observer of the insult, on the other hand, has only the overt behavior on which to base his or her attributions, and is more likely to infer that the actor possesses a trait which corresponds to the action.

Jones and Nisbett (1971) also discussed motivational rationales for their hypothesis that people will ascribe more traits to others than to themselves. Following Brehm (1966), among those discussed is the desire to perceive oneself as being free from the constraints of one's environment. According to Jones and Nisbett, "the perception of freedom is probably best maintained by simultaneously ascribing traits to others and denying them in oneself" (p. 92).

Support for the notion that people believe "personality traits are things other people have" (Jones & Nisbett, 1971, p. 92) was obtained in a subsequent experiment in which subjects were asked to attribute traits to themselves and an acquaintance (Nisbett, Caputo, Legant, & Maracek, 1973). Subjects in that experiment were given a list of 20 bipolar trait pairs and asked to indicate which trait was more descriptive of themselves. They were also given the option of choosing "depends on the situation" instead of choosing one of the traits:

serious	gay	depends on the situation
lenient	firm	depends on the situation
intense	calm	depends on the situation

On a separate sheet they described an acquaintance using the same scale. The results were that subjects checked one of the two trait adjectives more often when describing the acquaintance than when describing themselves, but chose the "depends on the situation" option more often when describing themselves than when describing the acquaintance. Those results were interpreted as supporting the hypothesis that people see themselves as possessing fewer traits than others.

The Multifaceted Self Interpretation

The purpose of this chapter is to offer a different interpretation of those results, to present three experiments that support this new perspective, and to integrate these findings with the arguments made by Jones and Nisbett. We begin with the suggestion that people perceive themselves as having a rich and multifaceted nature that allows them to act flexibility and adaptively in various situations. This is consistent with Jones and Nisbett's suggestion that people view themselves, "as acting in accord with the demands and opportunities inherent in each new situation" (p. 92), and this proposition is supported by the finding that people indicate that their own behavior depends on the situation. However, the proposal being advanced here is that people believe they have the capacity to respond adaptively to the requirements of different circumstances, not because they have few or no traits, but because they have many traits. Possessing many personality traits gives people, so to speak, many arrows in their behavioral quivers. People believe that they possess an extensive array of traits that allows them to show whatever aspect of themselves is appropriate to the situation. For example, whether I am energetic or relaxed depends on the situation because I am *both* energetic *and* relaxed. The requirements of the situation will determine which of those seemingly opposite traits is activated to guide my behavior.

According to this view then, when the subjects in the Nisbett et al. (1973) experiment circled the "depends on the situation" option to describe themselves, they may have been indicating that they believed they possessed both traits in the pair and not indicating that they possessed neither of the traits. This interpretation echoes a point made by Monson, Tanke, and Lund (1980). They also suggested that, given the opportunity, subjects would attribute more traits to themselves than to others. They presented to subjects a revised version of the Nisbett et al. (1973) measure which simply contained all 40 of the traits, randomly ordered and without the "depends on the situation" options. Subjects were asked to check off the traits that were self-descriptive, and descriptive of an acquaintance. Using this revised procedure, Monson et al. found that subjects attributed more traits to themselves than to their acquaintances.

Consistent with this new view of the inference process, not only do individuals attribute more traits to themselves than to others, they may also attribute apparently contradictory or polar opposite traits to themselves. For example, I might see myself as possessing both the traits of realism and idealism, as being both sociable and aloof, both energetic and relaxed. However, I would see other people as possessing one of those traits but not its opposite. Monson et al. (1980) found that, out of 20 opportunities, subjects checked off both traits of opposite trait pairs significantly more often when describing themselves than when describing their acquaintances (3.5 times vs. 2.6 times).

When we propose that people attribute many traits to themselves, and especially when we suggest that people see themselves as possessing some degree of opposite traits, we are also suggesting that lay persons think about traits differently than do most psychologists. Allport and Odbert (1936) defined traits as "consistent and stable modes of an individual's adjustment to his environment" (p. 26). In theory, possession of a trait leads to behavior that is stable over time and across situations. Thus, if a person possesses the trait of sociability, he or she should act in a relatively sociable manner in different situations and at different times. Behaving in an unsociable or aloof manner constitutes evidence that this person does not possess the trait of sociability, or at least is less sociable than he or she might be. According to that view, polar opposite traits are mutually exclusive. One can be sociable or aloof, but not both.

It has been suggested by some previous theorists that laypersons hold a similar view of traits, and perhaps an even more extreme view, namely, that possession of a trait is a virtual guarantee that it will be manifested in a person's behavior regardless of the circumstances (cf. Ross, 1977; Allen & Potkay, 1981). If one possesses the trait of sociability, one will always behave in a sociable manner because the trait overrides the constraints of the situation.

If people do, in fact, hold such a view of traits and their operation in causing behavior, then Jones and Nisbett are correct in arguing first, that exposure to variance in one's behavior will lead to the conclusion that the actor possesses few personality traits, and second, that individuals best maintain a perception of the self as being free and in control by ascribing few traits to themselves.

We suggest that laypersons have a different view. They may perceive traits, at least their own, as much less automatic in nature. They may view traits as behavioral potentials, or "determining tendencies" in the words of Allport and Odbert. Any particular trait that one possesses may or may not be shown in any given situation. For example, I may possess the trait of sociability, but I may not always act in a sociable manner. The nature of particular situations evokes or activates my trait of sociability, and I will then behave in a sociable manner. According to this view, having one trait does not preclude also possessing a trait that is quite the opposite. In some situations one's sociability may show through, in others one's aloofness may be elicited by the situation.

There is some support for the notion that laypersons may think of traits in less rigid terms than psychologists sometimes assume they do. Researchers have reported that people describe themselves with different traits on different occasions. Allen and Potkay (1973, 1977) asked university students to describe themselves each day for up to 47 days, and found that students used different trait words in making their self-descriptions on different days. Other evidence suggests that people do not view many traits as being highly stable. Greenberg, Saxe, and Bar–Tal (1978) asked subjects to rate the stability of 115 traits on a 7-point scale on which high numbers signified greater stability. Stability indexes ranged from a low of 1.59 to a high of 6.40 (the mean stability rating was 4.19, the median 4.17).

If laypersons do subscribe to the belief that personality traits are potentials that are evoked by situational characteristics, then one might come to conclusions about self and social trait inferences that are quite different from those reached by Jones and Nisbett. First, exposure to greater range or variability in one's conduct might lead to the conclusion that the actor possesses more, not fewer traits. As Jones and Nisbett point out, one is most familiar with one's own behavioral history; thus one would attribute more traits to oneself than to others.

For example, when I review my past conduct I may find that I have behaved cooperatively when, as Jones and Nisbett suggest, the situation made that behavior appropriate. I would also find that I have revealed my competitive streak when circumstances have made competitive behavior appropriate (or at least permissible). In both cases my behavior provides evidence that I possess a trait that corresponds to my actions. I may still report a situational cause for a specific action, in the sense that the demands of the situation determined which of my traits, cooperativeness or competitiveness, was evoked to guide my behavior. Thus, making correspondent trait inferences is not necessarily incompatible with making situational attributions for specific behaviors. Nevertheless, knowledge of behavioral variability can lead to the conclusion that the actor possesses more, not fewer traits, and that the actor possesses traits that seem to be polar opposites.

Where Jones and Nisbett (1971) suggest that knowledge about one's own internal states decreases the probability that one will ascribe traits to oneself, the new perspective put forth in this chapter proposes the opposite. For example, as I decide how to act in a new situation, I may be aware that more than one aspect of my nature is pushing to be expressed. I might have to suppress my competitive nature and cooperate with others if circumstances require. On the other hand, I might have to rouse my competitiveness and "get into the game." Still, these inner conflicts yield evidence that I possess both the traits of cooperativeness and competitiveness.

The third difference between this new perspective and that advanced by Jones and Nisbett concerns the motive for people to see themselves as enjoying freedom from and control over situational constraints. Jones and Nisbett stated that, "the individual would lose the sense of freedom to the extent that he acknowledged powerful dispositions in himself, traits that *imperiously* cause him to behave consistently across situations" (p. 92) [emphasis added]. If, however, people believe that traits operate in less than an "imperious" manner, their perceptions of freedom and control would be enhanced by attributing *more* rather than fewer traits to themselves. The perception that one has many traits and, in particular, many "opposite" traits, implies that one possesses a wide array of personal resources with which to respond to situational requirements. One is less subject to the whims of circumstance if one possesses a richness and depth of personality that allows one to respond adaptively in many different situations.

To recapitulate, the argument advanced here is that people believe they have more personality traits than others possess. This perception arises from both informational causes (greater knowledge of their own than others' behavioral histories, and greater awareness of internal thoughts and feelings) and motivational causes (a desire to see themselves as able to adapt to and control their environment). Furthermore, empirical results that have been interpreted as evidence that people ascribe fewer traits to themselves than to others may actually be consistent with the opposite proposition. The three experiments to be presented next test the basic notions advanced in this introduction and examine cognitive and motivational explanations for the tendency of people to see themselves as more multifaceted than others.[1]

EXPERIMENT 1

This experiment was designed to test the hypothesis that people would ascribe more traits to themselves than to others. It directly tested the prediction that people often perceive themselves as possessing both traits in polar opposite trait pairs, whereas they are likely to believe that other people possess one of the traits but not its opposite.

This experiment also tested another, related proposition. As has been stated, the perception that you possess a richer and more complex personality than others implies that you have more behavioral options on which to draw in any given situation. If subjects are asked, in general terms, to predict how they might behave in some future situation, they ought to see their own behavior as less predictable than the behavior of others. For example, if you see yourself as both sociable and aloof, it is difficult for you to predict whether you will act in a sociable or aloof manner without knowing the details of that future circumstance. On the other hand, if you believe that another person is either sociable or aloof, but not both, you can more readily predict his or her behavior, even without knowing the details of the situation. Hence, since you see yourself as possessing more behavioral flexibility than others, you will view your own behavior as less predictable than the behavior of others.

Method

Subjects were 20 male and 20 female students at Williams College. They were told that the experiment studied how people describe their acquaintances and themselves using common personality traits. In a variation of the Nisbett et al. (1973) procedure, subjects were presented with 11 pairs of trait adjectives and asked to indicate whether they would describe themselves as having the first trait, the second trait, both traits, or neither trait:

serious	carefree	both	neither
lenient	firm	both	neither
intense	calm	both	neither

---

[1]This research was conducted in collaboration with George R. Goethals and Christine E. Radloff from Williams College.

On a separate page, subjects described an acquaintance, using the same scale. When describing the acquaintance they were asked to call to mind "a specific person of the same sex, that you know fairly well but who is not a close friend, that is, someone who is more of an acquaintance than a friend." The order in which they described themselves and the acquaintance was counterbalanced.

In addition, subjects were asked to indicate the probability that their behavior, in an unspecified "typical" situation, would be characterized by each of the traits. For example, the first question asked, "In a typical situation how likely is it that you would act in a serious manner?" Subjects responded with percentage estimates (from 0% to 100%). They then indicated the probability that they would act in a carefree manner. Subjects also predicted the behavior of the acquaintance using the same kind of measure.

Results

Trait Scales

Analyses compared the number of times subjects circled the "both" and "neither" options for self and acquaintance (totaled across the 11 trait pairs). They circled "both" significantly more often for self ($M = 5.70$) than for acquaintance ($M = 3.93$), $F(1,36) = 17.95, p < .01$. They circled "neither" less often for self ($M = 0.03$) than for acquaintance ($M = 0.33$), $F(1,36) = 5.49$, $p < .03$.[2]

Probability Ratings

The difference between the two probability ratings for each trait pair was calculated, for example, the probability of acting in a serious manner minus the probability of acting in a carefree manner. The smaller the difference (the closer the two probabilities are to 50/50), the less predictable behavior is perceived to be.[3]

Probability differences, averaged across the 11 trait pairs, were significantly smaller for self ($M = 38.38$) than for the acquaintance ($M = 43.48$), $F(1,28) = 9.11, p < .01$. That is, subjects perceived their own behavior as less predictable than the behavior of the acquaintance.

Additional analyses examined another key hypothesis, namely that percep-

---

[2]The total number of traits attributed to a target is a constant (in this case 11), plus the number of "both" responses, minus the number of "neither" responses. The analyses of the total number of traits parallels, in all cases, those of the "both" responses.

[3]Eight subjects were excluded from the analyses of the probability ratings, two because they did not complete all of the scales and six because their average probability totals, across pairs, exceeded 100%. No subject's ratings totaled less than 100%.

tions of richness and depth in personality (as reflected in possession of "opposite" traits) are linked to flexibility or unpredictability in behavior. For example, if subjects indicate that they are both serious and carefree, will they see their behavior as less predictable than if they indicate that they are either serious or carefree, but not both? Probability estimates for trait pairs on which the subjects had circled the "both" option were contrasted to estimates corresponding to pairs on which the subject had circled one trait or the other.

The hypothesis was confirmed. When subjects circled the "both" option their behavior related to that trait dimension was perceived to be significantly less predictable ($M = 19.22$) than when they circled one of the traits ($M = 57.21$), $F(1,28) = 211.6, p < .01$. This confirms that, in the minds of our subjects, the possession of these apparently "opposite" traits is associated with greater behavioral flexibility.

Summary

Subjects indicated that, compared with an acquaintance, they more frequently possessed both traits in polar opposite trait pairs. Subjects also indicated that they perceived their own behavior to be less predictable than the behavior of the acquaintance (when the details of the future circumstance were not specified). In addition, decreased predictability in behavior was related to the possession of polar opposite traits. These results are consistent with the proposition that subjects in the Nisbett et al. (1973) experiment chose the "depends on the situation" option as a way of indicating that they believed they more often possessed both traits in a pair. They are also consistent with the notion that behavioral variability and the possession of personality traits are positively related.

EXPERIMENT 2

This experiment used the same basic procedure as the first in order to replicate the finding that people would attribute more traits, and more opposite traits to themselves than to others. It also tested two explanations for this effect.

It is possible that the results of the first experiment occurred because subjects, motivated by a desire to maintain a positive self-image, attributed more desirable traits to themselves than to others. That is, those subjects might have chosen the "both" option when describing themselves for the more desirable trait pairs but not for the less desirable trait pairs. To test this notion, after attributing traits to themselves and an acquaintance, subjects in this second experiment rated the social desirability of the traits. The results for trait pairs above and below the median on social desirability were contrasted to test if subjects described themselves as possessing both of the traits more frequently for desirable trait pairs than for less desirable trait pairs.

The second explanation examined in this experiment is a variation of one of the cognitive explanations that Jones and Nisbett (1971) advanced. They pointed out that the actor has unique access to his or her own internal thoughts, feelings, and emotions, and that this knowledge might influence trait ascription. This experiment examined the impact of trait visibility. Visibility refers to the fact that some traits are more easily inferred from observable behavior than are others (Andersen & Ross, 1984; Miller & McFarland, 1987). For example, it might be easier to observe if someone is talkative or clumsy than if they are sensitive or idealistic. When I make inferences about other people's traits I am usually limited to observable evidence (that is, from watching their behavior). It might be difficult to find evidence that someone is sensitive or idealistic. On the other hand, when I make inferences about my own traits, I have more sources of evidence. I can infer traits from my own behavior and, in addition, I have access to my private thoughts and feelings. For example, I may know from these internal sources of evidence that I am sensitive or idealistic, even though I may not often show that to others. Miller and McFarland (1987) found that people sometimes attribute more of these less "visible" traits to themselves than to others. This finding might help to account for the finding that subjects in Experiment 1 attributed more traits and more opposite traits to themselves than to an acquaintance.

To test this possibility, subjects in this experiment were asked to rate how "visible" each trait was (where high visibility characterized a trait that was reflected by observable behavior, and low visibility characterized traits that might not be as observable). The ascription of trait pairs above and below the median on visibility was compared to discover if subjects attributed more of the less visible trait pairs to themselves than to others.

Method

Subjects were 43 students in two separate classes at the University of Saskatchewan. They described themselves and a same-sex acquaintance on the same kind of trait attribution scales used in Experiment 1. Again the order in which subjects described themselves and the acquaintance was counterbalanced. Subjects' sex was not recorded. In this case, all 20 of the trait pairs from the original Nisbett et al. experiment were used (with the exception that serious/gay was again changed to serious/carefree). After completing the trait ascription measures, subjects rated the social desirability and the visibility of each of the traits, and from these ratings the desirability and visibility of each trait pair were calculated.

Results

As in the first experiment, subjects attributed both traits in a pair to themselves ($M = 7.12$) more often than to the acquaintance ($M = 4.60$), $F(1,39) = 20.35, p < .01$. They described themselves as having neither trait ($M = 2.07$) slightly but not significantly less often than the acquaintance ($M = 2.70$), $F(1,39) = 2.51, p = .12$.

As we have described, the social desirability of the trait pairs was calculated and a median split was used to divide the pairs into highly desirable and less desirable trait pairs. Subjects circled the "both" option significantly more often when describing themselves than when describing their acquaintances for the more desirable trait pairs (3.72 vs. 2.51), $t(39) = 5.21, p < .01$. They also chose the "both" option more often for themselves than for their acquaintances for the less desirable trait pairs (3.40 vs. 2.09) $t(39) = 3.13, p < .01$. In the case of the "neither" responses, for the more desirable trait pairs, subjects chose this option equally often when describing themselves and their acquaintances (both $Ms = 0.91$). For the less desirable traits, subjects chose this option less often when describing themselves than when describing their acquaintances (1.16 vs. 1.79), $t(39) = 2.16, p < .05$. That is, subjects were more willing to ascribe one of these less desirable traits to themselves than to their acquaintances.[4]

Subjects' attributions of trait pairs above and below the median on visibility were compared. Subjects chose the "both" option more often when describing themselves than their acquaintances for high-visibility trait pairs (3.72 vs. 2.23), $t(39) = 5.02, p < .01$. They also chose the "both" option more often for themselves than for their acquaintances for the low-visibility pairs (3.47 vs. 2.37), $t(39) = 3.26, p < .01$. Their choice of the "neither" option to describe themselves and their acquaintances was not significantly different for either the high- or low-visibility trait pairs.

Summary

These results replicated the effect found in Experiment 1, namely that subjects assigned more traits and more "opposite" traits to themselves than to their acquaintances. The tendency to attribute more traits to oneself than to another person was not limited to only highly desirable traits. This result parallels the finding by Nisbett et al. (1973) that subjects' choice of the "depends on the situation" was not affected by the desirability of the traits.

It should be noted at this point that the trait list used in this experiment (and used by Nisbett et al.) did not include highly undesirable traits. Other research (for example, that conducted by Brown, 1986) has shown that subjects are more willing to assign traits such as "rude" and "cruel" to "most other people" than

---

[4]We also compared (a) self and other ratings on those trait pairs in which the traits differed in desirability with (b) ratings on those pairs in which the traits were less discrepant. Because we included no highly undesirable traits, in general, the traits within pairs were not markedly discrepant. Trait pairs were divided into high- and low-discrepancy pairs (*Median* = 1). Subjects chose the "both" option significantly more often for self than for the acquaintance for high discrepancy pairs (3.02 vs. 2.11) and for low-discrepancy pairs (4.16 vs. 2.49).

to themselves. With that limitation noted, the social desirability of these particular traits cannot account for the tendency to see oneself as more multifaceted than others. Finally, the visibility of traits had no effect on the tendency for subjects to attribute more traits and more opposite traits to themselves than to their acquaintances.

EXPERIMENT 3

This final experiment expanded on the same basic procedure in order to test two explanations that we thought might account for the finding that subjects in Experiments 1 and 2 perceived themselves as more multifaceted than others.

The first explanation is a variation on the social desirability theme. Perhaps attributing many traits to oneself reflects a positive, flattering view of the self, and because we do not view others as positively as ourselves, we attribute fewer traits to them. One might have expected that a more positive view of the self than of others would lead to attributing more desirable traits to oneself, and less desirable traits to others. The results of Experiment 2 show that this did not happen. This experiment tested the proposition that a positive view of the self leads to the conclusion that one has *more* traits than others, not that one has better traits than others. This is consistent with the premise that attributing more traits to ourselves implies the very positive perception that we have more richness and depth of personality, and that this allows us to react to situations in a versatile and appropriate manner.

By extension, this explanation would predict that the more positive a view one has of any individual (or the better one likes that individual), the more traits one will attribute to him or her. In this experiment subjects described themselves on the trait measure, and they also described targets they liked and targets they disliked. It was expected that they would choose the "both" option more for liked than disliked targets, and the "neither" option less often for liked than for disliked targets.

The second explanation that was examined in this experiment is that the more familiar one is with an individual the more traits one will attribute to that person. Some evidence already exists to support this proposition. Monson et al. (1980) found a positive correlation between the number of traits assigned to a target and the length of time the subject had known that target. Jones and Nisbett (1971) proposed the opposite relation—that the better one knows an individual the fewer traits one would attribute to him or her. Nisbett et al. (1973) reported a follow-up study in which they found a negative correlation between the length of time subjects had known a friend and the tendency to ascribe more traits to that friend than to themselves. That is, the longer they had known the friend, the more often they chose the "depends on the situation" option when describing that friend. This finding was interpreted as supporting the proposition that greater familiarity is associated with the attribution of fewer traits. On the other hand, if in choosing the "depends on the situation" option subjects were indicating that they possessed both traits in the pair, the Nisbett et al. finding is consistent with the proposition that greater familiarity with an individual will lead to attributing more traits to him or her.

In this final experiment, the role of familiarity with the target was examined by comparing subjects' descriptions of people they knew well (that is, people they had known a long time) and people who were just acquaintances (people they had known for only a few months).

Method

Subjects were 23 male and 28 female students at the University of Saskatchewan. They used a trait ascription measure containing 20 trait pairs in the same format as the measure used in the first two experiments (serious/carefree/both/neither). The tests of the liking and familiarity explanations were combined by asking subjects to describe five targets: themselves, a liked well-known other, a disliked well-known other, a liked acquaintance, and a disliked acquaintance. After describing themselves and the four other individuals, they also rated the social desirability and visibility of each trait.

Results

A significant effect of target on attribution of "both" traits occurred because subjects chose that option more frequently for self and the two liked targets than for the two disliked targets, $F(4,156) = 30.15$, $p < .01$, (see Table 1.1). Contrasts were performed using the Newman–Keuls procedure (Winer, 1971, pp. 270–271). Subjects also chose the "neither" option less frequently for self and the two liked targets than for the two disliked targets, $F(4,156) = 20.61$, $p < .01$.

If we consider only targets other than the self, these data can be organized into a 2 × 2 (liking × familiarity) factorial design. There was a significant main effect for liking on assignment of both traits, with the liked targets being described with the "both" option more often than disliked targets, $F(1,39) = 32.25$, $p < .01$. There was also a significant main effect for familiarity, with well-known others being described with the "both" option more than acquaintances, $F(1,39) = 9.60$, $p < .01$. The interaction between familiarity and liking was also significant, $F(1,39) = 14.94$, $p < .01$. Familiarity had no effect on the description of disliked targets, but liked well-known others were described with the "both" option more than liked acquaintances.

It should be noted that manipulation checks showed that liking and familiarity were not independent. Specifically, liked well-known others were better liked

TABLE 1.1
Mean Frequency of "Both" and "Neither" Responses:
Experiment 3

| Response | Target | | | | |
	S	LWKO	LA	DWKO	DA
Both	7.08$_a$	6.22$_a$	4.18$_b$	2.31$_c$	2.55$_c$
Neither	1.25$_a$	1.59$_a$	1.78$_a$	3.63$_b$	3.67$_b$

Note: Within rows, means with different subscripts are signficantly different, $p < .01$. S = self; LWKO = liked well-known other; LA = liked acquaintance; DWKO = disliked well-known other; DA = disliked acquaintance.

From Sande, Goethals, and Radloff (1988). Perceiving one's own traits and others': The multifaceted self. *Journal of Personality and Social Psychology, 54*, No. 1. Copyright (1988). Reproduced by permission of the American Psychological Association.

than liked acquaintances. For this reason, an analysis of covariance was performed (looking at the familiarity effect while covarying out liking). It revealed that, even with liking covaried out, the liked well-known other was assigned more pairs of traits than the liked acquaintance.

The same kind of 2×2 analysis on the "neither" responses yielded only a main effect for the liking factor, with this option chosen less frequently for liked targets than for disliked targets.

As in Experiment 2, subjects rated the social desirability and visibility of all the traits so that the influence of these characteristics on the trait ascriptions could be determined. Once again the desirability and visibility of the trait pairs did not affect the results.

Summary

The results of this experiment reveal that both familiarity and liking affected the frequency with which traits were assigned to targets. The results of the Newman–Kuels tests suggest that the liking effect was the stronger of the two. Liking affected the "both" responses at both levels of familiarity (liked well-known others were assigned more traits than disliked well-known others; liked acquaintances were assigned more traits than disliked acquaintances). Familiarity affected responses for liked but not disliked targets (liked well-known others were assigned more traits than liked acquaintances). In addition, liking affected the "neither" responses but familiarity did not. Subjects ascribed about the same number of traits and opposite traits to themselves as to the liked well-known other.

GENERAL DISCUSSION

Taken together, the results of these three experiments lend strong support to the propositions that people not only attribute more traits to themselves than to others, but also perceive themselves as possessing traits that might ordinarily be considered to be opposites. The results of the third experiment suggest some ways in which these findings can be integrated with the theories set forward by Jones and Nisbett (1971) and with the research conducted by Nisbett et al. (1973).

First, these findings are not inconsistent with Jones and Nisbett's proposition that witnessing variability in an individual's actions will lead the observer to conclude that the actor's behavior is sensitive to and responsive to the situation. In addition, these findings are consistent with the idea that because they are most familiar with the variability in their own conduct, people will see their own behavior as most responsive to situational factors. However, these data seem incompatible with the hypothesis that this precludes the ascription of personality traits to the actor. Indeed, these data suggest that people believe they are able to respond to the requirements of various situations because they possess more traits than others.

This reconceptualization of the relation between knowledge of variability and the inferred possession of traits was supported by three findings. First, the consistent finding that subjects chose the "both" option more frequently when describing the self than when describing the acquaintance parallels the Nisbett et al. finding that subjects chose the "depends on the situation" option more often for self than for the acquaintance. Second, the results of Experiment 1 showed that the inferred possession of more opposing traits is associated with predictions of more variable behavior. Finally, just as subjects in the Nisbett et al. experiment perceived the behavior of more familiar others to be more responsive to the environment, subjects in Experiment 3 attributed more traits to people they had known a long time than to acquaintances.

In Experiment 3, the length of time subjects knew the target affected the attribution of traits to liked, but not disliked individuals. To the extent that one seeks to spend time with people whom one likes while avoiding those one dislikes, one should witness greater behavioral variability in the former group of individuals. In fact, one would be more familiar with the behavior of liked rather than disliked well-known others. In addition, we are probably more apt to interact with liked friends in a wider range of situations than liked acquaintances. Liked acquaintances are often people with whom we have some kind of role relationship within specific, well-defined situations. Liked well-known others are often those with whom we choose to interact in a variety of situations.[5] Thus,

---

[5]Thanks to Ned Jones for this suggestion.

these findings are consistent with the argument that the observation of behavioral variability leads to the ascription of a greater number of personality traits.

Although the results of the second experiment did not support the notion that the actor's privileged knowledge about less "visible" traits can account for the tendency for people to see themselves as possessing more traits than others, the familiarity effect in the third experiment is partly supportive of that explanation. Familiarity with an individual might also lead to internal evidence that he or she possesses a multifaceted nature. Ordinarily one would not have access to this evidence when making inferences about the traits of one's acquaintances. On the other hand, people I know well (and especially people I know well and like) might reveal those inner thoughts and feelings to me, making it more likely that I would ascribe more traits to them than to acquaintances.

The results of these experiments are also consistent with Jones and Nisbett's assertion that people see their own behavior as responsive to the situation partly in order to maintain a positive self-image. That notion is congruent with other lines of research that demonstrate self-serving attributional biases (cf. Fiske & Taylor, 1984; Ross & Fletcher, 1985). This research suggests, however, that the belief that one is less constrained by the situation than others is facilitated by the perception that one possesses more, not fewer traits than others. The finding that subjects consistently ascribed more traits to themselves than to others is congruent with the suggestion that people have more positive views of themselves than of others. So is the finding that subjects attributed more traits, and more opposite traits, to liked than to disliked others.

The parallels between the results of this research and those obtained by Nisbett et al. (1973) exemplify the principle that "the answer you get depends on the question you ask." The Nisbett et al. experiments solidly support Jones and Nisbett's hypotheses concerning the actor-observer effect and the tendency for individuals to see their own behavior as responsive to the situation. The present research indicates that the Nisbett et al. findings are also consistent with the notion that people believe that they are more multifaceted than others.

CONCLUSION

This chapter began with the hypothesis that people perceive themselves as being multifaceted, as possessing a wide array of personality traits that allow them to act flexibly and appropriately. It was proposed that, as a result of this view of the self, people would attribute more traits to themselves than to others, would see themselves as more often possessing traits that seem contradictory or opposite, and would view their own behavior as less predictable than others. The data from three experiments support these hypotheses. Traits are not simply things that other people have. Rather, the multifaceted self is richly appointed, well stocked, and prepared for action in a variety of situations.

ACKNOWLEDGMENT

I am grateful to Edward E. Jones, James Olson, and Mark Zanna for their insightful comments on an earlier version of this chapter. This research was conducted in collaboration with George R. Goethals and Christine E. Radloff from Williams College. It was funded by the Social Sciences and Humanities Research Council of Canada.

REFERENCES

Allen, B. P., & Potkay, C. R. (1973). Variability of self-description on a day-to-day basis: Longitudinal use of the adjective generation technique. *Journal of Personality, 41*, 638–652.

Allen, B. P., & Potkay, C. R. (1977). The relationship between AGT self-description and significant life events: A longitudinal study. *Journal of Personality, 45*, 207–219.

Allen, B. P., & Potkay, C. R. (1981). On the arbitrary distinction between states and traits. *Journal of Personality and Social Psychology, 41*, 916–928.

Allport, G. W., & Odbert, H. S. (1936). Trait-names: A psycholexical study. *Psychological Monographs, 47*(1, Whole No. 221).

Andersen, S., & Ross, L. (1984). Self-knowledge and social influence: 1. The impact of cognitive/affective and behavioral data. *Journal of Personality and Social Psychology, 46*, 280–293.

Brehm, J. (1966). *A theory of psychological reactance.* New York: Academic Press.

Brown, J. D. (1986). Evaluations of self and others: Self-enhancement biases in social judgments. *Social Cognition, 4*, 353–376.

Fiske, S., & Taylor, S. (1984). *Social cognition.* Reading, MA: Addison–Wesley.

Greenberg, M., Saxe, L., & Bar–Tal, D. (1978). Perceived stability of trait labels. *Personality and Social Psychology Bulletin, 4*, 59–62.

Heider, F. (1958). *The psychology of interpersonal relations.* New York: Wiley.

Jones, E. E., & Nisbett, R. (1971). The actor and the observer: Divergent perceptions of the causes of behavior. In E. E. Jones, D. Kanouse, H. Kelley, R. Nisbett, S. Valins, & B. Weiner (Eds.), *Attribution: Perceiving the causes of behavior* (pp. 79–94). Morristown, NJ: General Learning Press.

Miller, D. T., & McFarland, C. (1987). Pluralistic ignorance: When similarity is interpreted as dissimilarity. *Journal of Personality and Social Psychology, 2*, 298–305.

Monson, T., Tanke, E., & Lund, J. (1980). Determinants of social perception in a naturalistic setting. *Journal of Research in Personality, 14*, 104–120.

Nisbett, R., Caputo, C., Legant, P., & Maracek, J. (1973). Behavior as seen by the actor and as seen by the observer. *Journal of Personality and Social Psychology, 27*, 154–165.

Ross, L. (1977). The intuitive psychologist and his shortcomings: Distortion in the attribution process. In L. Berkowitz (Ed.), *Advances in experimental social psychology* (Vol. 10, pp. 173–220). New York: Academic Press.

Ross, M., & Fletcher, G. (1985). Attribution and social perception. In G. Lindzey & E. Aronson (Eds.), *Handbook of social psychology,* (3rd ed., Vol. 2, pp. 73–122). New York: Random House.

Sande, G., Goethals, G., & Radloff, C. (1988). Perceiving one's own traits and others': The multifaceted self. *Journal of Personality and Social Psychology, 54*(1).

Winer, B. (1971). *Statistical principles in experimental design* (2nd ed.). New York: McGraw–Hill.

2 Self-Inference Processes in Emotion

James M. Olson
University of Western Ontario

Attribution theorists propose that people have a natural interest in the causes of events and behaviors in their environment. Further, perceivers' causal judgments are presumed to follow systematic rules or principles and to have important consequences (such as influencing subsequent actions). The nature and effects of causal inference processes have been the focus of much research over the past 25 years (see Harvey & Weary, 1984; Olson & Ross, 1985; Ross & Fletcher, 1985).

One interesting hypothesis to emerge from the attribution literature has been the idea that individuals often use the same rules to infer the causes of their *own* behaviors as they use to infer the causes of *others'* actions (e.g., Bem, 1972; Kelley, 1967). In other words, self-inference processes often parallel social inference processes. This hypothesized similarity between self and social inference has intrigued researchers because phenomenological experience seems to contradict it. We rarely feel that deliberate, logical "inferences" are necessary to determine why we acted in a certain way—it seems as if we intuitively *know* the causes of our behaviors—whereas we do engage in deliberate analyses of the causes of others' actions. After all, most behavior is intentional, occurring for reasons of either personal desire or external demand. The "causes" of our own intended behaviors seem immediately obvious to us.

Yet, attribution theorists propose that self-inferences frequently occur in exactly the same way as social inferences. In support of this argument, researchers have obtained evidence that perceivers' judgments about the causes of their own behaviors can be altered by manipulations that implicate a causal factor which, in reality, probably played little role in the subjects' actions. For example, experiments on the "overjustification effect" have shown that giving someone an extrinsic reward for performing an enjoyable activity can reduce subsequent intrinsic interest in the activity (see Lepper, 1981; Lepper, Aspinwall, Mumme, & Chabay, Chapter 10, this volume; Lepper & Greene, 1978). Presumably, a salient reward leads subjects to infer that they did not perform the activity for intrinsic reasons. This self-inference phenomenon parallels findings in the social perception literature showing that perceivers see internal and external causes as inversely related—the more an external cause is implicated in a target's behavior, the less internal causes will be seen as important, and vice versa (e.g., Heider, 1958; Jones & Davis, 1965).

Thus, we often make inferences about the causes of our own behaviors in much the same way as we make inferences about the causes of others' actions. But what about our *emotions* (rather than our behaviors)—do self-inference processes play a role in this domain as well? Emotions qualify as one of our most private experiences and "feel" like they reflect physiological, as opposed to cognitive, processes. Yet, here, too, social psychologists have proposed that self-inference processes are important. In fact, numerous researchers, including Schachter (1964), Bem (1972), Weiner (1985), and Higgins (1987), have formulated theories that assign a significant role to attributional, self-inference processes in the experience of emotion. Although these theories may not constitute comprehensive analyses of emotion (which would require the inclusion of many other elements, including physiological and behavioral factors), they provide a useful perspective on emotional phenomena. For example, they imply that emotions may be more malleable than is generally assumed.

In this chapter, I describe three of my own experiments that were designed to examine the role of self-inference processes in emotion. In each case, cognitive manipulations were employed that should alter subjects' emotions if self-inferences do occur as postulated in the above theories. The focal emotion in the experiments was either speech anxiety or humor. In the first section of the chapter, two experiments derived from Schachter's (1964) attributional theory of emotion are presented. In the second section, an experiment derived from Bem's (1972) self-perception theory is described. Although these studies examined different emotions and evolved from different theoretical orientations, they shared the goal of documenting the importance of self-inference processes.

SCHACHTER'S THEORY OF EMOTION

In the early 1960s, Schachter (1964; Schachter & Singer, 1962; Schachter & Wheeler, 1962) proposed a "two-component" theory of emotion. According to Schachter, the phenomenological experience of emotion requires both physiological arousal and cognitions that label the arousal as a particular emotion. Thus, emotions will occur only when arousal is attributed to an emotional state (anger, fear, etc.). Usually, of course, whatever environmental event causes the arousal will also provide a label, so the two stages will rarely be discrete. Nevertheless, if Schachter's theory is valid, there may be circumstances where the arousal and the label can be separated or where more than one label for the arousal is plausible; investigation of these circumstances may help us to understand how emotions occur.

Schachter's theory was important because it emphasized cognitive rather than physiological processes in emotion. Indeed, Schachter proposed that the nature of the physiological arousal underlying different emotions is similar and that the cognitions determine which emotion is experienced. In an early demonstration of this reasoning, Schachter and Singer (1962) injected subjects with epinephrine, an arousing drug, and placed them in environmental circumstances that implied particular emotions. When subjects did not expect the injection to produce arousal symptoms, they seemed responsive to the environmental cues, behaving as if they were experiencing the implied emotion.

In the 25 years since it was proposed, Schachter's theory of emotion has been the target of some cogent critiques. It seems clear that there are limitations to the theory and problems with some of the underlying assumptions (see Cotton, 1981; Reisenzein, 1983; Ross & Fletcher, 1985). For example, physiological arousal does not seem necessary for subjective emotional experience to occur (e.g., Valins, 1966); young infants apparently experience emotions before they possess the cognitive skills necessary for labeling (Leventhal, 1980); feedback from facial muscles seems capable of influencing emotional experience (e.g., Laird, 1974; Rutledge & Hupka, 1985); and unexplained arousal generally produces negative affect, rather than stimulating an unbiased search for labels as proposed by Schachter (e.g., Marshall & Zimbardo, 1979; Maslach, 1979). Thus, as stated earlier in this chapter, Schachter's theory does not constitute a comprehensive analysis of emotion.

Misattribution Research

Despite the limitations to Schachter's theory, the basic idea that attributions about the causes of arousal can influence emotions may be valid. Several lines of research seem to indicate that self-inferences, in the form of labels for arousal, are important. These studies have tested the premise (derived from Schachter's model) that if people can be induced to *mislabel* the cause of their arousal symptoms, then their emotionality will be affected. This phenomenon—inducing subjects to mislabel the cause of their symptoms—is known as "misattribution" and has been demonstrated in several forms.

For example, Schachter and Singer's (1962) study showed that arousal from a nonemotional source (epinephrine) could be misattributed to an emotional cause, thereby heightening emotion. Similarly, Zillman (1978) has shown that nonemotional residual arousal from exercise can be misattributed to anger, increasing this emotion.

A second form of misattribution consists of mislabeling arousal that is actually caused by one emotion as being the result of some other emotion. For example, Dutton and Aron (1974) obtained evidence suggesting that arousal caused by fear could heighten attraction to a member of the opposite sex.

Finally, there is a third type of misattribution, which has been the focus of my research. This type of misattribution involves the reduction of emotionality by inducing subjects to label arousal that is actually caused by emotion as being nonemotional in nature. If, as Schachter suggests, emotions occur only when arousal symptoms are labeled as emotion, then it should be possible to reduce subjects' emotionality by giving them a neutral, nonemotional explanation for their arousal. For example, if subjects are placed in a situation where they will experience emotional arousal (fear, anger, or whatever) but are also given an alternative, nonemotional label for their arousal (e.g., that the arousal is the side-effect of a drug they have been given), then they should experience less emotion than they would have experienced without the neutral label. Of course, this reasoning assumes that subjects believe the alternative explanation of their arousal symptoms.

In 1970, Storms and Nisbett published a misattribution experiment that employed insomniac subjects. The typical sequence of events for insomniacs when they go to bed seems to be that they expect to have trouble falling asleep, lie awake thinking about their insomnia, begin to experience arousal symptoms such as a pounding heart, and become more and more anxious about their problem. In other words, a vicious cycle occurs, with symptoms of insomnia eliciting anxiety that exacerbates the insomnia. Storms and Nisbett gave subjects a pill to take before bedtime. The pill was actually a placebo. But some subjects were told that the pill would have the side-effect of making them feel aroused—their heart would pound, their mind would race, and so on. Paradoxically, but as predicted by a misattribution analysis, these subjects reported falling asleep faster than usual on the nights they took the allegedly arousing pills. Presumably, subjects misattributed arousal symptoms to the pill that were actually caused by insomnia and therefore felt less anxious.

A second group of subjects was given placebo pills and told that the pills would relax them. These subjects reported taking longer than usual to fall asleep on the nights they took the pills. Presumably, these subjects reasoned that since they were continuing to experience arousal symptoms despite having taken a relaxing drug, they must suffer from severe insomnia. In other words, symptoms of insomnia were even more disturbing than usual to these subjects.

Storms and Nisbett's experiment suggests that neutral labels for arousal have the potential to reduce emotion, as predicted by Schachter's (1964) theory. Unfortunately, these findings have proven difficult to replicate; at least two published studies with insomniacs have yielded either null effects or differences in the opposite direction of Storms and Nisbett's results (Bootzin, Herman, & Nicassio, 1976; Kellogg & Baron, 1975). Other emotional states have also yielded disappointing results in misattribution experiments. For example, three published experiments have failed to find that a misattribution manipulation reduced speech anxiety (Cotton, Baron, & Borkovec, 1980; Singerman, Borkovec, & Baron, 1976; Slivken & Buss, 1984). These negative results have led some researchers to question whether neutral labels can ameliorate emotion (see Cotton, 1981; Reisenzein, 1983).

Expectancy-attribution Model

In response to the inconsistent results in misattribution experiments, Michael Ross and I (Ross & Olson, 1981) proposed an expectancy-attribution model of the effects of placebos, which identified several interrelated preconditions for misattribution. We suggested that subjects will misattribute emotional symptoms to an erroneous source only when (1) the actual cause of arousal is not obvious, (2) the misattribution source is salient, (3) subjects consider the misattribution source to be a plausible cause of their arousal (e.g., the onset of the arousal is contiguous with the presentation of the misattribution source), and (4) subjects believe that the misattribution source is having more impact on their symptoms than is actually the case (i.e., the attributed impact exceeds any real effect of the placebo on subjects' symptoms). This last requirement is necessary because placebos can produce real changes in recipients' symptoms, termed "expectancy effects" or "standard placebo effects" (see Ross & Olson, 1981, 1982).

These factors have not typically been satisfied in past studies of misattribution and provide an explanation for the inconsistent results. For example, insomniacs constitute a group where, because of familiarity with the target symptoms, it will be difficult to induce misattribution (Cotton et al., 1980). Why should chronic insomniacs believe that a pill they took before going to bed caused the same symptoms that they have experienced on many previous nights? The actual cause of arousal may be obvious to these individuals. The experiments that failed to show misattribution of speech anxiety also can be criticized. For example, it can be argued that the placebos in these studies did not provide a plausible and salient explanation for subjects' arousal symptoms (see Olson, 1988).

Evidence supporting the expectancy-attribution model can be found in previous experiments, although the studies were not designed to test the model. For example, Nisbett and Schachter (1966) led subjects to anticipate either low- or high-intensity electrical shocks. Subjects were given a placebo pill that allegedly would produce either fear-relevant or fear-irrelevant symptoms. Subjects then completed a pain threshold task where they received increasingly painful electrical shocks. Nisbett and Schachter assumed that subjects who were fearful of the shocks would tolerate less intense shock. As predicted, subjects who believed that the placebo pill would produce fear-relevant symptoms exhibited higher pain thresholds than did fear-irrelevant placebo subjects, presumably because the former subjects could misattribute fear symptoms to the pill. This outcome occurred only in the low-intensity condition, however. When subjects anticipated high-intensity shocks, the alleged side-effects of the placebo did not affect pain thresholds. Stated in terms of the factors from the expectancy-attribution model, the actual cause of arousal may have been too obvious in the high-intensity condition for misattribution to occur.

White and Kight (1984) had male subjects run in place for 15 or 120 s. In the latter, high-arousal condition, subjects rated an attractive female confederate more positively if they expected to meet her and if cues associated with the preceding exercise were minimized. From the perspective of the expectancy-attribution model, these conditions served to increase the salience of the misattribution source while decreasing the salience of the actual cause of arousal (the first and second requirements).

Fries and Frey (1980) manipulated the perceived strength of the misattribution source. Subjects ingested a pill that was described as arousing and as having either a strong or a weak effect. Subjects then completed an intelligence test and received fictitious negative feedback. Fries and Frey assumed that subjects who were emotionally distressed by this feedback would derogate the validity of the intelligence test when given an opportunity to do so. Results showed less derogation of the test by subjects who had taken an allegedly strong pill than by subjects who had taken an allegedly weak pill, presumably because the former individuals misattributed their distress to the strong pill. In a second experiment using the intelligence test paradigm, Fries and Frey gave subjects a placebo pill that was described as either arousing or relaxing and as having either a short-lived or a long-lasting effect. Subjects showed less immediate derogation of the intelligence test when the pill was described as arousing than when it was described as relaxing, presumably because emotional distress could be misattributed only to an allegedly arousing pill. Moreover, these differences were maintained over time when the pill's effects were allegedly of long duration, but they disappeared over time when the pill's effects were allegedly temporary. Stated in terms of the factors from the expectancy-attribution model, these two experiments documented the importance of the third and fourth requirements, namely the plausibility of the misattribution source as a cause of arousal and the perceived impact of the misattribution source.

Thus, data supporting the expectancy-attribution model (and, therefore, supporting the role of self-inference processes in emotion) do exist, although the studies were not designed to test the model (see also Worchel & Yohai, 1979; Zanna & Cooper, 1974). One purpose of the two experiments reported herein was to provide planned, a priori tests of the model's factors, in particular the requirements that the placebo be seen as a plausible and substantial cause of arousal symptoms (the third and fourth prerequisites). A second purpose was to conduct such tests while focusing on an emotion that has yielded disappointing results in past studies. Recall that certain emotional states have not proven amenable to misattribution manipulations, including insomnia and speech anxiety. The two studies reported tested whether subjects could be induced to misattribute speech anxiety to a neutral source when the necessary preconditions for misattribution were satisfied.

In both of the experiments, subjects' task was to read a prepared speech in front of a camera. This task is novel to most introductory psychology students (the subject population in my research) and produces moderate levels of physiological arousal and subjective anxiety (Cotton et al., 1980; Singerman et al., 1976). Because the task was novel, subjects presumably did not have a clear idea of how nervous they "should" feel and, therefore, were potentially amenable to misattribution procedures. In other words, the actual cause of arousal was not obvious (or, at least, the amount of arousal that should be attributed to the actual cause was ambiguous).

The misattribution source in both experiments was the alleged presence of "subliminal noise" (see Worchel & Yohai, 1979). Pilot testing with my subject population showed almost universal belief in subliminal perception, including subconscious awareness of high-frequency sounds. This belief provided a convenient and plausible way to give subjects an alternative explanation for arousal symptoms—they were told that they were being exposed to subliminal stimulation. Subjects wore headphones during the procedure, and a quiet, high-pitched "hum" was presented through the headphones whenever the subliminal noise was allegedly playing. This hum kept the misattribution source salient to subjects as a possible cause of their arousal symptoms.

Speech anxiety was measured in both experiments by scoring the videotaped speeches for dysfluencies, such as stutters, stammers, and speech errors. Speech dysfluencies have proven to be a reliable concomitant of anxiety in past research (see Harper, Wiens, & Matarazzo, 1978; Mahl, 1956; Pope, Blass, Siegman, & Raher, 1970) and should be particularly sensitive when, as in my experiments, the content of the speech is controlled across subjects (everyone read the identical, prepared speech).

Experiment 1

The first experiment (Olson & Ross, 1988) manipulated the extent to which subjects believed that the placebo was causing their symptoms. This was achieved by giving subjects false feedback about how much the subliminal noise was affecting them personally. The previously described experiments by Fries and Frey (1980) also manipulated the perceived impact of the placebo, but did so by telling subjects that the placebo was either strong or weak (or long-lasting versus short-lived). The problem with manipulating the alleged strength of a placebo is that subjects' preparatory actions might be affected. For example, subjects who receive an initial description of a placebo making it sound powerful may engage in pretask behaviors designed to control the expected symptoms (e.g., to control oncoming arousal), which could result in fewer symptoms and less emotionality without any misattribution occurring (Leventhal, 1984). Therefore, in the present experiment, subjects were not given the false feedback until they began the experimental task, thereby minimizing possible differences between conditions in anticipatory control of the symptoms.

According to the expectancy-attribution model, subjects should misattribute their symptoms to a neutral source only if they believe that the source is truly active—that it is substantially affecting how they feel. Subjects must believe that the neutral source is having a perceptible effect on them before they will manifest reduced emotion. Therefore, if credible feedback from the experimenter indicates that the neutral source is not affecting them, subjects should have no option but to view the symptoms accurately, as emotion; misattribution and reduced emotionality should not occur if subjects believe that the placebo is having little or no impact on their symptoms.

Subjects in the first study were told that subliminal noise produces symptoms of either unpleasant arousal or pleasant relaxation. The "arousing noise" description was expected to parallel the symptoms of speech anxiety and, therefore, create the potential for misattribution. Thus, when subjects were given feedback indicating that the subliminal noise was affecting them strongly, the arousing noise condition was expected to yield reduced speech anxiety—as evidenced by fewer speech dysfluencies—than the relaxing noise condition. On the other hand, when subjects were given feedback indicating that the subliminal noise was having little impact, the arousing-versus-relaxing noise conditions were not expected to differ on the speech dysfluencies measure.

Procedure.   When subjects arrived at the laboratory, they were told that the experiment was investigating the physiological effects of subliminal noise, which was defined as high-frequency sound that lies outside the range of conscious hearing. The concept of subliminal perception was explained and illustrated with a couple of examples (e.g., subliminal advertising). Subjects were told that subliminal noise is important to study because it is produced by many machines and instruments of advanced technology. They were also told that they would be exposed to higher levels of subliminal noise than they would normally experience in everyday life so that the possible effects of the noise could be studied in a short period of time. Subjects were then given a 10-s "sample" of subliminal noise: The experimenter turned on a noise generator that fed into subjects' headphones, producing a quiet hum. Subjects were told that the noise generator produced both audible and subliminal sound and that they would know that the subliminal noise was playing whenever they could hear the hum.

Subjects were told that their physiological reactions to subliminal noise would be monitored by two machines. First, they were connected to a Grass Model 7 polygraph by attaching a plethysmograph to their nonpreferred hand. Next, the experimenter showed subjects a voltage indicator on the table in front of them, which appeared to be connected to the polygraph. On the face of this indicator was a meter, with a needle and a scale from 0 to 100 microamperes. Subjects were told that this machine was called an "electromyogram" and that it measured specific autonomic reactions that result from subliminal noise. Subjects were told that they would be able to tell how much the noise was affecting them by the movement of the needle on the meter.

The different descriptions of side-effects of the subliminal noise were then presented. Subjects in the arousing-noise condition were told:

There is substantial evidence that exposure to subliminal noise produces certain side-effects in some people. It has been found that exposure to subliminal noise makes some people feel unpleasantly aroused—such as experiencing a feeling of general agitation or anxiety. Therefore, if your autonomic nervous system is affected by the subliminal noise, which the electromyogram will measure, then you will feel somewhat tense or unpleasantly aroused when exposed to the subliminal noise.

Subjects in the relaxing noise condition were told:

There is substantial evidence that exposure to subliminal noise produces certain side-effects in some people. It has been found that exposure to subliminal noise makes some people feel relaxed. Actually, rather than calling it subliminal noise, it would be more correct to call it subliminal sound, because when one thinks of noise, this suggests something that is harsh and agitating rather than relaxing. So, if your autonomic nervous system is affected by the subliminal noise, which the electromyogram will measure, then you will feel rather pleasantly relaxed when exposed to the subliminal noise, which means that you will feel calm or at ease.

The experimenter then turned on the subliminal noise generator, which started the hum in subjects' headphones. While the subject sat quietly for 30 s, the experimenter slowly moved the needle on the voltage indicator to 10 microamperes (he controlled the needle via a dial on his desk, behind and outside the vision of the subject).

Subjects then learned about the speech task, which constituted the actual source of arousal. They were told that their task would be to read a prepared speech as clearly as possible into a camera at talking speed. While subjects listened to the instructions for the speech task (which were audiotaped and played into their headphones), the experimenter adjusted the needle on the voltage indicator to manipulate the alleged impact of the subliminal noise. One of three feedback levels was presented. In the "no impact" condition, the needle remained between 10 and 15 microamperes throughout the task. In the "some impact" condition, the needle slowly moved to 35 microamperes during the instructions and fluctuated between 35 and 40 throughout the task. In the "strong impact" condition, the needle slowly moved to 60 microamperes during the instructions and fluctuated between 60 and 65 throughout the task.

Following the instructions for the speech task, the experimenter pointed a camera at the subject (previously facing the wall) from a distance of 2 m. He then looked at the voltage indicator and commented on the impact of the subliminal noise, stating either: "The noise doesn't seem to be affecting you," "The noise is having some effect on you—an average amount," or "The noise is having a large effect on you—your physiological system seems to be activated strongly" in the no, some, and strong impact conditions, respectively. Subjects were then given a 650-word speech to read, which presented some of the positive and negative effects of television on our lives and life-styles.

Results.   Preliminary analyses showed that subjects in the "no impact" and "some impact" conditions behaved equivalently. The lack of difference between these groups does not pose serious problems for the expectancy-attribution model, since misattribution is posited to depend on an overestimation of the placebo's impact. Presumably, the intermediate impact condition was too weak to induce the perception of substantial impact. Consequently, for purposes of presentation, the "no impact" and "some impact" groups were combined to form the "weak impact" condition.

Table 2.1 presents the cell means on the speech dysfluencies measure. As expected, arousing-noise subjects made fewer speech errors than relaxing-noise subjects in the strong-impact condition but not in the weak-impact condition. A planned comparison testing this predicted pattern showed that arousing–noise subjects in the strong-impact condition made significantly fewer speech errors than subjects in the other three conditions, $t(82) = 1.89$, $p < .04$. Neither main effect (side-effects or false feedback) was reliable in the analyses of variance.

Thus, when the necessary preconditions were satisfied, speech anxiety was shown to be amenable to misattribution. In the strong-impact condition, arousing subliminal noise presumably provided a plausible explanation for a large amount of arousal, thereby leaving fewer symptoms to be labeled as anxiety. This reduction in subjective anxiety led to fewer speech dysfluencies. Moreover, the false feedback information was not presented until immediately before the speech

TABLE 2.1
Mean Speech Dysfluencies, Experiment 1

Alleged Side-effects	False Feedback	
	Strong Impact	Weak Impact
Arousing noise	11.80	18.27
	(15)	(30)
Relaxing noise	18.67	14.83
	(15)	(30)

Note: Cell *n*s are in parentheses.
Data from Olson & Ross, 1988.

task, a procedure that held constant subjects' initial expectancies about the strength of the placebo (i.e., the strong- and weak-impact conditions were identical until just before the speech task). Consequently, possible differences between conditions in anticipatory control of the symptoms were minimized.

Experiment 2

The second experiment (Olson, 1988, Experiment 2) also manipulated the plausibility of subliminal noise as a cause of arousal symptoms produced by speech anxiety, but did so in a different way. Specifically, the temporal contiguity between the onset of subjects' arousal and the presentation of the subliminal noise was varied.

In order for a neutral source to be seen as a plausible cause of arousal, it must occur contiguously with the arousal. If arousal symptoms do not occur at the same time as the introduction of the misattribution source, then subjects should not perceive a causal connection. Thus, a lack of temporal contiguity between a placebo and arousal symptoms should preclude misattribution of those symptoms to the placebo.

In the second experiment, two groups of subjects received the same subliminal noise cover story as was used in Experiment 1. Both groups were told that subliminal noise produces unpleasant arousal, thus making subliminal noise a possible misattribution source for speech anxiety. Instead of providing false feedback about the effects of the noise, all subjects were told that everyone is strongly affected by subliminal noise. One group, the "subliminal noise-immediate" condition, basically replicated the procedures from the first study (with the exception of the feedback manipulation). Thus, these subjects were told that subliminal noise would make them feel aroused; the noise generator was turned on; and they immediately learned about the speech task and read the speech into the camera. These subjects were expected to misattribute some of their speech anxiety to the noise and, consequently, make fewer speech errors.

The second subliminal noise group, the "subliminal noise-delay" condition, experienced a delay between the onset of the noise and the instructions informing them about the speech task (the actual source of arousal). Specifically, these subjects were told that subliminal noise would make them feel aroused; the noise generator was turned on; but they completed personality questionnaires for 10 min before learning about the speech task and reading the speech into the camera. These subjects were not expected to misattribute their speech anxiety to the noise. After all, the noise was on for 10 min before the arousal symptoms occurred (and the initial description of the subliminal noise, as in all subliminal noise conditions in my studies, stated that the noise would take effect very quickly). Thus, these subjects were expected to interpret the symptoms accurately—as nervousness caused by the speech task—and to make more speech errors than subjects in the "subliminal noise-immediate" condition.

Two additional conditions were also included in this experiment, which did not involve the subliminal noise cover story. Instead, these subjects were simply given advance warning of the symptoms they would experience.

In 1975, Calvert–Boyanowsky and Leventhal pointed out that "misattribution" manipulations give subjects accurate advance information about how they will be feeling. For example, if subjects are told that a pill (or subliminal noise or some other neutral source) will produce arousal symptoms and subsequently perform a task that makes them aroused, then the initial description of the placebo also provides accurate preparatory information about the oncoming arousal. Perhaps it is not misattribution that makes these subjects less emotional (compared with control subjects who are not told about the alleged impact of the neutral source), but instead advance warning about the symptoms. Arousal symptoms may be less surprising or distressing when they are expected (Leventhal, Brown, Shacham, & Engquist, 1979), and/or subjects may engage in preparatory actions designed to control the symptoms (Calvert–Boyanowsky & Leventhal, 1975). Either of these processes could ameliorate emotionality.

Thus, an important baseline in misattribution research is a group of subjects who are not given a possible misattribution source but who do receive the same accurate description of their oncoming symptoms as subjects in the misattribution conditions. In fact, this baseline is extremely rare in the misattribution literature; I know of only two published papers that have included it (Calvert–Boyanowsky & Leventhal, 1975; Rodin, 1976). Disconcertingly, the conclusion in both of these papers was that accurate information served to reduce emotion just as much as a misattribution manipulation.

In the present experiment, two groups of subjects were not exposed to the subliminal noise cover story, but did learn that the tasks to be completed would produce arousal symptoms. Thus, they were given accurate information about their oncoming arousal, but misattribution was not possible. One group, the "accurate information-immediate" condition, performed the speech task immediately after being told that the tasks would produce arousal. The second group, the "accurate information-delay" condition, completed personality questionnaires for 10 min after being told that the tasks would produce arousal, following which they performed the speech task.

Based on the expectancy-attribution model, I predicted that the "subliminal noise-immediate" condition would yield fewer speech dysfluencies than the other three groups. This prediction followed from the logic that the "subliminal noise-delay" group should not misattribute their symptoms to the noise, and the two "accurate information" groups did not have a misattribution source available.

Procedure. The procedure in the subliminal noise conditions closely paralleled that of the first experiment. Subjects were told that the study was investigating the physiological effects of subliminal noise. They were informed that previous research had shown that subliminal noise makes people feel unpleasantly aroused. The noise generator was then turned on, producing a hum in subjects' headphones. In the immediate condition, subjects immediately learned about the speech task and read the speech into the camera. In the delay condition, subjects were given three personality questionnaires to complete (e.g., Fenigstein, Scheier, & Buss's 1975 self-consciousness scale), during which time the hum continued in their headphones. After 10 min had elapsed, the experimenter told subjects that they could finish the questionnaires later because it was time to proceed to the next task. Subjects then learned about the speech task and read the speech into the camera.

In the accurate information conditions, subjects were told that the experiment was investigating individuals' physiological reactions during the performance of certain tasks. The experimenter stated that the tasks to be completed had been selected because past research had shown that they engender a particular emotional response. Specifically, subjects were told that the tasks make people feel unpleasantly aroused, such as experiencing a feeling of general agitation or anxiety (the identical pretask information that was given to subjects in the subliminal noise conditions). Subjects in the immediate condition then learned about the speech task and read the speech into the camera. Subjects in the delay condition completed personality questionnaires for 10 min, at which time they learned about and performed the speech task.

Results.   Table 2.2 presents the cell means on the speech dysfluencies measure. It can be seen that the pattern of means corresponded exactly to predictions, with "subliminal noise-immediate" subjects making fewer speech errors than subjects in the other three conditions. A planned comparison testing this specific pattern of interaction showed it to be statistically significant, $t(64) = 2.06, p <$ .03. Neither main effect was reliable in the analysis of variance.

Thus, misattribution was again shown to depend on the plausibility of the neutral source as a cause of subjects' arousal symptoms. When the subliminal noise was not introduced contiguously with the onset of subjects' arousal, subjects made more speech errors than when temporal contiguity was satisfied.

TABLE 2.2
Mean Speech Dysfluencies, Experiment 2

Timing	Condition	
	Subliminal Noise	*Accurate Information*
Immediate	15.50	21.00
Delay	20.11	21.78

Note: Cell *n*s are 18.
Data from Olson, 1988.

Also, this experiment showed that the ameliorative effects of the misattribution manipulation were not easily attributable to the fact that subjects were given accurate pretask information about their oncoming symptoms. Neither of the "accurate information" conditions yielded a level of speech dysfluencies that was as low as the level obtained in the "subliminal noise-immediate" condition.

Taken together, the two experiments reported herein provide strong support for the expectancy-attribution model. A neutral label for arousal symptoms reduced emotionality only when the preconditions specified in the model were satisfied.

Of course, since the expectancy-attribution model builds on Schachter's (1964) two-component theory of emotion, my experiments also provide some support for his theory. In particular, Schachter's basic assumption that attributions about the causes of symptoms can influence emotions seems valid. Thus, self-inference processes can play an important role in determining the nature of subjective emotional experience.

BEM'S SELF-PERCEPTION THEORY

Another social psychological theory that assigns a significant role to self-inference processes in emotion was proposed by Bem in 1972. Actually, self-perception theory can be applied to any internal state, including attitudes, beliefs, and emotions (see Fazio, 1987, for a recent review of the theory). The "overjustification effect" mentioned at the beginning of the chapter is an example of a phenomenon that was derived from self-perception theory.

Bem postulated that when an internal state is weak or ambiguous, individuals might infer the state from knowledge about their overt behavior and the circumstances in which the behavior occurred. That is, perceivers may infer their own internal states in exactly the same way as they are forced to infer others' internal states—by looking at behavior and taking into account environmental factors that could have facilitated or inhibited the behavior (see Jones, Chapter 4, this volume, for research examining the conditions under which individuals will infer dispositions from their own behavior).

For example, if someone is asked whether they liked a movie that they saw several weeks ago, they might answer by thinking back about their relevant behaviors. Did they laugh? Did they cry? Did they talk about the movie with friends afterwards? They might also think about environmental factors that could have affected these behaviors independently of the movie. Had anything happened to them before the movie that put them in an especially good or bad mood? Did they drink alcohol before going to the movie? Presumably, if no relevant environmental factors can be identified, then an internal state consistent with the overt behavior will be inferred (e.g., "I laughed a lot, so I must have liked the movie"). If facilitative environmental factors that might have caused the behaviors can be identified, then internal causes will be discounted (e.g., "I got a raise earlier that day and would have laughed at anything, so I'm not sure that I particularly liked the movie even though I laughed a lot"). If inhibitory environmental factors that should have inhibited the behavior (but did not) can be identified, then the inference of an internal state consistent with the behavior will be augmented (e.g., "I failed an exam that day and certainly didn't feel like laughing, so I must have liked the movie a lot to laugh so much").

There are similarities between Bem's model and Schachter's theory of emotion, although the theories focus on different elements of personal experience. Schachter addresses how attributions about *internal arousal symptoms* can affect feelings of emotion, whereas Bem addresses how attributions about *external behaviors* can affect inferences of emotion (and inferences of other internal states). In each case, the self-inference processes are assumed to occur in a logical fashion (just like social inferences). The targets of the causal judgments differ, however (internal arousal vs. overt behavior).

Bem's model provides a perspective on emotion that is reminiscent of James's (1890) suggestion that feedback from skeletal muscles contributes to emotion. For example, James argued that the experience of fear results, in part, from the perception that one is running away from a stimulus. Although James viewed these interpretations of skeletal reactions as automatic (rather than the more deliberate inferences postulated by Bem), the logic is similar in the two models.

To provide further evidence of the role of self-inference processes in emotion, I set out in the third study (Olson, 1989) to examine whether self-inferences about the causes of overt behavior can influence emotion as postulated by Bem. In addition to testing a different theoretical perspective, I focused on a positively valenced emotional state to increase the generality of the evidence. Specifically, I investigated humor, as reflected by laughter and smiling in response to written jokes.

One of the earliest self-perception experiments (Bem, 1965) also focused on humor reactions, although the procedures were very different from those of the present study. In an initial set of trials, Bem told subjects to answer simple questions about themselves truthfully when a green light was turned on during the question but to make up a false answer when an amber light was turned on during the question. In a subsequent set of trials, subjects were told to ignore the green and amber lights (which would continue to come on), and to give spontaneous evaluations of the funniness of cartoons. Subjects were then shown a series of cartoons that they had previously rated as neutral and were asked to choose between saying either "This cartoon is very funny" or "This cartoon is very unfunny," after which they rated the funniness of the cartoon. When given in the presence of the green light, the statements about the funniness of the cartoons influenced subsequent ratings: Subjects rated the cartoons as funnier when they had chosen to say they were funny than when they had chosen to say they were unfunny. In contrast, when the amber light was on during the statement, subjects continued to rate the cartoons neutrally irrespective of whether they had chosen to say they were funny or unfunny. Bem proposed that subjects came to regard the green light as indicative of "unmanded" (truthful) behavior, therefore inferring internal states consistent with the chosen expressions of funniness.

The problem with these data as support for self-perception theory is that subjects were told to ignore the lights in the second set of trials. Thus, since they presumably did not believe at a conscious level that the lights were affecting their answers, subjects should not, logically, have been affected by the light manipulation. Some sort of conditioning or priming effect must be posited, together with a self-perception explanation before the data make sense. Unfortunately, a simple demand explanation provides a compelling alternative to these more complex interpretations.

With a few exceptions (e.g., Bem, 1965; Schachter & Wheeler, 1962) most previous studies of self-inferences of emotion, especially in the misattribution literature, have examined negative or neutral states (see Ross & Olson, 1981). In fact, some theorists have suggested that misattribution may not occur at all with positive emotions (e.g., Schwarz & Clore, 1983). Although the present study did not examine misattribution of internal arousal to an erroneous cause (the typical focus of misattribution experiments derived from Schachter's theory), the procedures did attempt to induce misattribution of emotion-related behavior. Specifically, some subjects were given a nonemotional explanation for overt signs of mirth (laughter, etc.); the experiment tested whether this false label could influence subjects' inferred enjoyment of humorous materials.

Presumably, laughs and smiles in response to a joke usually reflect enjoyment of the joke. Thus, enjoyment can be logically inferred from the intensity of overt signs of mirth. Indeed, we normally assess others' enjoyment of jokes by noting their reaction along the continuum from stone-faced silence to knee-slapping hilarity. If such inferences occur in self-perception as well, then we may base our decision about how much we enjoyed a joke, at least in part, on the amount of our laughter and smiling. But what if, while reading the joke, we were exposed to an external factor that we believe increased laughter and smiling? In this circumstance, overt signs of mirth did not necessarily reflect enjoyment, and we must "correct" for the external factor when making our estimate of enjoyment (i.e., we should conclude that we did not enjoy the joke as much as our amount of laughter implied). In contrast, if we were exposed while reading the joke to an external factor that we believe decreased laughter and smiling, then overt signs of mirth were inhibited. Consequently, we should conclude that we enjoyed the joke even more than our amount of laughter implied. Experiment 3 tested this logic.

Experiment 3

Subjects were exposed to two sets of jokes, which were obtained from different books and selected to be about equally funny. While they read one set of jokes, subjects heard a "laugh track" (tape-recorded audience laughter) played through their headphones. Because a laugh track can have real effects on individuals' mirth responses (e.g., Cupchik & Leventhal, 1974; Donoghue, McCarrey, & Clement, 1983; Leventhal & Mace, 1970), I attempted to minimize its probable impact. Specifically, the laugh track consisted of an "endless loop" audiotape that repeated itself independently of subjects' behavior (e.g., independently of whether they were starting, finishing, or in between jokes). While subjects read the other set of jokes, no canned laughter was played through their headphones.

One group of subjects, the "increase mirth" condition, was told that laugh tracks have been shown to increase smiling and laughter. These individuals were expected to misattribute some of their mirth responses to the laugh track and, therefore, infer that the jokes they read while exposed to the laugh track were not actually as funny as they seemed (or not as funny as implied by the subject's mirth responses). A second group, the "no effect" condition, was told that laugh tracks have been shown to have no impact on smiling and laughter. These individuals were expected to infer funniness directly from their mirth responses. A third group, the "decrease mirth" condition, was told that laugh tracks have been shown to reduce smiling and laughter. These individuals were expected to augment the perceived funniness of the jokes they read while exposed to the laugh track. That is, they were expected to infer that the jokes accompanied by the laugh track were actually funnier than they seemed (or funnier than implied by the subject's mirth responses).

If we assume that the two sets of jokes were, in reality, equally funny (generated equal mirth) and that the laugh track did not actually affect mirth responses in any of the conditions, then the predictions for perceived funniness are straightforward. Subjects in the "increase mirth" condition should infer that the jokes accompanied by the laugh track were less funny than the jokes presented without canned laughter. After all, these subjects laughed equally at both sets of jokes, despite the facilitation of mirth for the laugh track set (which must therefore be less funny). Subjects in the "no effect" condition should find the two sets of jokes equally funny. Subjects in the "decrease mirth" condition should infer that the jokes accompanied by the laugh track were funnier than the jokes presented without canned laughter. After all, these subjects laughed equally at both sets of jokes, despite the inhibition of mirth for the laugh track set (which must, therefore, be funnier).

Based on the assumption that people would rather read funny jokes than unfunny jokes, a behavioral measure of the perceived relative funniness of the two sets of jokes was obtained in a "free play" period at the end of the experiment: Subjects were allowed free access to the two books from which the sets had been taken. I predicted that subjects in the "increase mirth" condition would spend most of their time reading the book that had *not* been accompanied by the laugh track, whereas subjects in the "decrease mirth" condition would spend most of their time reading the book that *had* been accompanied by the laugh track. The "no effect" subjects were expected to read the two books equally.

Procedure.   All subjects in this experiment were women, because past research has found that laugh tracks sometimes affect males and females differently (e.g., Cupchik & Leventhal, 1974; Leventhal & Cupchik, 1975; Leventhal & Mace, 1970). The instructions were audiotaped; subjects wore headphones throughout the procedure. Subjects were told that the experiment was investigating factors that affect how people react to humor, especially external or environmental factors. Thus, they would be shown humorous materials under different conditions and would rate them for funniness.

Subjects then learned that canned laughter was one external factor being examined in the study. Those in the "increase mirth" condition were told:

> The first factor we want to study is the presence of laughter from others. We are all familiar with "canned laughter" or "laugh tracks" on television shows. Why do producers add laughter to their programs? It turns out that smiling and laughter are, to a degree, "contagious." That is, humans instinctively respond with smiling or laughter to other people's laughter. This tendency can be seen as early as very young infants, who will smile in response to their mother's smile. So, television producers are actually employing a well-established fact when they add laughter to their programs. Such laughter does, in fact, increase quite substantially smiling and laughter by the listeners.

Subjects in the "decrease mirth" condition were told:

> The first factor we want to study is the presence of laughter from others. We are all familiar with "canned laughter" or "laugh tracks" on television shows. Is a laugh track really effective? That is, does it increase laughter by the audience? It turns out that the answer to this question depends on another factor—whether or not the listeners notice or become aware of the laugh track. If the laugh track is not noticed, if it more or less remains in the background, then there is some evidence that it does, in fact, increase listeners' smiling and laughter. If the laugh track is obvious, on the other hand, or if listeners become aware of the canned laughter, then the evidence shows that it actually decreases quite substantially people's smiling and laughter. This is probably because when we are aware of canned laughter, it seems stupid or fake, and it distracts us from the material. Also, we may feel manipulated, which further reduces our humor response. At any rate, obvious canned laughter reduces people's own smiling and laughter.

Using arguments similar to those presented in the "decrease mirth" condition, the "no effect" subjects were told that obvious laugh tracks have no impact on the listeners' smiling and laughter. To provide a rationale for why we were studying a factor that has no impact on mirth, these subjects were also told that they were in a control group and that other participants in the experiment were being exposed to laugh tracks that were not obvious.

All subjects then learned that they would read two sets of jokes, taken from different books. A laugh track would be presented through their headphones while they read one set of jokes but not while they read the other set. As appropriate to their condition, subjects were reminded that they would find themselves smiling and laughing either more, less, or the same when the laugh track was played.

The experimenter then placed in front of the subject a set of 12 index cards (10 × 15 cm), each of which contained a typewritten joke. The book from which the jokes were taken was also placed on the table. Subjects were asked to read the individual cards one at a time, placing them face down on the desk as they were finished. After reading all 12 jokes, subjects rated the entire set for funniness (no ratings of individual jokes were obtained). The experimenter then removed the index cards and rating sheet but left the book on the table. The second set of index cards, with its accompanying book, was then placed in front of the subject, and the reading-rating procedure was repeated.

One set of jokes was taken from *2,000 More Insults* (Safian, 1967); the other was taken from *The Offical Doctors' Joke Book* (Wilde, 1981). Based on pilot testing with subjects from the same population as the experimental subjects, the jokes were selected to be somewhat funny (i.e., rated at or just below the midpoint of a scale going from "not at all funny" to "very funny"). For example, one joke in the insults set was:

A Failure: He stayed awake nights trying to think of how to succeed. It would have been better if he had stayed awake days.

One joke in the doctor set was:

Nurse: Excuse me, Doctor, but that man you just gave a clean bill of health to walked out of the office and dropped dead. What should I do?
Doctor: Turn him around so he looks like he was walking in.

While they read one set of jokes, the "endless loop" laugh track was played through subjects' headphones. Whether the first or second set of jokes was accompanied by the laugh track was counterbalanced across subjects. Also, whether the insults set or the doctor set was accompanied by the laugh track was counterbalanced.

When subjects finished rating the second set of jokes, the experimenter removed the index cards and rating sheet, leaving the two books on the table. The experimenter then asked subjects to remove their headphones and said:

I have to change the instructions tape before we can continue with the next task. It will take me just a couple of minutes, so you can relax for a moment. Feel free to read the books while you wait, if you want to.

The experimenter then busied himself behind the subject, actually changing the tape on the tape-recorder. Subjects were given 3 min of "free time." Most subjects spent the entire 3-min period reading the joke books.

The subjects were videotaped throughout the experiment by a camera lying on a shelf beside their table, hidden among several other pieces of equipment and junk. Thus, we could unobtrusively measure exactly how much time subjects spent reading each book. We could also score subjects' mirth responses while they read the index cards, thereby testing whether the laugh track actually affected smiling and laughter.

Results.   Subjects' reactions while reading each set of index cards were scored for: (a) total number of smiles during the set, (b) total number of laughs during the set, and (c) total mirth for the set. Mirth scores were calculated for each single joke and then summed across the 12 jokes in each set; subjects' maximum mirth reaction to each joke was rated on a six-point scale: 1 = frown; 2 = no response; 3 = inhibited smile; 4 = half smile; 5 = full smile; 6 = laugh. This mirth scale was previously used by Leventhal and Cupchik (1975), although these authors did not distinguish between inhibited smile and half-smile (see also Cupchik & Leventhal, 1974; Donoghue et al., 1983; Zigler, Levine, & Gould, 1966).

Analyses of these measures of overt mirth while reading the index cards revealed no effects for the presence of a laugh track. That is, subjects' overt reactions to the jokes were similar, whether the jokes were accompanied by a laugh track or not, and whether subjects were in the "increase mirth," "decrease mirth," or "no effect" conditions. Of course, these null results validate the intended placebic nature of the laugh track. On average, subjects exhibited approximately three smiles and one laugh during each set of jokes.

The number of seconds that subjects spent reading (touching) each book was presumed to reflect their perceptions of the books' relative funniness.[1] Table 2.3 presents the means in each condition. The predicted interaction between conditions and books was significant, $F(2, 48) = 3.46$, $p < .04$, and the pattern of means corresponded exactly to predictions. In the "no effect" condition, subjects spent virtually identical amounts of time reading the books that had and had not been accompanied by the laugh track. In the "increase mirth" condition, subjects spent almost twice as much time reading the book that had *not* been accompanied by the laugh track as they did reading the laugh track book, although the within-cell variability on the behavioral measure was such that this difference was only marginally significant, $t(48) = 1.60$, $p < .06$. In the "decrease mirth" condition, subjects spent more than twice as much time reading the book that *had* been

---

[1]As part of the procedure, subjects also provided ratings of the funniness of each set of jokes. Unfortunately, these ratings could not be used to test the self-perception predictions because the rating of the first set was obtained before subjects had seen the second set. Comparative judgments of the relative funniness of the two sets of jokes are necessary to test the postulated inferences. Thus, the time that subjects spent reading each book, which presumably reflected their preferences for one alternative over the other, was the critical dependent measure.

TABLE 2.3
Mean Seconds Touching Each Book, Experiment 3

Book	Condition		
	Increase Mirth	No Effect	Decrease Mirth
Laugh track	54.50	88.30	117.60
No laugh track	107.15	90.00	48.10

Note: Cell *n*s are 20. Total duration of the free-play period was 180 s.
Data from Olson, 1989.

accompanied by the laugh track as they did reading the nonlaugh-track book, which was a reliable difference, $t(48) = 2.11$, $p < .03$.

Thus, the manipulation of the alleged impact of the laugh track on mirth reactions affected subjects' behavioral preferences for the two joke books in a manner consistent with Bem's (1972) self-perception theory. Presumably, subjects inferred the funniness of the jokes, in part, from their mirth reactions, but either discounted or augmented their reactions during the laugh track, depending on whether it was supposed to increase or decrease their mirth. These data support the role of self-inference processes in humor, one important type of emotional experience.

CONCLUSIONS

The three experiments described in this chapter indicate that self-inference processes, in the form of attributional judgments, can affect emotional experience. The studies investigated both positively and negatively valenced states (speech anxiety and humor) and attributions about the causes of both arousal symptoms and overt emotion-related behaviors. Taken together, the data make a strong case for the need to include cognitive, self-inference processes in models of emotion.

As mentioned at the beginning of the chapter, Schachter's theory of emotion and Bem's self-perception theory are not the only models that view self-inferences as critical in emotion. For example, Weiner (1985) has formulated an attributional model of achievement-related behaviors, in which he assumes that self-inferences about the causes of success and failure have important effects on emotion and subsequent motivation. Also, in his self-discrepancy theory, Higgins (1987) proposes that inferences about the nature and causes of discrepancies between self-state representations (e.g., between the "actual self" and the "ideal self") have important consequences for affect and emotion (see Higgins, Tykocinski, & Vookles, Chapter 8, this volume, for recent research testing self-discrepancy theory).

The existence of such a variety of theoretical approaches to self-inference processes in emotion underscores the fact that social psychologists have something worthwhile to say about the intensely private (and apparently nonsocial) phenomenon of emotion. Perceivers seem motivated to understand both themselves and their environment. This goal necessitates causal analyses, including analyses of one's own feelings and behaviors. The research described in this chapter shows that these attributional judgments have consequences not only for cognitive aspects of the self (e.g., for how one interprets one's actions), but also for affective aspects of the self, such as emotions. I conclude from these data that self-inference processes play a causal role in determining the subjective emotions that are experienced in particular settings.

ACKNOWLEDGMENTS

The research reported in this chapter was supported by grants from the Social Sciences and Humanities Research Council of Canada. I thank Ali Hammoud for serving as experimenter in the studies and Nigel Field, Carolyn L. Hafer, and J. Douglas Hazlewood for their assistance in scoring the data. Mark P. Zanna provided helpful comments on an earlier version of the chapter. Correspondence can be sent to James M. Olson, Department of Psychology, University of Western Ontario, London, Ontario, Canada N6A 5C2.

REFERENCES

Bem, D. J. (1965). An experimental analysis of self-persuasion. *Journal of Experimental Social Psychology, 1,* 199–218.

Bem, D. J. (1972). Self-perception theory. In L. Berkowitz (Ed.), *Advances in experimental social psychology* (Vol. 6, pp. 1–62). New York: Academic Press.

Bootzin, R. R., Herman, C. P., & Nicassio, P. (1976). The power of suggestion: Another examination of misattribution and insomnia. *Journal of Personality and Social Psychology, 34,* 673–679.

Calvert–Boyanowsky, J., & Leventhal, H. (1975). The role of information in attenuating behavioral responses to stress: A reinterpretation of the misattribution phenomenon. *Journal of Personality and Social Psychology, 32,* 214–221.

Cotton, J. L. (1981). A review of research on Schachter's theory of emotion and the misattribution of arousal. *European Journal of Social Psychology, 11,* 365–397.

Cotton, J. L., Baron, R. S., & Borkovec, T. D. (1980). Caffeine ingestion, misattribution therapy, and speech anxiety. *Journal of Research in Personality, 14,* 196–206.

Cupchik, G. C., & Leventhal, H. (1974). Consistency between expressive behavior and the evaluation of humorous stimuli: The role of sex and self-observation. *Journal of Personality and Social Psychology, 30,* 429–442.

Donoghue, E. E., McCarrey, M. W., & Clement, R. (1983). Humour appreciation as a function of canned laughter, a mirthful companion, and field dependence: Faciliation and inhibitory effects. *Canadian Journal of Behavioural Science, 15,* 150–162.

Dutton, D. G., & Aron, A. P. (1974). Some evidence for heightened sexual attraction under conditions of high anxiety. *Journal of Personality and Social Psychology, 30*, 510–517.

Fazio, R. H. (1987). Self-perception theory: A current perspective. In M. P. Zanna, J. M. Olson, & C. P. Herman (Eds.), *Social influence: The Ontario symposium* (Vol. 5, pp. 129–150). Hillsdale, NJ: Lawrence Erlbaum Associates.

Fenigstein, A., Scheier, M. F., & Buss, A. H. (1975). Public and private self-consciousness: Assessment and theory. *Journal of Consulting and Clinical Psychology, 43*, 522–527.

Fries, A., & Frey, D. (1980). Misattribution of arousal and the effects of self-threatening information. *Journal of Experimental Social Psychology, 16*, 405–416.

Harper, R. G., Wiens, A. N., & Matarazzo, J. D. (1978). *Nonverbal communication: The state of the art.* New York: Wiley.

Harvey, J. H., & Weary, G. (1984). Current issues in attribution theory and research. *Annual Review of Psychology, 35*, 427–459.

Heider, F. (1958). *The psychology of interpersonal relations.* New York: Wiley.

Higgins, E. T. (1987). Self-discrepancy: A theory relating self and affect. *Psychological Review, 94*, 319–340.

James, W. (1890). *The principles of psychology* (Vols. 1 and 2). New York: Holt.

Jones, E. E., & Davis, K. E. (1965). From acts to dispositions: The attribution process in person perception. In L. Berkowitz (Ed.), *Advances in experimental social psychology* (Vol. 2, pp. 219–266). New York: Academic Press.

Kelley, H. H. (1967). Attribution theory in social psychology. In D. Levine (Ed.), *Nebraska symposium on motivation* (pp. 192–240). Lincoln: University of Nebraska Press.

Kellogg, R., & Baron, R. S. (1975). Attribution theory, insomnia, and the reverse placebo effect: A reversal of Storms and Nisbett's findings. *Journal of Personality and Social Psychology, 32*, 231–236.

Laird, J. D. (1974). Self-attribution of emotion: The effects of expressive behavior on the quality of emotional experience. *Journal of Personality and Social Psychology, 29*, 475–486.

Lepper, M. R. (1981). Intrinsic and extrinsic motivation in children: Detrimental effects of superfluous social control. In W. A. Collins (Ed.), *Minnesota symposium on child psychology* (Vol. 14). Hillsdale, NJ: Lawrence Erlbaum Associates.

Lepper, M. R., & Greene, D. (Eds.). (1978). *The hidden costs of reward: New perspectives on the psychology of human motivation.* Hillsdale, NJ: Lawrence Erlbaum Associates.

Leventhal, H. (1980). Toward a comprehensive theory of emotion. In L. Berkowitz (Ed.), *Advances in experimental social psychology* (Vol. 13, pp. 139–207). New York: Academic Press.

Leventhal, H. (1984). A perceptual-motor theory of emotion. In L. Berkowitz (Ed.), *Advances in experimental social psychology* (Vol. 17, pp. 117–182). New York: Academic Press.

Leventhal, H., Brown, D., Shacham, S., & Engquist, G. (1979). Effects of preparatory information about sensations, threat of pain, and attention on cold pressor distress. *Journal of Personality and Social Psychology, 37*, 688–714.

Leventhal, H., & Cupchik, G. C. (1975). The informational and facilitative effects of an audience upon expression and the evaluation of humorous stimuli. *Journal of Experimental Social Psychology, 11*, 363–380.

Leventhal, H., & Mace, W. (1970). The effect of laughter on evaluation of a slapstick movie. *Journal of Personality, 38*, 16–30.

Mahl, G. F. (1956). Disturbances and silences in the patient's speech in psychotherapy. *Journal of Abnormal and Social Psychology, 53*, 1–15.

Marshall, G. D., & Zimbardo, P. G. (1979). Affective consequences of inadequately explained arousal. *Journal of Personality and Social Psychology, 37*, 970–988.

Maslach, C. (1979). Negative emotional biasing of unexplained arousal. *Journal of Personality and Social Psychology, 37*, 953–969.

Nisbett, R. E., & Schachter, S. (1966). Cognitive manipulation of pain. *Journal of Experimental Social Psychology, 2,* 227–236.

Olson, J. M. (1988). Misattribution, preparatory information, and speech anxiety. *Journal of Personality and Social Psychology, 54,* 758–767.

Olson, J. M. (1989). *Discounting and augmentation effects in the self-perception of humor.* Unpublished manuscript, University of Western Ontario, London, Ontario.

Olson, J. M., & Ross, M. (1985). Attribution research: Past contributions, current trends, and future prospects. In J. H. Harvey & G. Weary (Eds.), *Attribution: Basic issues and applications* (pp. 283–311). New York: Academic Press.

Olson, J. M., & Ross, M. (1988). False feedback about placebo effectiveness: Consequences for the misattribution of speech anxiety. *Journal of Experimental Social Psychology, 24,* 275–291.

Pope, B., Blass, T., Siegman, A. W., & Raher, J. (1970). Anxiety and depression in speech. *Journal of Consulting and Clinical Psychology, 35,* 128–133.

Reisenzein, R. (1983). The Schachter theory of emotion: Two decades later. *Psychological Bulletin, 94,* 239–264.

Rodin, J. (1976). Menstruation, reattribution, and competence. *Journal of Personality and Social Psychology, 33,* 345–353.

Ross, M., & Fletcher, G. J. O. (1985). Attribution and social perception. In G. Lindzey & E. Aronson (Eds.), *The handbook of social psychology* (3rd ed., Vol. 2, pp. 73–122). New York: Random House.

Ross, M., & Olson, J. M. (1981). An expectancy-attribution model of the effects of placebos. *Psychological Review, 88,* 408–437.

Ross, M., & Olson, J. M. (1982). Placebo effects in medical research and practice. In J. R. Eiser (Ed.), *Social psychology and behavioral medicine* (pp. 441–458). London: Wiley.

Rutledge, L. L., & Hupka, R. B. (1985). The facial feedback hypothesis: Methodological concerns and new supporting evidence. *Motivation and Emotion, 9,* 219–240.

Safian, L. (1967). *2,000 more insults.* New York: Pocket Books.

Schachter, S. (1964). The interaction of cognitive and physiological determinants of emotional state. In L. Berkowitz (Ed.), *Advances in experimental social psychology* (Vol. 1, pp. 48–81). New York: Academic Press.

Schachter, S., & Singer, J. E. (1962). Cognitive, social, and physiological determinants of emotional state. *Psychological Review, 69,* 379–399.

Schachter, S., & Wheeler, L. (1962). Epinephrine, chlorpromazine, and amusement. *Journal of Abnormal and Social Psychology, 65,* 121–128.

Schwarz, N., & Clore, G. L. (1983). Mood, misattribution, and judgments of well-being: Informative and directive functions of affective states. *Journal of Personality and Social Psychology, 45,* 513–523.

Singerman, K. J., Borkovec, T. D., & Baron, R. S. (1976). Failure of a "misattribution therapy" manipulation with a clinically relevant target behavior. *Behavior Therapy, 7,* 306–316.

Slivken, K. E., & Buss, A. H. (1984). Misattribution and speech anxiety. *Journal of Personality and Social Psychology, 47,* 396–402.

Storms, M. D., & Nisbett, R. E. (1970). Insomnia and the attribution process. *Journal of Personality and Social Psychology, 16,* 319–328.

Valins, S. (1966). Cognitive effects of false heart-rate feedback. *Journal of Personality and Social Psychology, 4,* 400–408.

Weiner, B. (1985). An attributional theory of achievement motivation and emotion. *Psychological Review, 92,* 548–573.

White, G. L., & Kight, T. D. (1984). Misattribution of arousal and attraction: Effects of salience of explanations for arousal. *Journal of Experimental Social Psychology, 20,* 55–64.

Wilde, L. (1981). *The official doctors' joke book.* New York: Bantam Books.

Worchel, S., & Yohai, S. M. L. (1979). The role of attribution in the experience of crowding. *Journal of Experimental Social Psychology, 15,* 91–104.

Zanna, M. P., & Cooper, J. (1974). Dissonance and the pill: An attribution approach to studying the arousal properties of dissonance. *Journal of Personality and Social Psychology, 29,* 703–709.

Zigler, E., Levine, J., & Gould, L. (1966). Cognitive processes in the development of children's appreciation of humor. *Child Development, 37,* 507–518.

Zillman, D. (1978). Attribution and misattribution of excitatory reactions. In J. H. Harvey, W. J. Ickes, & R. F. Kidd (Eds.), *New directions in attribution research* (Vol. 2, pp. 335–368). Hillsdale, NJ: Lawrence Erlbaum Associates.

3 Self-Persuasion Via Self-Reflection

Timothy D. Wilson
University of Virginia

Sometimes people come to believe what they are saying, even if their remarks are inconsistent with their attitudes, beliefs, or feelings. This phenomenon, known as self-persuasion, is a form of self-inference that has intrigued social psychologists for many years. In this chapter I will briefly review the literature on self-persuasion, and then present evidence for a new form of this type of attitude change. To anticipate, my students and I have found that when people try to explain why they feel the way they do they often bring to mind reasons that imply a new attitude, and as a result adopt this new outlook. I will discuss the reason this type of attitude change occurs, as well as its consequences for such areas as personal decision making.

Self-persuasion was first investigated in the early 1950s, as part of Carl Hovland's research project on communication and persuasion (Hovland, Janis, & Kelley, 1953). Janis and King (1954) and King and Janis (1956), for example, asked subjects to give a speech advocating a position that was against their own as part of a test of their debating skills. Those asked to generate their own arguments for the speech became more favorably disposed toward the position they advocated, as compared with subjects who read a prepared speech or listened to others give a speech. When preparing a speech people seem to engage in "biased scanning" (Janis & Gilmore, 1965), whereby they consider only the arguments on one side of the issue. These arguments seem to have greater force when people think of them themselves than when they simply read them, thus producing attitude change (Greenwald & Albert, 1968; O'Neill & Levings, 1979).

By far the best-known studies on self-persuasion have been those performed by dissonance theorists, who demonstrated that when people behave in a way that is silly, stupid, or immoral, without any good reason for doing so, they often justify this behavior to themselves by believing it had some merit (Aronson, 1980; Cooper & Fazio, 1984; Festinger, 1957). Some of the demonstrations of this phenomenon were similar to the Janis and King studies, in that people were induced to argue for positions against their beliefs. When people think they have a choice as to whether or not to argue the counterattitudinal position, and can find no compelling external reason for agreeing to do it, they reduce the resulting dissonance by coming to believe what they are saying (see, for example, Cohen's classic experiment, described in Brehm & Cohen, 1962). Similarly, self-perception theorists have documented several situations in which people change their attitudes, traits, and emotional states by drawing inferences from their behavior (Bem, 1972; Olson, this volume; Schachter, 1964).

Research on self-persuasion peaked in the late 1960s and early 1970s in a flurry of studies that attempted to distinguish between the dissonance, self-perception, and biased scanning interpretations of this phenomenon. This flurry subsided when it became clear that each approach was valid in its own, unique domain (see Petty & Cacioppo, 1981; Zanna & Cooper, 1976). There has continued to be, however, a trickle of new research on self-persuasion. For example, Jones and his students, as documented in this volume, demonstrated that even stable states such as self-esteem can be altered through self-persuasion. People instructed to respond in an especially self-enhancing or self-deprecating manner in an interview came to believe that their behavior was an accurate reflection of their self-esteem (Jones, this volume; Jones, Rhodewalt, Berglas, & Skelton, 1981; Rhodewalt, 1986; Rhodewalt & Agustsdottir, 1986).

Higgins (1981), in an earlier volume in this series, demonstrated a different form of self-persuasion. He argued that people often take into account other people's beliefs and attitudes when conversing with them, and tailor their message accordingly. For example, when Mary discusses Bill with Sue, she might present Bill in an especially positive light, because she knows that Sue is fond of Bill. Interestingly, these modifications of interpersonal communications have implications for the communicator's own attitudes. People either forget or don't realize that their messages were biased to suit their audience, and as a result come to believe what they are saying (Higgins & Rholes, 1978). Thus, Mary would like Bill more after presenting him in a positive light to Sue.

It is important to note that all of these different forms of self-persuasion, both new and old, share some common features. First, people initially behave in a fashion that is contrary to their beliefs because of an external constraint on their behavior. This external constraint usually takes the form of the experimenter instructing subjects to respond in a way that is not an accurate representation of their private beliefs—to argue a counterattitudinal position, to be especially self-deprecating in an interview, or even to eat a grasshopper (Zimbardo, Weisenberg,

Firestone, & Levy, 1965). Self-persuasion occurs in part because people do not fully appreciate the fact that their behavior has been constrained, and assume that it reflects their true nature or beliefs (Kelley, 1967). Second, there is a distinct interpersonal flavor to most demonstrations of self-persuasion. That is, people come to believe what they are saying after saying it in public, or at least in a form that they think will be made public. Indeed, one of the best ways to bring about self-persuasion, according to dissonance theory, is to convince people that others will witness their counterattitudinal behavior and be adversely affected by it (e.g., Nel, Helmreich, & Aronson, 1969).

In this chapter I will describe a type of self-persuasion that has many features in common with those already discussed, but is different in some important respects. As in the other studies in this area, I will demonstrate that people sometimes come to believe what they are saying. Unlike the other studies, people come to believe something they are saying to themselves, not to someone else. Further, rather than underestimating an external influence on their behavior, people in our studies seem to generate a counterattitudinal position on their own, without realizing they have done so. Thus, I hope to demonstrate that people's arms do not have to be twisted to write counterattitudinal essays, eat grasshoppers, or be self-deprecating to bring about self-persuasion: It is enough simply to ask people to explain why they feel the way they do. This simple act of self-reflection can, I suggest, cause people to generate a biased sample of reasons for their feelings, reasons which sometimes imply a different attitude than they previously held. Unaware that their reasons are not representative of their feelings, people then change their attitude to match their reasons. That is, much like previous research on self-persuasion, people come to believe what they are saying.

Before discussing this research in detail, it is important to mention another way in which it differs from previous research on self-persuasion. Compared with other studies, which have found that attitude change resulting from self-persuasion can be long lasting (e.g., Elms, 1966; Lepper, 1973; Watts, 1967), attitude change resulting from self-reflection may be short-lived. Why, then, should we bother to study it? Even though the change may be temporary, it can have important consequences. (As Jones argues elsewhere in this volume, in a similar context, "temporary and trivial are not the same thing.") For example, when people are faced with a choice, be it what car to buy, which job to accept, or whom to marry, they sometimes think about why they feel the way they do about each alternative. As a result of this self-reflection they might change their minds about which alternative is the best, and alter their choice accordingly. If this attitude change is temporary, however, and their initial preferences reassert themselves at some later point, people might come to regret the decision they made. Evidence in support of this hypothesis will be presented later in this chapter.

WHY CAN EXPLAINING AN ATTITUDE CHANGE IT?

Wilson, Dunn, Kraft, and Lisle (1989) offered the following account of how thinking about reasons can change people's attitudes: People have difficulty knowing exactly why they feel the way they do, thus the reasons they bring to mind are often incomplete or incorrect. Consequently, these reasons might imply a somewhat different attitude than they previously held. Unaware that their reasons are incomplete or inaccurate, people change their attitude in the direction implied by these reasons. Let us consider each component of this hypothesis:

The Reasons People Give Are Often Incomplete or Inaccurate

People's explanations of their own feelings, judgments, and behaviors are often incorrect (Nisbett & Wilson, 1977b; Wilson & Stone, 1985). Though some have found this conclusion to be too extreme (e.g., Ericsson & Simon, 1980; Smith & Miller, 1978), few would dispute the claim that people sometimes have difficulty knowing the exact determinants of their attitudes and feelings. A simple demonstration of this can be performed by asking one's married friends exactly why they love their spouses, or asking ourselves exactly why we feel the way we do about strawberry jam, old Cary Grant movies, or Picasso's "Guernica." Answers to such questions are surely not random—I am certain that my wife's cheerful nature is part of the reason I love her—but who is to say how much of a part? And how can I be certain that I am not underestimating the effects of other important factors? A little later I will argue that some types of attitudes are more difficult to explain than others, and are thus more susceptible to change as a result of thinking about reasons. For the moment, however, I simply suggest that there is a (sometimes substantial) margin of error in people's explanations of their attitudes.

The Reasons People Bring to Mind Can Imply a Somewhat Different Attitude

I do not mean to argue that as a result of being inaccurate, people bring to mind a set of reasons that are diametrically opposed to their attitudes. Even if people do not know why they feel the way they do, the desire to be consistent would cause them to come up with reasons that are at least roughly compatible with their attitude. My basic point is that there is room here for some slippage, and that the reasons people bring to mind can imply a somewhat different attitude than they held before. One reason this can occur is that there is a bias toward giving rational attributes of the attitude object as reasons for liking or disliking it, even when attitudes are caused by other factors. In the hundreds of reasons we have coded over the years, by far the majority of them are of this type, such as, "We get along well because we have common friends and enjoy many of the same activities," "I like this puzzle because it had a logical answer," "I don't like this painting because the flowers look like they're dying."

Curiously, however, there is ample evidence that attitudes are often caused by factors other than rational cognitions about the attributes of the attitude object. These other influences on attitudes include mere exposure (Zajonc, 1968), classical conditioning (Staats & Staats, 1958; Zanna, Kiesler, & Pilkonis, 1970), operant conditioning (Insko & Cialdini, 1971), halo effects (Nisbett & Wilson, 1977a), and attitudes stemming from people's core values such as their religious beliefs or the beliefs of their parents (Ellsworth & Ross, 1983; Herek, 1986; Rokeach, 1973; Sears, 1983). When people in our studies are asked to think about reasons, they rarely mention such factors.

This may explain why the reasons subjects bring to mind can imply a somewhat different attitude. People might feel favorably disposed toward a political candidate primarily due to mere exposure (i.e., they have seen the candidate on television many times) and the fact that the candidate belongs to the political party that they favor. When asked to explain their attitude, people might be unable to verbalize these factors. Instead, what comes to mind is the fact that the candidate holds different views on abortion than they do; that is, factors which imply a more negative attitude than they originally held. Again, I am not suggesting that people bring to mind reasons that are the opposite to their initial evaluation. Given that people often have a range of attitudes that they find acceptable at any given point in time, however (C. Sherif, M. Sherif, & Nebergall, 1965; M. Sherif & Hovland, 1961), any reason that is consistent with an attitude in this latitude of acceptance will seem plausible to people.

People Adopt the Attitude Implied by Their Reasons

Perhaps the most controversial part of our argument is that people come to adopt the attitude implied by the biased sample of reasons they bring to mind. I suggest that, possibly due to a general insensitivity to sample bias (Hamill, Wilson, & Nisbett, 1980), people do not realize that their reasons are sometimes incomplete or inaccurate, and thus assume that their attitude is the one implied by these reasons.

Evidence for this hypothesis has been obtained by Salancik (1974) and Seligman, Fazio, and Zanna (1980). Seligman et al., for example, asked subjects to think of reasons why they liked their dating partner. Unlike in our studies, these researchers attempted to bias the types of reasons subjects considered by the way the question was asked. Subjects answered either the question, "I go out with this person *because* I . . ." or, "I go out with this person *in order to* . . ." The former question elicited reasons that were primarily internal (i.e., having to do with one's own feelings and commitment), while the latter question elicited reasons that were primarily external (i.e., having to do with factors other than

FIG. 3.1. An example of attitude change following self-reflection (drawing by Cobean; © 1951, 1979, The New Yorker Magazine, Inc.).

love and commitment, such as the desire to impress one's friends). As predicted, subjects seem not to have realized that they had generated a biased set of reasons, and thus adopted the attitude implied by their reasons. That is, subjects who answered the "because I" question reported significantly more love and expressed more of an intention to marry their partners than did subjects who answered the "in order to" question.

Our hypothesis about self-persuasion via self-reflection is very similar to Salancik's (1974) and Seligman et al.'s (1980), with one important difference: We suggest that it is not necessary to direct subjects' reasons in any particular direction. Interestingly, people seem to come up with biased samples of reasons on their own, resulting in attitude change. As will be seen shortly this attitude change will not necessarily be in the same direction for all people, because the reasons that come to mind for one person might imply a different attitude than the reasons that come to mind for someone else. Nevertheless, people have been found to change their minds as a result of thinking about reasons. Before considering the experimental evidence for this proposition, an illustration of it can be found in the cartoon in Fig. 3.1. The man in the cartoon had a change of heart after thinking about why he felt the way he did about his betrothed. This is very close to the phenomenon we have found in our lab, proving that sometimes life imitates cartoons.

EXPERIMENTAL EVIDENCE

Let us take a more detailed look at the experimental evidence for the foregoing propositions. My students and I have conducted a series of studies in which some subjects are asked to think about why they feel the way they do about an attitude object. These attitude objects have included political candidates, dating partners, beverages, puzzles, consumer goods such as art posters and pens, and, immodestly, my vacation pictures. In one study, for example, subjects were asked "to list all of the reasons you can think of why your relationship with your dating partner is going the way it is" (Wilson, Dunn, Bybee, Hyman, & Rotondo, 1984, p. 11). Subjects are usually asked to write down their reasons, but the privacy and anonymity of these thoughts are stressed. In many studies subjects are told that we are asking them to think about reasons "to organize your thoughts," and that "you will not be asked to hand in this questionnaire." To reinforce this idea, the experimenter deposits the reasons questionnaire in the trash after the subject has completed it. Other subjects are randomly assigned to a control condition, where they spend a roughly equal amount of time completing a filler questionnaire. Often this questionnaire asks subjects to think about their reasons for some unrelated attitude, such as why they chose their major. All subjects then complete an attitude scale assessing evaluation of the attitude object in question, and the average attitudes reported by subjects in the reasons versus control conditions are compared.

Wilson et al. (1989) reviewed 20 studies that followed this design, and found that thinking about reasons caused a significant shift in attitudes in 11 of them. In addition, in several studies the reasons subjects gave were coded according to how positive an attitude toward the stimulus they conveyed. This "liking expressed in reasons" index was found to correlate significantly with subjects' subsequent attitudes in all of these studies, which is consistent with the idea that they adopted the attitude implied by their reasons. But what about the studies that found no evidence for attitude change? The studies reviewed by Wilson et al. measured attitudes only once, and thus could assess only one type of change: the case where subjects in the reasons condition became either more negative or more positive, on the average, compared with control subjects. They were unable to test another kind of change that might have occurred in some of the studies where there were no mean shifts in attitudes: The case where some subjects in the reasons condition became more positive and others became more negative, averaging out to an attitude that was no different than the average attitude in the control condition.

Either type of attitude change might be expected to occur as a result of thinking about reasons. The kinds of reasons that are most plausible for liking or disliking some attitude objects are fairly constant across subjects, so that when asked to give reasons, most subjects will come up with the same factors. Consequently, attitude change resulting from thinking about these reasons will be in a common direction across subjects. For example, in some of our studies subjects analyzed their reasons for liking or disliking five different puzzles (Wilson et al., 1984; Wilson & Dunn, 1986). Apparently the reasons that were most available in memory and most plausible were similar across subjects (e.g., that a particular puzzle was challenging), as evidenced by the fact that their evaluations of individual puzzles tended to change in the same direction as a result of thinking about reasons.

For other types of attitude objects, different kinds of reasons are likely to come to mind for different individuals. For example, the population of reasons for liking or disliking a political candidate is probably much larger than the population of reasons for liking or disliking a puzzle. Further, an attribute of a political candidate—such as his or her stance on abortion—is more likely to interact with people's own values and beliefs, such that it is viewed as a positive attribute by some people and a negative attribute by others. Therefore, when people think about why they feel the way they do about a political candidate, the attributes that come to mind might be primarily positive for some subjects and negative for others, producing attitude change in different directions for different individuals.[1]

_____

[1]Arguing that bidirectional attitude change can occur does not necessarily mean that attitudes will

This hypothesis was tested in a recent study by Wilson, Kraft, and Dunn (1989). As part of a group testing session in the early spring of 1987, subjects rated their attitudes toward several potential candidates for president in 1988. Several weeks later they took part in an ostensibly unrelated study, where half of the subjects were asked to think about why they liked or disliked six of these candidates. Subjects in the control condition completed an unrelated, filler questionnaire. All subjects then rated their attitudes toward the six candidates.

There is no reason to expect that the kinds of reasons that would come to mind for liking or disliking a particular candidate—such as George Bush—would be uniformly positive or negative for all of our subjects. Consistent with this expectation, the reasons manipulation did not produce a shift in attitude toward any of the candidates in a uniform direction. That is, the average shift in attitude between Time 2 and Time 1 was not significantly different in subjects in the reasons versus the control condition. As predicted, however, evidence was obtained for a bidirectional shift in attitude among subjects in the reasons condition. This was assessed by taking the absolute value of the difference in attitudes between Time 2 and Time 1, after converting both measures to standard scores. The average shift was significantly higher in the reasons than the control condition.

The reasons subjects gave were coded according to how positive an attitude toward the candidates they conveyed. If we are correct that subjects came to believe the attitude conveyed by their reasons, then this "liking expressed in reasons" index should correlate highly with their attitudes in the study, but less so with the attitudes expressed several weeks earlier. Consistent with this prediction, the average, within-subjects correlation between liking expressed in reasons and attitudes at Time 2 was higher (mean $r = .88$) than the average correlation between liking expressed in reasons and attitudes at Time 1 (mean $r = .71$), a difference that was nearly significant ($p = .06$).

Boundary Conditions on the Effects of Thinking about Reasons

If we are correct that self-persuasion follows self-reflection because people have difficulty knowing why they feel the way they do, thereby bringing to mind reasons that imply a somewhat different attitude, then a potential boundary condition is implicated: People are probably less likely to know why they feel the way they do about some attitudes than others, and if so, these attitudes should be most susceptible to change as a result of thinking about reasons. We hypoth-

---

become polarized (Tesser, 1978). A person with a moderately positive attitude might bring to mind reasons that are somewhat negative, causing moderation, or reasons that are extremely positive, causing polarization.

esized that a type of attitude fitting this description is one which is based on relatively little knowledge about the attitude object.

Knowledgeable people are more likely to have a strong cognitive component to their attitude that is well integrated with their affect. They have spent more time thinking about the attitude object, thus their attitude is more likely to be based on a consistent set of cognitions (Lusk & Judd, 1988). When asked to explain their attitude they may find it easier to do so, and may be less likely to bring to mind a biased sample of reasons than are unknowledgeable people. In contrast, unknowledgeable people are more likely to have attitudes that are not based on a well-articulated set of beliefs, and thus are more likely to be misled by having to phrase their attitude in cognitive terms. Finally, unknowledgeable people may have weaker attitudes that are more likely to change (Fazio, 1986; Fazio & Zanna, 1981), and are thus more susceptible to the effects of thinking about reasons.

We tested this hypothesis in the Wilson, Kraft, and Dunn (1989) political study by asking people during the group testing session how familiar they were with each of the candidates, and dividing them into two groups: those who were relatively knowledgeable and those who were not. As predicted, the reasons manipulation caused bidirectional attitude change only for unknowledgeable people; in fact, the results of this study referred to earlier were for this group of subjects only. Among knowledgeable subjects, there was little difference between the amount of change in the reasons and control subjects. This difference between the unknowledgeable and knowledgeable subjects was reflected by a significant Reasons × Knowledge interaction on the measure of bidirectional change. Further, as predicted, the liking expressed in the reasons of knowledgeable subjects correlated about equally with their attitudes at Time 2 and Time 1, $rs = .85$ and $.89$.

One reason knowledgeable people are less susceptible to the effects of explaining their attitudes is that they may have stronger attitudes, and are thus less likely to budge from their position in response to any attitude change technique (Fazio & Zanna, 1981). Alternatively, knowledgeable and unknowledgeable people may differ in other ways that contributed to the differential effect of thinking about reasons. For example, knowledgeable people may have a better grasp on why they feel the way they do, and thus are less likely to bring to mind a biased set of reasons. Unsure of why they feel the way they do, unknowledgeable people might be more likely to generate reasons that imply a different attitude than they previously held.

At present we cannot definitively distinguish between these different possibilities (for a more extended discussion of this issue, see Wilson, Kraft, and Dunn (1989). Wilson and Kraft (1988), however, have found evidence consistent with the idea that thinking about reasons is most likely to cause changes in attitudes that are difficult to explain. In this study we manipulated the basis of subjects' attitudes toward other students. Some subjects were given profiles describing the students' career goals and hobbies, whereas others formed their attitudes on the basis of information that was more difficult to verbalize (mere exposure; i.e., the frequency with which they saw pictures of the students). As predicted, having to explain why they felt the way they did was more likely to change the attitudes of subjects in the mere exposure condition, presumably because they found it difficult to explain their feelings, and thus came up with a list of reasons that was incomplete or inaccurate.

ANALYZING REASONS VERSUS OTHER FORMS OF SELF-REFLECTION

The type of self-reflection we have studied is similar to two other forms of introspection that have received a good deal of attention in the literature. The first is self-focus, or the case where people think about how they feel (as opposed to why they feel that way). Snyder and his colleagues, for example, have found that instructing people to think about their attitudes increased the consistency between attitudes and behavior, presumably by increasing the salience of the attitude and its implications for behavior (Snyder & Kendzierski, 1982; Snyder & Swann, 1976; see also Fazio, Chen, McDonel, & Sherman, 1982). Research generated by self-awareness theory (Duval & Wicklund, 1972, Wicklund, 1975) has also demonstrated that self-focused attention increases attitude-behavior correlations (e.g., Pryor, Gibbons, Wicklund, Fazio, & Hood, 1977; Scheier, Buss, & Buss, 1978). (For an extended discussion of these issues see Volume 2 in this series, especially Snyder, 1982, and Wicklund, 1982).

According to our model, thinking about reasons and focusing on feelings should have distinct effects. We have argued that attitude change results from analyzing reasons because people are not completely aware of why they feel the way they do, and thus bring to mind a set of reasons that are incomplete or inaccurate. When asked to focus only on how they feel, however, people should not have as much difficulty retrieving this affect. That is, even though people might not have perfect access to their internal states (Wilson, 1985), there probably is some truth to the old saw that "I may not know why but I know what I like." Thus, we would expect self-focus to leave an attitude unchanged or possibly even strengthen it, rather than causing the kind of change that results from analyzing reasons.

Support for this hypothesis has been found in several studies that compared instructions to focus on one's feelings and instructions to explain those feelings (Millar & Tesser, 1986a; Tesser, Leone, & Clary, 1978; Wilson & Dunn, 1986). In each of these studies the two types of self-reflection have been found to have distinct effects. Subjects in a study by Wilson and Dunn (1986), for example, familiarized themselves with a set of five puzzles, and then either (a) wrote down *why* they found each puzzle interesting or boring (reasons condition), (b) wrote down *how they felt* about each puzzle (focus condition), or (c) completed a filler questionnaire (control condition). As predicted by our model, subjects in the focus and control conditions reported very similar preferences for the five puzzles. Thinking about reasons, however, tended to change people's minds about which puzzles they like the best. (Another dependent measure in this study—the correlation between subjects' ratings of the puzzles and their behavior toward them—is discussed in a moment.)

Tesser (1978) has investigated another form of self-reflection, where people are asked merely to think about the attitude object. According to his model of self-generated attitude change, people who have a relatively complex schema about an attitude object will bring to mind evaluatively consistent cognitions when asked to think about the object, resulting in a more polarized (i.e., more extreme) attitude. This mere thought manipulation is more similar to the kind of self-focus manipulation discussed by Snyder (1982) and Wicklund (1982) than to our reasons manipulation; that is, subjects typically focus on their feelings, not on the reasons behind them. Therefore we would expect mere thought to have different effects than analyzing reasons. Tesser et al. (1978) found support for this hypothesis in a study of people who were anxious about public speaking. Some subjects were instructed to think about how they felt while speaking in public, whereas others were instructed to think about why they felt the way they did while speaking in public. The most attitude change (assessed with self-report measures of anxiety after giving a short speech) was found in the reasons analysis group. As in the Wilson and Dunn (1986) study, subjects in the condition that thought only about how they felt showed relatively little attitude change.

The relationship between analyzing reasons and mere thought was explored further in the Wilson, Kraft, and Dunn (1989) study of attitudes toward the 1988 presidential candidates. If the two kinds of self-reflection are similar, we should have found attitude polarization among subjects who were familiar with the candidates, because these people satisfied two conditions identified by Tesser (1978) and Millar and Tesser (1986b) for polarization: First, they were more likely to have complex schemata about the candidates, given their additional knowledge, and second, the thoughts about the candidates they listed were more evaluatively consistent than were the thoughts listed by people unfamiliar with the candidates. Analyzing reasons, however, did not lead to attitude polarization, suggesting that this type of self-reflection is not the same as mere thought. This is, of course, a null finding, but it is suggestive of the following conclusion: Analyzing reasons does not appear to polarize attitudes. Instead it changes attitudes—in a positive or negative direction—in people unfamiliar with the attitude object.

DOES EXPLAINING AN ATTITUDE
INFLUENCE BEHAVIOR?

To recap our argument to this point, we suggest that thinking about reasons brings to mind a biased sample of cognitions about the attitude object, producing attitude change in the direction of the biased sample. To this point we have been discussing attitude change on one type of dependent measure, namely self-reported attitudes. In several of our studies we also included behavioral measures of attitudes, such as the amount of time subjects played with the puzzles in the Wilson and Dunn (1986) study, or whether or not dating couples stayed together after being in the Wilson et al. (1984) experiment. A striking finding in these studies is that thinking about reasons appeared to change self-reported attitudes, but not behavioral measures of attitudes. As a result, the correlation between attitude reports and behavior has been very low among subjects who analyze reasons (see Wilson et al., 1989, for a review). In this section we explain why thinking about reasons often does not influence behavior, and outline the conditions under which it will.

One possibility is that thinking about reasons causes only weak, momentary attitude change, which is sufficient to move people a bit on 7-point attitude scales, but not to change behavior. This argument is similar to Campbell's (1963) differential threshold hypothesis, which holds that different types of attitudinal responses have different thresholds (that is, some require more effort or motivation to perform). From lowest to highest threshold, argued Campbell, are (1) autonomic-muscular reactions (e.g., GSR), (2) verbal reports about feelings toward the stimulus, (3) verbal reports about one's behavioral intentions, and (4) overt, locomotor behavior. Analyzing reasons may cause change that exceeds the threshold for self-report change, but which does not exceed the threshold for behavioral change.

There is reason to believe, however, that the differential threshold view cannot account fully for the effects of explaining attitudes. The first argument against this view concerns the earlier suggestion that analyzing reasons causes people to focus on cognitions about the attitude object, giving their new attitude a heavy cognitive flavor. Millar and Tesser (1986a) pointed out that behavior as well as attitudes can be the result of either the affective or cognitive component of an attitude, thus attitudes resulting from thinking about reasons should predict behavior that is cognitively based. Behavior change has not been found in our studies, they suggested, because we measured affectively based behaviors, which should not be expected to follow from a cognitively based attitude. Further, they demonstrated that analyzing reasons will change behavior, as long as the behavior is a function of the cognitions made salient by the reasons analysis manipulation.

In addition, we have found that analyzing reasons will affect behavior as long as the behavioral measure comes soon after the reasons manipulation (Wilson, Lisle, & Schooler, 1988). In many of our previous studies, behavior was measured after a delay, allowing people's initial evaluation to return. That is, as people continue to interact with the attitude object their initial evaluation of it may reassert itself, thereby driving their behavior in a way that is likely to be inconsistent with the attitude expressed after analyzing reasons.

An example of this process can be found in our studies that used Fazio's (e.g., Regan & Fazio, 1977) puzzle paradigm. In these studies subjects think about why they feel the way they do about five different types of puzzles. As a result of this reasons analysis they use different criteria to evaluate the puzzles, and end up evaluating them differently than do people in control conditions who do not think about reasons, as discussed earlier. After evaluating the puzzles subjects are left alone during a free-time period, where they can play with any of the puzzles they choose. We originally reported that subjects in the reasons analysis conditions choose to play with the same puzzles as subjects in the control conditions, and as a result exhibited less consistency between their evaluations and their behavior (Wilson & Dunn, 1986; Wilson et al., 1984). This is true if one averages subjects' behavior toward the puzzles during the entire 15-minute free-time period.

In a reanalysis of these studies, however, Wilson et al. (1989) found that when people thought about reasons, their *initial* choice of which puzzle to play with was predicted by their new attitude; that is, the reasons manipulation did change subjects' initial behavior. After playing with this puzzle for awhile, however, they tended to switch to the same puzzles chosen by subjects in the control condition, puzzles that they had not rated highly. It is as if subjects' initial evaluation (i.e., before they analyzed reasons) reasserted itself, such that they discovered that they didn't like their initial choice of puzzle as much as they thought they would. We will see later that this finding has important implications for personal decision making, when people analyze the alternatives before making their choice.

Thus, we and Millar and Tesser (1986a) have found evidence for behavioral change as a result of thinking about reasons, suggesting that Campbell's (1963) differential threshold view is not a satisfactory account of our results. An advantage of our hypothesis concerning initial versus later behavior change is that it specifies when behavior change should result from thinking about reasons and when it should not. If subjects have a relatively long period of time to interact with the attitude object, as in the puzzle studies and the Wilson et al. (1984) couples study (where the behavioral measure was whether subjects had broken up several months later), then people's initial evaluation of the stimulus has a chance to reassert itself. If the behavioral measure is a short-term one, such as subjects' choice between different attitude objects immediately after analyzing reasons, then this choice might well be driven by the new attitude, resulting in attitude–behavior consistency.

EFFECTS OF THINKING ABOUT REASONS
ON PERSONAL DECISION MAKING

To this point I have argued that thinking about reasons can change people's attitudes, at least temporarily. If the change is only temporary, however, then why should we get excited about it? Is it nothing more than the fleeting effects of momentary musing, or does it have some consequences to the muser? I suggest that it can have important consequences, some desirable, some undesirable.

Sometimes an attitude is unpleasant, either to the person who holds it (e.g., speech anxiety) or to the target of the attitude (e.g., racial prejudice). Having people explain these feelings might produce some attitude change in a desirable direction. Support for this prediction was found by Tesser et al. (1978), who asked women who were afraid of public speaking either to explain the reasons for their anxiety or simply to focus on their anxiety. As discussed earlier, those who explained their feelings reported significantly less anxiety after giving a speech than did those in either the focus or no-introspection control conditions. It is unlikely that simply asking people to explain why they are afraid of public speaking or why they have negative attitudes toward Blacks will lead to permanent attitude change. Thinking about the basis of such feelings, however, might prove to be a useful means of "unfreezing" them, making them more open to lasting change (Lewin, 1947).

I do not mean to suggest that we all walk around like monks with heads bowed, engaged in a constant questioning of our motives. In fact, there may be times when it is to our advantage *not* to analyze reasons. Occasionally we are faced with a choice between alternatives, such as automobiles to purchase, houses to live in, or spouses to marry. When deciding between alternatives, we are usually making an implicit prediction about what our affect toward these stimuli will be over time. That is, we want to choose the car or home or spouse that will give us the most pleasure in the long run. Would it be beneficial to analyze the reasons for our feelings when faced with such decisions?

To answer this question, it is important to note that when people analyze reasons, they appear to focus on a relatively small number of objective attributes of the attitude object. If these are the factors that will determine their affective reactions to the stimuli over the long run, then analyzing reasons would be a beneficial strategy. For example, consider the determinants of whether or not we are satisfied with a vacuum cleaner. There are probably a relatively small number of functional characteristics of vacuum cleaners that account for most of the variance in our satisfaction, such as whether they do a good job of picking up dirt, are convenient to use, and last a long time without needing repairs. Because analyzing our reasons for liking potential vacuum cleaners is likely to make us focus on features such as these, making such a decision reflectively is likely to increase the probability that we will be satisfied with our choice.

For other types of decisions, however, analyzing reasons might not be a desirable strategy to follow, for at least two reasons. First, if our future happiness with our choice is based on a large array of objective attributes of the stimuli, a strategy that highlights only a few of these attributes could be risky, because it might cause us to ignore important information. The answer here might be to do a much more formal, in-depth kind of reasons analysis of the type suggested by Janis and Mann (1977). They prescribed a "balance sheet" procedure designed to "stimulate [a] more thorough examination of the pros and cons of each alternative course of action" (p. 367), which involves a much longer and more careful examination of the stimuli than occurs in our studies, where subjects typically think about their reasons for only 10 minutes or so.

For still other kinds of decisions, however, it might be best to forgo any sort of reasons analysis, either in depth or off the cuff. This is likely to be true of any decision where people's eventual satisfaction with their choice is not a function of the objective attributes of the stimulus, but of factors that are more difficult to verbalize, or which do not seem like good, rational reasons for liking a stimulus. That is, if thinking about reasons focuses people on attributes of the stimulus that are irrelevant in determining their eventual satisfaction with their choice, then analyzing reasons could be risky. For example, when thinking about why we like or dislike a painting, most of us find it difficult to put into words exactly what it is that is determining our reaction. As a consequence we might focus on factors that are easy to verbalize but are not central to our reaction, such as some aspect of its composition, leading to the kind of attitude change we have observed in our other studies. That is, people might adopt the new attitude implied by their reasons.

There would be little consequence to such attitude change if it was long-lasting. People would adopt a new set of criteria for liking the painting, and presumably would be no worse off by doing so. Earlier, however, we saw that thinking about reasons can produce changes in attitudes and behavior in the short run, but over time people seem to revert back to their initial evaluation of the stimulus. When faced with a choice between stimuli that are difficult to analyze, then, people who explain their attitudes might be at a disadvantage: Their self-reflection might lead to a change in attitude that dictates which alternative they choose, whereas over time, their initial evaluation returns, leading to post decisional regret. People who make a choice based on their initial evaluation may be happiest with their decision, because this initial affect is a relatively good predictor of what their affect will be in the long run.

We recently tested these hypotheses in two studies in which subjects were asked to choose among an array of consumer items (Wilson, Lisle, & Schooler, 1988). In the first study, female subjects examined five posters of the type often seen in college dormitories. Two were reproductions of Impressionist art, which, we knew from pretesting, were very popular with our college student population. The other three were more contemporary posters (e.g., a photograph of a cat perched on a rope with the caption, "Gimme a Break"), which were unpopular with our population. Subjects examined the posters, and then rated how much they liked each one. Half of them were first asked to write down, privately and anonymously, why they liked or disliked each of the five posters, whereas the other half completed a filler questionnaire. After rating the posters, all subjects were told they could choose one to take home.

Consistent with our pretesting, subjects in the control, no-introspection condition rated the art posters higher than the contemporary posters, and, almost without exception, chose one of the art posters to take home (Table 3.1). As predicted, thinking about reasons produced a significant shift in attitudes: Those in the reasons condition rated the contemporary posters higher and the art posters lower, and were significantly more likely to choose one of the contemporary posters to take home.

Again, this attitude change would not be consequential if it persisted over time, such that both groups of subjects remained happy with their choice of poster. We predicted, however, that those in the reasons condition would come to regret their choice, because their initial evaluations of the posters—which, based on the reactions of the control subjects, were positive toward the art posters and negative toward the contemporary posters—would return. To test this, we telephoned subjects 3 weeks later and asked them how satisfied they were with the poster they had chosen. As seen in Table 3.1, subjects in the reasons condition were significantly less happy with this choice. This was particularly true among subjects who chose one of the contemporary posters, though the Reasons × Poster Type interaction was not significant.

These results are consistent with our prediction that it is sometimes undesirable to reflect too much about a decision. There are, however, some unanswered questions about the results of the poster study that were addressed in a second experiment. First, it was not entirely clear why the attitude change occurred in the direction it did. We have suggested that subjects who thought about reasons focused on attributes of the posters that were not central to their initial evaluation, causing attitude change. There is, however, at least one other possibility. Perhaps having to explain one's feelings reduced people's confidence in which posters were the best, causing them to rate all of the items close to the midpoint of the scale. The reduction in postchoice satisfaction may have stemmed from this bunching together of subjects' preferences; that is, it may have seemed like none of the posters was all that preferable to any other.

There were two sources of evidence against this "bunching" hypothesis.

TABLE 3.1
Results of the Wilson, Lisle, and Schooler (1988) Poster Study

Condition:	Control		Reasons	
Poster Type:	Art	Contemporary	Art	Contemporary
Choice (%)	95	5	64	36
Postchoice satisfaction[a]	2.68	3.00	2.21	2.17

[a]Subjects were asked whether they still had the poster, whether they had hung it up, and whether they planned to take it home with them at the end of the semester. They received a zero if they said no to these questions and a one if they said yes. The satisfaction index is the sum of their three responses.

First, the prechoice ratings of the posters subjects subsequently chose were as high in the reasons condition as in the control condition; it was only when they were called 3 weeks later that differences in satisfaction emerged. Second, a range score was computed for each subject by subtracting her lowest rating of a poster from her highest rating, and the difference between conditions in the mean range was nonsignificant. It would be desirable, however, to obtain more direct evidence for our hypothesis that subjects who think about reasons focus more on attributes that are not central to their initial evaluation.

In a second study we manipulated attributes of a stimulus (felt-tip pens) that we thought would be important to people's initial reaction, as well as attributes that we thought would not be as important, but were plausible as reasons for liking or disliking the pens. Based on pretesting, we used two pens that were of appealing colors (blue and black) and one that was unappealing (olive),[2] with the hypothesis that this would be an important determinant of subjects' initial liking for the pens. The pens were also said to differ in their tendency to smudge and how long they would last. These attributes, we hypothesized, would not be as important to subjects as the color of the pens, unless they focused on why they felt the way they did. The objective quality of a pen is a plausible reason for liking it, thus those instructed to think about reasons were hypothesized to weight this information more.

To test these hypotheses we manipulated whether the appeal of the colors was consistent with the objective quality of the pen. In the consistent condition, the pens that were of pleasing colors were also said to have the best objective characteristics, whereas in the inconsistent condition, the pens that were of pleasing colors were said to have the worst objective characteristics. If thinking about reasons causes people to focus more on the objective quality of the pens, then our reasons analysis manipulation should only influence people's attitudes in the inconsistent condition. When the color and objective information are consistent, thinking about reasons should make little difference.

The results were consistent with these predictions, as seen in Table 3.2. When there was a match between the appeal of the colors and the quality of the pens (i.e., in the consistent condition), thinking about reasons had no effect. All subjects in both the control and reasons condition chose one of the popular pens. When the appeal of the colors conflicted with the functional appeal of the pens, however, the poster study was replicated. Subjects in the control condition appear to have given more weight to the color, in that 92% of them chose a blue or black pen, even though its objective quality was ostensibly worse. More subjects

---

[2]Subjects also evaluated a brown-colored pen, which was intended to be unpopular. It turned out to be more popular than we thought, however; thus subjects who chose it were eliminated it from the analyses. The results were very similar if these subjects are included and the brown pen is categorized as popular.

TABLE 3.2
Results of the Wilson, Lisle, and Schooler Pen Study

Condition:	Control		Reasons	
Pen Color:	Popular	Unpopular	Popular	Unpopular
Percentage of People Who Chose Each Pen				
Consistent	100	0	100	0
Inconsistent	92	8	68	32
Post-choice Satisfaction[a]				
Consistent	.10	—	.23	—
Inconsistent	−.02	.47	.23	−.52

Note: The popular pens were blue or black, the unpopular pen was olive-colored.
[a]Average of the standardized ratings of (a) how often subjects reported using the pen in the past week, (b) whether or not they planned to buy a new pen of this type in the near future, (c) how satisfied they were with their choice of pen, and (d) how long it took them to retrieve their pen. The higher the score, the greater the satisfaction with the pen. It should be noted that these means are broken down by the number of people who chose each pen. Thus, there is missing data in the consistent/unpopular color cells, because no one in the consistent condition chose an olive-colored pen.

in the reasons condition, however, were swayed by the objective quality: Only 68% of them chose a blue or black pen, a difference that was significant.

Though subjects in the inconsistent/reasons condition were more likely to choose the olive-colored pen, those who chose this pen in this condition were the least satisfied with their choice when telephoned 3 weeks later (see bottom half of Table 3.2). The mean satisfaction score of −.52 was significantly lower than the mean of the satisfaction scores in the other five cells, supporting our prediction that thinking about reasons causes people to make choices that are based more on the objective characteristics of the stimuli, but that over time their initial evaluation reaction reasserts itself, leading to postchoice regret.

This result clarifies an equivocal finding from the poster study. According to our model, a reduction in postchoice satisfaction should occur primarily among subjects who analyze reasons *and* change their minds about which alternative is the best. Those for whom the reasons manipulation is ineffective—such as those who chose a blue or black pen in the reasons condition—should be relatively pleased with their pens. In the poster study there was only a trend in this direction; that is, there was a main effect of thinking about reasons on postchoice satisfaction rather than a Reasons × Poster Type interaction. The pen study found more definitively that only those who thought about reasons *and* chose a pen with an unappealing color came to regret their choice.

SUMMARY AND IMPLICATIONS

Several studies have found that people sometimes come to believe what they are saying, even when their utterances are contrary to their initial beliefs. In previous demonstrations of this self-persuasion effect there were constraints on what people could say; for example, an experimenter asked subjects to argue for a position contrary to their own. Because people did not fully recognize the extent to which their behavior was constrained, they assumed that what they said was what they believed. I have presented research indicating that even without any constraints on what they can say, people sometimes generate a biased sample of reasons for their feelings, reasons which imply a different attitude than they held previously. People then change their attitude to match their reasons, presumably because they are unaware that their reasons are not representative of their feelings.

Unlike previous demonstrations of self-persuasion, attitude change following self-reflection does not appear to be long-lasting. People adopt a new attitude based on a set of criteria that become salient when they analyze reasons, but over time, their initial evaluation is likely to return. This does not mean, however, that self-persuasion via self-reflection is inconsequential. We have demonstrated that after analyzing reasons people sometimes base a consumer decision on their new attitude, but that their initial evaluation returns at a later point, causing them to regret the decision they made.

Considerably more work is needed to establish the limits of these effects and the precise nature of the processes that mediate them. It will be particularly interesting to compare our findings with models of attitudes and decision making that view people as rational compilers of information. For example, Fishbein and Ajzen's (1975) theory of reasoned action posits that attitudes are the sum of people's evaluative beliefs, and that "human beings are usually quite rational and make systematic use of the information available to them" (Ajzen & Fishbein, 1980, p. 5). In contrast, we share the view of other recent theorists that attitudes are not always based solely on rational beliefs, but are often influenced by such factors as mere exposure, core values, conditioning, and past behavior (cf. Zajonc & Markus, 1982; Zanna & Rempel, 1988). Further, we have demonstrated that there may be a cost to attempting to make people rational: Reflecting about reasons can change people's attitudes, lower attitude-behavior consistency, and reduce postchoice satisfaction.

Interestingly, Fishbein & Ajzen (1975) anticipated the possible disruptive effects of reflection. When people focus on their beliefs about an attitude object, they argued, "previously nonsalient beliefs may become salient" and "the mere elicitation of beliefs may change a person's attitude" (pp. 218–219). To my knowledge, however, this possibility was never tested, and many studies of the theory of reasoned action focused subjects' attention on beliefs that might not have been part of their previous attitude, and thus might have changed subjects' minds about how they felt. Consistent with this possibility, Budd (1987) found that the order in which questions about subjects' beliefs, attitudes, subjective norms, and intentions were asked influenced the correlations between these variables, suggesting that "requiring people to think about the . . . components of the theory of reasoned action may cause them to create evaluative beliefs, intentions, subjective norms, and normative beliefs where none existed prior to measurement" (Budd, 1987, p. 98). Thus, the assessment techniques of the theory of reasoned action, as well as our reasons analysis manipulation, would appear to be candidates for a growing list of measures that have reactive effects (Feldman & Lynch, 1988).

Our findings also have important implications for decision making, by suggesting that there may be times when it is best to trust one's initial evaluation, rather than reflecting too much about a decision. I should emphasize, however, that I am not making an unbridled attack on self-reflection, and have no intention of challenging Socrates's oft-quoted statement that "the unexamined life is not worth living" (Loomis, 1942, p. 56). Earlier I outlined some conditions under which it would be desirable to unfreeze an attitude via self-reflection, and discussed some types of decisions that are best made reflectively. In addition, our studies so far have been limited to brief, off-the-cuff explanations of attitudes, and it may be that a more in depth analysis will not have the undesirable consequences we have found. For those of us who make most decisions armed with a list of reasons, however, it might sometimes be best to heed the advice I recently received in a fortune cookie: "Answer just what your heart prompts you."

ACKNOWLEDGMENTS

Most of the research discussed in this chapter was supported by National Science Foundation Grant BNS–8316189 or National Institute of Mental Health Grant MH41841. Several students and colleagues have made immeasurable contributions to this program of research, including Dana Dunn, Dolores Kraft, Doug Lisle, and Jonathan Schooler. Address correspondence to Timothy D. Wilson, Department of Psychology, Gilmer Hall, University of Virginia, Charlottesville, VA 22903–2477.

REFERENCES

Ajzen, I., & Fishbein, M. (1980). *Understanding attitudes and predicting social behavior.* Englewood Cliffs, NJ: Prentice-Hall.

Aronson, E. (1980). Persuasion via self-justification: Large commitments for small rewards. In L. Festinger (Ed.), *Retrospections on social psychology* (pp. 3–21). New York: Oxford University Press.

Bem, D. J. (1972). Self-perception theory. In L. Berkowitz (Ed.), *Advances in Experimental Social Psychology* (Vol. 6, pp. 1–62). New York: Academic Press.

Brehm, J. W., & Cohen, A. R. (1962). *Explorations in cognitive dissonance.* New York: Wiley.

Budd, R. J. (1987). Response bias and the theory of reasoned action. *Social Cognition, 5,* 95–107.

Campbell, D. T. (1963). Social attitudes and other acquired behavioral dispositions. In S. Koch (Ed.), *Psychology: A study of science* (Vol. 6, pp. 94–172). New York: McGraw–Hill.

Cooper, J., & Fazio, R. H. (1984). A new look at dissonance theory. In L. Berkowitz (Ed.), *Advances in experimental social psychology* (Vol. 17, pp. 229–266). Orlando, FL: Academic Press.

Duval, S., & Wicklund, R. A. (1972). *A theory of objective self-awareness.* New York: Academic Press.

Ellsworth, P. C., & Ross, L. (1983). Public opinion and capital punishment: A close examination of the views of abolitionists and retentionists. *Crime and Delinquency, 29,* 116–169.

Elms, A. C. (1966). Influence of fantasy ability on attitude change through role-playing. *Journal of Personality and Social Psychology, 4,* 36–43.

Ericsson, K. A., & Simon, H. A. (1980). Verbal reports as data. *Psychological Review, 87,* 215–251.

Fazio, R. H. (1986). How do attitudes guide behavior? In R. M. Sorrentino & E. T. Higgins (Eds.), *The handbook of motivation and cognition: Foundations of social behavior* (pp. 204–243). New York: Guilford Press.

Fazio, R. H., Chen, J., McDonel, E., & Sherman, S. J. (1982). Attitude accessibility, attitude-behavior consistency, and the strength of the object-evaluation association. *Journal of Experimental Social Psychology, 18,* 339–357.

Fazio, R. H., & Zanna, M. P. (1981). Direct experience and attitude-behavior consistency. In L. Berkowitz (Ed.), *Advances in experimental social psychology* (Vol. 14, pp. 161–202). New York: Academic Press.

Feldman, J. M., & Lynch, J. G. Jr. (1988). Self-generated validity and other effects of measurement on belief, attitude, intention, and behavior. *Journal of Applied Psychology, 73,* 421–435.

Festinger, L. (1957). *A theory of cognitive dissonance.* Stanford, CA: Stanford University Press.

Fishbein, M., & Ajzen, I. (1975). *Belief, attitude, intention, and behavior: An introduction to theory and research.* Reading, MA: Addison-Wesley.

Greenwald, A. G., & Albert, R. D. (1968). Acceptance and recall of improvised arguments. *Journal of Personality and Social Psychology, 8,* 31–34.

Hamill, R., Wilson, T. D., & Nisbett, R. E. (1980). Insensitivity to sample bias: Generalizing from atypical cases. *Journal of Personality and Social Psychology, 39,* 578–589.

Herek, G. (1986). The instrumentality of ideologies: Toward a neofunctional theory of attitudes and behavior. *Journal of Social Issues, 42,* 99–114.

Higgins, E. T. (1981). The "communication game": Implications for social cognition and persuasion. In E. T. Higgins, C. P. Herman, & M. P. Zanna (Eds.), *Social cognition: The Ontario Symposium* (Vol. 1, pp. 343–392). Hillsdale, NJ: Lawrence Erlbaum Associates.

Higgins, E. T., & Rholes, W. S. (1978). "Saying is believing": Effects of message modification on memory and liking for the person described. *Journal of Experimental Social Psychology, 14,* 363–378.

Hovland, C. I., Janis, I. L., & Kelley, H. H. (1953). *Communication and persuasion.* New Haven: Yale University Press.

Insko, C. A., & Cialdini, R. B. (1971). *Interpersonal influence in a controlled setting: The verbal reinforcement of attitude.* New York: General Learning Press.

Janis, I. L., & Gilmore, J. B. (1965). The influence in incentive conditions on the success of role-playing in modifying attitudes. *Journal of Personality and Social Psychology, 1,* 17–27.

Janis, I. L., & King, B. T. (1954). The influence of role-playing on opinion change. *Journal of Abnormal and Social Psychology, 49,* 211–218.

Janis, I. L., & Mann, L. (1977). *Decision making: A psychological analysis of conflict, choice, and commitment.* New York: Free Press.

Jones, E. E., Rhodewalt, F., Berglas, S., & Skelton, J. A. (1981). Effects of strategic self-presentation on subsequent self-esteem. *Journal of Personality and Social Psychology, 41*, 407–421.

Kelley, H. H. (1967). Attribution theory in social psychology. In D. Levine (Ed.), *Nebraska Symposium on Motivation* (Vol. 15, pp. 192–238). Lincoln: University of Nebraska Press.

King, B. T., & Janis, I. L. (1956). Comparison of the effectiveness of improvised versus non-improvised role-playing in producing opinion change. *Human Relations, 9*, 177–186.

Lepper, M. R. (1973). Dissonance, self-perception, and honesty in children. *Journal of Personality and Social Psychology, 25*, 65–74.

Lewin, K. (1947). Frontiers in group dynamics I. *Human Relations, 1*, 2–38.

Loomis, L. R. (Ed.). (1942). *Plato: Apology, Crito, Phaeda, Symposium, Republic* (B. Jowett, Trans.). New York: Walter J. Black.

Lusk, C. M., & Judd, C. M. (1988). Political expertise and the structural mediators of candidate evaluations. *Journal of Experimental Social Psychology, 24*, 105–126.

Millar, M. G., & Tesser, A. (1986a). Effects of affective and cognitive focus on the attitude-behavior relation. *Journal of Personality and Social Psychology, 51*, 270–276.

Millar, M. G., & Tesser, A. (1986b). Thought induced attitude change: The effects of schema structure and commitment. *Journal of Personality and Social Psychology, 51*, 259–269.

Nel, E., Helmreich, R., & Aronson, E. (1969). Opinion change in the advocate as a function of the persuasibility of his audience: A clarification of the meaning of dissonance. *Journal of Personality and Social Psychology, 12*, 117–124.

Nisbett, R. E., & Wilson, T. D. (1977a). The halo effect: Evidence for unconscious alternation of judgments. *Journal of Personality and Social Psychology, 35*, 250–256.

Nisbett, R. E., & Wilson, T. D. (1977b). Telling more than we can know: Verbal reports on mental processes. *Psychological Review, 84*, 231–259.

O'Neill, P., & Levings, D. E. (1979). Inducing biased scanning in a group setting to change attitudes toward bilingualism and capital punishment. *Journal of Personality and Social Psychology, 37*, 1432–1438.

Petty, R. E., & Cacioppo, J. T. (1981). *Attitudes and persuasion: Classic and contemporary approaches*. Dubuque, IA: William C. Brown.

Pryor, J. B., Gibbons, F. X., Wicklund, R. A., Fazio, R. H., & Hood, R. (1977). Self-focused attention and self-report validity. *Journal of Personality, 45*, 514–527.

Regan, D. T., & Fazio, R. H. (1977). On the consistency between attitudes and behavior: Look to the method of attitude formation. *Journal of Experimental Social Psychology, 13*, 38–45.

Rhodewalt, F. R. (1986). Self-presentation and the phenomenal self: On the stability and malleability of self-conceptions. In R. F. Baumeister (Ed.), *Public self and private self* (pp. 117–142). New York: Springer–Verlag.

Rhodewalt, F. R., & Agustsdottir, S. (1986). Effects of self-presentation on the phenomenal self. *Journal of Personality and Social Psychology, 50*, 47–55.

Rokeach, M. (1973). *The nature of human values*. New York: Free Press.

Salancik, G. R. (1974). Inference of one's attitude from behavior recalled under linguistically manipulated cognitive sets. *Journal of Experimental Social Psychology, 10*, 415–427.

Schachter, S. (1964). The interaction of cognitive and physiological determinants of emotional state. In L. Berkowitz (Ed.), *Advances in Experimental Social Psychology* (Vol. 1, pp. 49–80). New York: Academic Press.

Scheier, M. F., Buss, A. H., & Buss, D. M. (1978). Self-consciousness, self-report of aggressiveness, and aggression. *Journal of Research in Personality, 12*, 133–140.

Sears, D. O. (1983). The persistence of early political predispositions: The roles of attitude object and life stage. In L. Wheeler & P. Shaver (Eds.), *Review of personality and social psychology* (Vol. 4, pp. 79–116). Beverly Hills, CA: Sage.

Seligman, C., Fazio, R. H., & Zanna, M. P. (1980). Effects of salience of extrinsic rewards on liking and loving. *Journal of Personality and Social Psychology, 38*, 453–460.

Sherif, C. W., Sherif, M., & Nebergall, R. E. (1965). *Attitude and attitude change*. Philadelphia: W. B. Saunders.

Sherif, M. & Hovland, C. I. (1961). *Social Judgment: Assimilation and contrast effects in communication and attitude change*. New Haven: Yale University Press.

Smith, E. R., & Miller, F. D. (1978). Limits on perception of cognitive processes: A reply to Nisbett and Wilson, *Psychological Review, 85*, 355–362.

Snyder, M. (1982). When believing means doing: Creating links between attitudes and behavior. In M. P. Zanna, E. T. Higgins, & C. P. Herman (Eds.), *Consistency in social behavior: The Ontario Symposium* (Vol. 2, pp. 105–130). Hillsdale, NJ: Lawrence Erlbaum Associates.

Snyder, M., & Kendzierski, D. (1982). Acting on one's attitudes: Procedures for linking attitude and behavior. *Journal of Experimental Social Psychology, 18*, 165–183.

Snyder, M., & Swann, W. B. (1976). When actions reflect attitudes: The politics of impression management. *Journal of Personality and Social Psychology, 34*, 1034–1042.

Staats, A. W., & Staats, C. K. (1958). Attitudes established by classical conditioning. *Journal of Abnormal and Social Psychology, 57*, 37–40.

Tesser, A. (1978). Self-generated attitude change. In L. Berkowitz (Ed.), *Advances in experimental social psychology* (Vol. 11, pp. 289–338). New York: Academic Press.

Tesser, A., Leone, C., & Clary, G. (1978). Affect control: Process constraints versus catharsis. *Cognitive Therapy and Research, 2*, 265–274.

Watts, W. A. (1967). Relative persistence of opinion change induced by active compared to passive participation. *Journal of Personality and Social Psychology, 5*, 4–15.

Wicklund, R. A. (1975). Objective self-awareness. In L. Berkowitz (Ed.), *Advances in Experimental Social Psychology* (Vol. 8, pp. 233–275). New York: Academic Press.

Wicklund, R. A. (1982). Self-focused attention and the validity of self-reports. In M. P. Zanna, E. T. Higgins, & C. P. Herman (Eds.), *Consistency in social behavior: The Ontario Symposium* (Vol. 2, pp. 149–172). Hillsdale, NJ: Lawrence Erlbaum Associates.

Wilson, T. D. (1985). Strangers to ourselves: The origins and accuracy of beliefs about one's own mental states. In J. H. Harvey & G. Weary (Eds.), *Attribution in contemporary psychology* (pp. 9–36). New York: Academic Press.

Wilson, T. D., & Dunn, D. S. (1986). Effects of introspection on attitude-behavior consistency: Analyzing reasons versus focusing on feelings. *Journal of Experimental Social Psychology, 22*, 249–263.

Wilson, T. D., Dunn, D. S., Bybee, J. A., Hyman, D. B., & Rotondo, J. A. (1984). Effects of analyzing reasons on attitude-behavior consistency. *Journal of Personality and Social Psychology, 47*, 5–16.

Wilson, T. D., Dunn, D. S., Kraft, D., & Lisle, D. J. (1989). Introspection, attitude change, and attitude-behavior consistency: The disruptive effects of explaining why we feel the way we do. In L. Berkowitz (Ed.), *Advances in experimental social psychology* (Vol. 22, pp. 287–343). Orlando, FL: Academic Press.

Wilson, T. D., & Kraft, D. (1988). [Effects of thinking about reasons on affectively- and cognitively-based attitudes.] Unpublished raw data.

Wilson, T. D., Kraft, D., & Dunn, D. S. (1989). The disruptive effects of explaining attitudes: The moderating effect of knowledge about the attitude object. *Journal of Experimental Social Psychology, 25*, 379–400.

Wilson, T. D., Lisle, D. J., & Schooler, J. (1988). *Some undesirable effects of self-reflection*. Unpublished manuscript, University of Virginia.

Wilson, T. D., & Stone, J. I. (1985). More on telling more than we can know. In P. Shaver (Ed.), *Review of Personality and Social Psychology* (Vol. 6, pp. 167–183). Beverly Hills, CA: Sage.

Zajonc, R. B. (1968). Attitudinal effects of mere exposure. *Journal of Personality and Social Psychology Monograph, 9*, 1–28.

Zajonc, R. B., & Markus, H. (1982). Affective and cognitive factors in preferences. *Journal of Consumer Research, 9,* 123–131.

Zanna, M. P., & Cooper, J. (1976). Dissonance and the attribution process. In J. H. Harvey, W. J. Ickes, & R. F. Kidd (Eds.), *New directions in attribution research* (Vol. 1, pp. 199–221). Hillsdale, NJ: Lawrence Erlbaum Associates.

Zanna, M. P., Kiesler, C. A., & Pilkonis, P. A. (1970). Positive and negative attitudinal affect established by classical conditioning. *Journal of Personality and Social Psychology, 14,* 321–328.

Zanna, M. P., & Rempel, J. K. (1988). Attitudes: A new look at an old concept. In D. Bar–Tal & A. Kruglanksi (Eds.), *The social psychology of knowledge* (pp. 315–334). New York: Cambridge University Press.

Zimbardo, P., Weisenberg, M., Firestone, I., & Levy, B. (1965). Communicator effectiveness in producing public conformity and private attitude change. *Journal of Personality, 33,* 233–255.

4 Constrained Behavior and Self-Concept Change

Edward E. Jones
Princeton University

One of the most important themes in social psychology for the past three decades has been the conditions under which actions produce changes in the actor's dispositions. A major and distinctive contribution of our field has been to take the conventional view of attitudes affecting behavior and to stand it on its ear—or at least to recognize the companion truth that one's actions can bring about changes in one's attitudes. Most people in my generation grew up thinking that attitudes, values, and other dispositions grew out of experiences, out of things that happened to us and things that we were told. These attitudes were interesting because, we thought, they were good (though not infallible) predictors of behavior. Attitudes can be cheaply measured and such measurements can form bases of important predictions concerning consumption, voting behavior, ethnocentric discrimination and other consequential social decisions. Then along came Leon Festinger (1957) whose most important message (at least for me) was that people can be constrained to act in various "uncharacteristic" ways and, under some circumstances, the need to accommodate or to come to terms with those uncharacteristic actions results in various kinds of dispositional changes. This profound message was consolidated by Daryl Bem (1972) and is now part of the enduring legacy of experimental social psychology, so much of a part in fact that we forget that the message was indeed strange and controversial not very long ago.

The question I would like to address is whether the self-concept cannot also be changed in accommodation to constrained actions. On the face of it, there does not seem to be any logical or theoretical reason why self-concept changes should not reflect inductions of constrained behavior. After all, the self-concept is among other things a collection of attitudes and values. But there surely is debate about what kinds of self-concept changes are really possible, or even likely. Anything that we want to call a disposition would seem to have, almost by definition, some degree of built-in resistance to change. That is as true of attitudes as it is of other dispositional orientations, but many psychologists assumed that the self-concept is somehow more fundamental, more firmly anchored than a person's attitudes or beliefs. More than merely a disposition, one's self-concept is the housing, the framework within which other dispositions exist and in terms of which they are organized and defined.

The degree to which we resist self-concept change after constrained action depends not only on the inducing circumstances but also on what we mean by the self-concept. One can argue that each of us has an identity that remains stable, no matter what else changes (Baumeister, 1986). We know who we are, as defined by names and roles and capacities, and changes in this kind of identity knowledge can only occur over long periods of time. There are also definitions of the self-concept as a particular kind of cognitive structure (cf. Markus & Sentis, 1982), definitions that stress stability. The self is organized in certain ways to influence perception and interpretation, to shape rather than be shaped by experiences. Such structural approaches are appealing to those who have special interests in the determinants of memory, reaction time, and information integration.

But then there is what Gerard and I (Jones & Gerard, 1967) have called "the phenomenal self," a loose appellation that refers to features of the self-concept that are available and readily tapped. Surely when we ask someone to describe himself or herself, the result will be very much a function of context and recent experience. And that is particularly true of that feature of the phenomenal self we refer to as self-esteem.

Self-esteem can be conceptualized in various ways, but I think of it as a halo effect rather than some kind of separate structure. It is a pervasive self-rating tone or bias that is both an individual difference variable (suggesting some stability over time) and a variable that is also responsive to ongoing experiences, to achievements, to audience reactions of praise and punishment. Part of my identity—a small part—is that of a tennis player. But the tennis player part of my phenomenal self is not at all stable. My self-ratings of tennis ability still fluctuate wildly as a function of recent experiences on the court. Some features of the self-concept are more resistant to evaluative change than others, but nevertheless it is in the nature of phenomenal self-esteem that when I feel good about myself this tide of good feeling raises all of my attributional boats; when I am down, the halo effect is equally well distributed in the negative direction. (This is not, of course, entirely true but it may serve as a useful working assumption, and it avoids treating self-esteem as a special trait or component of the self-concept.)

With a minimum of stage setting, I should like to report a series of investigations into the nature and conditions of self-esteem change. The dependent variables will be laboratory-induced changes in self-esteem, the no doubt temporary responses to our clever experimental manipulations, but I shall attempt to argue later that temporary and trivial are not the same thing.

My interest in self-esteem change grew out of our research on ingratiation and other forms of self-presentation. When ingratiators are self-enhancing, when do they internalize these inflated appraisals of the self? When they are charmingly modest, when does their private view reflect this self-deprecation? Given the likely fact that people do not want to see themselves as dishonest, deceptive, or manipulative, it is rather easy to imagine changes in our self-concepts after an ingratiating encounter with someone whom we wish to impress. It is not comforting for any of us to believe that we tailored our behavior solely to make a good impression. But we know enough about self-perception in general and dissonance theory in particular to realize that this will depend on the ingratiator's perception of the degree of choice, constraint, or personal responsibility involved.

This was our starting point about fifteen years ago when Steve Berglas and I (Experiment 1, Jones, Rhodewalt, Berglas, & Skelton, 1981) induced subjects to describe themselves either positively or modestly in a selection interview. The induction involved a social comparison manipulation. Before their own interview, subjects were exposed to tape recordings of other applicants who were either self-enhancing or self-deprecating in the same interview situation that the subjects would soon confront. The results were dramatic, if not very interesting theoretically: subjects were enormously swayed by the consensus conveyed by the taped responses of the other applicants. Of greater interest was the subsequent companion shift in self-esteem. Prior to the experiment, in a group testing session, all subjects had completed the Self-Valuation Triads (SVT) test (Gergen, 1965). The complete test consists of 72 item-triads, each consisting of a relatively positive self-characterization (e.g., "exceptionally tolerant"), a more neutral description (e.g., "average childhood"), and one that was relatively negative (e.g., "unrealistic aspirations"). The favorability of each phrase had previously been established by the method of successive intervals. Subjects were asked to distribute 10 points among each triad, assigning these points as weights representing their judgment that the phrase is a valid self-description. Measures of self-esteem may be readily derived by adding the number of points assigned to the favorable phrase in each triad and subtracting the points assigned to the unfavorable phrase.

Subsequent to the experiment, presumably to help a colleague at a different institution, subjects were asked to fill out an adjective checklist and 22 of the 72 SVT items. By comparing point assignments on these items with those assigned on the subject's pretest, a measure of self-esteem change was obtained. Subjects who saw self-enhancing applicants were themselves very self-enhancing in their subsequent interviews (as measured by their responses to 10 selected SVT items) and this carried over to higher self-esteem ratings on a different sample of SVT items, and on an adjective checklist, in an unrelated setting.

Fred Rhodewalt and I (Jones, Rhodewalt, Berglas, & Skelton, 1981, Experiment 3) later did a modified replication of this study in which we introduced several manipulations designed to vary the subject's sense of responsibility for his interview behavior. Our general expectation was that subjects who felt in some way personally responsible for their self-deprecating behavior would show lower self-esteem after the interview. The procedure was to induce subjects in an interview (with a supposedly uninstructed student from a course on interviewing) to play the deliberately defined role of a self-enhancing or self-deprecating interviewee. The interview started with several open questions such as "How would you describe your ability to get along with others?" These were followed by an oral administration of 20 items from the SVT test. Subjects had no difficulty in presenting themselves as if it were "one of those days when you really feel good about yourself" or as if it were a time when "you feel really inadequate, unloved, incompetent, like anything you took on you'd likely mess up."

Cross-cutting this variation in the direction of self-description called for, half the subjects were introduced to a standard choice manipulation. They were told at a crucial point that they could, of course, leave the experiment with full credit or they were given no such choice. A final cross-cutting variable was the extent to which subjects were allowed to improvise the role—to choose their own way of impressing the interviewer that they were high or low in self-esteem. Half of the subjects chose the answers in line with the role they were assigned to play. The other half of the subjects were individually yoked to the first half. They were assigned either the self-enhancing or the self-deprecating role, and then given a script enabling them to give precisely the same interview answers as their yoked partners had. This was done in such a way that the interviewer could not tell whether the subject was in the spontaneous or yoked condition.

After the interview, subjects were again requested as a favor for another investigator in another institution to answer a series of questions about the self. As in the previous experiment, this consisted of 20 items from the 72-item SVT test that the subjects had filled out earlier in the semester.

The results, in terms of self-esteem change, were complicated but nevertheless striking. As Table 4.1 shows, self-enhancing subjects were essentially impervious to the dissonance manipulation but very responsive to the self-reference manipulation. Thus, spontaneous self-enhancing subjects showed a positive change in self-esteem, whereas yoked self-enhancing subjects did not. Self-deprecating subjects, on the other hand, were impervious to the self-reference manipulation but highly sensitive to the dissonance manipulation. Self-deprecating subjects who were reminded that they could leave if they wished, showed greater self-esteem change in the negative direction than those who were not given this choice.

Rhodewalt and I were struck by the ease with which the results could be mapped into the synthesis developed by Fazio, Zanna, and Cooper (1977) to

TABLE 4.1
Internalization of Self-presentational Behavior

	High Choice		Low Choice	
Instructions	Self-reference	Yoked	Self-reference	Yoked
Self-enhancing	20.8	2.8	22.4	8.6
Self-deprecating	−13.9	−16.5	9.2	−3.9

Note: Numbers are the adjusted cell means from an analysis of covariance of Self-Valuation Triads scores (from Jones, Rhodewalt, Berglas, & Skelton, 1981).

assign self-perception and dissonance theories to their "proper domains." They argued, and produced an experiment to support their argument, that behavior which is sufficiently uncharacteristic to be normally rejected by the individual gives rise to changes in attitude under the usual conditions of dissonance arousal—in particular under conditions of choice or personal responsibility. Behaviors that are mildly uncharacteristic but still generally acceptable to the subject, on the other hand, can induce a change in attitudes as long as the behavior itself is considered to be self-relevant. None of the aversiveness of dissonance arousal is presumably involved, and attitude change takes place as a kind of "biased scanning" of one's own recently enacted behavior. All that Rhodewalt and I needed to exploit this model was one crucial assumption—that most self-enhancing comments fall within the latitude of acceptable statements about the self whereas negative comments fall more readily into the latitude of rejection. It should follow, therefore, that the self-reference variations should affect esteem for the self-enhancers whereas the dissonance manipulation should affect esteem for the self-deprecators. If one thinks of the relevant variables that allegedly control dissonance reduction and self-perception, this is exactly what happened in our Princeton experiment.

As satisfying as this model appeared to be as an explanation for these results, I was not confident that such complicated findings could be replicated in any detail. But Rhodewalt went on to the University of Utah and did exactly that and more with a student named Agustdottir (Rhodewalt & Agustdottir, 1986). Following our Princeton procedure closely, the investigators were able to produce very similar results in a group of normally recruited subjects. And even more remarkable and fascinating, a sample of mildly depressed subjects showed the obverse pattern of results. Figs. 4.1 and 4.2 show these contrasting patterns.

Figure 4.1 shows clearly that the choice variable replicates for the non-depressed subjects. That is, choice strongly affects self-esteem in the self-deprecate condition, but not in the self-enhance condition. For the depressed subjects the reverse is true. Here the choice variable affects self-esteem only in the self-enhance condition. Fig. 4.2 presents the pattern of results comparing self-refer-

Choice vs. No-choice Conditions

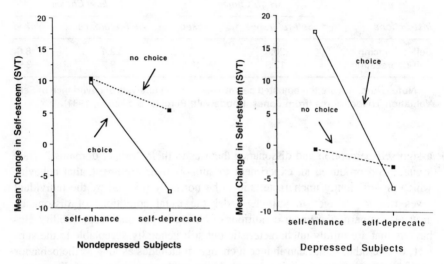

FIG. 4.1   Self-presentational choice (Adapted from Rhodewalt & Agustdottir, 1986).

Self-reference vs. Yoked Conditions

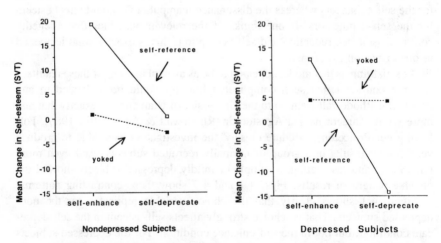

FIG. 4.2   Self-presentational spontaneity (Adapted from Rhodewalt & Agustdottir, 1986).

ence and yoked conditions. Again, the results for the nondepressed subjects replicate the original findings: The self-reference variable affects self-esteem in the self-enhance condition but not in the self-deprecate conditions. For depressed subjects, the opposite seems to be true. Here the self-deprecate subjects are more affected than those in the self-enhance condition by the self-reference variable.

Rhodewalt and Agustdottir summarize the theoretical assumptions intended to explain their results in Fig. 4.3. Given a reasonable set of assumptions about the different latitudes of acceptance and rejection of depressed and of nondepressed subjects, the results follow nicely from the Fazio, Zanna, and Cooper (1977) model. Thus the results make sense if we assume that depressed subjects find self-deprecation more acceptable than self-enhancement; with nondepressed subjects the reverse is true.

The Rhodewalt and Agustdottir results, combined with those from our earlier study, suggest that for each of us there is a range of actions that we can accept as

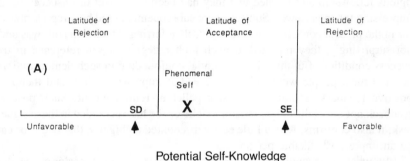

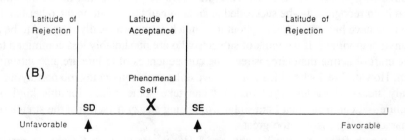

FIG. 4.3. Latitudes of acceptance and rejection of the phenomenal self. (SE = self-enhancement, SD = self-deprecation. Adapted from Rhodewalt & Agustdottir, 1986).

characteristic, and yet they are in fact uncharacteristic enough so that subsequent shifts in self-concept follow their enactment. Anything outside this range of acceptable self-reference requires the special tricks of dissonance arousal and reduction as a precondition for self-concept change.

The studies I have described so far all concern the conditions under which some uncharacteristic action is accepted as part of a shifted or newly expanded self-concept. In particular, we have shown that self-esteem changes can be induced by instructions to present oneself as self-enhancing or self-deprecating—as long as the context promotes either biased scanning or dissonance reduction. One feature of these experimental studies is that, although an audience is present, there is no definitive feedback concerning the success of the performance.

The question of self-presentational success versus failure is an intriguing one. In our very first study of ingratiation, done over 25 years ago (Jones, Gergen, & David, 1962), subjects role-played an interview with a gatekeeper of a prestigious fellowship and learned that they had been successful or unsuccessful in impressing the interviewer. Subjects were subsequently asked how representative (or in the present context we would say "self-referring") their behavior was and, not surprisingly, they reported a much higher degree of self-reference in the success condition. But there is an essential confounding in such demonstrations because most people would like to succeed at impressing others and therefore positive feedback is more than just a pellet of reinforcement. Such positive feedback not only tells the ingratiator that he or she has succeeded in the assigned task; it also confirms, with a little easily discounted ambiguity, that one is or can be an impressive, likable person.

But what if an audience confirms the authenticity of a performance that involves playing the role of an unpopular or unsavory character? How did an actor like Sidney Greenstreet feel when he was acclaimed for creating a truly convincing villain? On the one hand, he could be gratified that his acting skill had been recognized—he succeeded at an assigned task—but on the other hand, he may have had some doubts about how much acting was really required to be a convincing villain. If we think of subjects who are presumably less committed to the craft of acting than Greenstreet, the consequences of failure are also intriguing. How do I feel when I learn that I have done an unconvincing job portraying a truly sleazy character? Presumably I can take some solace for this kind of failure—it can mean that I am so far from being sleazy myself that the stretch of character acting is just too great.

Kenneth Brenner, John Knight, and I (Jones, Brenner, & Knight, in press) designed an experiment to explore the consequences for self-esteem of success and failure following an attempt to come across as a morally reprehensible person. In trying to get some purchase on how the dilemma might be resolved—that is, the dilemma of being rewarded for being something you don't want to see yourself as being—we thought of the relevance of individual differences in self-monitoring. After all, if Mark Snyder and his colleagues are correct (Snyder, 1987), the high self-monitor should be less concerned than the low self-monitor with the content of the role being played. The self-monitoring scale developed by Snyder (1974) has been shown to distinguish between those people (high scorers) who carefully monitor their own reactions to ensure their appropriateness to the situation and those (low scorers) who place a high value on personal consistency across settings. Thus the low self-monitor (LSM) is supposedly always concerned with "how I can be me" in every situation; the HSM is more exclusively concerned with reading what the situation calls for and responding accordingly. We expected, therefore, that high and low SMs would respond differently to feedback concerning the authenticity of their sleazy performances: The HSMs should show elevated self-esteem upon learning that they had convinced others of the authenticity of their performance. The LSMs, on the other hand, should feel better about themselves (and therefore have high self-esteem) after learning that they had failed in their role-playing task.

The performance involved responses to a set of moral dilemmas, each of which involved a choice between sacrificing one's own interests while upholding widely accepted moral principles versus cutting legal or moral corners to improve the chances of financial gain. For instance, one scenario asked the subject whether he would invent and report "lost items of high value" to increase the insurance settlement after a fire gutted the second floor of his home. Another involved the temptation to reveal business secrets about a former company to one that the subject had just joined because of its higher salary. These scenarios provided an obvious vehicle for enacting the role suggested by the following instructions:

> I would like you to imagine that the job you are interviewing for is truly a cutthroat position in a dog-eat-dog environment. Your task is to convince the interviewer (in this case those who will be listening to this tape) that you are a realistic, down-to-earth person. You are cynical enough to know that people on this job are, like yourself, out for number one. Therefore you have to convince the monitors that you are not some kind of head-in-the-clouds do-gooder, basking in self-righteousness. You are a practical, ambitious person, willing to cut corners if it promotes your success at getting ahead. . . . You should try to respond to [the moral dilemmas] as an ambitious, pragmatic realist would. Your eyes should read dollar signs as you try to be as convincing as possible. It is crucial that you play the role of this selfish, pragmatic person to the best of your ability. We are looking for subjects who can convince the monitors.

The subject's role playing responses were tape-recorded, supposedly to be played for students in an undergraduate person perception seminar, in order to have them try to estimate the true nature of the person responding to these moral dilemmas.

The subjects returned a week later to hear their own tape-recorded interview responses, followed by an apparent classroom discussion of students responding to their performance. This feedback tape, along with some rating sheets that were also handed to the subject, conveyed the success or failure manipulation. Subjects in the success condition learned that they came across as shrewd, willing to cut corners, and generally suited for a role in public relations or sales. One voice on the feedback tape commented that the subject wouldn't even mind "selling his mother down the river." Those in the failure condition learned that the authenticity of their performance was questioned. As one voice on the tape put it: "I get the feeling deep down that he wouldn't do any of the things he said he would." Another person noted that "you can almost feel the guy would not hurt people." There was general agreement that he would be best suited for a low-pressure profession where he wouldn't have to make decisions such as firing people.

All subjects had taken the self-monitoring scale and the Janis and Field (1959) self-esteem measure during the first session. After they were exposed to feedback in the second session, a second measure of self-esteem was obtained—the same SVT measure used successfully in our earlier studies of self-esteem change. As noted, we predicted that self-esteem of HSMs would be higher after success than after failure, whereas the self-esteem of LSMs would be higher after failure than after success.

The results exceeded our most optimistic expectations, even when we merely divided the subjects into highs and lows according to a median split on the self-monitoring scale. The results of the postfeedback, self-esteem scores (adjusted for the pretest scores) are shown in Fig. 4.4, confirming the prediction that high self-monitors feel good about themselves when they succeed whereas low self-monitors feel better about themselves when they fail.

Obviously the self-monitoring dimension is a crucial predictor of how one feels when he is told that he or she has succeeded or failed at projecting a believable image of greed and moral bankruptcy. Or, you could say, HSMs feel good about themselves after they have convinced others that they would sell their mothers down the river. Such feedback depresses the LSMs, who then report lowered self-esteem.

I have argued that the HSMs are insensitive, or at least only minimally concerned, with the content of the role they are playing. An obvious alternative is that the specified role is simply closer to their self-image as a manipulative person—or at least that they see nothing reprehensible about such persons. Therefore, they're naturally pleased and their self-esteem goes up when they are told that they succeeded in portraying a prototype that is congenial to them. A number of further experiments would have to be conducted in order to rule out this alternative completely, but one of our pretests certainly diminishes its plausibility. Pretest subjects were asked to evaluate someone who responded with the same consistent tendency to cut moral corners as our subjects later did in fulfilling this role playing task. These pretest subjects all found the person reprehensible, equally so whether they were high or low self-monitors. Thus even though

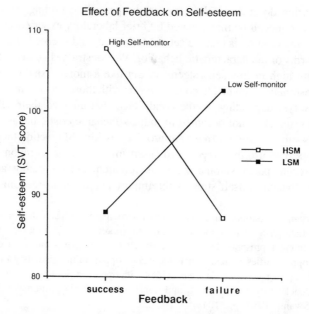

FIG. 4.4. Means represent SVT scores (post-feedback) adjusted for Janis and Field self-esteem test scores (premeasure). (Adapted from Jones, Brenner, and Knight, in press).

HSMs view the role content as reprehensible, they still are gratified to learn that they have portrayed it well.

The LSMs provide an interesting case of recoiling from the implications of a performance. Although we were unable to show that the LSMs became more ethical or more altruistic after attempting to act like a reprehensible person, it is not hard to imagine such an outcome. One wonders what might have happened if they were approached for contributions to a worthy cause as they left the experiment.

The evidence I have presented thus far seems to argue strongly for the malleability of self-esteem and its vulnerability to transient experimental arrangements. But there is a recent swing of the pendulum away from the notion that the self-concept is easily changed toward such notions as self-verification and self-affirmation. Swann, in particular, has forcefully argued that people do not like to be misunderstood (e.g., Swann, 1987). And when they are, they will reassert the misunderstood features of the self in acts of self-verification. He presents several sets of rather stunning results to back up his argument—results showing, for example, that low self-esteem people prefer to associate with others who are critical of them—in other words, others who agree that their low self-esteem is deserved.

What bearing do such results have on the preceding findings showing that self-esteem can indeed be manipulated by brief laboratory experiences? The key difference in my opinion is that we set out to induce, and succeeded in inducing, particular forms of uncharacteristic behavior. We constrained subjects to *act* like a person with high or low self esteem, or *act* like a morally shallow narcissist. Subjects presumably then had to come to terms with those actions and they did so in various ways, depending on the conditions, that affected their self-esteem.

Swann's research is not designed to induce uncharacteristic behavior. On the contrary, his subjects are left free to improvise any kind of reaction they want to, and they appear to use this freedom to assert misunderstood components of the self. In a recent paper summarizing his research and theorizing about self-verification, Swann himself stresses the importance of such freedom:

> Laboratory investigators commonly confront participants with self-discrepant feedback and then place them in interpersonal straitjackets. That is, in a typical study, the experimenter presents discrepant feedback to participants and then deprives them of opportunities to resist such feedback, opportunities that they ordinarily enjoy. Perhaps if participants were provided with opportunities to resist self-discrepant feedback, they would do so and consequently display minimal self-rating change (Swann, 1987, pp. 1043)

Although I think it is debatable that people "ordinarily enjoy" opportunities to resist discrepant feedback, the issue is an important one and worthy of additional systematic study. In a recent experiment relevant to the point, Nancy Schoenberger (1988) and I wanted to see how subjects responded to efforts to get them to recruit positive or negative self-relevant experiences in an interview context. These efforts were more subtle than the experiments I have first described, since they did not specifically instruct subjects to try to create a particular kind of impression. The manipulations were on the other hand somewhat more constraining than those in Swann's permissive experiments. Female subjects were interviewed about their Princeton experiences. A crucial part of the interview involved sets of loaded questions designed either to elicit positive self-references or negative self-references. The different questions, defining the two experimental conditions, are shown in Table 4.2. This part of the interview was bracketed by two measures of self-esteem; as in the Jones, Brenner, and Knight experiment, the first measure was the Janis and Field questionnaire and the second measure was the Self-Valuation Triads Test.

Turning to the results, did the loaded questions accomplish their mission of eliciting positive versus negative self-references? The answer is clearly yes. Transcripts of the answers—both including and not including the questions—showed that answers to the positive questions were more self-enhancing than answers to the negative questions. This is very clear in Fig. 4.5 which also shows that high self-esteem subjects were rated as showing higher apparent self-esteem in their interview answers than low self-esteem subjects.

TABLE 4.2
Interview Questions Creating Positive and Negative
Constraint Conditions (from Schoenberger)

1. **(positive condition)** Why don't you start by telling me about something that happened recently that made you feel really proud.

   (negative condition) Why don't you start by telling me about a recent situation in which you were really embarrassed.

2. **(positive condition)** Thinking about the past 3–4 years, what are some decisions you made that you think were especially good ones?

   (negative condition) Thinking about the past 3–4 years, what are some decisions you made that you would like to change if given the opportunity?

3. **(positive condition)** Often, people appear somewhat lacking in self-confidence when they actually have a strong sense of inner security. Do you think that others sometimes fail to recognize how secure and happy you really are? Can you give me an example?

   (negative condition) Often people project an image of self-confidence even when they feel rather insecure about themselves. Do you think that others see you as more secure and happy than you really believe yourself to be? Can you give me an example?

4. **(positive condition)** Tell me about an academic experience (in high school or at Princeton) in which you feel you did particularly well.

   (negative condition) Tell me about an academic experience (in high school or at Princeton) in which you did poorly.

5. **(positive condition)** What personal characteristic are you most proud of, would you most like to build on in the future?

   (negative condition) What personal characteristic are you most concerned about, would you most like to change in the future?

6. **(positive condition)** Let's think about the future. Take a few seconds to imagine that you are in an interview for a job that you really want, or for a graduate or professional school that you really want to get into. [pause] In that situation, what is your greatest strength which makes it more likely that you would be offered the position that you want?

   (negative condition) Let's think about the future. Take a few seconds to imagine that you are in an interview for a job that you really want, or for a graduate or professional school that you really want to get into. [pause] In that situation, what is your greatest weakness which makes it less likely that you would be offered the position that you want?

But what effects, if any, did these differences in self-referring remarks have on subsequent self-esteem? The answer? Clearly none. If we standardize scores on the Janis and Field and SVT measures, and subtract one from the other to get a change score, the amount of change is essentially zero in both the positive and negative question conditions. Alternatively, an analysis of covariance of the after

Mean Ratings of "Apparent Self-esteem" in the Interview

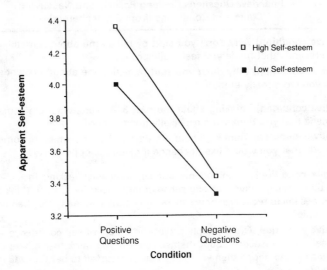

FIG. 4.5. The effects of constraining questions and "actual" (Janis and Field test) self-esteem on "apparent" self-esteem in the interview. (Data from Schoenberger, 1988).

(SVT) scores, covarying out the before (JF) scores, shows no effect of the different question conditions. And this deserves to be taken seriously since the two measures of self-esteem are highly intercorrelated (an r of .78 in the positive question condition, and an r of .61 in the negative question condition).

What makes the study interesting is that an analysis of the actual answers to the loaded questions gives us a glimpse of the processes of self-esteem maintenance when subjects are allowed sufficient response flexibility. Independent judges listened to tape recordings of the subjects' answers and rated the degree to which they transformed the questions in the process of answering them. Here it was apparent that high and low self-esteem subjects responded very differently. The results are shown in Fig. 4.6.

Here it is clear that high self-esteem subjects answered the positively biased questions in a very straightforward manner. But they transformed the negative questions into more positive ones. The low self-esteem subjects, on the other hand, transposed positive questions into negative ones. This helps us to see why there was no change in self-esteem (though unfortunately there is no clear evidence that those who "transformed" the most changed the least). Subjects exercised their freedom to give the impression they wanted to convey, regardless of the thrust of the questions confronting them. Unlike the subjects in the previous role-playing experiments I have described, these subjects see their task as one of

Mean Ratings of "Transforming the Question"

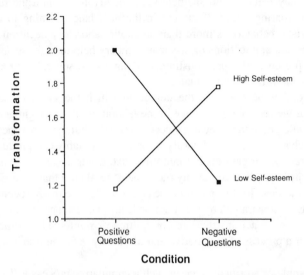

FIG. 4.6. The tendency to transform positive into negative and negative into positive questions as a function of self-esteem (Data from Schoenberger, 1988).

faithful self-disclosure. Though their responses were somewhat constrained by the questions asked, there was sufficient room to navigate for subjects to minimize the implications of their responses for their self-esteem. It should be noted, by the way, that all but one or two subjects were completely unaware that the questions were biased. This provides some evidence that self-verification processes are indeed very subtle and, perhaps, automatic in operation.

These last results do provide evidence for self-verification. But they do not, in my opinion, negate the real-world significance of all those studies (including our own) showing how one can induce changes in self-esteem by transient laboratory manipulations inducing subjects to present themselves in an uncharacteristic way.

There are at least two important issues involved here when attempting to generalize our experimental findings to the "real world." The first issue I have already identified: the extent to which our behavior is likely to be constrained so that we can be induced to behave in uncharacteristic ways. I would submit that we are frequently so constrained, often without awareness. In many of our interactions we are induced to play roles that display features we would normally prefer to disown. We fail to speak up when we later realize that our failure to be "authentic" was less than honorable. We nod our heads to opinions that we don't privately share. Though we think of ourselves as mature, cooperative citizens, as drivers we may behave with shameless competitiveness when the light finally turns green, roaring ahead of the car in the next lane. Coming to terms with uncharacteristic behavior is more than an exotic laboratory occurrence. All the implications and applications of dissonance theory help to make us aware of the ubiquitous presence of those constraints giving rise to self-relevant actions that are at the same time contra-valuant.

The second issue concerns the degree to which the kinds of self-concept changes that we are able to produce in the laboratory are transient and therefore trivial. I would argue that they are indeed reversible, but the experimental identification of change processes if hardly trivial. If we reliably can produce changes in the laboratory, we gain insight into how such changes can occur in everyday life. One hardly needs to argue any more the general case that induced behavior can affect attitudes. To this general case can be added the many specific cases in which behavior constrained by the situation leads to differences in self-perception that lead to further actions that are committing or reinforced and therefore become part of a process of cumulative and ultimately very important self-concept change.

One example of a critical stage in such a cumulative process is Tice's (1987) experimental demonstration involving the constrained elicitation of introverted or shy behavior (following procedures similar to those used by Kulik, Sledge, & Mahler, 1986). Male subjects were asked to wait in a hallway, where they sat near a female confederate who ignored them, burying her face in a book. After 3 minutes the experimenter returned, took the subjects to an experimental room, said that the person in the hall was an accomplice, and explained that the experiment was concerned with whether the subjects had spoken with the confederate (none of them had).

Subjects then watched videotapes purporting to show the behavior of four previous subjects in the same hallway situation. Two of the taped confederates had been previously presented as highly similar in personality, gender, and race to the subjects. The other two had been presented as very dissimilar in each of those respects. Cross-cutting these variations in similarity, there were variations in whether the taped "subjects" spoke to the confederate or remained silent like the naïve subjects themselves. Subjects were thus essentially confronted with similar or dissimilar others who were silent like themselves, or with similar or dissimilar others who engaged in conversation with the confederate.

When later asked a number of pertinent attributional questions, subjects showed that their current self-concepts were clearly affected by the contrived pattern of social comparison made available to them. The perceived actions of dissimilar others was especially influential. If the dissimilar others were silent, subjects rated themselves as more extraverted than if the dissimilar subjects engaged in conversation with the confederate. The perceived actions of similar subjects was less relevant for self-attribution. This seems reasonable: If a similar person behaves the way you did, you still don't know whether the situation called for this behavior; if the similar person behaves in a very different way, this is confusing but may quickly lead to doubts concerning the relevance of the particular dimensions of similarity for attributions of introversion/extraversion.

What is most important for our present discussion, subjects who became convinced, in response to the experimental manipulation, that they were dispositionally extraverted spoke more in a subsequent interview and sat closer to the interviewer. One can imagine conditions under which such behavioral reactions are reinforced by social labels or by the gratification they bring to the individual actor. Specifically, it is not hard to imagine important self-esteem carryover effects from transient experiences—and this is especially likely if such experiences are perhaps brief and transient, but repeated on many occasions. Alternatively, momentary changes in self-esteem may lead to consequential behavioral decisions or irrevocable commitments—like applying for a new job, asking a beauty queen for a date, or agreeing to give a colloquium speech.

The key may be, as I have tried to illustrate, the extent to which uncharacteristic self-relevant actions are induced or constrained, actions that are fairly specific but still not totally scripted for the actor. Our studies show, however, that if actors are given wide leeway to interpret the implications of the constraint, self-concept changes will be avoided and self-verification will be the result.

The main thrust of my argument in this chapter is that changes in the self-concept can be produced in brief laboratory situations in response to theoretically reasonable variables. Although I believe and certainly hope that these changes are reversible by careful "process debriefing," I do believe that such experiments offer one avenue toward understanding conditions of self-concept change in the real world. Self-verification processes undoubtedly do exist, and we should not be surprised when subjects take advantage of obvious self-verification opportunities—especially when they see their goal as that of honest self-disclosure. But I am convinced that such opportunities are not always available and there are many subtle and not so subtle circumstances that can induce us to behave in an uncharacteristic way. In such cases one can well imagine some of the changes actually taking place that I have tried to document in these experiments, and one can further imagine some of the conditions that would be important in sustaining those self-concept changes that do occur.

ACKNOWLEDGMENTS

The research reported in this chapter was supported by the U. S. National Science Foundation. I am especially indebted to Timothy Wilson for his comments.

REFERENCES

Baumeister, R. F. (1986). *Identity: Cultural change in the struggle for self.* New York: Oxford University Press.

Bem, D. (1972). Self-perception theory. In L. Berkowitz (Ed.), *Advances in experimental social psychology* (Vol. 6). New York: Academic Press.

Fazio, R. H., Zanna, M. P., & Cooper, J. (1977). Dissonance and self-perception: An integrative view of each theory's proper domain of application. *Journal of Experimental Social Psychology, 13,* 464–479.

Festinger, L. (1957). *A theory of cognitive dissonance.* Evanston, IL: Row–Peterson.

Gergen, K. J. (1965). The effects of interaction goals on personalistic feedback on the presentation of self. *Journal of Personality and Social Psychology, 1,* 413–424.

Janis, I. L., & Field, P. B. (1959). The Janis and Field personality questionnaire. In C. I. Hovland & I. L. Janis (Eds.), *Personality and persuasive ability.* New Haven, CN: Yale University Press.

Jones, E. E., Brenner, K., & Knight, J. G. (in press). When failure elevates self-esteem. *Personality and Social Psychology Bulletin.*

Jones, E. E., & Gerard, H. B. (1967). *Foundations of social psychology.* New York: Wiley.

Jones, E. E., Gergen, K. J., & Davis, K. E. (1962). Some determinants of reactions to being approved or disapproved as a person. *Psychological Monographs, 76*(Whole No. 521)

Jones, E. E., Rhodewalt, F., Berglas, S., & Skelton, J. A. (1981). Effects of strategic self-presentation on subsequent self-esteem. *Journal of Personality and Social Psychology, 41,* 407–421.

Kulik, J. A., Sledge, P., & Mahler, H. I. M. (1986). Self-confirmatory attribution, egocentrism, and the perpetuation of self-beliefs. *Journal of Personality and Social Psychology, 50,* 587–594.

Markus, H., & Sentis, K. (1982). The self in social information processing. In J. Suls (Ed.), *Psychological perspectives on the self* (Vol. 1). Hillsdale, NJ: Lawrence Erlbaum Associates.

Rhodewalt, F., & Agustdottir, S. (1986). Effects of self-presentation on the phenomenal self. *Journal of Personality and Social Psychology, 50,* 47–55.

Schoenberger, N. E. (1988). *Maintaining self-esteem in the face of behavioral pressures for change: Support for the theory of self-verification.* Unpublished senior thesis, Princeton University.

Snyder, M. (1974). The self-monitoring of expressional behavior. *Journal of Personality and Social Psychology, 30,* 526–537.

Snyder, M. (1987). *Public appearances/private realities.* New York: W. H. Freeman.

Swann, W. B. (1987). Identity negotiation: Where two roads meet. *Journal of Personality and Social Psychology, 53,* 1038–1051.

Tice, D. M. (1987). *Similarity of others and dispositional versus situational attributions.* Unpublished doctoral dissertation, Princeton University.

5 Perception and Evaluation of Body Image: The Meaning of Body Shape and Size

Janet Polivy
C. Peter Herman
Patricia Pliner
University of Toronto

It is impossible to discuss self-perception without some consideration of the perception of one's physical characteristics or judgments about one's own body. This particular self-perception or image of one's body is generally known as body image. However, as Lacey and Birtchnell (1986) point out, "body image is a complex concept, and although the term is widely used, its specific meaning remains unclear" (p. 623). Similarly, McCrea, Summerfield, and Rosen (1982) note that "the concept of body image is applied to a wide range of (phenomena). . . . Unfortunately, this breadth of interest has resulted in vague, equivocal definitions of the concept" (p. 225). Thus, any attempt at a truly thorough review of the construct of body image is likely to be more exhausting than exhaustive. Accordingly, this chapter will concentrate on the psychological and social dimensions of body image as they pertain to body shape and size, focusing particularly on overweight and normal weight subjects. (This restriction necessarily excludes many aspects of body image related to appearance, neurological issues, the phantom limb phenomenon, dysmorphophobia, psychotic disturbances of bodily perception, or physical deformities. See Lacey & Birtchnell, 1986, for a review.) Our working definition of body image is as one's self-perception of appearance, comprised of one's own perceptual experience and one's subjective response based on the reactions of others. Body image thus defined may be separated into two distinct components, perception per se, and one's evaluation of what one perceives.

Despite inconsistencies in the literature, it is fairly widely believed that obesity involves a disturbance of body image (e.g., Stunkard & Mendelson, 1967), and that young women in Western society are for the most part dissatisfied with their bodies (e.g., Polivy, Garner, & Garfinkel, 1986; Rodin, Silberstein, &

Striegel–Moore, 1985). It also seems to be widely believed that eating-disorder patients have distorted body images. In fact, this is one of the defining characteristics of anorexia nervosa and bulimia specified in DSM–III-R (APA, 1987). To what extent are all these assumptions justified?

As the following review will indicate, body-size estimation techniques do not seem to correlate well with each other, either because of poor reliability or because they are measuring different aspects of a complex construct. There is also the question of whether such tasks really assess simple perceptual or motivational factors. Given such methodological constraints, it may not be surprising to learn that subjects of all sizes appear to be somewhat inaccurate at indicating/perceiving their body size, with obese and eating-disorder patients not reliably different from normal individuals. On the other hand, dissatisfaction with one's shape and size does seem to be found with reasonable consistency in obese patients and normal-weight subjects, especially females and particularly in eating-disorder patients. Surprisingly, though, as will become apparent, the majority of women are actually satisfied with their body images and the ramifications of dissatisfaction are less than evident.

BODY-SIZE PERCEPTION
IN NORMAL-WEIGHT INDIVIDUALS

There have been several studies of normal-weight subjects' body-size perception, but the majority of data on this issue has been collected in studies of some other group, usually eating-disorder patients, with normal-weight subjects serving as a control group. In addition, some of the many studies on overweight subjects included normal-weight control subjects. In reviewing such studies, we find tremendous methodological/empirical variability. The methods used to assess accuracy of body-size perception or estimation include figure drawings, silhouette selection, image marking (visual size estimation), and distorted image techniques. Since the technique used seems to make a difference in what evidence of distortion is found, the various measures will be discussed separately.

Drawings

One of the earliest methods used for assessing body-size perception was the Draw-a-Person (DAP) test, in which subjects are asked to draw a person, and then (usually) to draw a second person of the opposite sex. The same-sex drawing (usually the first one done) is assumed to reflect the subjects' views of their own bodies. The drawings of normal-weight subjects were judged to be smaller and presumably more accurate than those of the obese in some studies (Bailey, Shinedling, & Payne, 1970; Shenker, Sonnenblick, & Fisichelli, 1978), or more whole and generally better or more mature (Gottesfeld, 1962; Nathan, 1973).

Since they were always being compared with overweight subjects, normal-weight subjects drawings have not been assessed for simple accuracy in and of themselves, though. Different criteria were applied in different studies, making it difficult to generalize from study to study.

Silhouettes

Another technique with less interpretive and scoring variability, but with greater discrepancies in results, requires subjects to choose the figure most like their own from a graded series of photographs or silhouettes. This technique is used frequently with normal-weight college student subjects. The silhouette selections of normal subjects were sometimes accurate (Bell, Kirkpatrick, & Rinn, 1986; Schonbuch & Schell, 1967), though underweight controls were found to overestimate their size (Schonbuch & Schell, 1967). However, using silhouettes ranging from very thin to very fat, Fallon and Rozin (1985) showed that college-age females overestimated their size, reporting that, on average, only 42.2% (rather than the expected 50%) of other students would be heavier than they (men reported 46.7% would be heavier, a significantly smaller underestimate). Dwyer, Feldman, Seltzer, & Mayer (1969) also found males to be more accurate than females, who tended to overestimate their size. Cohn et al. (1987) found less evidence of overestimation in their sample of junior high school students. Although girls tended to see themselves as too large, only 38% of them did so (compared with Fallon & Rozin's 70%). On the other hand, boys wanted to be heavier. As in Fallon and Rozin's sample, 20% of the girls chose an ideal figure thinner than the one they believed was most attractive to boys. Lippa (1983), in a slightly different kind of silhouette study, found both males and females to be inaccurate in estimating the figure (i.e., shoulder-to-waist ratio) of the average male or female, particularly for the female body. Subjects overestimated the extent of difference between the two sexes in average size as well. Silhouette selection thus yields varying results in normal-weight subjects, but the evidence of inaccuracy seems to be that women are more likely to overestimate their size with this technique.

Body-width Judgment

Using a simple measure wherein subjects mark on paper or movable bars the width of various body parts, most subjects tended to overestimate body size (Askevold, 1975; Dolan, Birtchnell, & Lacey, 1987).

Distorted Images

This technique involves presenting some sort of distorted image of themselves to subjects who must then adjust it correctly (to reflect reality). Shipman and Sohlkhah (1967) found normal-weight women to estimate their size accurately, using a distorting mirror. Glucksman and Hirsch (1969) found normals to underestimate slightly with a distorted photograph, but since no means are given, it is impossible to tell if this is significant or the subjects were essentially accurate (they were not different from obese subjects, at any rate). Garner, Garfinkel, Stancer, and Moldofsky (1976) found that normal (and underweight) subjects underestimated their size with a distorting photograph, but overestimated with a visual size estimation technique. In two studies on obese subjects by Gardner and his colleagues (1987a, 1987b) the normal controls were essentially accurate (means were not always given), as were the normal weight controls studied by Cash and Green (1986), although the underweight controls overestimated dramatically. The results for normal-weight subjects using a distorting image technique of body-size estimation are thus reasonably consistent: normals seem to be essentially accurate.

This pattern holds up for normal controls in studies of eating-disorder patients as well. For example, Garfinkel, Moldofsky, Garner, Stancer, and Coscina's (1978) normal controls gave accurate estimates with relatively low variability, as did Garfinkel, Moldofsky, and Garner's (1979) normals. Meerman (1983) found, like Garner et al. (1976), that anorexic patients and controls alike underestimated their size with a video distortion task, but overestimated with image marking and paper-and-pencil tasks. Touyz, Beaumont, Collins, McCabe, and Jupp (1984) found that their anorexic patients and controls showed no mean difference in estimation accuracy, both averaging around zero overestimation; however, the degree of variability and range of responses differed markedly between the two groups, with the normal estimates all falling within 11% of accurate, one way or the other, while the anorexics varied much more widely. Collins (1986) found that anorexics underestimated significantly, while normals underestimated only slightly, and the anorexic estimates were again more variable. Powers, Schulman, Gleghorn, and Prange (1987) also reported that their normal controls were accurate whereas bulimic subjects overestimated body size on several measures. Examination of the means (ranges are not given) indicates that the normals actually underestimated significantly on some measures, were accurate on some, and overestimated (but less than did bulimics) on others.

One study compared males' and females' accuracy with a video distortion method (Collins, 1986). Both sexes were essentially accurate, with males overestimating slightly (2.38%) and females underestimating to a minute extent (1.62%), for a marginal difference between groups. When asked to indicate their ideal sizes, both groups indicated that they wanted to be different: Males' ideal was close to 9% larger than their actual size, while females wished to be more than 16% smaller.

Taylor and Cooper's (1986) study of 50 normal-weight females with no history of weight or eating problems also found normal subjects to be quite accurate with a distorted photograph. When they divided their subjects on the basis of depression scores, they found that the highest scorers' estimates were significantly larger (103.6%) than were those of the lowest scorers (92.9%). There was a significant correlation between estimation and depression score, despite the limited range of both variables in this normal, healthy sample.

The various visual size estimation techniques seem to be uniform across subject populations: All subjects exhibit a tendency to overestimate their body size to a greater or lesser extent. Normal controls in obesity studies overestimated almost or actually as much as did the obese subjects (Dolan et al., 1987; Garner et al., 1976; Pearlson, Flournoy, Simonson, & Slavney, 1981), and Askevold's (1975) various patient groups all overestimated at least part of their bodies. Similarly, eating-disorder patients overestimate their body size with this technique, but so do the normal controls with whom they are compared, at least to some extent (Ben–Tovim & Crisp, 1984; Birtchnell, Lacey, & Harte, 1985; Cash & Brown, 1987; Casper, Halmi, Goldberg, Eckert, & Davis, 1979; Garner et al., 1987; Norris, 1984).

Looking exclusively at normal female adolescents, Halmi, Goldberg, and Cunningham (1977) found the usual overestimation on a visual size-estimation task. Overestimation was greater for younger subjects, especially 10-year-olds, but even the oldest (18-year-olds) were overestimating by about 10%. The authors speculate that there may be maturational development which leads to more accurate body-size estimation, and discuss Piaget's suggestion that perception is progressively constructed and improves with age. However, all subjects underestimated their arm and leg lengths, and this was unrelated to age.

Self-report

The tendency for subjects (females, at least—many of the studies on normals focus on sex differences) to overestimate their size is also consistently found in questionnaire surveys of normal subjects. Gray (1977) found that only half of the college students she studied perceived themselves correctly, with males tending to see themselves as lighter than they were, and females seeing themselves as heavier (despite the fact that the males were in fact objectively heavier, or perhaps because of it). Unfortunately, accuracy of perception was determined on the basis of self-reported height and weight and standardized norms tables, so misreporting may have distorted the results, especially if, for example, the heavier females were more likely to underreport their actual size. Desmond, Price, Gray, and O'Connell (1986) found essentially the same results in adolescent subjects, though, and their subjects were measured during the study. Mable, Balance, and Galgan (1986) also found that female college students overestimated their degree of overweight, while males were accurate. This study again relied upon self-reported heights and weights. However, Wardle and Beales (1986) did weigh and measure their 12- to 17-year-old normal subjects, and still found the same basic pattern: Males see themselves accurately and females see themselves as overweight. On the other hand, Gayton, Horner, and Laperrier

(1984) found that adults were generally inaccurate in estimating their body-frame size, tending to underestimate, which could result in many people thinking they are relatively more overweight (according to height–weight charts) than is the case.

Conclusion

On most measures of body-size estimation, then, normal-weight subjects seem to be reasonably accurate. The visual size estimation or image-marking technique consistently elicits overestimates, but this seems to be the case no matter who the subjects are, and probably should be considered an artifact of the technique. The more subjective self-report measures also seem to elicit consistent responses. Many normal-weight females perceive themselves as being larger than they actually are, and several measures indicate that they would prefer to be smaller (whereas males would like to be larger). It seems likely that such subjective measures of how subjects "see" themselves may be measuring more the evaluative, affective dimension of body image than any aspect of perception.

EVALUATION OF BODY SHAPE AND SIZE IN NORMAL-WEIGHT INDIVIDUALS

Although investigators such as Gray (1977) purport to be measuring both perceptual distortions and negative affective reactions to the body, subjects' self-ratings of fatness may reflect the same evaluative dimension as questionnaires about affect toward the body. The consistency of the results with such fatness ratings implies that there should be a similar reliable pattern of results with other measures of body-image satisfaction. Gray (1977) also reported, however, that in general, subjects' body affect was positive and unrelated to sex or accuracy of perception. In fact, distortion does not appear to be related to dissatisfaction even with other measures of distortion (Cash & Green, 1986; Dolan et al., 1987; Mable et al., 1986). How widespread is body dissatisfaction among normal-weight individuals?

Going back to the questionnaire surveys that have been mentioned, Gray (1977) reported generally positive body affect, but about 33% of her subjects also reported dieting with some frequency. Desmond et al. (1986) found that 50% of their normal-weight males and 55% of their normal-weight females were dieting and 52% of the males and 59% of the females were exercising to lose weight. Those who perceived their weight as higher were more likely to be trying to lose weight. Mable et al. (1986) found no differences between males and females on body dissatisfaction (and their mean levels of satisfaction were identical to Clifford's [1971] sample who were deemed generally satisfied), but Schwab and Harmeling (1968) found female medical patients to have more body dissatisfaction than males, and found all the patients to have lower than normal body-satisfaction levels. Wardle and Beasles (1986) found that females' preferred weight was below their current weight but males' preference was right at their actual level. Only 5% of the boys and 15% of the girls were dieting, however (in contrast to most of the other prevalence studies, which found higher levels of dieting).

Many surveys of general satisfaction with body shape have been conducted on normal samples. Dwyer et al. (1969) surveyed 446 female and 145 male high school students and measured height, weight, and fatness. All except the leanest girls (80%) wanted to weight less, whereas boys tended to want to be larger, connecting weight to desirable muscle and bone. The authors concluded that high levels of dissatisfaction were shown by most adolescents. Clifford (1971) reached the opposite conclusion. His junior high and high school students had some concerns, and the females were generally less satisfied than the males, but he concluded that the data indicate a positive cathexis toward self and body such that adolescents seem to be generally satisfied. Goldberg and Folkins (1974) found no sex difference in mean body evaluation scores.

Berscheid, Walster, and Bohrnstedt (1973) surveyed more than 62,000 *Psychology Today* readers and analyzed 2,013 of the responses. Almost half of the women and a third of the men said they were unhappy with their weight, and twice as many women as men were very dissatisfied. This dissatisfaction with weight correlated with body satisfaction in general. Looking at this from the other side of the glass though, one could also say that the majority of people are at least somewhat satisfied with their weight and bodies. Just over 10 years later, Wooley and Wooley (1984) conducted a similar survey in *Glamour* magazine. Their respondents were more likely to be happy with their bodies than unhappy: 59% to 41%. But 75% reported feeling overweight despite the fact that even by conservative criteria, only 25% actually were overweight. When asked what would make them happiest, 42% answered "losing weight," twice the number who chose success at work, a date with an admired man, and other seemingly desirable events. Finally, Cash, Winstead, and Janda (1986) replicated the Berscheid et al. (1973) survey. They reported that males seemed more concerned about being overweight than they had been in 1973, although not nearly as concerned as females, and that for both sexes, body dissatisfaction was most severe for those areas of the body most reflective of overweight (e.g., midtorso). Moreover, they found that a negative body image was associated with lower levels of personal adjustment.

Bailey and Hankins (1979) found males to be relatively satisfied with their body builds, and to see themselves as better than average, while females were somewhat more dissatisfied with their builds and saw themselves as just average. However, Hankins and Bailey (1979) found as many females to be extremely satisfied as were extremely dissatisfied. Satisfaction was related to a more ecto-morphic and mesomorphic and less endomorphic build for these females—the very satisfied females described their builds as more slender and athletic than average. A similar study by Young and Reeve (1980) showed the females with the highest percentage of body fat to be least satisfied with their body images and the leanest subjects to be more satisfied. On the other hand, Tucker's (1982) investigation of college males showed that almost 70% of them were dissatisfied with their bodies. The thinnest and fattest were equally dissatisfied, and those who saw themselves as normal or mesomorphic liked their bodies the most.

In a later factor analysis of a Body Cathexis Scale with college women, Tucker (1985) found the women most satisfied with aspects of their faces and total appearance but least satisfied with their weight and lower body. According to Hawkins, Turell, and Jackson (1983), women translate this dissatisfaction with weight into dieting and related concerns. Although no means were reported (so we cannot assess the extent of dissatisfaction), these authors reported that body-image dissatisfaction was correlated with weight and dieting tendency or restrained eating, as well as with lower social self-esteem.

Fallon and Rozin (1985) found that college women were dissatisfied with their size and wished to be smaller than they were, and this seemed to be motivated by more than a desire to be maximally attractive to males. They replicated these findings and surveyed subjects' parents as well, finding that sex rather than age is the major factor in dieting and concern about weight, and all subjects except the college males consider themselves to be overweight (Rozin & Fallon, 1988). Similarly, Eisele, Hertsgaard, and Light (1986) surveyed adolescent girls and found that although only 19% were overweight (and 53% were normal weight), 78% wanted to weigh less. Although 28% were underweight, only 8% indicated a desire to weigh more. Cohn et al. (1987), also found girls to want a thinner body, as did Collins (1986). Franzoi and Herzog (1987) generally found men to be more positive about their bodies than women. Drewnowski and Yee (1987) examined the connection between gender and perceived overweight and dissatisfaction with one's body; females were more likely than males to see themselves as overweight (48% to 26%) and much less likely to see themselves as underweight (3.1% to 20.9% for males). The women were significantly less satisfied with their shape and dieted much more to change it. Overall, 85% of the women sampled wanted to lose weight. Men, however, were evenly divided between wanting to lose weight and wanting to gain it. Men were also somewhat more likely to try to exercise to lose weight, whereas women were more likely to diet. The authors concluded that although women were rather dissatisfied with their bodies and primarily wanted to be thinner, men were also dissatisfied, although their dissatisfaction could reflect a desire for weight gain as easily as weight loss.

Ward and McKeown (1987) measured body-image evaluation in a very selected sample of females—students in an aerobic dance class. The group was satisfied about most aspects of their bodies, as would be expected in these lean, healthy women with good body images. Nonetheless, 32% had a negative body cathexis and even as a group they were dissatisfied with 8 aspects of their bodies (out of 32), particularly the midtorso region, body fatness, and weight.

Body dissatisfaction in normal-weight subjects has also been investigated in conjunction specifically with chronic dieting, or restrained eating. Blanchard and Frost (1983) reported that restraint scores were negatively correlated with body satisfaction and positively correlated with the extent to which female subjects perceived themselves as overweight (as well as with actual overweight).

Noles, Cash, and Winstead (1985) compared depressed and nondepressed college students on body-image evaluation. Depressed students were less satisfied with their bodies and felt less attractive than did nondepressed subjects; there was no difference between the groups, however, on observer-rated attractiveness. The authors interpreted these results as evidence that depressed individuals distort their body images, although apparently there was also substantial positive distortion in the nondepressed subjects (who saw themselves as more attractive than they were rated).

Kaplan, Busner, and Pollack (1988) looked at this phenomenon from another angle. They reported that female adolescents were more likely to see themselves as overweight, while males were more likely to see themselves as underweight; but weight perception interacted with sex to predict depression. Females who saw themselves as underweight were less depressed than those who saw themselves as normal or overweight, whereas males who saw themselves as underweight were somewhat more depressed than were those who saw themselves as normal or overweight.

There does seem to be some evidence then that females are more dissatisfied with their bodies than are males, although some of the most recent studies indicate that males may be beginning to share this dissatisfaction for one reason or another. A close look at the data, though, indicates that this dissatisfaction may not be quite as widespread as some of the survey authors have concluded. Several studies found all subjects, even female ones, to have a generally favorable view of their bodies (e.g., Berscheid et al., 1973; Clifford, 1971; Gray, 1977; Mabel et al., 1986; Wooley & Wooley, 1984), although the authors often focused on the degree of discontent. For example, Bailey and Hankins (1979) reported dissatisfaction of their female subjects with their bodies, but in fact, they generally regarded themselves as average, which does not seem very dissatisfied! Other investigators found no sex difference in satisfaction (Drewnowski & Yee, 1987; Goldberg & Folkins, 1974) but, again, some focused on the degree of dissatisfaction, rather than positive body cathexis. In short, it does not seem on the basis of the literature on body-image evaluation that women in general can be said to be dissatisfied with their bodies to any great extent, although a large minority of both sexes are at least somewhat unhappy.

One possible source of the assumption that Western women dislike their bodies is the evidence on the pervasiveness of a desire to be thinner, and the prevalence of dieting in women. Although men rarely diet, even if they are attempting to lose weight (apparently preferring to exercise, Drewnowski & Yee, 1987), many studies report higher levels of dieting behavior than of dissatisfaction (e.g., Desmond et al., 1986; Drewnowski & Yee, 1987; Dwyer et al., 1969; Hawkins et al., 1983; Wooley & Wooley, 1984), and most report that despite a generally positive evaluation of their bodies, the majority of females want to be thinner than they are (e.g., Clifford, 1971; Drewnowski & Yee, 1987; Dwyer et al., 1969; Fallon & Rozin, 1985; Hawkins et al., 1983; Wooley & Wooley, 1984). Apparently, even if they are reasonably satisfied with their bodies, women would still like to be thinner.

This desire to be thinner is often taken (mis-taken, perhaps) as evidence that females are dissatisfied with their bodies. The separate evidence from assessments of actual satisfaction and such preference for weight loss suggests that satisfaction should probably be regarded as a more relative concept that it currently is. We examined these issues in a group of 18 normal-weight restrained and unrestrained subjects. There was no difference between restrained and unrestrained eaters on their accuracy of body-size perception as measured by the image marking technique ($F1,17 = 0.49$), but the silhouette technique showed a difference in self-ideal discrepancy, with restrained individuals exhibiting a larger discrepancy. However, three measures of body cathexis or satisfaction showed no more than marginal differences (EDI body dissatisfaction subscale, no difference; Franzoi & Shields's 1984 Body Esteem Scale Total score, $F1,17 = 3.70$, $p < .08$, Attractiveness subscale, $F1,17 = 3.67$, $p < .08$), and although the dieters were somewhat less satisfied, the means for both groups were well within a normal or satisfied range. Apparently, women, even chronically dieting women, feel reasonably satisfied, but could feel *more* satisfied if they were thinner. This wish to be thinner may have been overinterpreted; a desire for weight loss is not necessarily an indication of discontent with the current reality.

The concept of satisfaction or dissatisfaction with one's body is thus not really a simple dichotomy. Whether one is seen as being satisfied or not depends on the question—women in general seem to be more satisfied than dissatisfied, but still not perfectly satisfied. Depending on how satisfaction is assessed, this may be manifested as a lack of (perfect) satisfaction or as relative satisfaction. One can look at the body-image evaluation glass as being a little more than half full, or almost half empty.

BODY WEIGHT AND ACCURACY OF PERCEPTION

Body image was first examined in overweight individuals in the early 1960s, when obesity was being explored psychologically by theorists such as Bruch (1957) and Stunkard (1957). Stunkard and Mendelson (1961) described "disturbances in body image of some obese persons." They suggested that a disturbance in body image is likely to be specifically related to obesity, but indicated that "we have yet to see an obese person with a disturbed body image who does not show other significant emotional disturbances" (p. 329). They reported that disturbed family environments and emotional problems contributed to body-image distortions in the obese. Conversely, they pointed out that in families where obesity is valued, self-esteem (and body satisfaction) can actually be enhanced by excess weight. (At this early point, body-image disturbance was not separated into evaluation and perception, and the two were treated as one phenomenon.) In a more detailed presentation of their findings (Stunkard & Mendelson, 1967), they stated that only a minority of neurotic obese have a disturbed body image. Similarly, Stunkard and Burt (1967) mentioned that any distinguishing physical characteristic could become the focus of a negative body image; glasses, pigtails, braces, skin blemishes, and pigeon toes were objects of self-derogation in their preadolescent sample. By 1969, however, the perception in the literature was that "disturbances of body image are *often* observed in obese patients," (Glucksman & Hirsch, 1969, p. 1, italics added); since then the presumption of disturbance (again, meaning perception, evaluation, or both) has become normative.

As with normal-weight persons, the literature on body image in overweight persons involves the same wide variety of techniques for the measurement of accuracy of perceived body image or size estimation. The findings tend to be equally or even more varied.

Drawings

Silverstein and Robinson (1961) found a small negative correlation between degree of obesity and dimensions of the figure drawn by children. The more overweight subjects drew figures that were thinner than average. Nathan (1973) studied the drawings of 36 obese and 36 normal-weight children aged 7, 10, or 13 and found less detailed, inadequate, immature figures portrayed by the obese at all ages. Although performance improved with age (as one would expect when drawing ability is involved), the 7-year-old obese were more similar to their age mates than were the older obese children. These obese subjects were clinic patients, brought in for treatment because someone in their family was concerned about their weight. Nathan noted that nonpatient obese children made excellent, accurate drawings.

In a study of obese adolescents (Shenker et al., 1978) the males drew appropriately larger male (but not female) figures than normal, but the females drew normal-sized figures of both sexes, which was interpreted as denial of their obesity. Bailey et al. (1970), using older (college student) subjects divided into underweight, normal, and overweight groups, found that the overweight subjects drew larger heads and torsos (analyzed together) than did the other subjects. They concluded that this supports the research on overweight subjects indicating that they tend to "enlarge the dimensions of body size" (p. 618).

Gottesfeld (1962) found that obese adults were more likely to draw a person with a missing body part or lower level of differentiation of body features. The clinical interpretation of these drawings was that they indicated a negative attitude toward the body (as opposed to a distorted perception of it and its size). A questionnaire assessing attitudes toward one's personality was also given to these subjects, and the obese, surprisingly, rated their personalities more positively than did the neurotic controls. Since they also rated themselves equal to the controls on "good-looking," this was interpreted as defensive denial on the part of the obese, who presumably were less able to hide their perceptions of themselves on the projective DAP test.

Glucksman, Hirsch, McCully, Barron, and Knittle (1968) had six obese adults draw pictures before, during, and after a hospitalized weight loss program. They found that the pictures grew progressively bigger for five of the patients, and that four of them drew larger waist diameters after than before weight loss. These patients also tended to become more depressed as they lost weight, and showed other evidence of concern about their new body size. The figure drawing data were interpreted as indicating either that there was a delay in alteration of body-size perception as it changed with weight loss, or that subjects were compensating perceptually by "restoring" the lost weight to their drawings. In contrast to this, studies on the drawings of superobese patients (100 or more pounds overweight) treated with intestinal bypass surgery indicate that such patients are reasonably accurate in their perceptions of body size (although some overestimate and some underestimate, and there is an overall tendency to overestimate initially), and that they are able to assess accurately the progressive changes in their body size as they lose weight after surgery (Castelnuovo–Tedesco, 1980; Castelnuovo–Tedesco, & Schiebel, 1976, 1978).

What is most striking about these studies of obese body image as reflected in their drawings of human figures is the diversity of scoring and interpretive techniques used: size of head and torso (Bailey et al., 1970), total drawing size (Glucksman et al., 1968), ratio of height to width (Shenker et al., 1978), ratio of abdominal widths in a picture of the self and one of an average person (Castelnuovo–Tedesco, 1980; Castelnuovo–Tedesco & Schiebel, 1976, 1978), clinician judgments, number of missing parts, and differentiation scores (Gottesfeld, 1962). The findings were likewise diverse. The obese were shown to draw thinner pictures (Silverstein & Robinson, 1961), larger figures (Bailey et al., 1970; after weight loss, Glucksman et al., 1968; males only, Shenker et al., 1978) or same-sized figures (females only, Shenker et al., 1978) compared with normal-weight subjects of the same age. These results are interpreted variously as denial of obesity, accurate self-perception, or overestimation of body size. Finally, Nathan (1973) distinguished between obese patients seeking treatment for their overweight and nonpatients who are (or whose families are) unconcerned about losing weight, indicating that only the former draw distorted bodies (and presumably have disturbed body images).

Silhouettes

Schonbuch and Schell (1967) found that while normal-weight males were accurate at this task, underweight and overweight subjects both overestimated their size. Bell, Kirkpatrick, and Rinn (1986) used a similar procedure with anorexic, normal, and obese females and found that while the normals were again accurate, the anorexics overestimated but the obese underestimated their body size.

Self-report

Gray (1977) found that overweight subjects, particularly males, tended to report themselves as being lighter than they actually were. Females in general were more likely to see themselves as overweight, though males were more likely to be overweight (and see themselves as lighter). Normal-weight subjects were most likely to be correct about their appearance, and underweight subjects, especially females, were more likely to see themselves as heavier than they actually were. Desmond et al. (1986) found their heavy subjects to be accurate at perceiving themselves as overweight.

Body-width Judgment

Askevold (1975) developed another measure of body image wherein subjects simply mark on paper taped to a wall the width of various body parts, as if they were marking these dimensions on a mirror. Obese patients, like those with anorexia nervosa, were found to overestimate the size of all measured body parts. Pearlson et al. (1981), using a similar procedure wherein subjects moved lights along a bar to indicate the widths of various body parts, also found that obese subjects (particularly women) in a weight-loss program overestimated their size. Finally, Dolan et al. (1987) found that while all subjects overestimated all body widths, the most overweight and most underweight subjects overestimated to a greater extent than did normal-weight subjects.

Distorted Images

Shipman and Sohlkhah (1967) found that obese women overestimated their body size with a distorting mirror. Glucksman and Hirsch (1969) used slides distorted with an anamorphic lens. Initially (before weight loss), both normal and obese subjects apparently underestimated their size slightly (no means are given) and did not differ from each other. After they had lost weight, however, the obese patients overestimated their body size, continuing to see themselves as they were before they reduced.

Garner, Garfinkel, Stancer, and Moldofsky (1976) used both the distorted photograph (anamorphic lens) and the image-marking technique to measure body-size estimation in obese and thin anorexia nervosa) patients, and normal-weight controls. On the average, with the photograph technique, the controls exhibited significant underestimation, while the obese and anorexic patients were accurate. However, half of each patient group underestimated and half overestimated, producing an average estimation score of zero distortion. It is clearly important to examine not only group means, but the distribution of scores as well. The visual marking task did not reveal any differences between groups; both the normal-weight controls and the two patient groups overestimated all four body parts tested.

Using the more standard distorted image technique (two to four trials), Cash and Green (1986) found that overweight subjects overestimated by about 11%, but did not differ significantly from normal-weight subjects (mean overestimation of 1%). Both groups gave smaller estimates than did underweight subjects, who overestimated their own size by 24% and a mannequin's size by 32%; normals estimated the mannequin at 110%, the obese at 116% of its actual size.

Speaker, Schultz, Grinker, and Stern (1983) tested obese boys 12 to 14 years old who were attending a weight-loss camp. Their subjects did not distort their body size at the start of camp, but underestimated their sizes at the end of camp, after losing an average of close to 30 pounds. The authors attribute this underestimation to the exercise program at the camp (although Herman, 1983, questioned just how exercise would produce underestimation).

Collins, McCabe, Jupp, and Sutton (1983) assessed female students in a weight-reducing course. The more obese subjects overestimated their size to a greater extent than did the less obese subjects initially, although all subjects overestimated. Over time though, all subjects reduced their ratings, becoming more accurate. This might indicate that practice lessens the tendency to overestimate. However, a recent series of studies clouds this issue. Gardner, Martinez, and Espinoza (1987) gave obese and normal-weight subjects 20 practice trials before a series of 100 self-estimations (plus estimates of an obese and a normal mannequin). The obese and normal subjects were equally accurate, overestimating slightly on average. The authors speculated that the feedback on the task may have prevented the obese from overestimating. On the other hand, Gardner, Martinez, and Sandoval (1987) found that normal subjects were accurate on average, but obese subjects overestimated by 11.52%. They interpreted these data to indicate that obese subjects experience a sensory distortion, but did not mention their other study where this was not found. (Complications due to the inclusion of practice trials with feedback may be partially responsible for the difference between studies.) No data on variability were provided in either study.

Conclusions

It is obviously difficult to draw conclusions about how accurately overweight people perceive themselves, since the data are so variable. Analysis of figure drawings (based on the *assumption* that these reflect the self) shows that overweight subjects draw unduly thin portraits (e.g., females in Shenker et al., 1978; all subjects in Silverstein & Robinson, 1961), or accurate portraits (Castelnuovo–Tedesco, 1980; Castelnuovo–Tedesco, & Schiebel, 1978), or larger portraits than others draw (although this "error" may well produce an accurate self-portrait) (Bailey et al., 1970; males in Shenker et al., 1978), or a portrait that grows larger over time despite a reduction in the subject's own size (Glucksman et al., 1968), or negative or immature pictures (Gottesfeld, 1962; Nathan, 1973) or even normal pictures (Nathan, 1973). Over time during weight reduction, obese patients either draw progressively larger drawings (Glucksman et al. 1968), accurate representations of their decreasing size (Castelnuovo–Tedesco, 1980; Castelnuovo–Tedesco, & Schiebel, 1976, 1978), or do not change their drawings (Nathan & Pisula, 1970). There is apparently no consistent difference between the drawings of obese and normal individuals, and no clear conclusion one can draw from these drawings, whatever they may actually represent to the artist. Underweight subjects do not appear to have been tested with this technique.

The results of simply asking subjects their size are equally confusing. The heavier subjects may underestimate their size (Gray, 1977), or they may be accurate (Desmond et al., 1986), apparently depending on whether more males or females in the sample are overweight. Underweight subjects, on the other hand, tend to see themselves as heavier (more normal) than they actually are.

Using something with more apparent face validity, such as silhouettes, does not clarify the situation much. Overweight subjects may overestimate their size (Schonbuch & Schell, 1967), or they may underestimate their size (Bell et al., 1986). What seems most consistent is the tendency of underweight subjects to overestimate their size.

Even the most sophisticated techniques do not reveal much. Image-marking or visual size-estimation tasks are the only consistent ones in the literature—obese subjects overestimate their body size (Askevold, 1975; Dolan et al., 1987; Garner et al., 1976; Pearlson et al., 1981). It is not clear what this means, though, since normal-weight controls and underweight or anorexic subjects also consistently overestimate their size with this task (Askevold, 1975; Dolan et al., 1987; Garner, Garfinkel, & Bonato, 1987; Garner et al., 1976), suggesting that this may be simply an artifact of the technique.

The even more sophisticated image-distorting techniques are not especially consistent. The obese may overestimate (Collins et al., 1983; Gardner et al., 1987b; Glucksman & Hirsch, 1969; Shipman & Sohlkhah, 1967) or be as accurate as normal weight subjects (Cash & Green, 1986; Gardner et al., 1987a; Garner et al., 1976; Speaker, Schultz, Grinker, & Stern, et al., 1983), or underestimate (Glucksman & Hirsch, 1969, before weight loss). They may become more accurate after weight loss (Collins et al., 1987), or underestimate after weight loss (Speaker et al., 1983), or overestimate after weight loss (Glucksman & Hirsch, 1969). Underweight subjects again seem most likely to overestimate their size, except for anorexic patients, who are exceptionally variable. In general, though, with distorted image techniques, as with most of the other techniques, where subjects are not accurate, they seem more likely to perceive themselves as larger than reality, not smaller.

Despite early speculations and popular views, there is thus no real evidence that overweight persons perceive or visualize or represent their bodies any less accurately (or more inaccurately) than do normal-weight individuals under any given circumstances. Even a change in actual body size (such as weight loss) does not produce a corresponding reliable change in the overweight person's body-size estimate or perception. If the obese have a distinctive body-image distortion, it does not seem to be at the level of perception. Underweight subjects, on the other hand, seem to be consistent in their overestimation of their body size.

BODY WEIGHT AND EVALUATION OF BODY SHAPE AND SIZE

When Stunkard and his colleagues initially discussed the possibility of body-image disturbances in the obese, they actually seemed to mean a disorder of evaluation rather than of perception (Stunkard & Burt, 1967; Stunkard & Mendelson, 1961, 1967). They discussed body-image derogation, and attributed the development of disturbances to derogatory comments of others, concluding that such disturbances are affective, not cognitive (Stunkard & Burt, 1967). They saw such body-image devaluation as related to other emotional disorders, and did not expect emotionally healthy obese to exhibit them (Stunkard & Mendelson, 1961, 1967). Others concur. Craft (1972) concluded that it is not true that all obese have negative feelings about their bodies. Wadden and Stunkard (1987) acknowledged that, owing to intense societal pressures toward slimness, one might expect all obese individuals to be dissatisfied with their appearance; but this is not in fact the case. Rather, obese middle- and upper-class young women, for whom the pressures to be thin are particularly strong and the sanctions against obesity especially severe, are the ones likely to despise their bodies. Even among these women, such dissatisfaction is usually seen only in those who have been overweight since childhood or adolescence, who are also neurotic, and who have been negatively evaluated for their weight by family or friends.

Others disagree, however. Altshul (1981) observed that obese people tend to loathe their bodies, and see the body as an enemy. Brownell (1979) called body-image disparagement the most common psychological disturbance in the obese. He attributes low self-esteem and self-consciousness to disturbed body image in obese patients. Weiss (1986) observed that some patients consciously see themselves as fat but unconsciously still see themselves as thin. This different sort of distortion interferes with therapy and weight loss, as do unrealistic fantasies about being thin.

Many investigators have collected data on the extent of body dissatisfaction in obese subjects. Through a series of interviews with 94 obese patients, Stunkard and Mendelson (1967) concluded that derogation of the body occurs only in a minority of neurotic obese, not in emotionally healthy obese patients. Moreover, while weight loss did not seem to diminish whatever disturbances exist, if the body-image problem was cured in psychotherapy, weight loss seemed easier to achieve and maintain. The main feature of these disturbances, which characterize childhood or adolescent onset obesity, but not adult onset obesity, seemed to be a preoccupation with one's obesity to the exclusion of other characteristics.

This was explicitly investigated by Stunkard and Burt (1967), in adult-onset obese patients plus a group of juvenile-onset obese patients divided into those who were obese in both childhood and adolescence, obese in adolescence only, or those who were obese in childhood only. The adult-onset obese were least likely to have even mild body-image derogation, while the juvenile onset patients were unlikely to be problem-free. The one individual who was overweight only as a child and an adult did not evince any dissatisfaction though. (Screening 115 more obese patients, the authors found only one more such patient, and this person also had no disturbance.) This seemed to pinpoint adolescence as a critical period. They then studied preadolescent obese and normal girls (grades 4 to 6). No real body-image disparagement comparable with that found in the adults was noted. Some disturbance was noted but no more in the obese than the normals, and even the obese girls were not always upset about their weight (as opposed to glasses, pigtails, braces or other distinguishing physical characteristics). Finally, the authors found 10 normal-weight adults who had been obese at 12 years of age. Only three reported a body-image disturbance (in adolescence). Stunkard and Burt (1967) concluded that disturbances in body image in the obese originate in adolescence, probably from derogatory comments by parents, peers, or others, and that any physical defects (real or imagined) can cause body-image disparagement in adolescence.

Dwyer et al. (1969) investigated adolescents' attitudes toward weight and their bodies and found the obese to be most dissatisfied with their bodies, as well as being more likely to see themselves as larger than others of their height. Overweight boys were less dissatisfied with their bodies than were overweight girls, but underweight boys wanted to be larger (more muscular).

Similar interviews and surveys have been conducted more recently. Allon (1979) studied children and teen-agers and found a negative body image present in everyone but the preadolescent males. Being overweight was seen as a reason for loathing one's body, and as what others focus on in social interactions, arousing mixed feelings of pity and repugnance and overwhelming other (positive) attributes of the fat individual. Blyth et al., (1981) found obese junior high school boys to be the most dissatisfied with their weight, while thin boys were slightly more dissatisfied than were normal weight boys. The fatter, heavier males were more self-conscious, more likely to have an unstable sense of self, and self-esteem was negatively correlated with weight. However, in Doell and Hawkins's (1981) college students, the overweight subjects' global self-ratings were about as positive as were those of normal-weight subjects, although subjects who thought they were fat (defined as having a negative body image) reported a more negative self-concept. Overweight subjects were more likely to have such negative body images, since their descriptions of their physical bodies were accurate, yet not negative enough to differ from normal-weight subjects.

Obese individuals who have lost weight have also been examined, usually with a view to establishing the salutary effect of weight loss on their body images (in terms of increased satisfaction). Restrained eating (chronic dieting) was positively related to both body dissatisfaction and the frequency and enjoyability of pleasurable activities in overweight patients at a weight loss clinic (Doell & Hawkins, 1982); dieters disliked their bodies more but seemed to have more fun than nondieters.

Rohrbacher investigated the effect of a weight-loss camp program on overweight boys aged 8 to 18. Subjects lost an average of 33 pounds during the 8-week program and were followed up for an additional 16 weeks. Weight loss per se was not associated with a change in body-image evaluation or self-concept, although weight change after camp was related to body image such that those who lost weight after camp felt better about their bodies while those who gained felt worse. Overall, body-image evaluation was significantly correlated with self-concept, despite the failure of self-concept to change over the course of the study.

Leon (1975) compared subjects at their first weight-loss session with a control group of normal, stable-weight individuals, and then split the overweight group into two groups who lost more (change) or less (no change) than 14 pounds in the first 6 months. There were few body-image differences between obese and control subjects at the first session. The only effects of weight loss seemed to be that the change group saw themselves as less heavy, more self-controlled and had fewer cues for eating than the no-change group, and did not differ from the controls (though they had differed on these variables initially). On the other hand, Castelnuovo–Tedesco and Schiebel (1976, 1978) found that after intestinal-bypass surgery but before weight loss had occurred, obese patients felt slimmer, more self-confident, and mildly euphoric (implying that the surgery marked an improvement over what they had felt before). Over time, however, while their self-confidence remained elevated, and their MMPI scores did not change, patients became more emotional, in particular more likely to become angry or (to a lesser extent) depressed or anxious. These patients also tended to show a reluctance to mingle with fat people after their surgery, claiming that they were developing new, "normal" identities and did not want to be reminded of when they had been fat.

Conclusion

Body-image evaluation in the obese presents a somewhat clearer picture than does body-image perception. Although it is by no means true that all—or even perhaps most, depending on the sample—obese individuals are dissatisfied with their bodies, overweight people do seem as a group to be more dissatisfied than are normal-weight people. This generalization seems to hold especially for females, and particularly for female adolescents or females who were overweight as adolescents. As Stunkard and Burt (1967) noted, adolescence is time when any physical characteristic which differs from the norm causes self-consciousness and derogation (by self and others), which can result in a negative body evaluation. Excess weight appears to be particularly prone to this derogation. Underweight, on the other hand, is less of a problem, causing discomfort only to thin males, if at all.

BODY IMAGE AND EATING DISORDERS— A BRIEF OVERVIEW

The recent upsurge of interest in body image has been fostered by the presumed presence of body-image distortions in extremely thin eating-disorder patients (this literature has been ably reviewed quite recently; see Cash & Brown, 1987, or Garner et al. 1987). In this area as elsewhere, though, conceptual confusion is a problem. Garner and Garfinkel (1981) point out that the lack of clarity of the body-image construct has posed particular difficulties for the study of anorexia nervosa and bulimia because there appear to be at least two ways in which a body-image disturbance may be manifested in this population (corresponding to the perception and evaluation components of body image discussed earlier). Some patients appear to exhibit a perceptual disturbance such that they are unable to estimate their body size and shape accurately (mostly a matter of overestimation), while others see themselves accurately enough but have a disturbance in that they experience loathing and disgust for their own bodies. Different investigators have focused on one or the other of these manifestations of body-image disturbance, often without recognizing the distinction.

These conceptual shortcomings are exacerbated by methodological complications and limitations. As Garner et al. (1987), stated, "body image has been operationally defined or measured using a range of different methods including projective techniques, figure drawings, questionnaires, sensory perception tests, critical interviews, and size estimation tasks using visual and tactile cues" (p. 119).

Finally, even using similar methodologies on similar subject groups, investigators have reported conflicting results. Despite theoretical expectations (e.g., Bruch, 1962; Garner, et al., 1987), some studies find that eating-disorder patients overestimate their body size, some find that they underestimate, and some find that they are accurate. At the same time, normal controls often show the same aberrations as do the patient groups being studied (see Cash & Brown, 1987; or Garner et al., 1987 for reviews), leading Cash and Brown to conclude that there is no "unequivocal evidence that eating-disordered groups have a more perceptually distorted body image than various comparison groups" (p. 493) although the evidence of greater dissatisfaction in the patient groups is more consistent. Eating-disorder patients thus seem more likely than normals to be dissatisfied with their bodies, but show great variability in their perceptual accuracy, as do normals.

Despite this variability, there are some reliable findings in this area. In terms of personality, overestimation in (thin) patients is positively correlated with neuroticism, external locus of control, depression, anxiety, eating pathology, somatization, and introversion and negatively correlated with ego strength and self-esteem (Garner et al., 1987; Strober, 1981). Overestimation is also associated with number of prior therapeutic failures, lack of clinical progress, early relapse following hospitalization, and poor treatment outcome (Garner et al., 1987), although Ben–Tovim & Crisp (1984) argue that the relation between overestimation and clinical prognosis may be artifactually inflated as patients gain weight, owing to the use of a Body Perception Index based on actual width.

In addition, there is some evidence that bulimia nervosa may be even more strongly related to body dissatisfaction and pathology than anorexia nervosa (Eckert, Halmi, Marchi, & Cohen, 1987; Katzman & Wolchik, 1984).

CONCLUSIONS:
WHAT DOES BODY IMAGE SIGNIFY?

The common beliefs about body image mentioned earlier do not appear to be borne out by the literature. Eating-disorder patients may or may not have a body-image disturbance of perception or evaluation. When distorted perception is present, it seems to be associated with a poor prognosis, but it is not clear that it is a defining characteristic of the eating disorders (Garner et al., 1987; Hsu, 1982). Dissatisfaction is more uniformly present in these patients (Garner et al., 1987), but is less clearly connected to pathology or prognosis (or distortion). Obesity also may or may not be associated with disturbed body perception or evaluation, but these are neither reliably present nor notably widespread among the obese. Their relation to any other pathology in the obese has yet to be demonstrated, and weight loss does not seem to improve them anyway. And finally, the majority of women are relatively satisfied with their body images, although the obese are somewhat less satisfied than are normals. Why, then, is so much attention focused on the study of body image? And why is the literature so inconclusive?

While we are not able to say that there is any distortion of body image in general in any particular group, when such disturbance is present perhaps there are consequences which merit attention (leaving aside for the moment eating-disorder patients, who are naturally more pathological in most respects). Possibly there are undesirable personality traits, attitudes or behaviors which accompany a distorted self-perception in otherwise normal or merely overweight populations.

One might expect increased dissatisfaction to lead to distorted perception, or vice versa. Are the two types of body-image disturbance related to each other? Some of the studies included measures of both perception and evaluation and addressed this issue. The answer seems to be that they are not. Cash and Green (1986), Mabel et al. (1986), and Dolan et al. (1987) all found little or no association between accuracy of size estimation and satisfaction with what one sees. The two types of distortion are thus unrelated, and their correlates are likely to be different.

Body-size Perception

Body-size estimation techniques do not seem to correlate well with each other (Garner et al., 1987), either because of poor reliability or because they are measuring different aspects of a complex construct. There is also the question of whether such tasks really assess simple perceptual or motivational factors. Their influencability by such factors as instructions, feedback, and other cognitive interventions implies that there is indeed a significant motivational component to such estimates (Garner et al., 1987).

It is noteworthy that only overestimation is seen as pathological in any population (and the scant evidence for pathology is only related to overestimation). Underestimation is found in some eating-disorder patients, obese subjects, and normals but somehow does not appear to be regarded as problematical.

Garner and Garfinkel (1981) review several explanations of the possible meaning to eating-disorder patients of faulty size estimation (i.e., overestimation), ranging from avoidance of biological maturity to denial of illness. They also mention Bruch's (1973) hypothesis that many individuals with eating disorders or obesity have learned to misperceive their internal bodily sensations due to unresponsive or faulty parenting, and that their development is actually arrested. This last theory is supported somewhat by data that body-size estimation becomes more accurate with age (since all size estimation seems developmentally determined and improves with age). Disturbed size estimation should then be correlated with other faulty perceptions of internal experiences. There does seem to be some evidence of this in eating-disorder patients, at least for those who overestimate. Such patients typically score high on measures of faulty internal sensitivity (Garner, Olmstead, Polivy, & Garfinkel, 1984) and external locus of control, fail to exhibit sucrose aversion after a glucose load (Garner et al., 1987), and show evidence of physical anhedonia (Garner & Garfinkel, 1981).

There is less evidence of any such association in normal and obese subjects, however. The consistent overestimation of underweight (normal) subjects has neither been remarked upon nor investigated. Overestimation of body size in obese subjects has been shown to correlate with external locus of control scores (Garner et al., 1976; Speaker et al., 1983), but no other personality measure (Mable et al., 1986). Taylor and Cooper (1986) did find that lower estimators had lower depression scores than higher estimators, and that the most depressed subjects had higher estimates than the least-depressed subjects, though this was due more to the underestimation of the low depressed subjects. Unfortunately most of the studies which examined body-size estimation failed to correlate it with anything else, and many reported only means and no ranges, so that even the extent of distortion is difficult to assess. Except for the eating-disorder literature, where outcome of treatment is frequently examined with respect to body-image disturbance, little or no actual behavior has been studied in conjunction with body-size estimation. In one exception, Pearlson et al. (1981) found that overestimation in obese women did not predict success in a weight-loss program, and was not even related to age of onset of obesity. Perception of body size thus has not been shown to be of particular significance for most individuals as a diagnostic or prognostic indicator.

Body-image Evaluation

Some dissatisfaction with one's shape and size does seem to be found with reasonable consistency in both obese patients and normal-weight subjects, especially females. Many of the studies demonstrating this imply in their conclusions that the presence of such a self-evaluation indicates something pathological or is somehow problematical for the individuals who feel this way. To what extent, though, is this implication supported by any data?

A negative body image seems to be associated with a desire to lose weight, particularly in females. One would therefore expect to find an association between such dissatisfaction and dieting tendencies or behaviors. In fact, where this has been measured, this does seem to be true. Doell and Hawkins (1982), Blanchard and Frost (1983), and Wardle and Beales (1986) all reported strong correlations between body-image dissatisfaction and restrained eating. Garner et al. (1984) found an association between drive for thinness and body dissatisfaction in normal subjects on the Eating Disorder Inventory. As described earlier, data just collected in our own laboratory corroborate this as well. Body dissatisfaction was significantly correlated with drive for thinness, and with restraint scores in a group of 18 normal college females. Restraint scores also correlated negatively with a general body feelings scale and a subscale of body attractiveness. However, Pearlson et al. (1981) found that dislike of one's body did not predict weight loss for obese subjects (although it could perhaps be argued that dieting and drive for thinness might not predict actual weight loss either).

Body-image satisfaction, or body concept as it is sometimes called, has frequently been shown to be related to self-esteem or self-concept. Zion (1964) reported a significant positive linear relationship between body concept and self-concept on a variety of measures. In Blyth et al.'s (1981) study, satisfaction with weight was associated with higher self-esteem, lower self-consciousness, and a more stable self-image. These authors concluded that "satisfaction with weight is always advantageous for the self-image" (p. 69) (although causality remains unproven). Franzoi and Herzog (1986) found a significant relation between body esteem and general self-esteem, and Mable et al. (1986) reported that body dissatisfaction was associated with low self-esteem, as well as external locus of control, and depression. The only contradictory finding was Rohrbacher's (1973) summer camp study wherein body image improved but self-concept remained unchanged. There seems, then, to be a general tendency for dissatisfaction with one's body to be associated with a lower overall self-concept or self-esteem. This accords with Polivy, Heatherton, & Herman's (1988) findings that restrained eating is associated with lower self-esteem, and the combination of low self-esteem and dieting leads to disinhibitory eating.

Depression and body dissatisfaction have been found to be associated in several investigations. Mable et al. (1986), as mentioned, reported such an association, and Kaplan et al.'s (1988) data can be similarly interpreted. Noles et al. (1985) found that depressed subjects were less satisfied with their bodies on several indexes of body-image evaluation, and assessed themselves as less attractive than did observers. In a similar vein, Butters and Cash (1987) reported that a negative body image was related to low levels of psychosocial well-being or adjustment.

Body dissatisfaction appears to have some negative correlates in addition to being reasonably widespread. Although it is present in a minority of subjects, this is a sizable minority (ranging from 25% to nearly 50%). Apparently these individuals are more likely to be depressed, much more likely to be dieting, with all the hazards that entails (see, e.g., Polivy & Herman, 1987), and likely to have generally lower self-esteem.

This description brings to mind Schonfeld's (1964) description of body image as reflecting internalized psychological factors from an individual's personal, perceptual, and emotional experiences, plus the influence of others' reactions. This sounds like a description of an evaluative body image which would be connected to one's general self-image. Similarly, Van der Velde (1985) emphasized the importance of body image for the development of self-concept and personality, and Gallagher (1986) indicated its conscious, personal nature. These conceptions of body image thus seem most consistent with what we have been discussing here as the evaluative aspect of body image. Accuracy of perception of one's body size may be more of an artifact of its own measurement (as Gallagher, 1986, proposes) than a true reflection of the individual's self-perception, which may be better reflected in the evaluative dimension of body image.

Our self-perceptions and self-inferences about our own appearance must naturally reflect our comparisons of ourselves with others, and the feedback we receive from them. These seem to be more likely to be incorporated into body-image evaluation than into size perception.

And finally, although there are negative correlates of body-image dissatisfaction, there is insufficient evidence at present to conclude that body image causes these. In fact, the studies on depression suggest that it may be a consequence of either depression itself, or a negative general self-concept. Future studies on body image could attempt to determine whether it is a causal influence or a mere consequence of development.

Body image appears to be a more complex phenomenon than has generally been believed. Of its two components, body-size estimation seem to be of little theoretical or practical value for any but a small number of anorexia nervosa patients. This aspect has been perhaps overinvestigated. Body-shape evaluation, however, may still yield some interesting or important information. Its relation to self-esteem needs further exploration—does body dissatisfaction cause low self-esteem or is it a result of it? How do these factors relate to the widespread dieting in our society? Would changing body image (evaluation) change one's general feelings about oneself, relieve depression, and reduce dieting and its negative sequelae? Are there other behavioral or personality correlates of body dissatisfaction? It is perhaps time to stop measuring body image and start assessing its impact.

REFERENCES

Allon, N. (1979). Self-perceptions of the stigma of overweight in relationship to weight-losing patterns. *American Journal of Clinical Nutrition, 32,* 470–480.

Altshul, V. A. (1981). The body as enemy in obese patients: Physician entanglement. *Psychosomatics, 22.*

American Psychiatric Association. (1987). *Diagnostic and statistical manual of mental disorders,* revision (DSM–IIIR). American Psychiatric Association, Washington, DC.

Askevold, E. (1975). Measuring body image. *Psychotherapy and Psychosomatics, 26,* 71–77.

Bailey, R. C., & Hankins, N. E. (1979). Body build perceptions in male and female college students. *Social Behavior and Personality, 7,* 153–156.

Bailey, W. H., Shinedling, M. M., & Payne, J. R. (1970). Obese individuals' perception of body image. *Perceptual and Motor Skills, 31,* 617–618.

Bell, C., Kirkpatrick, S. W., & Rinn, R. C. (1986). Body image of anorexic, obese, and normal females. *Journal of Clinical Psychology, 42,* 431–439.

Ben–Tovim, D. I., & Crisp, A. H. (1984). The reliability of estimates of body width and their relationship to current measured body size among anorexic and normal subjects. *Psychological Medicine, 14,* 843–846.

Berscheid, E., Walster, E., & Bohrnstedt, G. (1973). Body image: The happy American body: A survey report. *Psychology Today, 7,* 119–131.

Birtchnell, S. A., Lacey, J. H., & Harte, A. (1985). Body image distortion in bulimia nervosa. *British Journal of Psychiatry, 147,* 408–412.

Blanchard, F. A., & Frost, R. O. (1983). Two factors of restraint: Concern for dieting and weight fluctuation. *Behavior Research & Therapy, 21*, 259–267.

Blyth, D. A., Simmons, R. G., Bulcroft, R., Felt, D., Van Cleave, E. F., & Bush, D. M. (1981). The effects of physical development on self-image and satisfaction with body-image for early adolescent males. *Research in Community and Mental Health, 2*, 43–73.

Brownell, K. D. (1979). *Obesity as a social and emotional disability.* Testimony before the Pennsylvania Human Relations Committee, Aug. 8.

Bruch, H. (1957). *The importance of overweight.* New York: W. W. Norton.

Bruch, H. (1962). Perceptual and conceptual disturbances in anorexia nervosa. *Psychosomatic Medicine, 24*, 187–194.

Bruch, H. (1973). *Eating disorders: Obesity, anorexia and the person within.* New York: Basic Books.

Butters, J. W., & Cash, T. F. (1987). Cognitive-behavioral treatment of women's body image dissatisfaction. *Journal of Consulting and Clinical Psychology, 55*, 889–897.

Cash, T. F., & Brown, T. A. (1987). Body image in anorexia nervosa and bulimia nervosa: A review of the literature. *Behavior Modification, 11*, 487–521.

Cash, T. F., & Green, G. K. (1986). Body weight and body image among college women: Perception, cognition, and affect. *Journal of Personality Assessment, 50*, 290–301.

Cash, T. F., Winstead, B. A., & Janda, L. H. (1986, April). Body image survey report: The great American shape-up. *Psychology Today*, pp. 20, 30–37.

Casper, R. C., Halmi, K. A., Goldberg, S. C., Eckert, E. D., & Davis, J. M. (1979). Disturbances in body image estimation as related to other characteristics and outcome in anorexia nervosa. *British Journal of Psychiatry, 134*, 60–66.

Castelnuovo–Tedesco, P. (1980). Jejuno-ileal bypass for superobesity: A psychiatric assessment. *Advances in Psychosomatic Medicine, 10*, 196–206.

Castelnuovo–Tedesco, P., & Scheibel, D. (1976). Studies of superobesity: II. Psychiatric appraisal of jejuno-ileal bypass surgery. *American Journal of Psychiatry, 133*, 26–31.

Castelnuovo–Tedesco, P., & Scheibel, D. (1978). Body image changes after jejuno-ileal bypass surgery. *International Journal of Psychiatry in Medicine, 8*, 117–123.

Clifford, E. (1971). Body satisfaction in adolescence. *Perceptual and Motor Skills, 33*, 119–125.

Cohn, L. D., Adler, N. E., Irwin, C. E., Jr., Millstein, S. G., Kegeles, S. M., & Stone, G. (1987). Body figure preferences in adolescent males and females. *Journal of Abnormal Psychology, 96*, 276–279.

Collins, J. K. (1986). The objective measurement of body image using a video technique: Reliability and validity studies. *British Journal of Psychology, 77*, 199–205.

Collins, J. K., McCabe, M. P., Jupp, J. J., & Sutton, J. E. (1983). Body percept change in obese females after weight reduction therapy. *Journal of Clinical Psychology, 39*, 507–511.

Craft, C. A. (1972). Body image and obesity. *Nursing Clinics of North America, 7*, 677–685.

Desmond, S. M., Price, J. H., Gray, N., & O'Connell, J. K. (1986). The etiology of adolescents' perceptions of their weight. *Journal of Youth and Adolescence, 15*, 461–474.

Doell, S. R., & Hawkins, R. C., II. (1981). *Obesity, slimness, and self-protective bias: A semantic differential analysis.* Paper presented at the annual meeting of the American Psychological Association.

Doell, S. R., & Hawkins, R. C., II. (1982). Pleasures and pounds: An exploratory study. *Addictive Behaviors, 7*, 65–69.

Dolan, B. M., Birtchnell, S. A., & Lacey, J. H. (1987). Body image distortion in noneating disordered women and men. *Journal of Psychosomatic Research, 31*, 513–520.

Drewnowski, A., & Yee, D. K. (1987). Men and body image: Are males satisfied with their body weight? *Psychosomatic Medicine, 49*, 626–634.

Dwyer, J. T., Feldman, J. J., Seltzer, C. C., & Mayer, J. (1969). Adolescent attitudes toward weight and appearance. *Journal of Nutrition Education, 1*, 14–19.

Eckert, E. D., Halmi, K. A., Marchi, P., & Cohen, J. (1987). Comparison of bulimic and non-bulimic anorexia nervosa patients during treatment. *Psychological Medicine, 17,* 891–898.

Eisele, J., Hertsgaard, D., & Light, H. K. (1986). Factors related to eating disorders in young adolescent girls. *Adolescence, 21,* 283–290.

Fallon, A. E., & Rozin, P. (1985). Sex differences in perceptions of desirable body shape. *Journal of Abnormal Psychology, 94,* 102–104.

Franzoi, S. L., & Herzog, M. E. (1987). Judging physical attractiveness: What body aspects do we use? *Personality and Social Psychology Bulleting, 13,* 19–33.

Franzoi, S. L., and Shields, S. A. (1984). The body esteem scale: Multidimensional structure and sex differences in a college population. *Journal of Personality Assessment, 48,* 173–178.

Gallagher, S. (1986). Body image and body schema—A conceptual clarification. *Journal of Mind and Behavior, 7,* 541–554.

Gardner, R. M., Martinez, R., & Espinoza, T. (1987). Psychological measurement of body image of self and others in obese subjects. *Journal of Social Behavior and Personality, 2,* 205–218.

Gardner, R. M., Martinez, R., & Sandoval, Y. (1987). Obesity and body image: An evaluation of sensory and non-sensory components. *Psychological Medicine, 17,* 927–932.

Garfinkel, P. E., Moldofsky, H., & Garner, D. M. (1979). The stability of perceptual disturbances in anorexia nervosa. *Psychological Medicine, 9,* 703–708.

Garfinkel, P. E., Moldofsky, H., Garner, D. M., Stancer, H. C., & Coscina, D. V. (1978). Body awareness in anorexia nervosa: Disturbances in "body image" and "satiety." *Psychosomatic Medicine, 40,* 487–498.

Garner, D. M., & Garfinkel, P. E. (1981). Body image in anorexia nervosa. Measurement, theory, and clinical implications. *International Journal of Psychiatric Medicine, 11,* 263–284.

Garner, D. M., Garfinkel, P. E., & Bonato, D. P. (1987). Body image measurement in eating disorders. *Advances in Psychosomatic Medicine, 17,* 119–133.

Garner, D. M., Garfinkel, P. E., Stancer, H. C., & Moldofsky, H. (1976). Body image disturbance in anorexia nervosa and obesity. *Psychomatic Medicine, 38,* 329–336.

Garner, D. M., Olmstead, M. P., Polivy, J., & Garfinkel, P. E. (1984). Comparison between weight preoccupied women and anorexia nervosa. *Psychosomatic Medicine, 46,* 255–266.

Gayton, W. F., Horner, C., & Laperrier, A. (1984). Accuracy in self-appraisal of body-frame size. *Perceptual and Motor Skills, 59,* 706.

Glucksman, M. L., & Hirsch, J. (1969). The response of obese patients to weight reduction: III. The perception of body size. *Psychosomatic Medicine, 31,* 1–7.

Glucksman, M. L., Hirsch, J., McCully, R. S., Barron, B. A., & Knittle, J. L. (1968). The response of obese patients to weight reduction: II. A quantitative evaluation of behavior. *Psychosomatic Medicine, 30,* 359–373.

Goldberg, B., & Folkins, C. (1974). Relationship of body image to negative emotional attitudes. *Perceptual and Motor Skills, 39,* 1053–1054.

Gottesfeld, H. (1962). Body and self-cathexis of super obese patients. *Journal of Psychosomatic Research, 6,* 356–363.

Gray, S. H. (1977). Social aspects of body image: Perception of normalcy of weight and affect of college undergraduates. *Perceptual and Motor Skills, 45,* 1035–1040.

Halmi, K. A., Goldberg, S. C., & Cunningham, S. (1977). Perceptual distortion of body image in adolescent girls: Distortion of body image in adolescence. *Psychological Medicine, 7,* 253–257.

Hankins, N. E., & Bailey, R. C. (1979). Body build satisfaction and the congruency of body build perceptions. *Social Behavior and Personality, 7,* 77–80.

Hawkins, R. C., II, Turell, S., & Jackson, L. J. (1983). Desirable and undesirable masculine and feminine traits in relation to students' dieting tendencies and body image dissatisfaction. *Sex Roles, 9,* 705–717.

Herman, C. P. (1983). Editorial comment. *International Journal of Obesity, 7,* 81–83.

Hsu, L. K. G. (1982). Is there a disturbance in body image anorexia nervosa? *The Journal of Nervous and Mental Disease, 170,* 305–307.

Kaplan, S. L., Busner, J., & Pollack, S. (1988). Perceived weight, actual weight, and depressive symptoms in a general adolescent sample. *International Journal of Eating Disorders, 7,* 107–113.

Katzman, M. A., & Wolchik, S. A. (1984). Bulimia and binge eating in college women: A comparison of personality and behavioral characteristics. *Journal of Consulting and Clinical Psychology, 52,* 423–428.

Lacey, J. H., & Birtchnell, S. A. (1986). Body image and its disturbances. *Journal of Psychosomatic Research, 30,* 623–631.

Leon, G. (1975). Personality, body image, and eating pattern changes in overweight persons after weight loss. *Journal of Clinical Psychology, 31,* 618–623.

Lippa, R. (1983). Sex typing and the perception of body outlines. *Journal of Personality, 51,* 668–682.

Mable, H. M., Balance, W. D. G., & Galgan, R. J. (1986). Body-image distortion and dissatisfaction in university students. *Perceptual and Motor Skills, 63,* 907–911.

McCrea, C. W., Summerfield, A. B., & Rosen, B. (1982). Body image: A selective review of existing measurement techniques. *Journal of Medical Psychology, 55,* 225–233.

Meerman, R. (1983). Experimental investigation of disturbances in body image estimation in anorexia nervosa patients, and ballet and gymnastics pupils. *International Journal of Eating Disorders, 2,* 91–100.

Nathan, S. (1973). Body image in chronically obese children as reflected in figure drawings. *Journal of Personality Assessment, 37,* 456–463.

Nathan, S., & Pisula, D. (1970). Psychological observations of obese adolescents during starvation treatment. *Journal of the American Academy of Child Psychiatry, 9,* 722–740.

Noles, S. W., Cash, T. F., & Winstead, B. A. (1985). Body image, physical attractiveness, and depression. *Journal of Consulting and Clinical Psychology, 53,* 88–94.

Norris, D. L. (1984). The effects of mirror confrontation on self-estimation of body dimensions in anorexia nervosa, bulimia, and two control groups. *Psychological Medicine, 14,* 835–842.

Pearlson, G. D., Flournoy, L. H., Simonson, M., & Slavney, P. R. (1981). Body image in obese adults. *Psychological Medicine, 11,* 147–154.

Polivy, J., Garner, D. M., & Garfinkel, P. E. (1986). Thinness and social behavior. In C. P. Herman, M. P. Zanna, & E. T. Higgins (Eds.) *Physical appearance, stigma, and social behavior: The Ontario Symposium* (Vol. 3). Hillsdale, NJ: Lawrence Erlbaum Associates.

Polivy, J., Heatherton, T. F., & Herman, C. P. (1988). Self-esteem, restraint, and eating behavior. *Journal of Abnormal Psychology, 97,* 354–356,.

Polivy, J., & Herman, C. P. (1987). The diagnosis and treatment of normal eating. *Journal of Consulting and Clinical Psychology, 55,* 635–644.

Powers, P. S., Schulman, R. G., Gleghorn, A. A., & Prange, M. E. (1987). Perceptual and cognitive abnormalities in bulimia. *American Journal of Psychiatry, 144,* 1456–1460.

Rodin, J., Silberstein, L. R., & Striegel–Moore, R. H. (1985). Women and weight: A normative discontent. In T. B. Sonderegger (Ed.), *Nebraska symposium on motivation: Vol. 32. Psychology and gender* (pp. 267–307). Lincoln: University of Nebraska Press.

Rohrbacher, R. (1973). Influence of a special camp program for obese boys on weight loss, self-concept, and body image. *Research Quarterly, 44,* 150–157.

Rozin, P., & Fallon, A. E. (1988). Body image, attitudes to weight, and misperceptions of figure preferences of the opposite sex: A comparison of men and women in two generations. *Journal of Abnormal Psychology, 97,* 342–345.

Schonbuch, S. S., & Schell, R. E. (1967). Judgments of body appearance by fat and skinny male college students. *Perceptual and Motor Skills, 24,* 999–1002.

Schonfeld, W. A. (1964). Body image disturbance in adolescents with inappropriate sexual development. *American Journal of Orthopsychiatry, 34,* 493–502.

Schwab, J. J., & Harmeling, J. D. (1968). Body image and medical illness. *Psychosomatic Medicine, 30,* 51–61.

Shenker, I. R., Sonnenblick, M., & Fisichelli, V. (1978). Self-perception of obese adolescents as measured by human figure drawings. *Obesity/Bariatric Medicine, 7,* 217–220.

Shipman, W. G., & Sohlkhah, N. (1967). Body image distortion in obese women. *Psychosomatic Medicine, 29,* 540.

Silverstein, A., & Robinson, H. (1961). The representation of physique in children's figure drawings. *Journal of Consulting Psychology, 25,* 146–151.

Speaker, J. G., Schultz, C., Grinker, J. A., & Stern, J. S. (1983). Body size estimation and locus of control in obese adolescent boys undergoing weight reduction. *International Journal of Obesity, 7,* 73–83.

Strober, M. (1981). The relation of personality characteristics to body image disturbances in juvenile anorexia nervosa: A multivariate analysis. *Psychosomatic Medicine, 43,* 323–330.

Stunkard, A. J. (1957). The dieting depression: Incidence and clinical characteristics of untoward responses in weight reduction regimens. *American Journal of Medicine, 23,* 77–86.

Stunkard, A. J., & Burt, V. (1967). Obesity and the body image: Age at onset of disturbances in the body image. *American Journal of Psychiatry, 123,* 1443–1447.

Stunkard, A. J., & Mendelson, M. (1961). Disturbances in body image of some obese persons. *Journal of the American Dietetic Association, 38,* 328–331.

Stunkard, A. J., & Mendelson, M. (1967). Obesity and the body image: I. Characteristics of disturbances in the body image of some obese persons. *American Journal of Psychiatry, 123,* 1296–1300.

Taylor, M. J., & Cooper, P. J. (1986). Body size overestimation and depressed mood. *British Journal of Clinical Psychology, 25,* 153–154.

Touyz, S. W., Beaumont, P. J. V., Collins, J. K., McCabe, M., & Jupp, J. (1984). Body shape perception and its disturbance in anorexia nervosa. *British Journal of Psychiatry, 144,* 167–171.

Tucker, L. A. (1982). Relationship between perceived somatotype and body cathexis of college males. *Psychological Reports, 50,* 983–989.

Tucker, L. A. (1985). Dimensionality and factor structure of the body image construct: A gender comparison. *Sex Roles, 12,* 931–937.

Van der Velde, C. D. (1985). Body images of one's self and of others: Developmental and clinical significance. *American Journal of Psychiatry, 142,* 527–537.

Wadden, T. A., & Stunkard, A. J. (1987). Psychopathology and obesity. In R. J. Wurtman & J. J. Wurtman, (Eds.) *Human obesity.* New York Academy of Sciences, pp. 55–65.

Ward, T. E., & McKeown, D. C. (1987). Association of body cathexis and morphological variables on college-aged females in an exercise setting. *Perceptual & Motor Skills, 64,* 179–190.

Wardle, J., & Beales, S. (1986). Restraint, body image and food attitudes in children from 12 to 18 years. *Appetite, 7,* 209–217.

Weiss, F. (1986). Body-image disturbances among obese adults: Evaluation and treatment. *American Journal of Psychotherapy, 15,* 521–542.

Wooley, O. W., & Wooley, S. C. (1984). Feeling fat in a thin society. *Glamour,* 198–201, 204–205.

Young, M., & Reeve, T. G. (1980). Discriminant analysis of personality and body-image factors of females differing in percent body fat. *Perceptual and Motor Skills, 50,* 547–552.

Zion, L. C. (1964). Body concept as it relates to self-concept. *Research Quarterly, 36,* 490–495.

6 Population-Distinctiveness, Identity, and Bonding

William Turnbull
Simon Fraser University

Dale T. Miller
Princeton University

Cathy McFarland
Simon Fraser University

Images of the self, one's self-description, differ from person to person. Self-images differ also within persons. Central aspects of self-image are likely to be highly accessible in most situations, whereas peripheral aspects of self-image will vary in their accessibility (Markus & Wurf, 1987). What is a central attribute of one person's self-image might be a peripheral aspect of the self-image of someone else. The factors that determine individuals' perceptions of the central aspects of their self-images are not well understood. In this chapter, we identify attribute population-distinctiveness as one major determinant of the perceived centrality of attributes in the self-image and examine the impact of sharing such attributes with others.

Consideration of the following example provides an orientation to the major issues addressed in this chapter. Recently, a friend reported that while driving to work, he had stopped to help a stranded motorist. Our friend found the incident to be most noteworthy because he viewed his behavior as entirely out of character; indeed, he could remember no other occasion on which he had offered help to a stranded motorist. Searching for an explanation of his unusual behavior, our friend was struck by the fact that, unlike other stranded motorists he had encountered, both he and the motorist were driving Maseratis. The only explanation our friend could offer for his unusual behavior was that the sharing of this rare possession somehow created a sense of camaraderie, belongingness, or bond that, in turn, led to a concern for the other's fate. Believing himself to be rational, he was troubled by this explanation: The sharing of a rare characteristic seemed to him a completely inadequate determinant of the feeling of having a bond with another person. Ultimately, he concluded that he had succumbed to the effects of a *granfalloon* (Vonnegut, 1974), a proud yet arbitrary association of human beings.

Rather than being based on an "arbitrary" association, we propose that experiences of this type depend critically on orderly principles of the structure of the self-image. Specifically, the basic claim of the present chapter is that those attributes that are rare in a population (i.e., *population-distinctive* attributes) tend to be perceived as central and important aspects of self-image and personal identity. Individuals who perceive themselves as sharing central and important aspects of their self-images, share an important identity. Further, we suggest that the more individuals believe that they share central aspects of self, the greater the bond they experience with others who share those attributes (i.e., the more they care about and are influenced by those others). These claims may help explain our friend's action by positing: (1) That since it is rare to be the owner of a Maserati, that attribute is seen by our friend to be an important part of his self-image or identity, (2) The threatening nature of the stranded motorist's situation triggered in our friend the recognition that he shared an important identity with the stranded motorist, and (3) This recognition of shared identity resulted in a feeling of being strongly bonded to the motorist, with the consequence that our friend was motivated to help someone whose negative outcome he symbolically was experiencing.

But why would attributes that are rare or distinctive in a population be perceived as central and important aspects of one's self-image? The explanation, we suggest, lies in the informativeness of population-distinctive attributes. In terms of a phenomenological conception of self, the self-image is the way one describes oneself to oneself. In cooperative interactions, descriptions tend to follow certain principles, one of which is that they consist of attributes that are informative in the context (Adler, 1986; Grice, 1975). With respect to descriptions of persons, informative attributes are those that distinguish one person from others in a particular situation. An attribute that is distinctive in a context (i.e., a *situationally distinctive* attribute) will be highly informative in that context and, as prescribed by the informativeness principle, such attributes do tend to dominate descriptions of others given to others (Bruner & Perlmutter, 1957) and descriptions of oneself given to others (McGuire & McGuire, 1982). In describing oneself to oneself, a similar principle of informativeness can be expected to apply (Turnbull, 1986). For example, the only person wearing a hat in a room full of bare-headed people is likely to be described both by others and himself or herself as "wearing a hat." Further, the greater the distinctiveness of an attribute in a population, the greater will be the number of particular contexts (i.e., samples drawn from the population) in which that attribute is distinctive. As a consequence, population-distinctive attributes of the self will be employed in self-descriptions with great frequency, thereby becoming chronically highly accessible. The greater the number of contexts in which a self-attribute is evoked, the greater the perceived centrality of that attribute in the self-image. Thus, since

population-distinctive attributes are highly accessible across situations, population-distinctive attributes are likely to be perceived as central aspects of self-
image.

Indirect evidence for the impact on self-image of population-distinctiveness is
provided by research concerned with the different feelings that members of
minorities and majorities have toward their own group. In these studies, subjects
were led to believe either that they possessed an attribute that was statistically
rare (minority status) or common (majority status) in the population. The critical
attribute was equally represented in each experimental session (i.e., it was not
situationally distinctive). Under these conditions, Jellison and Zeisset (1969)
found that members of a successful minority were more strongly attracted to one
another than were members of a successful majority. Similarly, Kaplan and
Olczak (1971) found that minority subjects cared more than did majority subjects
whether or not ingroup members agreed with them. Finally, Gerard and Hoyt
(1974) found that members of minority groups evaluated each other more favorably relative to out-group members than did members of majority groups. There
is little theorizing in these papers as to why minority- and majority-group members responded differently. Nonetheless, because subjects' minority or majority
status was defined relative to a population, the pattern of results is consistent
with the proposition that the fewer the number of people in a population who
share an attribute, the more important that attribute is in their self-images and the
greater will be the impact of that shared identity.

The studies to be reported in this chapter provide support for the hypotheses
that attributes that are distinctive in a population are perceived to be central and
important components of the self-image, and that the perception of a shared
identity creates a bond. Our general strategy was to manipulate the distinctiveness of an attribute in a population while holding constant the situational distinctiveness of that attribute. The first study examined the impact of distinctiveness on self-image. The second and third studies focused on the
heightened impact on the self of the outcomes of a group with whom one shares a
distinctive as compared with a nondistinctive attribute.[1]

STUDY 1

In this study, subjects learned that they belonged to each of two groups (in
actuality, categorization was random), one grouping purportedly based on an
attribute that was distinctive in the population and the other based on an attribute
that was nondistinctive in the population. Subjects were unfamiliar with the
attributes on the basis of which they had been categorized. We have proposed that

---

[1]Studies 1 and 2 are reported in Miller, Turnbull, and McFarland, 1988.

individuals believe that population-distinctive attributes are more central and important aspects of themselves than are population-nondistinctive attributes. This proposition, combined with the claim that people should be particularly interested in knowing about aspects of themselves that they believe to be central and important, leads to a clear prediction; namely, that subjects should be more interested in learning about their distinctive than nondistinctive group. This hypothesis was tested in the first study. Additionally, we assessed directly whether or not individuals do believe that their population-distinctive attributes are more central and important components of their self-image than are population-nondistinctive attributes.

Method

Subjects

Subjects were 31 male and female undergraduate volunteers from Simon Fraser University who participated individually.

Procedure

The study was described to subjects as concerned with the relation between perceptual style, described as "the way in which a person categorizes and processes information" and social perceptiveness, described as "the ability to make accurate judgments of other's personalities." Subjects first completed the test of social perceptiveness, and then the two tests of perceptual style.

Social Perceptiveness Test. The social perceptiveness test required subjects to read a biographical description of a person and then answer 15 multiple-choice questions regarding the individual's past and present life experiences (e.g., whether his or her parents were strict or lenient). After completing the test, all subjects learned that they had obtained a score of 42 out of 60.

Perceptual Style Test. Once subjects received their bogus score on the social perceptiveness test, the experimenter elaborated on the alleged purposes of the research. She described perceptual styles as being important characteristics of people because of their relation to a wide variety of social and personality characteristics. Subjects were informed that the purpose of the study was to discover why each of the two different perceptual style dimensions relates to social perceptiveness. In accord with this fiction, subjects were told that once they had been categorized on the two perceptual style dimensions they would be asked to describe the strategies that they had employed in answering the questions on the social perceptiveness test. Subjects were told that their responses on these latter measures would allow the researchers to assess whether people with different perceptual styles employ different test-taking strategies. The experimenter stressed that both perceptual style dimensions were *equally* related to social perceptiveness, and that the major goal of the study was to explore why these relationships exist.

The first test of perceptual style required subjects to estimate the number of dots appearing on 10 slides that were each projected for approximately 1 second. Subjects were informed that people tend to either overestimate or underestimate the number of dots. Following the presentation, the experimenter told subjects that they were *overestimators* (as opposed to *underestimators*). The second test required them to estimate the size of objects presented on each of 10 slides. Subjects were informed that people tend to judge the objects to be either larger or smaller than they actually are. Following the presentation of these slides, all subjects were told that their estimates indicated that they were *reducers* (as opposed to *enlargers*). It was stressed that no perceptual style is any better, in a general sense, than any other and all styles were described in an evaluatively neutral tone.

Distinctiveness Manipulation. In addition to informing subjects that they were characterized by the overestimator and reducer perceptual styles, the feedback sheet also informed subjects that one of their perceptual styles was distinctive and that the other was nondistinctive. For the purpose of counterbalancing, half were told that overestimators were a distinctive group (overestimators make up 9% of the population and underestimators the other 91%) and that reducers were a nondistinctive group (reducers making up 88% of the population and enlargers making up the remaining 12%). The other half of the subjects learned that reducers were the distinctive group (reducers making up 12% of the population and enlargers making up the remaining 88%) and that overestimators were a nondistinctive group (overestimators making up 91% of the population and underestimators the remaining 9%).

Dependent Measures. Following the feedback, the experimenter indicated that she possessed several pamphlets, each containing information about a different perceptual style. She then explained that since she needed a few minutes to prepare the test materials, the subject would be allowed to read one of the pamphlets. Subjects were asked to indicate which of their two perceptual styles they would most like to learn about. In addition, they were asked to indicate which of their perceptual styles they thought was "more central and important in their personality." Following this, all subjects were debriefed thoroughly.

Results and Discussion

Before presenting the results it should be noted that in this and all subsequent studies, preliminary analyses indicated that there were no gender effects that approached significance. Consequently, the reported analyses collapse across this variable. Also, preliminary analysis in this and all subsequent studies indicated that the perceptual style dimension did not qualify the distinctiveness effect; hence, all reported analyses collapse across this variable.

It was predicted that subjects would be more interested in learning about their distinctive characteristic than their nondistinctive characteristic. This prediction was confirmed. Eighty-seven percent of the subjects chose to read the pamphlet containing the information about their distinctive perceptual style, whereas only 13% chose to read the pamphlet containing information about their nondistinctive perceptual style., χ^2 (1) = 17.06, p < .001.

We predicted also that subjects would view their distinctive characteristic as more important and central to their personality than their nondistinctive characteristic. This prediction also was confirmed. Sixty-eight percent of the subjects indicated that their distinctive perceptual style was more central and important in their personality, and only 32% of the subjects indicated that their nondistinctive style was more important and central in their personality, χ^2 (1) = 3.9, p < .05. These data strongly support the hypothesis that one's attributes that are distinctive in a population are perceived to be important components of self-image.

STUDY 2

Study 1 examined the impact of population distinctiveness on people's images of themselves. Study 2 pursued the link between distinctiveness, shared identity, and bonding by examining the impact that learning about the average level of performance of one's group in an important domain has on mood and self-esteem.

We have proposed that the greater the strength of the bond between individuals, the greater will be the impact of one person's outcomes on others. Given these claims, it follows that, in a performance situation, the successes and failures of others should have a greater or lesser effect on one's feelings of pride and shame, depending on the bond one shares with them. Given our claims about the relation of shared distinctive qualities to bonding, it can be predicted, therefore, that a member of a group should be more strongly affected by the fate of his or her group when the attribute shared by the group is distinctive rather than nondistinctive in the population. Study 2 tested this hypothesis.

Method

Subjects

Subjects were 40 male and female undergraduate volunteers from Simon Fraser University who participated individually.

Procedure

Initially, subjects were informed that they would be participating in two separate research projects that were being conducted by different researchers in the psychology department. The first experiment allegedly was concerned with social perceptiveness. Specifically, the research was described as attempting to assess the strategies people employ in solving social perceptiveness problems. The second experiment allegedly was concerned with the interrelationships among perceptual style, age, sex and family composition.

Subjects began by completing the social perceptiveness test, after which they were asked to describe briefly the strategies they had used in answering the questions on the test. Once subjects had finished this task, the experimenter indicated that the first experiment was completed.

Distinctiveness Manipulation. The researchers involved in the second study were said to be interested in whether people of differing ages, sexes or family composition tend to have different perceptual styles. Accordingly, after subjects described themselves in terms of these demographic categories, they were given the dot estimation test (as in Study 1). All subjects were informed that the test indicated they were overestimators. In addition they learned that this style was either distinctive or nondistinctive (as in Study 1).

Performance-level Manipulation. The experimenter continued by announcing that many previous participants had asked if they could see their score on the social perceptiveness test. This, he indicated, he could not do because the calculations would take too long. However, he indicated that what he could do was allow them to see the average scores of the overestimators and underestimators who had participated in the study thus far. Subjects were then reminded that social perceptiveness was unrelated to perceptual style and, consistent with this, told that the average score of the overestimators and underestimators was the same, either 56 points out of 60 points or 26 points out of 60 points.

Perceptual style was described as being unrelated to social perceptiveness in order to avoid a potential alternative account of the findings. This account focuses on subjects' beliefs about their own level of performance rather than their beliefs about the average performance of their group. If perceptual style and social perceptiveness were related, those individuals sharing a distinctive perceptual style would occupy a more extreme position (high or low percentile score) in the general distribution of social perceptiveness scores than would the group of individuals sharing a nondistinctive perceptual style. Consequently, stronger affective reactions to the performance scores of a distinctively similar group could be mediated by subjects' inferences concerning the relative position of their group and hence themselves, rather than by their feelings of fraternal bond. This interpretation is obviated when the variables are described as being unrelated because the relative standings in the overall distribution of the distinctive and nondistinctive groups would not be expected to differ.

Dependent Measures. Once subjects learned the average score of the previous overestimators and underestimators, they completed a questionnaire that asked them to indicate their current mood. Specifically, they were asked to indicate on 7-point scales the degree to which they felt *satisfied, happy, pleased, disappointed, sad, proud,* and *competent.*

Research by Simon and Brown (1987) suggests another alternative account for the predicted results. These authors had members of experimentally created minority and majority groups estimate the variability of the scores of minority and majority group members in a set of performance domains. Subjects were led to believe that scores in these performance domains were related to the attribute on which they had been assigned their minority/majority status. The results indicated that minority-group members predicted a smaller variability for the minority group than majority-group members predicted for the majority group. Based on this research, it is possible that subjects in the distinctive condition of the present study believed themselves to be more similar to their group than did subjects in the nondistinctive condition. If they did believe this, then they might have expected their *own* score to be more similar to the average of their own group than would subjects in the nondistinctive condition. Given this expectation, the predicted greater impact of the group average on distinctive subjects might occur, not because of the vicarious sharing of group outcomes, but rather because these subjects were responding to a belief about their own score. In order to assess this possibility, after completing the mood questions, subjects were asked to indicate (a) The score out of 60 that they thought they themselves would receive on the social perceptiveness test, and (b) The highest and lowest score they thought would be obtained by those sharing their perceptual style. Subjects were then debriefed.

Results and Discussion

The internal consistency among the 7 mood scales was very high (alpha = .74), and thus the items were collapsed to yield a single mood index. All subsequent analyses of mood effects were performed on this index. We hypothesized that the performance level of the group would influence the affective responses of group members more when the attribute the group members shared was distinctive than when it was nondistinctive. A 2×2 ANOVA (Performance Level: high versus low X Distinctiveness of group: distinctive versus nondistinctive) performed on the mood index revealed a significant interaction that supported this prediction, $F(1, 36) = 4.24, p < .05$. The means pertinent to this interaction are presented in Table 6.1.

Simple effects analyses provided further support for the hypothesis. Subjects

TABLE 6.1
Mean Mood Ratings as a Function of Group
Distinctiveness and Group Performance Level

	Performance Level	
	Low	High
Group Distinctiveness		
Nondistinctive	4.45 (11)	4.90 (10)
Distinctive	3.92 (9)	5.24 (10)

Note: Higher numbers indicate more positive mood.
The number of subjects in each condition is presented in
parentheses.

belonging to the group sharing a distinctive attribute reported experiencing a significantly more positive mood when their group performed well ($M = 5.24$) than when it performed poorly ($M = 3.92$), $t(36) = 4.29$, $p < .001$. In contrast, the mood of the subjects belonging to the group sharing a nondistinctive attribute was not significantly affected by the performance level of their group, $t(36) = 1.55$, ns.

Prediction.   Our position is that subjects did not learn any more about their own score in the distinctive than nondistinctive condition. Accordingly, predictions of their own score should not have been influenced more by learning the average score of distinctive others than the average score of nondistinctive others. A 2 × 2 ANOVA performed on the prediction scores confirmed this effect. The mean predicted score of subjects in the high-performance-level condition was significantly greater than that of subjects in the low-performance-level condition ($Ms = 48.09$ and 27.74, respectively; $F(1, 36) = 102.32$, $p < .001$), but there was no statistically significant effect of distinctiveness ($Ms = 37.35$ and 38.48 for the nondistinctive and distinctive conditions, respectively; $F < 1$). The interaction between group performance level and group distinctiveness was nonsignificant also, $F < 1$.

It is instructive to examine the relationship between subjects' predictions of their own scores and the group averages they received. In the low-performance condition (group average $= 26/60$), subjects' predictions in both the distinctive and nondistinctive conditions ($Ms = 28.87$ and 26.82, respectively) closely paralleled the group average. However, in the high-performance condition (group average $= 58/60$), subjects' predictions in both the distinctive and nondistinctive conditions ($Ms = 48.30$ and 47.89, respectively) were significantly lower than their group's average, $t(35) = 4.89$, $p < .01$ and $t(35) = 4.86$, $p < .01$, respectively. The fact that subject's estimates, at least in the high-performance condition, deviated from the group average suggests that these estimates were not simply restatements of the group average. This is important because it counters the charge that experimental constraints would have prohibited group distinctiveness from having an effect on subjects' predictions even if it was perceived to relate to group variability.

Group Range.   A second means of exploring subjects' beliefs about the link between distinctiveness on a predictor variable (perceptual style) and variability on a criterion variable (social perceptiveness) is to examine subjects' estimates of the range of social perception scores for groups varying in distinctiveness. A 2 × 2 ANOVA on subjects' estimates of the range of social perception scores in their group failed to support the hypothesis that subjects believe there is less variability in distinctive than nondistinctive groups. This analysis revealed no main effect of group distinctiveness (Ms = 35.72 and 29.85 for the low- and high-performance level conditions, respectively; $F(1, 35)$ = 1.8, ns.), nor an interaction between these two factors, $F(1, 35)$ = 1.61, ns.

The results of Study 2 provide support for the claim that the sharing of a distinctive attribute creates a bond that, in turn, may lead to the vicarious sharing of group outcomes. In general, we feel happy when our group does well and sad when our group does badly.

STUDY 3

Imagine what might occur if, in contrast to the previous study, subjects were informed about their own score as well as the scores of distinctively and nondistinctively similar others. One possibility is that subjects' reactions to performance feedback would be dominated by the *egoistic* comparison of their own score to that of distinctively similar others. For example, in the case where individuals perform better than other members of their group, we might expect more positive affective reactions when their group is distinctive than when it is nondistinctive. Another possibility, however, is that subjects' reactions might be dominated by the *fraternal* comparison of the scores of distinctively similar group members to that of other groups. Thus, when members of their own group perform well, individuals might react more positively when their group is distinctive than when it is nondistinctive.

We have suggested that individuals may feel bonded to those with whom they share distinctive attributes, one consequence of which is that what happens to these special others symbolically happens to the self. Thus, when people share population-distinctive attributes, it is predicted that fraternal comparisons are a more important determinant of reactions to performance feedback than egoistic comparisons.

To test this prediction, we created the following situation. Subjects learned that they belonged to two groups, one possessing a distinctive attribute, the other possessing a nondistinctive attribute. In the first experimental condition, subjects were provided with feedback indicating that they personally had performed better on a test than someone in their distinctive group, but that this group member had performed worse than someone in their nondistinctive group. In a second condition, subjects were informed that they personally had performed worse than someone in their distinctive group, but that this group member had performed better than someone in their nondistinctive group. All subjects received the same individual score.

If subjects' affective reactions to performance feedback were dominated by egoistic comparisons, they should react more favorably when they perform better than someone in their distinctive group (condition 1) than when they perform worse than that person (condition 2). However, if their reactions are dominated by fraternal comparisons, they should react more favorably when a member of their distinctive group outperforms a member of their nondistinctive group (condition 2) than when a member of their distinctive group is outperformed by a member of their nondistinctive group (condition 1).

Method

Subjects

Subjects were 21 male and female undergraduate volunteers from Simon Fraser University who participated individually.

Procedure

As in Study 1, subjects were informed that the purpose of the study was an investigation of the relation between perceptual style and social perceptiveness. They began by completing the social perceptiveness test, and all subjects were informed that they had received a score of 42 out of 60 on the test. Next, the experimenter described more fully the nature of perceptual style, the way perceptual style was assessed, and the various perceptual styles someone could have. Subjects were told that they would take both the dot estimation and size estimation tests of perceptual style. Before taking the tests of perceptual style, subjects were informed that overestimators perform differently on the social perceptiveness test than do underestimators, and reducers perform differently than do enlargers. Indeed, it was explained that the major purpose of the study was to examine why these differences existed. Subjects subsequently were provided with feedback indicating that they were an overestimator on the first dimension of perceptual style and a reducer on the second. Additionally, the overestimator style was described as distinctive and the reducer style as nondistinctive for half of the subjects, whereas for the others the overestimator style was nondistinctive and the reducer style distinctive (see Study 1 for details).

Performance Feedback.   The experimenter continued by telling subjects that many previous participants had found their score on the social perceptiveness test difficult to interpret and had expressed a desire to see the scores of other people in the study. It was explained that this could not be done because the scores of everyone who had taken the test had not been calculated yet. However, it was possible to show the subject the scores of the last overestimator and the last reducer who had taken part in the study. Subjects learned either that the overestimator had a score of 30 and the reducer a score of 54, or vice versa. In effect, these manipulations created two experimental conditions: *Condition A,* in which subjects received feedback indicating that they had performed better than the distinctively similar other but worse than the nondistinctively similar other in a situation in which the distinctive other performed less well than the nondistinctive other; or *Condition B,* in which subjects received feedback that they had performed worse than the distinctively similar other but better than the nondistinctively similar other in a situation in which the distinctive other had performed better than the nondistinctive other.

Subjects were provided with the alleged scores of the last overestimator and last reducer rather than the average scores of overestimators and reducers in order to avoid an alternative interpretation of the results. Consider the case in which the subject gets a score of 42 and learns also that the distinctive group average is 30 and the nondistinctive group average is 54. Under these circumstances, subjects have been provided with enough information about the distribution of social perceptiveness scores to conclude that their score was better than that of only a few people but worse than that of most people. Similarly, in the other condition of the study, they would have enough information to conclude that their score was worse than only a few people but better than that of most people. If judgments of this sort were to occur, the expected pattern of results would be identical to that predicted on the basis of fraternal comparisons. In order to inhibit subjects from making judgments about their relative position in the overall distribution, they were given the scores of only two individuals.

Dependent Measures.   After receiving the feedback, subjects completed a questionnaire that assessed their current mood (see Study 2 for details of the mood assessment). Additionally, subjects were asked to indicate on 7-point scales (a) *Relative to other university students, how much social perceptiveness ability they felt they had,* and (b) *Relative to other university students, how well they thought they performed on the social perceptiveness test.* Following this, subjects were debriefed and thanked for their participation.

Results and Discussion

Mood.   If subject's reactions were determined by egoistic comparisons, they should have rated their mood as more positive in Condition A, where they outperformed the distinctively similar other and did less well than the nondistinctively similar other, than in Condition B, where they did less well than the distinctively similar other but outperformed the nondistinctively similar other. Alternatively, if subjects' reactions were based mainly on fraternal comparisons, the mood ratings should be more positive in Condition B than A because the distinctively similar other outperformed the nondistinctively similar other in Condition B. As in Study 2, the mood items were collapsed to yield a single mood index. This mood index was significantly higher, indicating a more positive mood, in Condition B, where the distinctively similar other outperformed the nondistinctively similar other, than in Condition A, where the nondistinctively similar other outperformed the distinctively similar other ($t(19) = 3.8$ $p < .001$; $Ms = 5.03$ and 4.27, respectively). These results offer support for the view that subjects' reactions to feedback about their own and others' performance were determined mainly by fraternal comparisons.

Relative Standing. In spite of trying to prevent them from drawing conclusions about their own standing in the population, it is possible that subjects did so anyway. The data do not support this possibility. There were no statistically significant differences on either of the two dependent measures that assessed the subjects' perceptions of relative standing (both $ts < 1$, ns).

GENERAL DISCUSSION

In the present chapter we have argued that an individual's attributes that are distinctive in the population are perceived as central aspects of self-image. Because population-distinctive attributes are central to one's self-image, those with whom individuals share distinctive attributes are those with whom they share an identity. One potential consequence of the perception of a shared identity is a sense of bonding.

Data from three studies support these claims. Subjects who believed that they possessed a distinctive attribute rated that attribute as more central and important in their personalities than did those who possessed a nondistinctive attribute. Further, the average performance (high or low) of the group to which subjects belonged had a more polarizing effect on the mood ratings of subjects who shared a distinctive as opposed to nondistinctive attribute. Finally, subjects' reactions to performance feedback pertaining to their own score and that of their distinctive group seem to have been based mainly on fraternal rather than egoistic comparisons. In particular, subjects' reactions appear to have been based on a comparison of the scores of someone with whom they shared a distinctive attribute to that of someone with whom they shared a nondistinctive attribute, rather than a comparison of their own score to that of a distinctive other.

Population-distinctiveness and Identity

Certain attributes of persons are likely to be perceived as central and important aspects of self-image whether or not these attributes are distinctive in a population. For example, many North Americans would consider their nationality (e.g., American), sex (e.g., female), and race (e.g., Caucasian) to be central aspects of their identity even though these attributes are population-nondistinctive. Other attributes, such as owning a car or having a pet, are attributes around which we would not expect people to build their identity. The major claim we are making in this chapter is that even attributes that would be an unlikely basis for an identity can become central and important if those attributes are population-distinctive. Thus, for example, owning a Maserati, or having a pit bull or a python for a pet, are attributes that may become central in one's self-image, whereas being the owner of a Ford or having a mutt or a canary for a pet are likely to be perceived as only peripheral aspects of self.

Negative Distinctiveness

It is a virtual truism that people are motivated to view themselves positively. Thus, it might be expected, contrary to our claims, that only distinctive attributes that are evaluated positively will be perceived as central aspects of self-image. Nothing in our experimental results contradicts this possibility since both distinctive and nondistinctive perceptual styles were described in evaluatively neutral or slightly positive terms. However, the literature on negative or "spoiled" identities (Goffman, 1963; Jones et al. 1984) offers strong support for the view that identities can form around distinctive attributes that are highly negative, including both identities/statuses that are achieved, such as *ex-con, hooker* or *pimp,* and those that are ascribed, such as *deaf-mute, paraplegic* or *mental retardate.* Of course, it is possible that minority-group members do not themselves consider the attribute that makes them distinctive to be negative. On the other hand, the well-documented adverse effects of negative self-labels suggest that central aspects of self-image can be negative (Jones et al., 1984; Swann, 1987).

One clear implication of the position adopted in this chapter is that individuals should be more affected by the belief that they possess a negative population-distinctive attribute than by the belief that they possess a positive population-nondistinctive attribute. One possible direction for this effect is that minority-group members will be more likely to identify themselves in terms of the negative attribute that makes them distinctive (e.g., physically disabled) than majority-group members will be to identify themselves in terms of the positive attribute that makes them nondistinctive (e.g., able-bodied). Alternatively, individuals who possess a negative attribute may be more likely to deny that they possess that quality and to dissociate themselves from other members of their group when the attribute is rare rather than common in the population. Clearly a model of the motivational and informational factors influencing the impact of population-distinctive attributes on self-image needs to be developed.

Situational and Population-Distinctiveness

There is considerable evidence supporting the claim that the greater the statistical distinctiveness of an attribute in a context, the greater the perceptual salience of that attribute (Campbell, 1958; Diener, 1980; Gerard & Hoyt, 1974; Taylor, Fiske, Etcoff, & Ruderman, 1978; Wegner & Schaefer, 1978; Wicklund, 1980; Ziller, 1964). When an attribute is made perceptually salient, its accessibility increases. Thus, situationally distinctive attributes, because of their perceptual salience and associated high accessibility (and also, as noted previously, their high informational value) are likely to be employed in self-descriptions even when they are *not* central aspects of self-image. For example, being brown-haired is not likely to be a central part of the identity of most Canadians. In spite of this lack of perceived centrality in the self-image, a brown-haired Canadian in a room of blonds is likely to describe oneself as having brown hair (cf., McGuire & McGuire, 1982), and we could expect two brown-haired individuals in such a situation to experience a sense of shared identity.

The effects of the situational-distinctiveness of an attribute on self-image that are mediated by perceptual salience are to be differentiated from the influence of an attribute's population-distinctiveness. We have proposed that attributes of self that are population-distinctive are perceived to be central components of self-image because, being evoked in many contexts, they become chronically highly accessible. An important consequence is that population-distinctive attributes are likely to be highly accessible in contexts in which they are nondistinctive (i.e., even when they are situationally nondistinctive). Consider this with respect to the opening example of our friend who helped a stranded motorist. We suggest that our friend considers being a Maserati owner to be a central aspect of his self-image. As such, that attribute is a highly accessible attribute across most, if not all, situations for our friend. Because of this, he should be as likely to experience a shared identity if 10 Maseratis were pulled over at the side of the road rather than only one. In sum, perception of a shared identity can occur either because of the situational salience of an attribute or because of the centrality of an attribute in a self-image.

Social Identity and Bonding

Although sharing an identity always leads to some degree of bonding, the strength of the bond is subject to a number of influences. In discussing the relationship between shared identity and bonding, it is useful to consider *social identity theory,* as propounded by Henri Tajfel and his colleagues (Tajfel, 1978, 1979, 1982a, 1982b; Tajfel & Turner, 1986; Turner, 1982; Turner & Giles, 1981). Following William James (1890/1950), the social identity theorists assume that the self-image is composed of a personal identity and a social identity. Thinking about the self as an individual without regard to group identifications evokes one's personal identity, whereas thinking of the self as a member of one or more social groups evokes one's social identity.

Most typically, the conception of the self at any particular moment will consist of aspects of both personal and social identity. However, there are conditions under which the self-image is dominated by either the personal or the social identity, with predictable consequences. The factors that have been shown to evoke social identity include the situational distinctiveness of one's group (Brown & Turner, 1981, pp. 42–43), the presence of a salient out-group (Wilder & Shapiro, 1984), and competition and out-group threat (Dion, Earn & Yee, 1978; Doise, 1978).

The main consequence of one's identity being dominated by social identity is that bonding occurs. For example, Turner (1978; see also Brown & Deschamps, cited in Turner, 1982) found that when social identity is strongly evoked, subjects tend to allocate equal amounts to self and an anonymous ingroup member but less to an out-group member, and when personal identity is strongly evoked, subjects tend to allocate more to themselves than to others irrespective of the group to which those others belong. In other words, people are more likely to act fraternally (i.e., act on the basis of a perceived bond) when social identity dominates self-image but egoistically when personal identity dominates self-image.

The social identity analysis of shared identity carries with it an additional important proposal; namely, that the perception of a shared social identity can occur in the absence of the perception of global similarity. No doubt, those who share a social identity, such as two Maserati owners, may feel similar to one another with respect to car ownership but this does not imply that they feel similar to one another in general. We suggest that there are many instances of bonding that occur as a consequence of a perceived shared identity in the absence of perceived global similarity. A recent example is the outrage felt by many Canadians over what was viewed as the violation of territorial waters and the grossly unfair treatment of Canadian, east coast fishermen by the French fishing fleet. Without feeling any overall similarity to those Canadian fishermen (e.g., what does a university professor living in Vancouver have in common with east coast fishermen?), people felt personally offended. The point is that the offense was felt personally because of a shared identity, not a global similarity.

It is important to be clear about what we are *not* claiming. Although global similarity is neither a necessary precondition for bonding nor a necessary concomitant of sharing an identity, shared identity and global similarity can co-occur. Consider people who have received a heart transplant, or those who have won a Nobel prize or the world heavyweight boxing title. Here are instances of bonding in which the individuals involved share both a population-distinctive attribute and a high level of global similarity. In addition, although we have distinguished between the effects of situational salience and population-distinctiveness on self-image, there is no implication that each of these factors must operate to the exclusion of the other. Indeed, making a population-distinctive attribute situationally salient should be an extremely potent means of activating social identity. Thus, for example, we would expect a stronger bond to exist between two Maserati owners than between two Ford owners who happen to meet at a Dodge dealership, or between two paraplegics in a group of able-bodied persons than between two able-bodied persons in a group of paraplegics.

Social Comparison

The data from our three studies also have implications for the social comparison process. Festinger (1954) argued that to evaluate the "goodness or badness" of their abilities, individuals often must compare themselves with similar others. The preference for comparison with similar others occurs because they provide the greatest cognitive clarity concerning one's abilities. But people may be similar to one another in many respects, and Goethals and Darley (1977) proposed that people compare themselves with others who are similar on attributes that are related to, or predictive of, the to-be-evaluated ability. By doing this, individuals can determine what Miller, Turnbull, and McFarland (1988) refer to as their *universalistic* standing; that is, their standing relative to people in general.

People may care at times about their universalistic standing, but this is not the only kind of standing they seem motivated to assess. Consider, in this regard, a study by Carol Miller (1984). Subjects characterized as schematic or aschematic for sex were asked to choose which of several group norms they wanted to see in order to evaluate their performance. Schematics, those who incorporated masculine or feminine characteristics into their self-concepts, made same-sex comparisons *regardless* of the relationship of sex to performance. In contrast, aschematics made same-sex comparisons only when sex was related to performance. Clearly, the aschematics made comparisons only with those who could give them information about their overall standing, whereas the schematics sometimes made a comparison that would appear not to allow them to do so. Focusing on those schematics who compared their own score with the score of a same-sex other when sex was unrelated to ability, it is interesting to speculate as to what they hoped to learn. Because masculinity/femininity is an important attribute of the self-image of schematics, these subjects may have felt that they shared an identity with those of the same sex. Those with whom we share an identity may function as a reference group. Furthermore, quite independently of concerns about their overall standing, people may care about their *local* or *particularistic* standing—their standing relative to those with whom they identify (Frank, 1985; Miller et al. 1988). In support of this hypothesis, Miller et al. (1988) demonstrated in a series of studies that subjects preferred to see the scores of others with whom they shared an identity even when that choice could give them no more information about their universalistic standing than choosing to see the scores of others with whom they did not share an identity.

What information could one gain by comparing oneself with others who do not share attributes related to the performance domain at issue? It seems possible that the impact of knowing where one stands relative to one's reference others may differ from the impact of knowing one's universal standing. Specifically, individuals might define themselves and measure their self-worth in relation to their reference others. Consider, for example, a golfer who has played for many years with a 36 handicap. This golfer can discover little more about his or her universal standing by comparing oneself with others similar on related attributes (e.g., others who have played as much, or are the same age or sex). However, he or she might well feel good having beaten a friend and longtime rival. In a similar vein, providing students with GRE or SAT percentile scores, even if they are broken down in terms of related attributes, will not eliminate the students' desire to compare their scores with those of their friends.

CONCLUSION

As indicated earlier in the chapter, there has been a considerable amount of research investigating situational-distinctiveness. To date, however, psychologists generally have ignored the role of population-distinctiveness in individual, interpersonal, and intergroup phenomena. It is our hope that the present chapter may motivate researchers to examine the many interesting and unresolved issues relating to population-distinctiveness.

REFERENCES

Adler, J. E. (1984). Abstraction is uncooperative. *Journal for the Theory of Social Behaviour, 14,* 165–181.

Brown, R. J., & Turner, J. C. (1981). Interpersonal and intergroup behavior. In J. C. Turner & H. Giles (Eds.), *Intergroup behavior* (pp. 33–65). Oxford, England: Blackwell.

Bruner, J. S., & Perlmutter, H. V. (1957). Compatriot and foreigner: A study of impression formation in three countries. *Journal of Abnormal and Social Psychology, 55,* 253–260.

Campbell, D. T. (1958). Common fate, similarity, and other indices of the status of aggregates of persons as social entities. *Behavioral Science, 3,* 14–25.

Diener, E. (1980). Deindividuation: The absence of self-awareness and self-regulation in group members. In P. B. Paulus (Ed.), *Psychology of group influence* (pp. 209–242). Hillsdale, NJ: Lawrence Erlbaum Associates.

Dion, K. L., Earn, B. M., & Yee, P. H. N. (1978). The experience of being a victim of prejudice: An experimental approach. *International Journal of Psychology, 13,* 197–214.

Doise, W. (1978). *Groups and individuals: Explanations in social psychology.* Cambridge, England: Cambridge University Press.

Festinger, L. (1954). A theory of social comparison processes. *Human Relations, 7,* 117–140.

Frank, R. (1985). *Choosing the right pond: Human behavior and the quest for status.* Oxford, England: Oxford University Press.

Gerard, H. B., & Hoyt, M. F. (1974). Distinctiveness of social categorization and attitude toward ingroup members. *Journal of Personality and Social Psychology, 29,* 836–842.

Goethals, G. R., & Darley, J. M. (1977). Social comparison theory: An attributional approach. In J. M. Suls & R. L. Miller (Eds.), *Social comparison processes: Theoretical and empirical perspectives.* (pp. 259–278). Washington, DC: Hemisphere.

Goffman, E. (1963). *Stigma: Notes on the management of spoiled identity.* Englewood Cliffs, NJ: Prentice-Hall.

Grice, H. P. (1975). Logic and conversation. In P. Cole & J. Morgan (Eds.), *Syntax and semantics* (pp. 41–58). New York: Academic Press.

James, W. (1890/1950). *The principles of psychology.* (Vol. 1). New York: Dover.

Jellison, J. M., & Zeisset, P. T. (1969). Attraction as a function of the commonality and desirability of a trait shared with another. *Journal of Personality and Social Psychology, 11*, 115–120.

Jones, E. E., Farina, A., Hastorf, A. H., Markus, H., Miller, D. T., & Scott, R. A. (1984). *Social stigma: The psychology of marked relationships.* New York: Freeman.

Kaplan, M. F., & Olczak, P. V. (1971). Attraction toward another as a function of similarity and commonality of attitudes. *Psychological Reports, 28*, 515–521.

Markus, H., & Wurf, E. (1987). The dynamic self-concept: A social psychological perspective. *Annual Review of Psychology, 38*, 299–337.

McGuire, W. J., & McGuire, C. V. (1982). Significant others in self space: Sex differences and developmental trends in the social self. In J. Suls (Ed.), *Psychological perspectives on the self* (Vol. 1, pp. 71–96). Hillsdale, NJ: Lawrence Erlbaum Associates.

Miller, C. T. (1984). Self-schemas, gender, and social comparison: A clarification of the related attributes hypothesis. *Journal of Personality and Social Psychology, 46*, 1222–1229.

Miller, D. T., Turnbull, W., & McFarland, C. (1988). Particularistic and universalistic evaluation in the social comparison process. *Journal of Personality and Social Psychology, 55*, 908–917.

Simon, B., & Brown, R. (1987). Perceived intragroup homogeneity in minority-majority contexts. *Journal of Personality and Social Psychology, 53*, 703–711.

Swann, W. B. (1987). Identity negotiation: Where two roads meet. *Journal of Personality and Social Psychology, 53*, 1038–1051.

Tajfel, H. (Ed.). (1978). *Differentiation between social groups: Studies in the social psychology of intergroup relations.* London: Academic Press.

Tajfel, H. (1979). Individuals and groups in social psychology, *British Journal of Social and Clinical Psychology, 18*, 183–190.

Tajfel, H. (1982a). *Social identity and intergroup relations.* Cambridge, England: Cambridge University Press.

Tajfel, H. (1982b). Social psychology of intergroup relations. In M. R. Rosenzweig & L. W. Porter (Eds.), *Annual Review of Psychology, 33*, 1–39.

Tajfel, H., & Turner, J. C. (1986). The social identity theory of intergroup behavior. In W. Worchel & W. G. Austin (Eds.), *Psychology of intergroup relations* (pp. 7–24). Chicago: Nelson–Hall.

Taylor, S. E., Fiske, S. T., Etcoff, N. L., & Ruderman, A. J. (1978). Categorical and contextual bases of person memory and stereotyping. *Journal of Personality and Social Psychology, 36*, 778–793.

Turnbull, W. (1986). Everyday explanation: The pragmatics of puzzle resolution. *Journal for the Theory of Social Behaviour, 16*, 141–160.

Turner, J. C. (1978). Social categorization and social discrimination in the minimal group paradigm. In H. Tajfel (Ed.), *Differentiation between social groups: Studies in the social psychology of intergroup relations* (pp. 94–121). London: Academic Press.

Turner, J. C. (1982). Towards a cognitive redefinition of the social group. In H. Tajfel (Ed.), *Social identity and intergroup relations* (pp. 15–40). Cambridge, England: Cambridge University Press.

Turner, J. C., & Giles, H. (Eds.). (1981). *Intergroup behavior.* Oxford: Basil Blackwell.

Vonnegut, K., Jr. (1974). *Wampeters, foma and granfalloons.* New York: Delcorte Press.

Wegner, D. M., & Schaefer, D. (1978). The concentration of responsibility: An objective self-awareness analysis of group size effects in helping situations. *Journal of Personality and Social Psychology, 36*, 147–155.

Wicklund, R. A. (1980). Group contact and self-focused attention. In P. B. Paulus (Ed.), *Psychology of group influence* (pp. 189–208). Hillsdale, NJ: Lawrence Erlbaum Associates.

Wilder, D. A., & Shapiro, P. N. (1984). Role of out-group cues in determining social identity. *Journal of Personality and Social Psychology, 47*, 342–348.

Ziller, R. C. (1964). Individuation and socialization: A theory of assimilation in large organizations. *Human Relations, 17*, 341–360.

Recounting the Past: Gender Differences in the Recall of Events in the History of a Close Relationship

7

Michael Ross
Diane Holmberg
University of Waterloo, Ontario

Francis Galton is generally recognized as one of the great, albeit misguided, geniuses of the last century (misguided because he expressed an enthusiasm for eugenics that offends our modern sensibilities). He is also known for his outstanding memory. Galton was a child prodigy who memorized, at an early age, a great deal of Scott, Milton, and of the *Iliad* and the *Odyssey*. In this context, it is interesting to note that he begins his memoirs by bemoaning the death of his latest surviving sisters (Galton, 1908/1974). According to Galton, the "minds [of these sisters] were sure storehouses of family events" (p. 1). He observes that he depended on his sisters when he wanted a "date or particulars of a long-past fact" (p. 1).

Galton's comments intrigued us because they were consistent with data emerging from research in which we examined married couples' recall of events in their relationship. Our interest in studying the stories people tell about their pasts stemmed from a general concern with self and social perception. People's accounts of their personal histories may help us understand how they view themselves and others. Recall of shared events in a close relationship may be particularly informative. These accounts may both reflect and influence people's views of themselves, their partner, and their relationship.

In presenting our study, we begin with the procedure and data, and subsequently attempt to place the findings in a broader context. The results that we describe were largely unanticipated; our reversal of the typical ordering of theory and data is intended to emphasize the post hoc nature of our theorizing.

During the spring and summer of 1988, we asked married couples to participate in a study of autobiographical memory. Participants were selected from a list of couples who had applied for a marriage license in the city of Waterloo in 1984 and 1985. Of the 624 couples who applied for licenses in those 2 years, we found current local addresses for 236. These couples were sent an initial letter describing the study and asking them to consider participating. We contacted 173 of the couples with a follow-up phone call and 43% of those eligible for the study agreed to participate (5 couples were now separated, divorced, or widowed). We were unable to schedule 7 couples at a mutually convenient time and another 5 couples were assigned to a pretest. Sixty couples participated in the experiment. Some of the characteristics of this sample are shown in Table 7.1.

Each couple was asked to recall three incidents from their past: their first date together, their last vacation together, and a recent argument between the two of them. The events were presented in counterbalanced order. We selected these particular events for several reasons: they involved both participants, they varied in importance and affect, and they were at least somewhat memorable and meaningful for the relationship. Participants' estimates of the length of time that had elapsed since the target events averaged 6.8 years for the first date (range: 2.3–15.4 years), 9.4 months for the argument (range: less than a day–7.8 years), and 10.0 months for the vacation (range: 4 days–3.9 years).

The participants were asked to recall each event in detail, speaking into a tape recorder for up to 10 minutes per episode. The study included two between-group, experimental manipulations. First, participants were either alone or together with their spouses when they tape-recorded their recall. In the together condition, spouses discussed their memories with each other during the recall period. The together-alone manipulation allowed us to evaluate the impact of differing perspectives on recall and to observe how idiosyncratic memories are merged to form a common story. In both conditions, the experimenter asked participants to come to an agreement on the particular event to be recalled (e.g., which argument or vacation) before beginning the tape recording. The experi-

TABLE 7.1
Characteristics of Sample

		Husbands	Wives
Age	Mean:	32.3	30.1
	Range:	22–76	23–70
Years of education	Mean:	13.6	13.0
	Range:	9–20	9–21
Percentage employed		95	80

Notes:
1. Participants were employed in a broad range of jobs. Examples include floor installer and principal (for men), and custodian and university professor (for women).
2. The mean number of children per couple was 1.12, with a range of 0–5 (including children from previous marriages).

TABLE 7.2
Items Assessing Clarity of Memory

---

1. How clear is your memory of your first date with your spouse?

   vague   1   2   3   4   5   6   7   clear/distinct

2. Is your memory of this first date sketchy or highly detailed? (i.e., Can you remember only bits and pieces, or can you recall the entire sequence of events?)

   sketchy   1   2   3   4   5   6   7   highly detailed

3. Overall, how well do you remember your first date with your spouse?

   hardly   1   2   3   4   5   6   7   very well

4. Do you have any doubts about the accuracy of your memory for the date?

   a great deal   1   2   3   4   5   6   7   no doubt
      of doubt   whatsoever

5. Do you remember what you thought during the course of the date?

   not at all   1   2   3   4   5   6   7   clearly

6. How clearly or vividly can you recall the emotions you experienced during the course of your first date?

   not at all   1   2   3   4   5   6   7   very clearly
      clearly

---

menter then retired to another room, leaving the participants on their own during the recording periods.

In addition to the open-ended recall, participants completed questionnaires individually in which they reported their impressions of each event. The second experimental manipulation involved the timing of these questionnaires. Participants answered the questionnaires either immediately *before* they tape-recorded their recall of each event, or immediately *after* their recording. The timing manipulation enabled us to assess whether participants' private impressions of the events were influenced by their tape-recorded recall.

Finally, participants completed a brief questionnaire at the conclusion of the study in which they were asked general questions about the accuracy of their memory and about the effects of social context on recall. Participants' responses to all of the questionnaires were private and were not shown to their spouses.

In this chapter, we focus on participants' questionnaire responses. In the questionnaires associated with each event, six items were designed to assess respondents' impressions of the clarity and vividness of their recall. Several of these questions are modified versions of items used by Johnson in her research on the clarity of memories for perceived and imagined events (e.g., Johnson, Foley, Suengas, & Raye, 1988; Suengas & Johnson, 1988). Table 7.2 shows the questions we asked respondents about their first date. Similar items appeared on the argument and vacation questionnaires.

As well as obtaining this subjective measure of clarity of memory, we obtained more objective evidence. Two research assistants examined typed transcripts of the tape-recorded recall. For each couple, the assistants completed the same clarity and vividness of memory questions as did the participants. In addition, the assistants recorded the number of times in each transcript that respondents explicitly stated an inability to recall an aspect of the target event.

CLARITY OF MEMORY

Participants' responses to the six clarity questions were all highly intercorrelated. Consequently, we created an index of clarity by averaging the six responses. Means and significance levels are shown in Table 7.3. The data were analyzed treating gender (husbands vs. wives) as a within-subjects factor and the experimental manipulations as between-subjects factors.

The results are easy to summarize: Females reported more detailed and vivid memories of all three events than did males. The two experimental manipulations failed to influence the strength of this effect. Females reported more vivid memories than did males whether the clarity measure was assessed before or after the tape-recorded recall, and whether participants recalled the events alone or together with their spouses.

The gender effect is not simply in the minds of our subjects. Averaging across all three of the events, our research assistants rated typed transcripts of the women's memories as more vivid and detailed, $M = 5.63$, than their spouses' memories for the same events, $M = 5.26$, $p < .01$. In addition, we examined observers' ratings of each event separately. Females' memories of the date and the argument were rated as significantly more vivid than those of their spouses. No gender difference was obtained for memories of the vacation.

The assistants also counted the number of times that each respondent explicitly stated that he or she could not recall a particular detail (e.g., "I forget what day it was," or "I can't remember whose house we went to.") An analysis of these data revealed a significant main effect for experimental condition. Spouses were more likely to report forgetting aspects of the events when they

TABLE 7.3
Mean Clarity of Recall

Event recalled	Husbands' Ratings	Wives' Ratings	p <
Argument	4.69	5.37	.01
First date	4.32	5.00	.001
Vacation	5.52	5.86	.01
All 3 events	4.84	5.44	.0001

Note: Higher numbers indicate greater clarity of memory. Possible range is 1–7.

TABLE 7.4
Evaluation of Own and Partner's Memory
for Details from the Past

		Rater	
		Husband	Wife
Target	Husband	4.05	4.33
	Wife	5.12	4.98

Note: Higher numbers indicate better memory on a 7-point scale. Both partners agreed that the wife has the better memory, $F = 16.4$, $p < .001$.

recalled the events together, $M = 4.99$, than when they recalled the events alone, $M = 2.58$. In addition, a significant interaction was found between experimental condition and gender. When spouses recalled the events together, a gender effect was obtained that paralleled the results found on the vividness ratings. Males reported a significantly greater number of memory failures, $M = 6.26$, than did females, $M = 3.71$. When spouses recalled the events alone, the gender difference was nonsignificant (male $M = 2.31$; female $M = 2.86$).

The increase in reports of forgetting in the together condition appears to reflect, in part, efforts to elicit information from one's spouse, a process that Wegner (1986) has labeled "transactive retrieval" (p. 190). In the alone condition, there is no possibility of help, and reports of forgetting are relatively infrequent. Furthermore, in the together condition males were more likely than females to report forgetting details of the events. Presumably, males, with their less vivid memories, felt a greater need to call on their spouses for aid.

After recalling all three of the events, respondents independently completed a final questionnaire in which they were asked to assess their own and their spouse's overall memory for "details from the past." Both spouses rated the female partner's memory as superior (Table 7.4). This result is worthy of comment. Available research indicates that males and females expect women to perform less well than men on a wide variety of tasks (e.g., Bem & Bem, 1970; Feldman–Summers & Kiesler, 1974). The present finding that both sexes praised females' memories suggests that males have convincing evidence of their inferiority on this dimension and females of their superiority.

To indicate how the discussions proceeded in the together condition, we present excerpts from one couple's recall of their first date together:

Wife: Here's your memory test. When was our first date?
Husband: When? Do we have to know dates?
Wife: No, not when exactly.

Husband: I thought it was in wintertime.
Wife: Good, yes. . . . We met in January.
Husband: Ya, I remember that. January 8th.
Wife: On the 8th. And our first date was about the 16th or 17th.
Husband: Oh, I don't remember the first.
• •
Wife: Do you remember how you asked me out?
Husband: No, I don't remember that.
Wife: You said "Gee, I really like the way you dress. You want to take me shopping for clothes?" . . . Ok, so we went shopping.
Husband: Ya, we went to Conestoga Mall. I remember that.
Wife: And Fairview Mall too, I think.
Husband: Fairview too?
Wife: I think so.
Husband: I don't remember going to Fair . . . wait a minute. Ya, I do remember going to Fairview because . . .
Wife: We went to Star's Men's Shop. That's where you bought . . .
Husband: you commented, you commented twice . . .
Wife: your leather tie.
Husband: ya, you commented twice when we were in Conestoga. You said "everybody's staring at me" and then we went to Fairview and you said the same thing. I remember.
• • • ` • • • • • • • • • • • • • ‹ • • • › • • • • • • • •
Wife: Do you remember how the evening ended?
Husband: No.
Wife: It didn't. It lasted until the next morning. You fell asleep on the couch.
Husband: Oh that's right. Ya, we . . . that's right.

This exchange between a couple in our sample may sound familiar to readers who are fans of Broadway musicals. Below are the words of the song *I Remember it Well,* as we transcribed them from the 1958 film of Lerner and Loewe's *Gigi.* The song records an exchange between two former lovers, Maurice Chevalier, who plays an aging roué, and Hermione Gingold, who plays Gigi's grandmother. They recall their final date together, many years earlier.

He: I can remember everything, as if it were yesterday.
      We met at nine.
She: We met at eight.
He: I was on time.
She: No, you were late.
He: Ah yes, I remember it well.
      We dined with friends.
She: We dined alone.
He: A tenor sang.
She: A baritone.

He: Ah yes, I remember it well.
That dazzling April moon. . . .
She: There was none that night
And the month was June.
He: That's right, that's right.
She: It warms my heart to know that you
Remember still the way you do.
He: Ah yes, I remember it well.
How often I've thought of that Friday. . .
She: Monday.
He: Night when we had our last rendezvous.
And somehow I foolishly wondered if you might
By some chance be thinking of it too.
That carriage ride. . .
She: You walked me home.
He: You lost a glove.
She: I lost a comb.
He: Ah yes, I remember it well.
That brilliant sky. . .
She: We had some rain.
He: Those Russian songs. . .
She: From sunny Spain.
He: Ah yes, I remember it well.
You wore a gown of gold.
She: I was all in blue.
He: Am I getting old?
She: Oh no, not you.
How strong you were,
How young and gay
A prince of love in every way.
He: Ah yes, I remember it well.

WHY ARE FEMALES' MEMORIES MORE VIVID?

Both song and data indicate that women possess more detailed and vivid memories of interactions within intimate relationships than do men. The evidence suggests that women tend to be the interpersonal historians in our culture. Why might this be the case?

There have been many studies examining cultural stereotypes of males and females in North American society. Generally, men are described as independent, rational, and competent; in contrast, women are seen as dependent and emotional. Women are also depicted as more concerned with interpersonal relationships, more aware of the feelings of others, and more expressive of their own feelings (e.g., Deaux, 1976; Parsons & Bales, 1955). The evidence does not necessarily indicate that men and women possess different values; it does suggest that the sexes are socialized to assume somewhat different roles in the pursuit of common values within the family (Parsons & Bales, 1955).

If women are socialized to be more concerned with interpersonal relationships, they may attend more closely to an ongoing social interaction and/or think about it more afterwards than do men. Women may then possess a more vivid memory of the interaction than males.

Additional items on our questionnaires asked respondents how often they had thought and how often they had talked about each event (with their spouse or with others) since it had occurred. The responses to the thought and talk questions were highly correlated; we combined them into a single measure of reminiscence. Participants were also asked to assess the personal importance of each event at the time it had occurred. The means shown in Table 7.5 reveal a gender difference. In comparison with their husbands, wives tended to report that they were more likely to reminisce about the events. Women also rated the events as more important.

A closer scrutiny of the results suggests that differential rehearsal and importance may not account for the gender effect on vividness of recall. Ratings of

TABLE 7.5
Reminiscence and Personal Importance

| Event Recalled | Mean Frequency of Reminiscence | | $p <$ |
	Husbands' Ratings	Wives' Ratings	
Argument	2.46	2.84	n.s.[a]
First date	3.95	4.57	.05
Vacation	4.20	4.76	.01
All 3 events	3.54	4.06	.01

| Event Recalled | Mean Personal Importance | | $p <$ |
	Husbands' Ratings	Wives' Ratings	
Argument	4.40	5.56	.01
First date	5.10	5.23	n.s.[b]
Vacation	5.40	5.91	.05
All 3 events	4.96	5.57	.05

Notes:
1. [a]$F = 1.34$; [b]$F < 1$
2. Frequency of reminiscence could range from 1 (not at all) to 7 (many times).
3. Ratings of personal importance could range from 1 (not at all important) to 7 (very important).

personal importance did not correlate significantly with ratings of vividness for any of the recalled events; averaging across the three events, $r = .18$, $p =$ n.s. Ratings of frequency of reminiscence were correlated with ratings of vividness for each event, $ps < .01$; averaging across the three events, $r = .47$. However, the impact of gender on vividness of recall remained strong when ratings of frequency of reminiscence were entered into the analyses as a covariate. Thus, we suspect that these two variables do not fully explain the vividness effect. Our conclusions remain tentative, however, because the reliability and validity of our measures of importance and frequency of reminiscence are unknown.

A second possible explanation for the vividness effect can be dismissed with greater confidence. The males in our sample were somewhat older than the females (see Table 7.1). Conceivably, vividness of recall decreases with age. The effect of gender on vividness did not decline in strength, though, when age of subject was entered as a covariate in the analyses. Evidently, age does not account for the gender difference in vividness.

A third and more interesting possibility is that women may be relationship experts (Parsons & Bales, 1955). Experts in domains such as chess, physics, and soccer possess detailed cognitive schemata that facilitate fast, accurate judgments and superior memory in their area of expertise (Charness, 1988; Morris, 1988). Similarly, women may develop a more articulated and complex understanding of relationships than do men. Observations that can be related to such a well-differentiated memory structure are more likely to be recalled.

Conceivably women become relationship experts as a result of culturally mediated gender differences in social roles and power. In our culture, women have been traditionally assigned to the roles of caring for the family and social functions (Kidder, Fagan & Cohn, 1981). The degree of task specialization should not be exaggerated. Couples share responsibilities in many areas (Aronoff & Crano, 1975; Davis, 1976) and there is no doubt a good deal of variability across families. Nonetheless, women may be socialized to accept somewhat more responsibility for social and family activities, and thus develop a greater degree of expertise in the interpersonal domain. In addition, women have tended to be the less powerful member of the marital relationship, in both physical and economic terms (Frieze, Parsons, Johnson, Ruble, & Zellman, 1978; Turner, 1970). It is important for less powerful members of a relationship to become knowledgeable about their partner's feelings and behaviors (Thibaut & Kelley, 1959; Turner, 1970). They must learn how to influence and not to offend their high power partner.

We have suggested that women possess more vivid memories of events in a relationship because of culturally mediated sex differences in roles and power. Another possibility must be addressed. Perhaps women simply have better memories than men. The evidence does not seem to support this interpretation. Maccoby and Jacklin's (1974) review indicates that traditional tests of memory have generally failed to show systematic sex differences.

The possibility that women possess superior memories cannot be totally discounted, however. The Maccoby and Jacklin review suggested that verbal memory may be better in females than in males. Furthermore, the research summarized by Maccoby and Jacklin was conducted primarily with children.

Evidence from the adult memory literature is sparse. Tests for sex differences are typically not reported in published studies of memory. We recently examined the journal entitled *Memory and Cognition*. Many researchers simply noted that their subjects were undergraduates; the researchers failed to indicate the ratio of males to females in their sample. Not a single study of the more than 100 that we scanned reported a significance test for gender. Similarly, Johnson (personal communication) has not tested for sex differences in her research on the vividness of people's memories for perceived and imagined events.

Researchers in the gerontology area have been somewhat more interested in gender differences in accuracy of recall (e.g., Botwinick & Storandt, 1974; Storandt, Grant, & Gordon, 1978). The data are mixed. In one study (Storandt et al., 1978), for example, adult males of all ages remembered historical events more accurately than their female counterparts (e.g., the date of Pearl Harbor and the name of the ship that hit an iceberg and sank on its maiden voyage in 1912). In contrast, there was no gender difference in recall of people or events from the entertainment industry (e.g., the names of the author of *Gone With The Wind* and of the actress who played the wife of Jackie Gleason in the "Honeymooners"). Botwinick and Storandt (1980) attribute the gender difference in recall of historical events to differential encoding. They infer that females probably pay less attention to historical events than do males.

Finally, consider the self-reports of the participants in our study. Spouses were asked to evaluate the accuracy of each other's memory for "details from the past" on the final questionnaire. Both spouses rated the female's memory as superior (Table 7.4). The item was posed as a general memory question; it did not specify memory for interpersonal episodes. Nonetheless, the question was asked in a context in which participants had recently been required to describe and evaluate their memories of interpersonal events. It is likely that spouses' responses to the general memory question were influenced by the vividness of their recall of these target events.

We conclude that a gender effect in vividness of recall probably reflects a difference in process, rather than faculty. Vividness will vary with expertise, interest, rehearsal, and other variables that will sometimes, but not always, be associated with gender. This conclusion remains tentative, however, because of a lack of available data.

It is important to emphasize that the findings that we have reported concern the vividness of recall, rather than its accuracy. We have no basis for concluding that women's memories of the events are more accurate than those of their husbands. Women report a greater tendency to reminisce about the events, but such rehearsal may lead to increased amounts of fabrication, as well as to the preservation of the original information (Johnson, 1988). In addition, past research on flashbulb memories (Neisser, 1982b) and eyewitness testimony (Wells & Loftus, 1984) reveals that it can be a mistake to equate detailed and vivid recall with accuracy.

In everyday life, this caveat may often be ignored. Vivid memories are likely to be accepted as genuine, unless other evidence casts doubt upon them. However, autobiographical memories are typically not open to objective forms of verification.[1] For example, the married couples in our study probably cannot obtain a documentary record of their first date. Consensual verification is more readily available, but we suspect that people rarely seek it. Research on the false consensus effect suggests that individuals commonly assume that their own view of reality would be shared by others (Ross, Greene, & House, 1977). Therefore, people may rarely feel a need to verify their memories. It is evident from transcripts of discussions in the together condition that our experiment was the first occasion on which some of the couples had discussed and become aware of their differing perspectives on the events in question.

Cognitive psychologists who study recall are perhaps more skeptical than most people about the veracity of memory. Yet even they were slow to doubt the validity of highly detailed, flashbulb memories (Neisser, 1982b, 1986). Vivid memories often assume a reality of their own.

THE FUNCTIONS OF PUBLIC RECOLLECTIONS

To this point, we have assumed that people attempt to recall accurately past events in their lives. On occasion, though, goals other than accuracy may take precedence. Much of our social discourse involves recounting our experiences; think, for instance, of cocktail party chatter. For others' amusement we fashion stories out of our lives. Indeed, entertainment is a common goal of various forms of communication (Higgins, 1981).

There is a problem, though. Most people's personal experiences are fairly mundane and are of little interest to anyone other than perhaps their spouses or parents. Individuals may sometimes solve the dilemma by offering embellished or exaggerated accounts of events. They are, after all, not testifying on the witness stand. Given a choice, their listeners would probably opt for an embellished but interesting account, rather than a stunningly accurate but boring one.

---

[1]Occasionally, a record is available. In a recent book, Richard Feynman (1988) recounts how he outfoxed a group of pickets with a clever speech. He reports the beginning of the talk, as he remembers it. He then notes that he discovered a transcript of his speech and "what I said at the beginning doesn't seem anywhere near as dramatic as the way I remember it. . . . What I remember saying is much more wonderful than what I actually said! (p. 75)" It is interesting that Feynman chose to present the improved version and never tells the reader what he actually said.

In his delightful autobiography entitled *Growing Up,* Russell Baker (1984) offered the following description of a favorite uncle: "I found him irresistible. It was his intuitive refusal to spoil a good story by slavish adherence to fact that enchanted me" (p. 176).

On the final questionnaire in our study, we asked respondents to indicate how they, their spouse, and most males and females describe the past to other people. The end points of the scales were labeled "almost always alter details to make a point or be entertaining" and "almost always describe events as accurately as possible." Not surprisingly, perhaps, individuals rated themselves and their spouses as significantly more truthful than males and females in general (Table 7.6). In addition, individuals reported a sex difference in people's tendency to improve the past while engaging in public recollections. Both spouses indicated that males are significantly more likely to alter details than females, and that they and their spouse evidence this same trend (Table 7.6). Finally, on average, respondents placed themselves and their spouses toward the middle of the accuracy dimension. Apparently, the goal of telling a good story often takes away from the goal of accuracy.[2]

We have no objective evidence that men are more likely than women to alter the past. On the other hand, we have no reason to doubt the reports of our participants. For the present, we are inclined to accept them at face value, which leads us to our next question. Why might men be more inclined than women to revise their histories in the presence of an audience? There are obviously many possible answers. It is tempting to speculate, however, that women are sometimes constrained by their vivid and detailed recall. People are hesitant to make statements that they consider to be clearly untrue (DePaulo et al., 1985). Men, with their fuzzier memories of interpersonal events, may feel greater freedom to fill in the gaps in their memories in ways that suit their current purposes.

Verbal communication serves a number of social functions other than entertainment; for example, it is used to facilitate the achievement of social relationship and self-presentational goals (Higgins, 1981). Public recollections can serve similar purposes. Remembering helps people define their relationships with others. Reminiscing with friends and family can remind people of the ties that connect them and thereby strengthen their commitment to each other (Neisser, 1988). At a societal level, history can be interpreted in a manner that justifies present status and role differences (Mead, 1964).

Furthermore, acts of remembering and forgetting are often interpreted as providing information about people's feelings toward each other. Acknowledgment of birthdays, anniversaries, and other important dates is seen to indicate caring; a failure to remember a significant date may be viewed as reflecting a lack

---

[2]Along the same lines, Neisser (1988) has recently proposed that any act of remembering lies on a continuum between "utility (using the past to accomplish some present end) and verity (using memory to recapture what really happened in the past)" (p. 557).

TABLE 7.6
Functions of Public Recollections

	Target	
	Male	Female
Own marriage	4.28	4.79
People in general	3.25	4.40

Notes:

1. Ratings were provided on a 7-point scale, with higher numbers indicating a greater concern for accuracy (1 = almost always alter details to make a point or to be entertaining; 7 = almost always describe events as accurately as possible).

2. Females were evaluated as more inclined than males to strive for accuracy, $F = 11.70$, $p < .001$. Self and spouse were evaluated as more concerned with accuracy than people in general, $F = 30.69$, $p < .001$.

3. The data are reported collapsed over the person doing the ratings (husband or wife). Main effects and interactions involving rater did not approach statistical significance.

of affection. Similarly, an inability to remember a person's name[3] or to recognize his face may be interpreted by that individual as indicating a lack of interest or concern.

These examples suggest that, like Freud, social observers believe that remembering and forgetting reflect a person's underlying attitudes and motives. This interpretation would most certainly be wrong some of the time. Remembering and forgetting are multiply determined phenomena—but try explaining that to your spouse when you forget your wedding anniversary. Valid or not, motivational interpretations of remembering have important implications for self as well as social perception. Others' reactions can affect people's self-perceptions and self-esteem (Mead, 1934).

Remembering can also be used in the service of self-presentational goals. Individuals can vary their accounts to project particular images of themselves

---

[3]A couple of months before their marriage, the senior author's fiancée forgot his name while introducing him to a friend. The shock that he experienced in response to this aphasia is reflected in his ability to remember the event more than 20 years later. (Note that the author bases his belief that the memory is accurate on the vividness of his recall. In the spirit of this chapter, it is only fair to note that his spouse disputes his version of the story.)

(Greenwald, 1980). Such public memory performances are doubly important because they may affect the rememberer's self-perceptions, as well as his or her public personae. Saying sometimes leads to believing (Higgins, 1981; Higgins & Rholes, 1978; Jones, Rhodewalt, Berglas, & Skelton, 1981; Schlenker, 1980). Individuals who initially alter details of an event to create a better story may, in time, come to believe those alterations themselves. As Bruner (1987) has observed, "in the end we *become* the autobiographical narratives by which we 'tell about' our lives" (p. 15).

People's efforts to construct histories that suit their purposes may have implications for the profession of psychology. Mahony (1986) has contrasted Freud's published case histories to his private process notes. The case histories apparently create an impression of greater treatment completeness, effectiveness, and orderliness than was the case. No doubt, the alterations reflect a variety of motivations. We suspect, though, that part of the orderliness is derived from Freud's desire to tell a "good" story, which means, at least in part, a coherent and interesting narrative.

In a similar vein, psychological researchers are often dismayed by the portrayal of their work in textbooks. Case histories have been written of the embellishments and distortions that creep into textbook descriptions of classic experiments, such as Watson's study of little Albert (Harris, 1979). Textbook authors are historians of our discipline; we, researchers, demand accuracy. However, writers have multiple goals. Accuracy may be sacrificed in the effort to tell an interesting, convincing, and comprehensible story. Some of the critics of textbook authors may well introduce comparable distortions into their own classroom presentations of research.

TWO CONTRADICTORY PHENOMENA?

We have proposed that females' recall of interpersonal events is more vivid and detailed than is males' recall of the same events. We have also suggested that males are more likely than females to embellish their stories of the past to make a point or be entertaining. The two phenomena seem contradictory. If men embellish the past, shouldn't their accounts be rated by observers as more vivid than those of females?

The answer may be that vividness depends on the goal of recall, as well as on the more cognitive variables (such as expertise) that we discussed earlier. The couples in our research were asked to participate in a study of memory. The implicit and explicit demands were for accurate recall. In such circumstances, deliberate embellishment may be seen as inappropriate. When rememberers strive for veridical recall, women's accounts of interpersonal episodes are likely to be more vivid than those of their spouses, for the reasons we described earlier. On the other hand, men may engage in greater fabrication and produce more vivid recall in many everyday social settings. One implication of this reasoning is that the vividness of men's accounts of interpersonal events may be more affected than women's by social context and goals.

TOWARD A SOCIAL PSYCHOLOGY OF MEMORY

It has been recognized for a long time that social psychological factors influence memory. For instance, Bartlett (1932) and George Herbert Mead (1934, 1964) suggested that remembering is affected by social context, current knowledge, motives, and goals.

Although cognitive psychology has flourished since Bartlett and Mead, the influence of social factors on memory has tended to be neglected. The major thrust of cognitive psychologists has been to develop a general theory of memory and its organization in the brain (Neisser, 1982a).

In this chapter, we have provided evidence that remembering is a social as well as a cognitive phenomenon. It is important to know how memory is represented in the brain; but it is also important to understand the functions and nature of recall in its social context. In 1982, Neisser wrote that "if X is an interesting or socially significant aspect of memory, then psychologists have hardly ever studied X" (1982a, p. 4). Prompted in part by Neisser's challenge, an increasing number of psychologists are studying autobiographical recall and memory in naturalistic settings (e.g., Gruneberg, Morris, & Sykes, 1988; Rubin, 1986).

For the most part, though, this research continues to overlook the social aspects of recall. Ironically, much the same can be said about research on memory conducted by social psychologists. In a typical social psychology experiment, subjects are asked to recall information that has been presented to them by an experimenter. The only thing social about such research is that the information being recalled concerns another, often hypothetical, human being.

In everyday life, remembering frequently occurs during social interactions. The group transcript presented earlier and the data that we provided on reports of forgetting indicate that people contribute to each other's recall and negotiate a common story about their shared past (see also Berger & Kellner, 1964; Edwards & Middleton, 1986, 1988; Wegner, 1986). To understand memory in its natural contexts, researchers need to consider the quality of this transactive process, as well as the impact on recall of cultural mores, individual differences, goals, and motives.

In addition, the study of remembering in ongoing relationships offers the promise of increased understanding of the nature, bases, and functions of social relationships. Relationships influence recall and recall, in turn, helps define and shape relationships. The study of memory is important to social psychologists precisely because of the reciprocal association between recall, on the one hand, and self and social perception on the other.

FACT OR FICTION?

We began with quotes from Galton's autobiography. In the middle of the chapter we burst into song. It seems fitting to close with the words of a contemporary novelist who specializes in stories of marital relationships. In Updike's (1963) short story entitled *Walter Briggs*, a husband and wife engage in a competitive memory game to enliven a boring car trip. They try to recall a summer, 5 years earlier. The husband observes that his wife "danced ahead, calling into color vast faded tracts of that distant experience. . . . It made him jealous, her store of explicit memories. . . . Their past was so much more vivid to her presumably because it was more precious" (pp. 15–16).

ACKNOWLEDGMENTS

The research in this chapter was supported by a Social Sciences and Humanities Research Council Grant to Michael Ross. We thank Phil Costanzo and Jim Olson for their comments and suggestions. Parts of the chapter are based on an invited address presented at the American Psychological Association, 1988, in Atlanta.

REFERENCES

Aronoff, J., & Crano, W. D. (1975). A re-examination of the cross-cultural principles of task segregation and sex role differentiation in the family. *American Sociological Review, 40,* 12–20.

Baker, R. (1984). *Growing up.* New York: New American Library.

Bartlett, F. C. (1932). *Remembering: A study in experimental and social psychology.* London: Cambridge University Press.

Bem, S. L., & Bem, D. J. (1970). Case study of a non-conscious ideology: Training the woman to know her place. In D. J. Bem (Ed.), *Beliefs, attitudes, and human affairs* (pp. 80–99). Monterey, CA: Brooks/Cole.

Berger, P. L., & Kellner, M. (1964). Marriage and the construction of reality. *Diogenes, 46,* 1–24.

Botwinick, J., & Storandt, M. (1974). *Memory related functions and age.* Springfield, IL: C. Thomas.

Botwinick, J., & Storandt, M. (1980). Recall and recognition of old information in relation to age and sex. *Journal of Gerontology, 35,* 70–76.

Bruner, J. (1987). Life as a narrative. *Social Research, 54,* 11–32.

Charness, N. (1988). Expertise in chess, music and physics: A cognitive perspective. In L. Obler & D. Fein (Eds.), *The exceptional brain.* New York: Guilford Press (pp. 399–426).

Davis, H. L. (1976). Decision making within the household. *Journal of Consumer Research, 2,* 241–260.

Deaux, K. (1976). *The behavior of women and men.* Monterey, CA: Brooks/Cole.

DePaulo, B. M., Zuckerman, M., & Lassiter, G. D. (1985). Deceiving and detecting deceit. In B. R. Schlenker (Ed.), *The self and social life* (pp. 323–370). New York: McGraw Hill.

Edwards, D., & Middleton, D. (1986). Joint remembering: Constructing an account of shared experience through conversational discourse. *Discourse Processes, 9,* 423–459.

Edwards, D. & Middleton, D. (1988). Conversational remembering and family relationships: How children learn to remember. *Journal of Social and Personal Relationships, 5,* 3–25.

Feldman–Summers, S. & Kiesler, S. (1974). Those who are number two try harder: The effects of sex on attributions of causality. *Journal of Personality and Social Psychology, 30,* 846–855.

Feynman, R. P. (1988). *What do you care what other people think?* New York: W. W. Norton.

Frieze, I. H., Parsons, J. E., Johnson, P. B., Ruble, D. N., & Zellman, G. L. (1978). *Women and sex roles: A social psychological perspective.* New York: Norton.

Galton, F. (1974). *Memories of my life.* New York: A.M.S. (Original work published 1908)

Greenwald, A. G. (1980). The totalitarian ego: Fabrication and revision of personal history. *American Psychologist, 35,* 603–618.

Gruneberg, M. M., Morris, P. M., & Sykes, R. N. (Eds.). (1988). *Practical aspects of memory: Current research and issues.* London: Academic Press.

Harris, B. (1979). Whatever happened to Little Albert? *American Psychologist, 34,* 151–160.

Higgins, E. T. (1981). The "communication game": Implications for social cognition and persuasion. In E. T. Higgins, C. P. Herman, & M. P. Zanna (Eds.), *Social cognition: The Ontario symposium* (Vol. 1, pp. 343–392). Hillsdale, NJ: Lawrence Erlbaum Associates.

Higgins, E. T. & Rholes, W. S. (1978). Saying is believing: Effects of message modification on memory and liking for the person described. *Journal of Experimental Social Psychology, 14,* 363–378.

Johnson, M. K. (1988). Reality monitoring: An experimental phenomenological approach. *Journal of Experimental Psychology: General, 117,* 390–394.

Johnson, M. K., Foley, M. A., Suengas, A. G., & Raye, C. L. (1988). Phenomenal characteristics of memories for perceived and imagined autobiographical events. *Journal of Experimental Psychology: General, 117,* 371–376.

Jones, E. E., Rhodewalt, F., Berglas, S., & Skelton, J. A. (1981). Effects of strategic self-presentation on subsequent self-esteem. *Journal of Personality and Social Psychology, 41,* 407–421.

Kidder, L. H., Fagan, M. A., & Cohn, E. S. (1981). Giving and receiving: Social justice in close relationships. In M. J. Lerner & S. C. Lerner (Eds.), *The justice motive in social behavior* (pp. 235–256). New York: Plenum.

Maccoby, E. E., & Jacklin, C. N. (1974). *The psychology of sex differences.* Stanford, CA: Stanford University Press.

Mahony, P. J. (1986). *Freud and the rat man.* New Haven, CN: Yale University Press.

Mead, G. H. (1934). *Mind, self and society.* Chicago: University of Chicago Press.

Mead, G. H. (1964). *Selected writings* (A. J. Reck, Ed.). Chicago: University of Chicago Press.

Morris, P. (1988). Expertise and everyday memory. In M. M. Gruneberg, P. M. Morris, & R. N. Sykes (Eds.), *Practical aspects of memory: Current research and issues* (Vol. 1, pp. 459–465).

Neisser, U. (1982a). Memory: What are the important questions? In U. Neisser (Ed.), *Memory Observed.* San Francisco: W. H. Freeman (pp. 3–19).

Neisser, U. (1982b). Snapshots or benchmarks? In U. Neisser (Ed.), *Memory Observed.* San Francisco: W. H. Freeman (pp. 43–48).

Neisser, U. (1986). Remembering Pearl Harbor: Reply to Thompson and Cowan. *Cognition, 23,* 285–286.

Neisser, U. (1988). Time present and time past. In M. M. Gruneberg, P. M. Morris, & R. N. Sykes (Eds.), *Practical aspects of memory: Current research and issues,* (Vol. 2, pp. 545–560).

Parsons, T., & Bales, R. F. (1955). *Family, socialization and interaction process.* Glencoe, IL: Free Press.

Ross, L., Greene, D., & House, P. (1977). The "false consensus effect": An egocentric bias in social perception and attribution processes. *Journal of Experimental Social Psychology, 13,* 279–301.

Rubin, D. C. (1986). *Autobiographical memory.* New York: Cambridge University Press.

Schlenker, B. R. (1980). *Impression management: The self-concept, social identity, and interpersonal relations*. Belmont, CA.: Brooks/Cole.

Storandt, M., Grant, E. A., & Gordon, B. C. (1978). Remote memory as a function of age and sex. *Experimental Aging Research, 4,* 365–375.

Suengas, A. G., & Johnson, M. K. (1988). Qualitative effects of rehearsal on memories for perceived and imagined complex events. *Journal of Experimental Psychology: General, 117,* 377–389.

Thibaut, J. W., & Kelley, H. H. (1959). *The social psychology of groups*. New York: Wiley.

Turner, R. H. (1970). *Family interaction*. New York: Wiley.

Updike, J. (1963). *Pigeon feathers and other stories*. New York: Ballantine Books.

Wegner, D. M. (1986). Transactive memory. In B. Mullen & G. R. Goethals (Eds.), *General theories of group behavior* (pp. 185–208). New York: Springer–Verlag.

Wells, G. L. & Loftus, E. F. (1984). *Eyewitness Testimony*. Cambridge, England: Cambridge University Press.

Patterns of Self-Beliefs: The Psychological Significance of Relations Among the Actual, Ideal, Ought, Can, and Future Selves

8

E. Tory Higgins
Columbia University

Orit Tykocinski
Jennifer Vookles
New York University

Of all the psychological characteristics of people, perhaps the most fundamental is that they derive meanings from the events in their lives and then respond to those meanings. Although this insight into the nature of people has a long history in Western thought, it was most clearly developed at the turn of the century in the work of Weber, Durkheim, Freud, James, Cooley, and others. Thomas and Thomas (1928) expressed the essence of this insight as follows: "If men define situations as real, they are real in their consequences." In social psychology as well, Lewin (1935) early on emphasized the importance of the psychological situation in determining people's motivations and actions.

Social objects and events not only have meaning. They also have importance. The term "significance" refers to both the quality of conveying meaning and the quality of being important. Thus the concept, *psychological significance,* captures both the meaning and importance aspects of subjective experience. What determines which psychological significances people will experience? In part, psychological significances derive from momentary factors, such as the particular features of the stimuli being perceived and the specific context of perception. But psychological significances also derive from socialization histories that cause certain meanings and consequences to become available and chronically accessible.

It is these chronic psychological significances, especially, that are the source of individual, developmental, and cultural differences in responding to the social world. How might these chronic psychological significances be conceptualized? Is there a way to distinguish systematically among different types of chronic psychological significances? What are the emotional/motivational consequences of people possessing different types of chronic psychological significances? As a first step in answering these general questions, this chapter considers the particular case of chronic psychological significances associated with the self-system. This will involve an extension and elaboration of self-discrepancy theory (see Higgins, 1987). The first section discusses how social interactions with significant others shape both the meaning and importance of self-beliefs. The second section describes different patterns of self-beliefs and relates these patterns to distinct meanings and emotional/motivational consequences.

INTERPERSONAL HISTORY
OF PSYCHOLOGICAL SIGNIFICANCES

Self-discrepancy theory (Higgins, 1987, 1989a) distinguishes between people's representations of their current or actual self and their representations of valued end-states or self-directive standards. The former representation is the self-concept and the latter representations are self-guides. The theory distinguishes between two basic types of self-guides: (a) An *Ideal* self-guide—your representation of the attributes that someone (yourself or another) would like you, ideally, to possess (i.e., someone's hopes, wishes, or aspirations for you); and (b) An *Ought* self-guide—your representation of the attributes that someone (yourself or another) believes you should or ought to possess (i.e., a representation of someone's sense of your duty, obligations, or responsibilities).

A basic assumption of the theory is that people are motivated to reach a condition where their self-concept matches their personally relevant self-guides. A discrepancy between the self-concept and a self-guide is predicted to produce discomfort. It is also predicted that the kind of discomfort produced by a discrepancy depends on the type of self-guide involved in the discrepancy. An actual–ideal discrepancy is predicted to produce dejection-related discomfort, such as feeling sad, disappointed, dissatisfied, or discouraged, whereas an actual–ought discrepancy is predicted to produce agitation-related discomfort, such as feeling worried, nervous, edgy, tense. These predicted relations have been found in a number of studies (see Higgins, 1987, 1989a).

Why is it that an actual–ideal discrepancy produces dejection-related discomfort whereas an actual–ought discrepancy produces agitation-related discomfort? Why do these two types of self-belief patterns have different psychological significance to people? To answer these questions, one must consider the developmental history of the self-system in general and these self-beliefs in particular. This history involves both general developmental shifts in the self-system associated with changes in children's mental representational system and individual differences in the self-system associated with modes of socialization. In both cases, it is the child's history of social interactions and interpersonal relations that is the critical determinant of psychological significances.

Intellectual Development and the Psychological Significance of the Self

Self-system development from infancy to adolescence can be described in terms of five major shifts in children's capacity for mentally representing events (see Higgins, in press, 1989c; Moretti & Higgins, 1989, for fuller discussions of these shifts). These shifts are consistent with various models of intellectual development (e.g., Damon & Hart, 1986; Fischer, 1980; Piaget, 1965; Selman, 1980) but rely most heavily on Case's (1985) model. The use of distinct levels is an expositional device for describing some basic changes in the psychological significance of the self that can occur because of changes in children's mental representational capacity.

Level 1: Early Sensorimotor Development

By the end of the first year of life, children are capable of representing the relation between two events, such as the relation between a behavior produced by them and their mother's reaction to their behavior. Even at this early stage, then, children are capable of the preliminary form of role taking described by Mead (1934), the ability to anticipate the responses of a significant other with whom one is interacting. Children during this stage are also able to experience all four major types of actual and anticipated psychological situations:

1. The *presence of positive outcomes,* as when children feel their mother's nipple between their lips or anticipate their mother's face when playing peek-a-boo, which is associated with a feeling of satisfaction and joy (e.g., Case, 1988; Sroufe, 1984).

2. The *absence of positive outcomes,* as when a child's mother changes from affectionate face-to-face play to withholding communication from the child or when a child's sought after (but not visible) toy cannot be found, which is associated with the child's feeling of sadness, disappointment, and frustration/anger (e.g., Campos & Barrett, 1984; Kagan, 1984; Sroufe, 1984; Trevarthen, 1984).

3. The *presence of negative outcomes,* as when a child suffers from noxious stimulation or is confronted by an unexpected and potentially harmful person or situation, which is associated with the child's feeling of distress and fear (Emde, 1984; Kagan, 1984).

4. The *absence of negative outcomes,* as when a mother removes noxious stimulation from a child or removes a child from a situation that the child finds threatening, which is associated with the child's feeling calm, secure, reassured (e.g., Case, 1988; Sroufe, 1984).

Level 2: Late Sensorimotor and Early Interrelational Development

Between 1½ and 2 years of age there is a dramatic shift in children's ability to represent events, a shift traditionally associated with the emergence of symbolic representation (e.g., Bruner, 1964; Case, 1985; Fischer, 1980; Huttenlocher & Higgins, 1978; Piaget, 1951; Werner & Kaplan, 1963). Children become capable of recognizing the higher-order relation that exists between two other relations, of using a scheme representing the relation between two objects as a *means* to obtaining a represented and specified goal pertaining to two other objects (see Case, 1985). At this stage, children can represent *the relation between two relations:* (1) The relation between a particular kind of self-feature (action, response, physical appearance, mood, etc.) and a particular kind of response by another person, such as the relation between the child making a fuss or a mess at mealtime and mother frowning, yelling, or leaving; and (2) The relation between a particular kind of response by another person and a particular kind of psychological situation they will experience, such as the relation between mother's frowning, yelling, or leaving and the child experiencing a negative psychological situation.

The shift between children's ability at Level 1 to represent relation (1) and their ability at Level 2 to represent the higher-order relationship between relation (1) and relation (2) is illustrated in Fig. 8.1.

At Level 2, then, children are capable of anticipating the consequences for themselves of their own actions. The significant others in the child's life respond to the child's features, which in turn places the child into particular psychological situations. Thus, the significant others link the child to the larger society by providing the *social meanings* of the child's features. This occurs because children can now represent *self–other contingencies,* as follows:

My displaying Feature X is associated with Person A displaying Feature Y, and Person A displaying Feature Y is associated with my experiencing Psychological Situation Z.

In representing such self–other contingencies, children learn the interpersonal significance of their self-features. Their self-features now have *psychological significance.* At this stage, the meaning of a self-feature to a child is determined by how others respond to the feature, and the importance of a self-feature to a child is determined by the psychological situations produced in the child by others' responses to the feature. Because children's self-features can now have this new psychological significance, they can experience new emotions such as pride, joy, shame, fear of punishment, and feelings of abandonment and rejection (see Campos & Barrett, 1984; Case, 1988; Kagan, 1984; Sroufe, 1984).

LEVEL 5: LATE VECTORIAL DEVELOPMENT

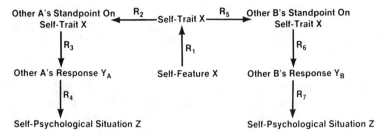

LEVEL 4: LATE DIMENSIONAL AND EARLY VECTORIAL DEVELOPMENT

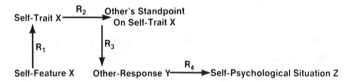

LEVEL 3: LATE INTERRELATIONAL AND EARLY DIMENSIONAL DEVELOPMENT

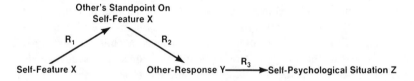

LEVEL 2: LATE SENSORIMOTOR AND EARLY INTERRELATIONAL DEVELOPMENT

Self-Feature X $\xrightarrow{R_1}$ Other-Response Y $\xrightarrow{R_2}$ Self-Psychological Situation Z

LEVEL 1: EARLY SENSORIMOTOR DEVELOPMENT

Self-Feature X $\xrightarrow{R_1}$ Other-Response Y

FIG. 8.1. Illustration of developmental changes in children's ability to represent self–other contingencies.

Level 3: Late Interrelational and Early Dimensional Development

Another dramatic shift in children's mental representational capacity occurs between 4 and 6 (see Case, 1985; Feffer, 1970; Fischer, 1980; Flavell, Botkin, Fry, Wright, & Jarvis, 1968; Piaget, 1965; Selman & Byrne, 1974; Werner, 1957).

During this stage, children become capable of inferring the thoughts, expectations, motives, and intentions of others (see Higgins, 1981; Shantz, 1983). This
new inferential ability can be applied to the case of self–other contingency
knowledge. In order to regulate their features so as to obtain others' responses
that are associated with positive psychological situations and to avoid others'
responses that are associated with negative psychological situations, children are
motivated to learn what kinds of self-features are expected, valued, and preferred
by the significant others in their life (e.g., their parents). Thus, children at this
stage have both the ability and motivation to acquire internalized standards or
self-guides (see Fischer & Watson, 1981; Gesell & Ilg, 1946).

As illustrated in Fig. 8.1, children can now represent another person's view-
point or standpoint on their features, which are those features of the child that the
other person values or prefers (as inferred by the child). Now the relation between self-feature X and other-response Y is understood to be mediated by the
relation between self-feature X and the other's standpoint on self-feature X.
Thus, at this stage, children not only anticipate others' responses to their features. Now they also represent *others' valued end-states for them*. It is these
representations of others' valued or preferred end-states for them that now provide the social meanings of their features. And it is children's representations of
the consequences for them of others' standpoint on them—their representation of
the psychological situations they will experience by meeting or failing to meet
others' valued end-states for them—that provide the importance of their features.
At this stage, then, the psychological significance to children of their self-
features is tied to their representations of others' valued end-states for them.
These valued end-states or *self-guides* can take the form of either wishes and
hopes (Ideals) or duties and obligations (Oughts).

Level 4: Late Dimensional
and Early Vectorial Development

Between 9 and 11 children become capable of coordinating values along two
distinct dimensions (see Case, 1985; Fischer, 1980; Higgins, 1981; Piaget,
1970). It is during this period that children first begin to represent their attributes
as being both temporally stable and cross-situationally consistent (see Ruble &
Rholes, 1981). Thus, *children can now possess a dispositional self-concept* (see
Harter, 1983; Rosenberg, 1979; Ruble & Rholes, 1981; Shantz, 1983).

As illustrated in Fig. 8.1, children at Level 4 can compare their represented
self-concept attributes as a whole with a representation of another person's standpoint on their self-attributes as a whole. Children's capacity at this level to
interrelate distinct dimensions means that true *self-concept–self-guide structures*
can be formed. Children can not only emotionally appraise a particular feature
that they have just displayed by considering another person's likely response to or
feelings about the action, but they can also use a self-guide to appraise a trait that

they believe they generally possess. In addition, one trait dimension involving a match or a mismatch between a self-concept trait and a self-guide can become interconnected with other trait dimensions involving matches or mismatches. For this reason, children at this stage may evaluate themselves in more global, overall terms.

Now the psychological significance of a self-feature is not determined only by its relation to others' valued end-state for that feature. The self-feature can be related to a general self-trait, the general self-trait can be related to other self-traits, and the self-traits as a whole can be related to some significant other's standpoint on those traits. Thus, for the first time there can be *a pattern of structural interconnections among actual self-traits and a self-guide that as a whole has psychological significance.*

If children are more likely to pay attention to and mull over problematical self-attributes (i.e., actual self-traits–self-guide mismatches) than nonproblematical self-attributes, then it is more likely that problematical self-attributes would become structurally interconnected than nonproblematical self-attributes (see Higgins, Van Hook, & Dorfman, 1988). Because of spreading activation among interconnected elements in a unitized self-structure (see Collins & Loftus, 1975; Hayes–Roth, 1977; Higgins et al., 1988), the self-evaluative process for a single mismatching self-feature could now activate a child's general self-discrepancy system as a whole (see Higgins, 1989b; Strauman & Higgins, 1987).

Self-discrepancy theory proposes that a discrepancy between actual self-traits and an ideal self-guide is a meaningful pattern of self-beliefs. The theory proposes that this pattern represents a particular psychological situation. If a person possesses this discrepancy, the current state of his or her actual attributes, from the person's own standpoint, does not match the ideal self that someone wishes or hopes that he or she would attain. Thus, an *actual–ideal discrepancy* as a whole represents the absence of something positive, *the absence of positive outcomes*. The theory also proposes that if a person possesses an *actual–ought discrepancy,* then the current state of his or her actual attributes, from the person's own standpoint, does not match the state that someone believes is his or her duty or obligation to attain. Because violation of prescribed duties or obligations is associated with sanctions such as punishment or criticism, this discrepancy as a whole represents the expected presence of something negative, the *presence of negative outcomes*.

Level 5: Late Vectorial Development

Between 13 and 16 children become capable of interrelating different perspectives on the same object, including the self as an object (Fischer, 1980; Inhelder & Piaget, 1958; Selman & Byrne, 1974). They become capable of interrelating different systems of distinct dimensions (Case, 1985), of constructing abstract mappings in which two abstractions are related to each other (Fischer & Lamborn, 1987). Adolescents' new ability to interrelate distinct dimensional systems has a consequence of major significance. Now more than one standpoint on the actual self can be represented simultaneously. For the first time, two distinct self-guide systems, such as one actual self–self-guide system involving a peer stand-point and another actual self–self-guide system involving a parental standpoint, can themselves be interrelated. As illustrated in Fig. 8.1, now the relation be-tween self-feature X and other-response Y can not only be part of a higher-level system relating self-trait X and the standpoint of a particular other on self-trait X, but this higher-level system can itself be related to another system relating self-trait X and the standpoint of another person on self-trait X.

This new ability of adolescents to represent the relation between two self-systems introduces a new possible pattern of self-beliefs—a self-guide–self-guide discrepancy. For example, a daughter might have a conflict between her personal wish to be assertive and her father's belief that she ought to be passive, which would involve an ideal/own–ought/other discrepancy (see Horney, 1946). Given that adolescents are capable of experiencing such conflicts between others' guides for them, they are motivated to resolve the conflicts. And by searching for solutions to such conflicts adolescents are more likely to construct self-chosen principles to which they are personally committed (see Kohlberg, 1976) and to become conscientious (Loevinger, 1976). Each adolescent can now construct his or her *own* standpoint that is distinct from the standpoint of others and can function as the integrated, coordinated solution to the complex array of alter-native self-guides.

In summary, self-discrepancy theory identifies five major levels in the devel-opment of the self-system (see also Higgins, in press; 1989c; Moretti & Higgins, 1989). A key assumption of the theory is that self-guides are based on a history of social interactions between a child and significant others involving interpersonal contingencies. It is these interactions and representations of self–other con-tingencies that provide the underlying meaning and importance of people's self-attributes. The developmental levels of mental representational capacity are nec-essary conditions for the acquisition of self–other contingency knowledge and self-guides. They are not, however, sufficient conditions. Children must also be exposed to the kinds of information that promote learning of such self-system knowledge. The next section describes how different modes of caretaker–child interaction vary in this regard as well as in the psychological significances that they attach to self-discrepancies.

Modes of Socialization and the Psychological Significance of the Self

To understand how different modes of interaction between children and their significant others produce differences in children's acquisition of self-guides and in the psychological significance of the self, one must consider how a child would acquire strong self-guides (see Higgins, in press, 1989c; Moretti & Higgins, 1989). Strong self-guides are uniform procedural forces of high accessibility and magnitude. If one assumes that the acquisition of self–other contingency knowledge is a function of the same basic factors that determine knowledge acquisition in general, then the following features of children's interactions with their significant others would be expected to influence children's acquisition of self-guides:

1. *Frequency* of exposure to social interactions that instantiate a self–other contingency. The more frequently a child is exposed to instances of a particular type of contingency, the more likely it is that the child will acquire knowledge of the contingency.

2. *Consistency* of the instantiations of a self–other contingency. The more consistently self-feature X and other-response Y are associated and the more consistently other-response Y and self-psychological situation Z are associated, the more likely it is that a child will acquire the contingency.

3. *Clarity* of presentation of the instantiations of a self–other contingency. A contingency is more likely to be acquired if the instantiations present the contingent information clearly and occur under conditions that both draw attention to the contingency event and distinguish it from other events (i.e., make the contingency event salient). A contingency is also more likely to be acquired if the instantiations and communications about the contingency occur under circumstances facilitating comprehension (e.g., without background noise, distractions or disruptions).

4. *Significance* of the instantiations of a self–other contingency. A self–other contingency is more likely to be acquired if the instantiations of the contingency are significant, in the sense that the other-response Y is meaningful and produces a motivationally important self-psychological situation Z.

Type of "Self-Psychological Situation Z" as a function of socialization mode.   As described earlier, a key element of child–caretaker contingent interactions is the self-psychological situation Z that the child experiences as a consequence of the caretaker's other-response Y to the child's self-feature X. This psychological situation of the child is also reflected in the "significance" feature of self–other contingency events by both contributing to the meaning element associated with the other-response Y and providing the importance element. Socialization modes vary in the type of psychological situation they produce in the child.

When a *match* occurs between a child's features and those child features valued by the caretaker, the caretaker is likely to respond to the child in a manner that places the child in a *positive psychological situation* (e.g., hugging, holding, reassuring). When a *mismatch* occurs, the caretaker is likely to respond to the child in a manner that places the child in a *negative psychological situation* (e.g., punishing, criticizing, withholding). Socialization modes vary in the extent to which they involve management sequences (i.e., engineering and planning the child's environment to bring out valued attributes in the child) versus disciplinary sequences. Managing modes produce matches for the child whereas disciplinary modes produce mismatches for the child (see Higgins, in press, 1989c).

Socialization modes also vary in terms of the *type of outcome orientation* that underlies the child's psychological situation:

1. *Presence and absence of positive outcomes*—In this mode, the caretaker responds to the child in such a way that the child experiences either the presence of positive outcomes (a positive psychological situation) or the absence of positive outcomes (a negative psychological situation). For example, a child smiles at the mother, the mother picks up and hugs the child, and the child feels happy (presence of positive outcomes); a child spills some food, the mother stops feeding the child and stops smiling at the child and the child feels sad (absence of positive outcomes).

2. *Presence and absence of negative outcomes*—In this mode, the caretaker responds to the child in such a way that the child experiences either the presence of negative outcomes (a negative psychological situation) or the absence of negative outcomes (a positive psychological situation). For example, a child looks away, the mother plays roughly with the child to get his or her attention, and the child feels scared (presence of negative outcomes); a child cries out in distress, the mother removes the source of distress and reassures the child, and the child now feels safe and secure (the absence of negative outcomes).

Self-discrepancy theory postulates that caretakers who chronically appraise a child in terms of *how they would ideally like the child to be,* in terms of their hopes and aspirations for the child, are likely to respond to the child in a way that the child experiences the presence or absence of positive outcomes. For example, if a child's behavior fails to fulfill (mismatches) a mother's hopes for the child, the mother is likely to feel disappointed in the child and withdraw love and attention from the child, which would cause the child to experience the absence of positive outcomes. In contrast, caretakers who chronically appraise a child in terms of *how they believe the child ought to be,* in terms of their beliefs about the child's duty and obligations, are likely to respond to the child in a way that the child experiences the presence or absence of negative outcomes. For example, if a child's behavior violates (mismatches) what a mother believes the child ought to do, the mother is likely to feel angry at the child and criticize or punish the child, which would cause the child to experience the presence of negative outcomes.

In sum, the psychological significance of people's self-attributes is based on a history of interactions with others. Initially, it is the actual responses of others to children's attributes and the psychological situations these responses produce in the children that instill children's attributes with meaning and importance. Later, it is children's inferences about others' valued end-states for them (hopes or demands) and their beliefs about the consequences of meeting or failing to meet those valued end-states that infuse children's attributes with psychological significance. Still later, it is patterns of self-beliefs that in themselves have psychological significance for older children and adults. Let us turn now to a closer examination of different types of self-belief patterns.

EMOTIONAL/MOTIVATIONAL CONSEQUENCES OF SELF-BELIEF PATTERNS

Self-discrepancy theory initially focused on distinguishing between the actual–ideal discrepancy and actual–ought discrepancy patterns. As discussed earlier, the actual–ideal discrepancy pattern as a whole represents the "absence of positive outcomes." Therefore, for individuals possessing this self-belief pattern, it was hypothesized that when this pattern was activated a person would experience the absence of positive outcomes, which would induce dejection-related emotions. The actual–ought discrepancy as a whole represents the "presence of negative outcomes." For individuals possessing this self-belief pattern, then, it was hypothesized that when this pattern was activated a person would experience the presence of negative outcomes, which would induce agitation-related emotions. These hypotheses have been tested in a number of studies (see Higgins, 1987, 1989a, for fuller reviews).

Distinguishing the Actual–Ideal and Actual–Ought Patterns

In most of our studies, introductory psychology undergraduates filled out a "Selves Questionnaire" that was included in a general battery of measures handed out at the beginning of the semester, and then 6 to 8 weeks later the dependent measures were collected during an experimental session. The Selves Questionnaire simply asks respondents to list up to 8 or 10 attributes for each of a number of different self-states. It is administered in two sections, the first involving the respondent's own standpoint and the second involving the standpoints of the respondent's significant others (e.g., mother, father). On the first page of the questionnaire the different types of selves are defined (e.g., the actual, ideal, and ought self-states). On each subsequent page there is a question about a different self-state, such as "Please list the attributes of the type of person *you* think you *actually* are" or "Please list the attributes of the type of person your *Mother* thinks you *should or ought* to be." The respondents were also asked to rate for each listed attribute the extent to which the standpoint person (self or other) believed they actually possessed that attribute, ought to possess that attribute, wanted them ideally to possess that attribute, and so on. The basic coding procedure for calculating the magnitude of a self-discrepancy involved a two-step procedure:

1. For each self-discrepancy, the attributes in one self-state (e.g., actual/own) were compared with the attributes in the other self-state (e.g., ideal/mother) to determine which attributes were synonyms and which were antonyms according to Roget's thesaurus. Attributes across the two self-states that were neither synonyms or antonyms (i.e., attributes in one self-state that had no relation to the attributes in the other self-state) were considered to be *nonmatches*. Antonyms were considered to be *antonymous mismatches*. Synonyms where the attributes had the same basic extent ratings were considered to be *matches*. Synonyms where the attributes had very different extent ratings (e.g., actual/own: "slightly attractive" versus ideal/mother: "extremely attractive") were considered to be *synonymous mismatches*.

2. The magnitude of self-discrepancy for the two self-states was calculated by summing the total number of mismatches and subtracting the total number of matches.

In order for people to experience the psychological significance associated with a particular self-belief pattern, the self-belief pattern must be activated. As for any stored social knowledge (see Higgins, 1989b; Higgins & King, 1981), there are various factors that can increase the likelihood that a self-belief pattern will be activated. One source of activation is the *applicability* of the self-belief pattern to a stimulus event. Self-discrepancy theory predicts that the psychological significance represented in a self-belief pattern is more likely to be activated when the pattern is applicable to a stimulus event than when it is nonapplicable. This prediction was tested in a study by Higgins, Bond, Klein, and Strauman (1986, Study 1).

Undergraduates were asked to imagine either a positive event in which performance matched a common standard (e.g., receiving a grade of A in a course) or a negative event in which performance failed to match a common standard (e.g., receiving a grade of D in a course that was necessary for obtaining an important job). It was hypothesized that the negative psychological significance represented in an actual–self-guide discrepancy would be applicable to the negative event but not to the positive event. Thus, it was predicted that significant relations between the magnitude of subjects' discrepancies and mood change would be found only when subjects' focused on the negative event. It was also predicted that in the negative event condition, the greater was the magnitude of a particular type of self-belief pattern possessed by an individual, the more he or she would experience the kind of discomfort associated with the psychological significance represented in that pattern—dejection-related emotions (e.g., feeling discouraged, blue, dissatisfied) in the case of actual–ideal discrepancy, and agitation-related emotions (e.g., feeling afraid, desperate) in the case of actual–ought discrepancy.

Subjects' mood was measured both before and after they engaged in imagining the positive or negative event. To measure change in mood, the contribution to subjects' postmanipulation mood from their premanipulation mood was statistically removed. The partial correlational analyses on the mood "change" measures are shown in Table 8.1, where the contribution to the relation between one type of discrepancy and a mood measure from their common association to the other type of discrepancy was also statistically removed. As Table 8.1 shows, the predictions were confirmed. The magnitude and type of subjects' actual–self-guide discrepancies predicted the amount and particular kind of change in mood that they would experience *weeks later*. Moreover, these relations were only clearly evident when subjects focused on an event to which the negative psychological significances represented in the self-belief patterns were applicable (i.e., the negative event condition).

If self-belief patterns are cognitive structures, as hypothesized, then it should also be possible to activate an entire pattern by activating only one of its parts (see Higgins, 1989b). Thus, activation of a self-guide that is part of an actual–self-guide discrepancy should, through spreading activation among interconnected parts (see Collins & Loftus, 1975), be sufficient to activate the whole discrepancy. In addition, the greater the accessibility of a particular type of self-belief pattern, the more likely it is that the individual possessing the pattern will experience the psychological significance represented in that pattern. Thus, if an individual possesses more than one type of self-discrepancy, he or she should experience the emotional/motivational state associated with whichever self-dis-

TABLE 8.1
Partial Correlations Between Types of Self-Discrepancies
and Types of Postmanipulation Mood in the Positive Event
and Negative Event Conditions[1]

	Guided-imagery Manipulation Task			
	Positive Event		Negative Event	
Type of Postmood	Dejection Emotions	Agitation Emotions	Dejection Emotions	Agitation Emotions
Type of Self-discrepancy				
Actual–ideal	.17	.13	.39**	−.33*
Actual–ought	.05	.26#	−.04	.46**

[1]Partial correlations shown have premanipulation mood and the alternative type of self-discrepancy partialled out of each.
#$p < .10$.
*$p < .05$.
**$p < .01$.

crepancy is temporarily more accessible. These predictions were tested in another study by Higgins, Bond, Klein, and Strauman (1986, Study 2).

Undergraduates completed the Selves Questionnaire 4 to 6 weeks before the experimental session. On the basis of their responses, two groups of subjects were recruited for the experiment: (a) Subjects who were relatively high on both actual–ideal discrepancy and actual–ought discrepancy; and (b) Subjects who were relatively low on both types of discrepancies. Ostensibly as part of a life-span developmental study, subjects were asked either to describe the kind of person that they and their parents would ideally like them to be, the attributes that they hoped they would have (the Ideal Priming condition), or to describe the kind of person that they and their parents believed they ought to be, the attributes that they believed it was their duty or obligation to have (the Ought Priming condition). Both before and after this priming manipulation, subjects filled out a mood questionnaire that identified both dejection-related emotions and agitation-related emotions, and subjects rated the extent to which they now were feeling each emotion.

As shown in Table 8.2, the results of the study revealed a significant three-way interaction that was consistent with our predictions. For those subjects that had self-discrepancies available to be activated (i.e., the subjects who were high in both types of self-discrepancies), activation of a self-guide through priming was sufficient to produce an increase in discomfort. Moreover, the kind of discomfort that these subjects experienced depended on which type of self-guide was activated, with subjects experiencing an increase in dejection-related emotions when the Ideal self-guide was activated and an increase in agitation-related emotions when the Ought self-guide was activated.

If self-discrepancy patterns are fully unitized, cognitive structures (see Fiske & Dyer, 1985; Hayes–Roth, 1977), as their hypothesized wholistic nature would suggest, then it should be possible to activate the entire pattern by simply activat-

TABLE 8.2
Mean Change in Dejection-related Emotions
and Agitation-related Emotions as a Function of Level
of Self-Discrepancies and Type of Priming

Self-Discrepancies	Ideal Priming		Ought Priming	
	Dejection	Agitation	Dejection	Agitation
High actual–ideal and actual–ought discrepancies	3.2	−0.8	0.9	5.1
Low actual–ideal and actual–ought discrepancies	−1.2	0.9	0.3	−2.6

Note: Each emotion was measured on a 6-point scale from *not at all* to *a great deal*, and there were eight dejection emotions and eight agitation emotions. The more positive the number the greater the increase in discomfort.

ing a single discrepant attribute in the pattern. Strauman and Higgins (1987) used a covert, idiographic priming technique to activate self-attributes in a task supposedly investigating the "physiological effects of thinking about other people." Subjects were given phrases of the form, "An X person is _____" (where X would be a trait adjective such as "friendly" or "intelligent"), and were asked to complete each sentence as quickly as possible. For each sentence, each subject's total verbalization time and skin conductance amplitude were recorded. Subjects also reported their mood on scales measuring dejection-related and agitation-related emotions at both the beginning and end of the session. Subjects were preselected on the basis of their responses to the Selves Questionnaire obtained weeks before the experimental session. Subjects were selected who were either high in actual–ideal discrepancy and low in actual–ought discrepancy, or high in actual–ought discrepancy and low in actual–ideal discrepancy.

In one of the studies, subjects were primed either with positive self-guide attributes from which subjects' actual-self attributes were discrepant (i.e., priming of *mismatching, self-related* attributes) or with positive attributes that did not appear among subjects' listed actual-self attributes (i.e., priming of *self-unrelated* attributes). (For other comparison and control conditions, see Strauman & Higgins, 1987). This study found a dejection-related syndrome (i.e., mood, skin conductance amplitude, and total verbalization time all changing in the dejection-related direction) for the actual–ideal discrepant subjects and an agitation-related syndrome for the actual–ought discrepant subjects. For the standardized skin conductance amplitude measure and the total verbalization time measure, this study permitted a trial-by-trial analysis of the effects of priming self-related mismatches. These results are shown in Figs. 8.2 and 8.3. As is evident from

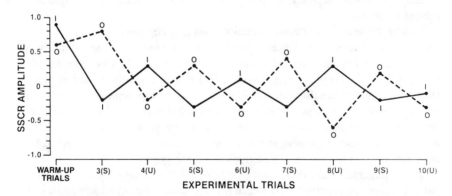

FIG. 8.2. Standardized spontaneous skin conductance response amplitude during warm-up and experimental trials for subjects in the mismatch priming condition. (I = actual/own–ideal/own-discrepant subjects' central tendency. O = actual/own–ought/other-discrepant subjects' central tendency. S = subject-related trial. U = subject-unrelated trial.)

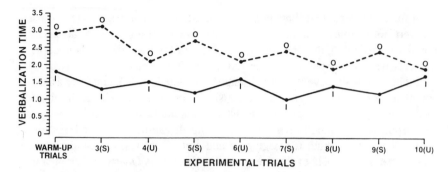

FIG. 8.3. Total verbalization time (in S) during warm-up and experimental trials for subjects in the mismatch priming condition. (I = actual/own–ideal/own- discrepant subjects' central tendency. O = actual/own–ought/other-discrepant subjects' central tendency. S = subject-related trial. U = subject-unrelated trial.)

these figures, there was a striking shift into and out of the syndromes as subjects received subject-related mismatching priming versus subject-unrelated priming, respectively, with the direction of the shifts being opposite for the actual–ideal discrepant subjects than for the actual–ought discrepant subjects as predicted.

These basic findings have recently been replicated by Strauman (1988) in a study using depressed and social phobic clinical samples as well as a "normal" undergraduate sample. The depressed subjects, who had the highest level of actual–ideal discrepancy, generally experienced an increase in the dejection-related syndrome, whereas the social phobic subjects, who had the highest level of actual–ought discrepancy, generally experienced an increase in the agitation-related syndrome.

In sum, these and other correlational studies (see Higgins, 1987, 1989a) have provided considerable evidence supporting the proposal that the actual–ideal discrepancy and actual–ought discrepancy patterns of self-beliefs represent distinct psychological significances associated with distinct emotional/motivational states. The actual–ideal pattern is hypothesized to represent the absence of positive outcomes, and, as would be expected, it has been found to be associated with dejection-related symptoms. The actual–ought pattern is hypothesized to represent the presence of negative outcomes, and, as would be expected, it has been found to be associated with agitation-related symptoms.

Both the actual–ideal discrepancy pattern and the actual–ought discrepancy pattern involve an interrelation between *two self-states*, the actual self and a self-guide. Other mental elements are, however, contained in the mental representation as a whole (see Fig. 8.1). In particular, the inferred consequences of the discrepancy, the self-psychological situation Z, are also represented. This additional, importance element is assumed to contribute to the overall psychological significance of the discrepancy pattern. Indeed, there is some evidence suggesting that people's beliefs about the consequences of possessing a discrepancy may be an additional and critical determinant of the intensity of the emotional/motivational states produced by a discrepancy (see Higgins, 1989a). For example, one study with undergraduates found that the subjects with the highest levels of depression (indeed, the only group who were in the moderately depressed range) were those who possessed *both* a high magnitude of actual–ideal discrepancy and a strong belief concerning the negative interpersonal consequences of possessing a discrepancy (see Higgins, Klein, & Strauman, 1987).

Self-belief patterns are not restricted to those involving interrelations among two self-states. Once individuals reach Level 5 of intellectual development, self-belief patterns can involve interrelations among three or more self-states. One such pattern was briefly described earlier: conflicts between alternative self-guides for the same actual self (see Fig. 8.1). Let us now consider these more complex self-belief patterns involving *interrelations among multiple self-states*. We will begin with considering self-guide–self-guide discrepancies more fully.

Self-guide–Self-guide Discrepancies:
A Multiple Self-state Pattern

As described earlier, by adolescence people become capable of representing a conflict between two self-guide systems. In its simplest form, a discrepancy between two self-guides represents an approach–approach conflict where a person is motivated to reach two valued end-states that cannot be simultaneously approached (see Lewin, 1935), such as being motivated to meet both your own ideal for yourself and your father's ought for you when they are opposite. But meeting one self-guide also means failing to meet the other self-guide. Thus, each of the alternative self-guides has a latent aspect, which is the negative psychological situation associated with failing to meet the alternative self-guide (e.g., punishment from failing to meet one's father's ought for you or disappointment in oneself from failing to meet one's own ideal).

Thus, when self-guides are opposite to each other, a distinct negative psychological situation is created (see Miller, 1944), a double approach–avoidance conflict. The emotional/motivational consequences of possessing this self-belief pattern, then, should be those that are associated with the psychological significance of a double approach–avoidance conflict (see Van Hook & Higgins, 1988). This type of conflict has been associated in the response competition literature with a number of consequences, including vaciilation, blocking, and entrapment in the conflict area (see Epstein, 1978; Heilizer, 1977; Miller, 1959). There would be some motivation to "flee the field" entirely (Lewin, 1935) or to reject one end-state (or self-guide) at a time in order to pursue at least temporarily the alternative end-state.

One might also expect that such a conflict would have long-term consequences for the self-concept. Because there would be vacillation in the predominance of the conflicting self-guides, there would be vacillation or inconsistency
in which self-guide was used for self-evaluation. Given that the self-guides are
opposite, the same attribute would be evaluated as a "success" when one self-
guide was used but as a "failure" when the other self-guide was used, which
over time is likely to yield self-perceptions of possessing only moderate levels of
"mismatching" attributes (i.e., neither a clear success nor a clear failure on the
attribute). Such an effect would be revealed by subjects' extent ratings of those
attributes among their actual-self attributes that also appear in a self-guide–self-
guide mismatch being lower or more moderate than their other actual-self
attributes.

Thus, a conflict between self-guides would be predicted to be associated with
individuals generally feeling confused, muddled, and unsure of themselves and
their goals, with their being distractible and rebellious, and with their having
identity confusion and moderate ratings of the extent to which they possessed
"mismatching" attributes. This cluster of symptoms, in turn, resembles clinical
descriptions of the hysterical personality style (e.g., Horowitz, 1976; Magaro &
Smith, 1981; Shapiro, 1965). Thus, it was also predicted that people who possessed a chronic conflict between self-guides would have higher levels of this
personality disorder than those who did not.

Two studies were conducted to test these predictions (see Van Hook & Higgins, 1988). Undergraduates who possessed self-guide–self-guide discrepancies
were compared with a control group of undergraduates who did not. Each of the
predicted relations between possessing self-guide–self-guide discrepancies and
suffering from *confusion-related* and hysterical personality symptoms was confirmed. Moreover, through the use of both statistical and sampling methods,
these relations were shown to be independent of both subjects' level of other
kinds of emotional /motivational problems (i.e., dejection-related, agitation-
related, anger-related problems) and their level of both actual–ideal discrepancy
and actual–ought discrepancy. Thus, self-guide–self-guide discrepancy is a distinctive self-belief pattern that predicts vulnerability to a distinct emo-
tional/motivational syndrome.

All the self-belief patterns considered so far have involved beliefs about two
or more of the following self-states: (a) the Actual self; (b) the Ideal self; and (c)
the Ought self. But these are not the only self-state beliefs. Two additional self-
state beliefs that may also be involved in self-belief patterns are beliefs about the
kind of person one has the potential to be and beliefs about the kind of person one
will be in the future. Let us now consider these two new self-beliefs, their
involvement in some new multiple self-state patterns, and the distinct psychological significances of these new patterns.

Self-belief Patterns Involving the Can and Future Selves

Descriptions of self-beliefs in the literature have not been restricted to the self-concept (the current actual self) or to self-guides. The literature has also described people's beliefs about what they can and cannot do and people's beliefs about what type of person they might become or expect to become. These "potential" (James 1890/1948) or "possible" (Markus and Nurius, 1987) actual selves have been described as having important motivational effects (Bandura, 1982; Markus & Nurius, 1986; for a review, see Markus & Wurf, 1987). Previous models, however, have not considered the psychological significance of the *relations* between these types of self-beliefs and other types of self-beliefs. In addition, previous models have rarely *distinguished* between the emotional /motivational vulnerabilities associated with these types of self-beliefs and those associated with other types of "possible" selves, such as imaginary or fantasized selves (see Freud, 1923/1961; Levinson, 1978). Indeed, as Markus and Nurius (1986) point out, until recently it has even been unusual for these types of self-beliefs to be directly measured.

In order to consider the implications of these additional types of self-beliefs, self-discrepancy theory has recently been expanded to include the following two self-domains:

1. The *Can* self, which is your representation of the attributes that someone (yourself or another) believes you can possess (i.e., a representation of someone's beliefs about your capabilities or potential).

2. The *Future* self, which is your representation of the attributes that someone (yourself or another) believes you are likely to possess in the future (i.e., a representation of someone's expectations about the type of person you will become).

The Can self and the Future self are *not* two additional self-guides. Indeed, some people possess Can and Future selves that are discrepant from the end-states they value (e.g., they do not believe that they have the potential to fulfill their Ideal). The Can and Future self are also not the same as the actual self. Some people believe that their potential or future self is quite different from their current self. Rather than representing either a current self-state or a valued end-state, the Can and Future selves represent a view of actual-self attributes that a person does not possess but possibly could possess—*self-possibilities*.

Although previous descriptions of the self have included these types of self-beliefs (e.g., Bandura, 1982; Markus & Nurius, 1986), no previous model of the self to our knowledge has explicitly distinguished among the actual, can, and future self-state representations to make differentiated predictions concerning how their relations to other self-beliefs produce vulnerabilities. Markus and Nurius (1986) assessed both subjects' "now" self and their "probable possible self," which are most similar to the actual self and future self, respectively. A separate can self was not assessed and how the *relations* among these self-state representations was associated with emotional/motivational problems was not examined.

Bandura (e.g., 1982) identifies perceived self-efficacy as a motivational factor and distinguishes it from actual capabilities or actual performance. It is not clear whether "perceived self-efficacy" as a self-belief is more similar to the can self or the future self as defined here. Bandura (1982) describes this self-belief as an appraisal of one's own capabilities and as a judgment about how well one can organize and execute a course of action. Although this description sounds closer to the can self, other descriptions suggest that it is one's expectations of personal agency that is being judged, which would bring the concept closer to the future self. In any case, the can self and the future self are not differentially related to other self-beliefs to predict distinct emotional/motivational predispositions.

The purpose of including distinct can and future selves in self-discrepancy theory was to identify new self-belief patterns that were associated with specific vulnerabilities. As described earlier, an actual–ideal discrepancy is a two-element relation representing the subjective belief that one's current attributes have chronically failed to fulfill one's hopes, wishes, or aspirations. This relation represents the general psychological situation of "absence of positive outcomes." This general psychological situation, in turn, is associated with dejection-related feelings. If one added a third element to this relation, creating a multiple-element pattern, would this general psychological situation take on a more specific meaning? And, if so, would different kinds of dejection-related feelings be associated with different multiple-element patterns that varied in which particular third element was added? We felt that addressing these questions for the actual–ideal relation was especially interesting and important because the voluminous literature on self-esteem has traditionally focused on this particular relation without considering the implications of adding additional elements to it.

If one considered just the can self alone, one would expect that the greater the subjective positivity of the can self, the more positive a person would feel. From this perspective, one might expect that people with high actual–ideal discrepancy would be better off if they at least had can–ideal congruence than if they also had high can–ideal discrepancy. This expectation, however, is based on an "elementistic" logic which assumes that the independent significances of the pair of two-element relations—level of actual–ideal discrepancy and level of can–ideal discrepancy—can be simply combined.

In contrast, self-discrepancy theory follows an "holistic" logic (see Higgins & Rholes, 1976). From this holistic perspective, what is critical is the psychological significance of the pattern as a whole, the multiple-element interrelation among the actual, ideal, and can selves. How does the psychological significance of an actual–ideal discrepancy change when a can self-belief element is added to the pattern? Because the psychological significance of chronic failure to meet one's ideal depends on the meaning of such failure, it is necessary to consider how the relation of the can self to the actual and ideal selves changes the meaning of an actual–ideal discrepancy. Let us consider, then, the psychological significance of an actual–ideal discrepancy when the relation of the can self to the actual and ideal selves varies:

(a) Actual–can congruency with can–ideal discrepancy [A = C < I]: A can–ideal discrepancy (i.e., C < I) represents the subjective belief that one's ideal self is beyond one's capability, that one does not have the potential to meet one's ideal. But an actual–can congruency (i.e., A = C) represents the subjective belief that one is at least fulfilling one's potential. As a whole, then, this pattern of self-beliefs represents the psychological situation of fulfillment of limited potential.

(b) Actual–can discrepancy with can–ideal congruency [A < C(=I)]: A can–ideal congruency (i.e., C = I) represents the subjective belief that one has the capability, the potential to meet one's ideal. Given this relation between the can and ideal selves, the can self takes on the meaning of one's positive potential. But the actual self is perceived as being discrepant from the can self (i.e., A < C). As a whole, then, this pattern of self-beliefs represents the psychological situation of chronic failure to meet one's positive potential.

As described, the psychological situation represented by each of these patterns is somewhat unpleasant. This is to be expected given that both patterns involve the general "absence of positive outcomes" represented by an actual–ideal discrepancy. But when one considers the more specific meaning represented by each pattern as a whole, the "A < C(=I)" pattern is more unpleasant than the "A = C < I" pattern despite the can self as an independent element being more positive in the "A < C(=I)" pattern. This is because the "A = C < I" pattern as a whole represents fulfillment of one's potential even though the potential is limited, whereas the "A = C < I" pattern as a whole represents a chronic failure to meet one's positive potential. Indeed, the psychological situation of believing that one has failed to meet one's positive potential has been associated with depression in the clinical literature (e.g., Blatt, D'Afflitti, & Quinlan, 1976). And Bandura (1986) suggests that people with high self-perceived capability who experience repeated failure are especially likely to become depressed.

Thus, contrary to what one would predict from an elementistic perspective, we predicted that possession of an "A < C(=I)" pattern would be associated with greater dejection-related emotions than possession of an "A = C < I" pattern. This prediction was initially tested in a study by Higgins and Tykocinsky

(1987; see Higgins, 1989a). As part of filling out the Selves Questionnaire, subjects were asked to "list the attributes of the type of person *you* think you *can* be" (after being asked to list their actual self-attributes and before listing their ideal self-attributes). Thus, it was possible to identify different patterns by measuring both subjects' can–ideal and actual–can discrepancies (the actual, can, and ideal selves all involved the "own" standpoint). For example, when people's can self is congruent with their ideal self (i.e., C = I) but their actual self is discrepant from their can self (i.e., A < C), then they possess an actual–ideal discrepancy involving the "A < C(=I)" pattern.

The results indicated that the *smaller* was subjects' can–ideal discrepancies, the *higher* was their level of depression as measured weeks later by the Beck Depression Inventory, $r(60) = -.39$, $p = .001$. The subjects' beliefs that they possessed "positive" capabilities, then, was associated with suffering! As just discussed, self-discrepancy theory would predict this relation to the extent that people were especially likely to suffer from depression and dejection if they possessed both a can–ideal congruency *and* an actual–can discrepancy (i.e., "I have the capacity to be the kind of person that I would ideally like to be, but I am *not* fulfilling my potential"). A simultaneous multiple regression analysis including as factors can–ideal discrepancy, actual–can discrepancy, and their interaction, revealed that the interaction between can–ideal discrepancy and actual–can discrepancy was indeed uniquely related to depression and chronic dejection-related emotions as measured weeks later.

To clarify the nature of this interaction, median splits were performed on the scores for each type of discrepancy and the scores of the high and low subjects for each type of discrepancy were averaged. As shown in Table 8.3, a low level of can–ideal discrepancy (i.e., can–ideal congruency) combined with a high level of actual–can discrepancy, which constitutes the "A < C(=I)" pattern representing "chronic failure to meet one's (positive) potential," was predictive of the highest levels of depression and chronic dejection-related emotions.

In a recent study by the present authors, the prediction that the "A < C(=I)" pattern would be associated with greater suffering than the "A = C < I" pattern was tested more directly. This study also examined other actual–ideal discrepancy patterns involving the *future* self as the additional element. A major goal of this study was to consider whether the psychological significance of actual–ideal discrepancy patterns would vary depending on the particular type of self-possibility that was added to the actual–ideal relation (i.e., the can self versus the future self). Might it be that actual–ideal discrepancies would be associated with *different kinds of dejection-related problems*, depending on whether the pattern as a whole included a can self-belief or a future self-belief as the third element?

To begin with, let us consider the psychological significance of an actual–ideal discrepancy when a *future* self-belief element is added to the pattern that is either congruent with or discrepant from the ideal:

(a) Actual–ideal discrepancy with future–ideal discrepancy [A < I(>F)]: A

TABLE 8.3
Means of Symptoms Involving Interactions of Can–Ideal
and Actual–Can Discrepancies in Predicting Depression (BDI)
and Dejection[a]

	High Can–Ideal		Low Can–Ideal	
	High Actual–Can	Low Actual–Can[c]	High Actual–Can[d]	Low Actual–Can
Depression (BDI)	8.2	9.3	19.9	8.3
Overall dejection[b]	1.6	1.5	2.6	1.5
(Feeling) low	0.8	1.3	2.4	1.1
Disappointed	1.3	1.8	2.7	1.5
(Not) happy	1.8	1.8	2.6	1.4
(Not) satisfied	1.7	2.1	3.2	1.8
(Not) optimistic	1.7	1.8	2.7	1.9

[a]The table includes only those interactions of can–ideal and actual–can discrepancies that are significant ($p < .05$) when level of actual–ideal discrepancy is statistically controlled.

[b]All emotions were rated on scale from 0 (almost never) to 4 (almost always). (Can–ideal = can/own–ideal/own discrepancy; Actual–Can = actual/own–can/own discrepancy; Actual–ideal = actual/own–ideal/own discrepancy).

[c]This combination—low actual–can (actual–can congruency) with high can–ideal (can–ideal discrepancy)—constitutes the "A = C < I" pattern.

[d]This combination—high actual–can (actual–can discrepancy) with low can–ideal (can–ideal congruency)—constitutes the "A < C(=I)" pattern.

future–ideal discrepancy represents the subjective belief that one will not reach one's ideal in the future. The ideal is a desired end-state that one does not expect to attain. Given this relation between the ideal and future selves, the ideal self takes on the meaning of a "wish." As a whole, then, this pattern of self-beliefs represents the psychological situation of doing less well than wished for but not less than expected.

(b) Actual–ideal discrepancy with future–ideal congruency [A < I(=F)]: A future–ideal congruency represents the subjective belief that one's ideal is a desired end-state that one *does* expect to attain. Given this relation between the ideal and future selves, the ideal self takes on the meaning of a "hope." As a whole, then, this pattern of self-beliefs represents the psychological situation of chronically unfulfilled hopes.

It is likely that each of these psychological situations would be unpleasant, once again because they both involve the general negative psychological situation of the "absence of positive outcomes." But when one considers the more specific meaning of each pattern, the "A < I(=F)" pattern is likely to be more unpleasant than the "A < I(>F)" pattern. For the "A < I(=F)" pattern, the "absence of positive outcomes" involves not just a failure to meet desires but a chronic thwarting of hopes because the desires are expected to be attained. For the "A < I(>F)" pattern on the other hand, the "absence of positive outcomes" also involves a failure to meet desires, but these desires are only wishes because they are not expected to be attained. Unfulfilled hopes are likely to produce more suffering than unfulfilled wishes.

Consistent with this analysis, Bandura (1986) suggests that people feel disappointed when there are wide disparities between their current level of performance and their lofty future standards (see also Mandler's [1982] discussion of disconfirmed expectancies). Olson and Ross (1984) found in a couple of experiments that moderately high hopes (from a perception of abundant resources) combined with a negative actual self involving low perceived ability to fulfill the hopes (from a perception of low qualifications) yielded especially high levels of feelings of deprivation. Heider (1958) suggests that "hope" arises when people believe that a desired object will come within their reach, when they expect to obtain a desired object in the future. When hopes are not fulfilled, people feel disappointed, and when hopes are chronically unfulfilled people feel despondent (see Heider, 1958). In contrast, a "wish" arises when people do not necessarily expect a desired object but believe that its obtainment is possible, when they believe that with luck they might obtain it (Heider, 1958). Unfulfilled wishes produce frustration, but the amount of frustration decreases as the perceived possibility of fulfilling one's wishes decreases (Heider, 1958). Therefore, since the perceived possibility of fulfilling one's wishes would be low for people possessing the "A < I(>F)" pattern (i.e., the evidence from chronic past unfulfillment does not support the possibility of a favorable future outcome), the amount of frustration associated with this pattern should be low.

The prediction that the "A < I(=F)" pattern would be associated with greater discomfort than the "A < I (>F)" pattern was also tested in our recent study. Undergraduates in the introductory psychology course answered the Selves Questionnaire as part of a battery of questionnaires that they filled out at the beginning of the term. In this questionnaire, the can and future selves were defined as follows:

(a) The *Can* self—the attributes that you believe you can possess; your capabilities or potential.

(b) The *Future* self—the attributes that you believe you are likely to possess in the future; the type of person you believe you *will* actually become.

Our procedure for calculating self-discrepancy patterns in this study was more configurational than that used in our previous studies. For each of the four types of actual–ideal discrepancy patterns described—the "A = C < I" pattern, the "A < C(=I)" pattern, the "A < I(>F)" pattern, and the "A < I(=F)" pattern—a subjects's attribute responses to all three self-belief elements in a particular pattern were considered together (the actual, ideal, can, and future selves all involved the "own" standpoint). To calculate the "A < I(=F)" pattern, for example, a subjects's list of attributes for the ideal self was compared with their list of attributes for the future self and those attributes were identified for which there was a match between the future and ideal selves. A discrepancy score between these attributes and the attributes listed for the actual self (i.e., mismatches minus matches) was then calculated in the same way as our standard method for calculating self-discrepancy scores.

The rationale underlying this method of calculating self-discrepancies involves first identifying self-belief attributes that have a particular meaning as defined by a specific relation to another self-belief (e.g., an ideal-self attribute that is a "hope" as defined by its matching a future-self attribute; a can-self attribute that is a "positive potential" as defined by its matching an ideal-self attribute). Then, the overall discrepancy (mismatches minus matches) between the attributes listed in the actual self and those attributes listed in the ideal self or the can self that have this particular meaning is hypothesized to have the psychological significance of nonobtainment of this type of self-state (e.g., chronically unfulfilled hopes; chronic failure to meet one's positive potential).

As discussed earlier, we predicted that the "A < I(=F)" pattern would be more strongly related to dejection-related suffering than the "A < I(>F)" pattern. This prediction was confirmed. As shown in Table 8.4, on a general measure of depression (the Beck Depression Inventory) as well as on a number of more specific dejection-related emotions and beliefs, the "A < I(=F)" pattern was more strongly correlated with suffering than the "A < I(>F)" pattern, even though both patterns involve an actual–ideal discrepancy. Indeed, when the contribution of the alternative pattern to the relation between a particular pattern and dejection measure was statistically removed (the partial correlations in the

TABLE 8.4
Predictive Relations to Dejection-related Symptoms and Beliefs
of Two Types of Actual–Ideal Discrepancy Patterns Involving
the Future Self—the "A < I(>F)" Pattern and the "A < I(=F)" Pattern

Symptoms and Beliefs	Zero-order Correlations		Partial Correlations	
	A < I(>F)	A < I(=F)	A < I(>F)	A < I(=F)
BDI	.19*	.41***	.18	.41***
Feeling sad	.02	.36***	−.01	.36***
Feeling discouraged	.05	.32**	.04	.31**
Feeling frustrated	−.01	.29**	−.02	.29**
Feeling disappointed	.11	.31**	.11	.30**
Hopeless	−.05	.33**	−.07	.33**
Regretful	−.01	.28**	−.02	.28**

$*p < .05.$
$**p < .01.$
$***p < .001.$

right half of Table 8.4), it is evident that only the "A < I(=F)" pattern was uniquely associated with dejection-related suffering.

Previous studies have not directly compared the "A < I(=F)" and "A < I(>F)" patterns in regard to their association with dejection-related feelings. The Olson and Ross (1984) experiments on feelings of deprivation mentioned earlier, however, did find an intriguing pattern of results that is generally consistent with our findings. In these experiments, half of the subjects perceived that they were unqualified with respect to a particular area of performance. These subjects, then, might be considered to possess a negative actual self in relation to their aspirations (i.e., an actual–ideal discrepancy). Half of these subjects believed that the opportunity for obtaining their valued end-state was good (abundant resources) and half believed that the opportunity was poor (scarce resources). Consistent with our findings, the former subjects had higher hopes but experienced greater feelings of deprivation than the latter subjects.

Our recent study also retested the prediction that the "A < C(=I)" pattern would be more strongly associated with dejection-related suffering than the "A = C < I" pattern. As shown in Table 8.5, this prediction was again confirmed.

TABLE 8.5
Predictive Relations to Dejection-related Symptoms and Beliefs
of Two Types of Actual–Ideal Discrepancy Patterns Involving
the Can Self—the "A < C(=I)" Pattern and the "A = C < I" Pattern

Symptoms and Beliefs	Zero-order Correlations		Partial Correlations	
	A = C < I	A < C(=I)	A = C < I	A < C(=I)
BDI	.25*	.36***	−.01	.27**
Feel like a failure	.14	.35***	.15	.35***
Not satisfied with myself and my accomplishments	.11	.24*	−.08	.23*
Have to push myself to do anything	.18	.43***	−.17	.42***
(Not) Driven	−.03	.30**	−.08	.27**
(Not) Alert	.09	.21*	−.08	.21*
Listless	.25*	.31**	.05	.20*
(Not) Energetic	.09	.28**	−.14	.30**
There is something wrong with me that prevents me from fulfilling my potential	.08	.26**	−.14	.28**
(Not) Self-controlled	.12	.23*	−.05	.20*
Helpless	.17	.33***	−.08	.30**

*$p < .05$.
**$p < .01$.
***$p < .001$.

Indeed, the partial correlations (shown in the right half of Table 8.5) indicate that only the "A < C(=I)" pattern was uniquely associated in general with dejection-related emotions and beliefs.

These results indicate that different types of actual–ideal discrepancy patterns vary in their strength of association to dejection-related suffering, depending on the specific relation of the third self-belief element to the ideal self. Interestingly, for actual–ideal discrepancy patterns involving either the can self or the future self as the third element, the pattern is associated with greater dejection-related suffering when the third element itself is *more* positive in the sense of being congruent with rather than discrepant from the ideal self. This is because the can self or the future self combines with the ideal self to define a positive end-state, which makes chronic nonattainment of this state all the more distressing. When self-possibilities (i.e., the can and future selves) match the ideal self, the end-state combinations have both positivity and subjective reality. This in turn may increase commitment to the end-state. Thus, nonattainment of such end-states produces greater discomfort. Once again, this highlights the importance of considering the significance of the pattern as a whole rather than the significance of the independent elements contained in the pattern.

When one considers the specific meaning of each actual–ideal discrepancy pattern as a whole, the "A < C(=I)" and the "A < I(=F)" patterns appear to be especially problematical, as discussed earlier. The "A < C(=I)" pattern as a whole represents the negative psychological situation of "chronic failure to meet (positive) potential." The "A < I(=F)" pattern as a whole represents the negative psychological situation of "chronically unfulfilled hopes." As predicted, our study found that these patterns were strongly associated with dejection-related suffering. But the logic of self-discrepancy theory makes an even stronger prediction. The theory predicts that even though both the "A < C(=I)" pattern and the "A < I(=F)" pattern involve an actual–ideal discrepancy, and even though both patterns are expected to be strongly associated with dejection-related emotions and beliefs, these two patterns should be associated with *different* kinds of dejection-related emotions and beliefs because the specific meanings of these patterns are different.

The "A < C(=I)" pattern should be associated with dejection-related symptoms that reflect the negative psychological situation of "chronic failure to meet (positive) potential" whereas the "A < I(=F)" pattern should be associated with dejection-related symptoms that reflect the negative psychological situation of "chronically unfulfilled hopes." Table 8.6 shows the results of a direct comparison of the correlations of the "A < C(=I)" and "A < I(=F)" patterns with dejection-related emotions and beliefs. The partial correlations shown on the right half of Table 8.6 reveal that, as predicted, each pattern was uniquely associated with those particular dejection-related emotions and beliefs that reflected its specific negative psychological situation. At the same time, both patterns were independently associated with overall depression as measured by

TABLE 8.6
Predictive Relations to Dejection-related Symptoms and Beliefs
of Two Types of Actual–Ideal Discrepancy Patterns Involving
the Can Self Versus the Future Self—the "A < C(=I)" Pattern
and the "A < I(=F)" Pattern

Symptoms and Beliefs	Zero-order Correlations		Partial Correlations	
	A < C(=I)	A < I(=F)	A < C(=I)	A < I(=F)
BDI	.36***	.41***	.18	.27**
Feel like a failure	.35***	.31**	.22*	.15
Not satisfied with myself and my accomplishments	.24*	.02	.27**	−.14
Have to push myself to do anything	.43***	.33**	.31**	.13
(Not) Driven	.30**	.13	.28**	−.04
(Not) Alert	.21*	.02	.24*	−.12
Listless	.31**	.21*	.24*	.05
(Not) Energetic	.28**	.19*	.21*	.05
There is something wrong with me that prevents me from fulfilling my potential	.26**	−.06	.36***	−.26**
(Not) Self-controlled	.23*	.11	.20*	−.02
Helpless	.33***	.30**	.21*	.15
Feeling sad	.17	.36***	−.04	.33**
Feeling discouraged	.25*	.32**	.09	.22*
Feeling frustrated	.25*	.29**	.11	.19*
Feeling disappointed	.23*	.31**	.08	.22*
Hopeless	.19*	.33**	.02	.27**
Regretful	.13	.28**	−.03	.25*

*p < .05.
**p < .01.
***p < .001.

the Beck Depression Inventory, although the partial correlation was only borderline significant ($p < .10$) for the "A < C(=I)" pattern.

Consistent with its specific meaning of "chronic failure to meet (positive) potential," the "A < C(=I)" pattern was uniquely associated with "feeling like a failure," *not* feeling "satisfied with myself and my accomplishments," believing that "there is something wrong with me that prevents me from fulfilling my potential," feeling "listless," helpless," and so on. Consistent with its specific meaning of "chronically unfulfilled hopes," the "A < I(=F)" pattern was uniquely associated with feeling "disappointed," "discouraged," "hopeless," and so on.

What is rather remarkable about these two sets of unique correlations is that they clearly distinguish two kinds of dejection—a "feeling weak" (e.g., helpless; listless) kind of dejection and a "feeling despondent" (e.g., hopeless; discouraged) kind of dejection. And these two distinct kinds of dejection were found to be uniquely associated with two actual–ideal discrepancy patterns that differ only in the content of the additional self-belief element—the can self and the future self, respectively. Moreover, these distinct sets of unique correlations make sense psychologically. The "feeling weak" kind of dejection was found to be uniquely associated with the "A < C(=I)" pattern that was hypothesized to reflect the negative psychological situation of "chronic failure to meet (positive) potential." And the "feeling despondent" kind of dejection was found to be uniquely associated with the "A < I(=F)" pattern that was hypothesized to reflect the negative psychological situation of "chronically unfulfilled hopes."

In sum, the results of our recent study demonstrate the importance of moving beyond "two-element" patterns to "multiple-element" patterns in identifying self-belief interrelations with psychological significance. Four different patterns were examined that all involved an actual–ideal discrepancy. And yet it was the specific relation of the third self-belief element to the ideal self that determined the psychological significance of the actual–ideal discrepancy. Vulnerability to dejection-related suffering was greatest when either the can self or the future self matched the ideal self and the actual self was chronically discrepant from the positive end-state defined by this match.

The results of this study also demonstrate that the content of the third self-belief element is a further determinant of the particular significance of the actual–ideal multiple-element pattern. Given the presence of the basic actual–ideal discrepancy, both patterns include "the absence of positive outcomes" as part of their general meaning. And, as predicted, both patterns were associated with vulnerability to dejection-related suffering. But the particular psychological significance of the pattern varies, depending on whether the meaning of the positive end-state is defined by the ideal self matching the can self or the future self. When the can self matches the ideal self in an actual–ideal discrepancy, the psychological significance of the pattern as a whole is "chronic failure to meet (positive) potential," and this pattern is associated specifically with vulnerability to a "feeling weak" syndrome. When the future self matches the ideal self in an actual–ideal discrepancy, the psychological significance of the pattern as a whole is "chronically unfulfilled hopes," and this pattern is associated specifically with vulnerability to a "feeling despondent" syndrome.

IMPLICATIONS AND CONCLUSIONS

This chapter has considered the chronic psychological significances associated with the self-system. Two basic assumptions of self-discrepancy theory (Higgins, 1987, 1989a) are that people have interrelations among their self-beliefs that function like cognitive-structural units, and that these cognitive-structural units have both meaning and importance, that is, *psychological significance,* to those who possess them. The theory proposes that people's interpretation and evaluation of self-relevant life events, whether past, present or future, are influenced by these self-system structural units. Thus, the same event can produce different emotional and motivational responses in different people or even in the same person at different times depending on which particular type of self-belief *pattern* is activated by the event. This proposal has received considerable support. There is now substantial evidence that different types of self-belief patterns are associated with vulnerability to distinct kinds of emotional and motivational problems. The fact that independent self-beliefs can become interrelated to form psychologically significant patterns has a number of theoretical and practical implications that need to be considered.

An important implication of the notion that people possess self-belief patterns with psychological significance is that the psychological significance of an event would not depend solely on the features of the event itself (e.g., low score on a test necessary to pass in order to graduate) and its interpretation as a single event (e.g., "I could have passed this test if I had studied harder for it"). Rather, the psychological significance of an event, and thus its emotional and motivational consequences, would also depend on whether the event activated a pattern of self-beliefs that placed the event into a broader framework that went beyond the information available in this single instance. Indeed, the broader framework provided by self-belief patterns could change the psychological significance of an event.

There is considerable evidence, for example, that when people have failed on a particular task, especially a relatively novel task, their subsequent motivation on the task will often be higher if they believe they can succeed on the task than if they believe they cannot succeed (see Bandura, 1986). In momentary situations, the belief that one has the capability to fulfill one's goal despite having just failed to do so has been found to produce a more positive emotional/motivational state than the belief that one does not have the capability to fulfill one's goal. In such momentary situations it is possible to consider one's current performance as being just temporary and thus direct one's attention away from the performance to the relation between one's goal and one's capability to fulfill the goal. When performance capability is perceived to match the goal, a person could simply focus on his or her positive potential. But the "A < C(=I)" self-belief pattern represents a chronic rather than a momentary situation. The actual-self element in the pattern is a summary representation of many past performance outcomes and thus cannot be perceived as simply temporary. It is likely, then, that the actual-self element will be considered together with the can and ideal elements. When "positive potential" is considered together with chronic failure to meet it, the significance of the total pattern becomes "chronic failure to meet (positive) potential," which is experienced as unpleasant.

Therefore, if people who possessed the "A < C(=I)" self-belief pattern perceived the momentary event as an instance of the more general psychological situation represented by this pattern, the significance of the event would change. We predict that they would experience the "feeling weak" syndrome. This syndrome definitely involves unpleasant feelings. The motivational consequences of experiencing such feelings is less clear, however. These feelings could increase motivation on the task because success on the task would reduce the discrepancy and thus improve the emotional state. Moreover, the "C = I" positive potential unit could itself increase motivation (see Bandura, 1986). High-need achievers may experience precisely this combination of negative feelings but increased motivation (see Higgins et al., 1986). It is also possible that when the unpleasant feelings are intense, people might deal just with the feelings themselves (e.g., distract themselves from the unpleasant task) rather than try to reduce the underlying self-discrepancy. In such cases, motivation to perform the task could be impaired. Thus, the possible motivational consequences of perceiving the momentary event as an instance of the more general "A < C(=I)" pattern need to be distinguished from the likely emotional consequences.

Even for people who did not initially possess the "A < C(=I)" self-belief pattern, if they failed on a task continuously over a prolonged period, it is likely that they would begin to focus on their stable performance together with the other self-belief elements and thus begin to experience the negative psychological significance associated with this pattern. People who did possess the self-belief pattern would be expected both to need less instances of failure to begin to experience failure in terms of this negative psychological significance and to experience the significance more intensely.

A similar case can be made with respect to the future self. In a momentary situation, the expectancy that one *will* meet one's goal in the future despite having just failed to do so is likely to produce a more positive emotional /motivational state than the belief that one will never meet one's goal. If a single performance is considered to be just temporary, then a perceived match between future performance and goal could be the focus of attention. This perception would produce the pleasant state of "hope." But this momentary situation could be perceived as an instance of the more general psychological situation of "chronically unfulfilled hopes" represented by the "A < I(=F)" self-belief pattern. If people who possessed an "A < I(=F)" pattern perceived this single event in terms of this more general psychological situation, we predict that they would experience the "feeling despondent" syndrome. Such feelings are definitely unpleasant. But, once again, the motivation to perform the task could be either enhanced or impaired, depending on the intensity of the distress and how the distress is dealt with.

People who possess the "A < I(=F)" pattern experience the "feeling despondent" syndrome that includes feeling less hope. Some people suffer so intensely from this pattern that they apparently give up the "I = F" unit as a way of dealing with it. When people give up this unit, they abandon "hope" entirely. Thus, feeling "hopeless" in the sense of feeling less hope or feeling discouraged needs to be distinguished from the feeling of hopelessness that people experience when they have no hope at all. When hope is abandoned entirely, people move from feeling despondent to feeling complete despair (see Heider, 1958). People who give up the "I = F" unit may actually be less likely to suffer such self-evaluative emotions as "disappointment" because they are less likely to judge themselves in reference to this unit, to compare their current state with their hopes. This solution to suffering, then, may have some self-evaluative benefits. But this solution also has the major self-regulatory cost of reducing motivation, purpose, and meaning in life, which produces a unique kind of suffering associated with severe depression.

One might wonder why people with the "A < I(=F)" pattern who chronically fail to fulfill their positive self-expectancies and their hopes, do not simply lower their expectancies. After all, it is normal to lower expectancies after repeated failure (see Bandura, 1986). Moreover, it would be more realistic to do so, and these people would suffer less if their self-expectancies were more realistic. It may be, in fact, that some of the individuals with the "A < I(>F)" pattern are people who previously possessed the "A < I(=F)" pattern but eventually lowered their expectancies. Those individuals with the "A < I(=F)" pattern who do not lower their expectancies despite continual failure may have a history of interpersonal relations that has led them to believe that others' love and respect depends on their maintaining high hopes for themselves. For example, a woman may have a history of interaction with her parents in which the parents relate most positively to her when they focus on the positive end-state that they expect she will attain in the future. To avoid conflict and unpleasantness, the woman must incorporate these positive self-expectancies into her own system even if they are unrealistic. The woman may believe that a positive relationship with her parents (and, perhaps, with others as well) depends on her accepting and maintaining these high hopes for her. Under these circumstances, a person may not be willing to give up his or her hopes even after repeated failure and suffering.

It is also possible that individuals who believe that they are making *progress* toward meeting their ideal self would not suffer as much from unfulfilled positive self-expectancies. Because they believe that they are making progress, that their actual self is improving, such individuals would not possess a stable actual-self representation. As their actual-self representation is not stable, they could possess the "I(=F)" component of the "A < I(=F)" pattern but would not possess the whole pattern as a chronic structure. Thus, our model would predict that they would not suffer to the same extent as those who did possess this pattern as a chronic structure.

The notion that people possess psychologically significant *patterns* of self-beliefs that increase vulnerability to different kinds of suffering has implications as well for treating people with emotional/motivational problems. Cognitive-behavioral perspectives on therapeutic intervention have tended to emphasize the importance of changing people's negative or irrational beliefs, cognitions, and attitudes (e.g., Beck, Rush, Shaw, & Emery, 1979; Ellis, 1962). Such beliefs, cognitions, and attitudes typically are treated, both conceptually and therapeutically, as independent units. There are some serious limitations with this "elementistic" approach.

First, focusing on the negativity of independent self-beliefs rather than on the negative relations between self-beliefs can be inefficient. For example, not all negative actual-self attributes are psychologically significant. Moretti and Higgins (in press) found, for instance, that individuals' negative actual-self attributes predicted low self-esteem only when the attributes were also discrepant from the individuals' ideal self. Thus, intervention would be more efficient if it concentrated on self-beliefs involved in actual self–self-guide discrepancies rather than simply on negative self-beliefs. In addition, it would be reasonable to focus on self-beliefs involved in actual self–ideal discrepancies when patients suffer mostly from a dejection syndrome and to focus on self-beliefs involved in actual self–ought discrepancies when patients suffer mostly from an agitation syndrome. By distinguishing between these and other specific types of self-belief relations, even greater efficiency might be achieved.

Second, identifying functional and dysfunctional self-beliefs in terms of their positivity and negativity as independent elements could lead to errors in intervention. Imagine, for example, a male client who describes himself as having few skills and low potential and another female client who describes herself as being highly capable and having high potential. Both clients are performing quite well in their various roles but are nevertheless seriously depressed. From a strict cognitive-behavioral perspective, the male client's poor view of his capabilities and potential might be seen as a problem that needs to be addressed whereas the female client's positive view of her capabilities and potential might be seen as a positive indicator that could be strengthened and used to improve her condition. For example, the female client might be reminded of her own positive view of her capability in order to provide evidence against her current claim that she is worthless.

Such an approach would be reasonable when considering these self-beliefs alone. But when these self-beliefs are considered in relation to other self-beliefs, different self-belief patterns could be identified that would lead to very different conclusions. It may be, for example, that the female client's can self is an element in an "$A < C(=I)$" self-belief pattern whereas the male's can self is an element in an "$A = C < I$" self-belief pattern. Thus the can self could be more problematical for the female client than the male client. By considering how a particular self-belief is related to other self-beliefs, it is possible to determine its true psychological significance for the client. The key question for intervention is whether the self-belief is an element in a pattern that *as a whole* has negative psychological significance rather than whether the self-belief by itself is negative or "unrealistic" (i.e., unsupported by objective evidence). Indeed, without considering the role of a particular self-belief within a client's self-system as a whole, there is the risk of strengthening a positive self-belief element only to produce a more negative self-belief pattern that increases the client's suffering.

For both theoretical and practical reasons, it is important to recognize that self-beliefs do not function independently. Different types of self-beliefs become structurally interconnected to form specific self-belief patterns that have distinct psychological significances. This chapter has presented research investigating the unique psychological significances of not only two-element patterns but also three-element patterns involving actual–ideal discrepancies combined with beliefs about either the can self or the future self. Currently we are doing research exploring other three-element patterns involving actual–ought discrepancies. In addition, we have begun to explore the psychological significances of four-element patterns. And self-beliefs are not the only beliefs that become structurally interconnected to form psychologically significant patterns. Other kinds of social beliefs do so as well, such as ideals and oughts that people hold for others. By identifying these other social-belief patterns, we will better understand the contribution of chronic psychological significances to people's social reality.

ACKNOWLEDGMENT

The preparation of this chapter and the research reported herein were supported by Grant MH 39429 from the National Institute of Mental Health.

REFERENCES

Baldwin, A. L. (1955). *Behavior and development in childhood*. New York: Dreyden Press.

Bandura, A. (1982). The self and mechanisms of agency. In J. Suls (Ed.), *Psychological perspectives on the self* (Vol. 1). Hillsdale, NJ: Lawrence Erlbaum Associates.

Bandura, A. (1986). *Social foundations of thought and action: A social cognitive theory*. Englewood Cliffs, NJ: Prentice–Hall.

Beck, A. T., Rush, A. J., Shaw, B. F., & Emery, G. (1979). *Cognitive therapy of depression*. New York: Guilford Press.

Blatt, S. J., D'Afflitti, J. P., & Quinlan, D. M. (1976). Experiences of depression in normal young adults. *Journal of Abnormal Psychology, 86*, 203–223.

Bruner, J. S. (1964). The course of cognitive growth. *American Psychologist, 19*, 1–15.

Campos, J. J., & Barrett, K. C. (1984). Toward a new understanding of emotions and their development. In C. E. Izard, J. Kagan, & R. B. Zajonc (Eds.), *Emotions, cognition, and behavior* (pp. 229–263). New York: Cambridge University Press.

Case, R. (1985). *Intellectual development: Birth to adulthood*. New York: Academic Press.

Case, R. (1988). The whole child: Toward an integrated view of young children's cognitive, social, and emotional development. In A. D. Pellegrini (Ed.), *Psychological bases for early education* (pp. 155–184). Chichester, England: Wiley.

Collins, A. M., & Loftus, E. F. (1975). A spreading-activation theory of semantic processing. *Psychological review, 82,* 407–428.

Damon, W., & Hart, D. (1986). Stability and change in children's self-understanding. *Social Cognition, 4,* 102–118.

Ellis, A. (1962). *Reason and emotion in psychotherapy.* New York: Lyle Stuart.

Emde, R. N. (1984). Levels of meaning for infant emotions: A biosocial view. In K. R. Scherer & P. Ekman (Eds.), *Approaches to emotion* (pp. 77–107). Hillsdale, NJ: Lawrence Erlbaum Associates.

Epstein, S. (1978). Avoidance-approach: The fifth basic conflict. *Journal of Consulting and Clinical Psychology, 46,* 1016–1022.

Feffer, M. (1970). Developmental analysis of interpersonal behavior. *Psychological Review, 77,* 197–214.

Fischer, K. W. (1980). A theory of cognitive development: The control and construction of hierarchies of skills. *Psychological Review, 87,* 477–531.

Fischer, K. W., & Lamborn, S. D. (1987). Sources of variation in developmental levels: Cognitive and emotional transitions during adolescence. In A. de Ribaupierre, K. Scherer, & P. Mounod (Eds.), *Transition mechanisms in cognitive-emotional child development: The longitudinal approach.* Paris: European Science Foundation.

Fischer, K. W., & Watson, M. W. (1981). Explaining the Oedipus conflict. In K. W. Fischer (Ed.), *Cognitive development.* New Directions for Child Development, No. 12. San Francisco: Jossey–Bass.

Fiske, S. T., & Dyer, L. M. (1985). Structure and development of social schemata: Evidence from positive and negative transfer effects. *Journal of Personality and Social Psychology, 48,* 839–852.

Flavell, J. H., Botkin, P. T., Fry, C. L., Wright, J. W., & Jarvis, P. E. (1968). *The development of role-taking and communication skills in children.* New York:

Freud, S. (1961). The ego and the id. In J. Strachey (Ed. and Trans.), *Standard edition of the complete psychological works of Sigmund Freud* (Vol. 19, pp. 3–66). London: Hogarth Press. (Original work published 1923)

Gesell, A., & Ilg, F. (1946). *The child from five to ten.* New York: Harper & Row.

Harter, S. (1983). Developmental perspectives on the self-system. In P. H. Mussen (Ed.), *Handbook of child psychology, Vol. 4: Socialization, personality, and social development* (pp. 275–385). New York: Wiley.

Hayes–Roth, B. (1977). Evolution of cognitive structures and processes. *Psychological Review, 84,* 260–278.

Heider, F. (1958). *The psychology of interpersonal relations.* New York: Wiley.

Heilizer, F. (1977). A review of theory and research on Miller's response competition (conflict) models. *Journal of General Psychology, 97,* 227–280.

Higgins, E. T. (1981). Role-taking and social judgment: Alternative developmental perspectives and processes. In J. H. Flavell & L. Ross (Eds.), *Social cognitive development: Frontiers and possible futures* (pp. 119–153). Cambridge, England: Cambridge University Press.

Higgins, E. T. (1987). Self-discrepancy: A theory relating self and affect. *Psychological Review, 94,* 319–340.

Higgins, E. T. (1989a). Self-discrepancy theory: What patterns of self-beliefs cause people to suffer? In L. Berkowitz (Ed.), *Advances in experimental social psychology, (Vol. 22),* (pp. 93–136). New York: Academic Press.

Higgins, E. T. (1989b). Knowledge accessibility and activation: Subjectivity and suffering from unconscious sources. In J. S. Uleman & J. A. Bargh (Eds.), *Unintended thought* (pp. 75–123). New York: Guilford Press.

Higgins, E. T. (1989c). Risks and trade-offs in self-regulatory and self-evaluative processes: A developmental model. In M. R. Gunnar & A. Sroufe (Eds.), *Minnesota symposium on child psychology.* Hillsdale, NJ.: Lawrence Erlbaum Associates.

Higgins, E. T. (in press). Continuities and discontinuities in self-regulatory and self-evaluative processes: A developmental theory relating self and affect. *Journal of Personality.*

Higgins, E. T., Bond, R. N., Klein, R., & Strauman, T. (1986). Self-discrepancies and emotional vulnerability: How magnitude, accessibility, and type of discrepancy influence affect. *Journal of Personality and Social Psychology, 51,* 5–15.

Higgins, E. T., & King, G. (1981). Accessibility of social constructs: Information processing consequences of individual and contextual variability. In N. Cantor & J. Kihlstrom (Eds.), *Personality, cognition, and social interaction* (pp. 69–121). Hillsdale, NJ.: Lawrence Erlabum Associates.

Higgins, E. T., King, G. A., & Mavin, G. H. (1982). Individual construct accessibility and subjective impressions and recall. *Journal of Personality and Social Psychology, 43,* 35–47.

Higgins, E. T., Klein, R., & Strauman, T. (1987). Self-discrepancies: Distinguishing among self-states, self-state conflicts, and emotional vulnerabilities. In K. M. Yardley & T. M. Honess (Eds.), *Self and identity: Psychosocial perspectives* (pp. 173–186). New York: Wiley.

Higgins, E. T., & Rholes, W. S. (1976). Impression formation and role fulfillment: A "Holistic reference" approach. *Journal of Experimental Social Psychology, 12,* 422–435.

Higgins, E. T., Strauman, T., & Klein, R. (1986). Standards and the process of self-evaluation: Multiple affects from multiple stages. In R. M. Sorrentino & E. T. Higgins (Eds.), *Handbook of motivation and cognition: Foundations of social behavior* (pp. 23–63). New York: Guilford Press.

Higgins, E. T., Van Hook, E., & Dorfman, D. (1988). Do self attributes form a cognitive structure? *Social Cognition, 6,* 177–207.

Higgins, E. T., & Wells, R. S. (1986). Social construct availability and accessibility as a function of social life phase: Emphasizing the "how" versus the "can" of social cognition. *Social Cognition, 4,* 201–226.

Hoffman, M. L. (1970). Moral development. In P. H. Mussen (Ed.), *Carmichael's manual of child psychology* (Vol. 2, pp. 261–359). New York: Wiley.

Horney, K. (1946). *Our inner conflicts: A constructive theory of neurosis.* London: Routledge & Kegan Paul.

Horowitz, M. (1976). *Stress response syndromes.* New York: Jason–Aronson.

Huttenlocher, J., & Higgins, E. T. (1978). Issues in the study of symbolic development. In W. A. Collins (Ed.), *Minnesota symposia on child psychology* (Vol. 2, pp. 98–140). Hillsdale, NJ: Lawrence Erlbaum Associates.

Inhelder, B., & Piaget, J. (1958). *The growth of logical thinking from childhood to adolescence.* New York: Basic Books.

James, W. (1948). *Psychology.* New York: World Publishing Co. (Original publication, 1890)

Kagan, J. (1984). The idea of emotion in human development. In C. E. Izard, J. Kagan, & R. B. Zajonc (Eds.), *Emotions, cognition, and behavior* (pp. 38–72). New York: Cambridge University Press.

Kohlberg, L. (1976). Moral stages and moralization. In T. Lickona (Ed.), *Moral development and behavior.* New York: Holt, Rinehart, & Winston.

Levinson, D. J. (1978). *The seasons of a man's life.* New York: Ballantine Books.

Lewin, K. (1935). *A dynamic theory of personality.* New York: McGraw–Hill.

Lewin, K., Lippitt, R., & White, R. (1939). Patterns of aggressive behavior in experimentally created social disasters. *Journal of Social Psychology, 10,* 271–299.

Loevinger, J. (1976). *Ego development: Conceptions and theories.* San Francisco: Jossey–Bass.

Maccoby, E. E., & Martin, J. A. (1983). Socialization in the context of the family: Parent-child interaction. In P. H. Mussen (Ed.), *Handbook of child psychology, Vol. 4: Socialization, personality, and social development* (pp. 643–691). New York: Wiley.

Magaro, P., & Smith, P. (1981). The personality of clinical types: An empirically derived taxonomy. *Journal of Clinical Psychology, 37,* 796–809.

Mandler, G. (1982). The structure of value: Accounting for taste. In M. S. Clark & S. T. Fiske, (Eds.), *Affect and cognition* (pp. 3–36). Hillsdale, NJ: Lawrence Erlbaum Associates.

Markus, H., & Nurius, P. (1986). Possible selves. *American Psychologist, 41,* 954–969.

Markus, H., & Wurf, E. (1987). The dynamic self-concept: A social psychological perspective. *Annual Review of psychology, 38,* 299–337.

Mead, G. H. (1934). *Mind, self, and society.* Chicago: University of Chicago Press.

Miller, N. E. (1944). Experimental studies of conflict. In J. M. Hunt (Ed.), *Personality and the behavior disorders* (Vol. 1). New York: Ronald Press.

Miller, N. E. (1959). Liberalization of basic S–R concepts: Extensions to conflict behavior, motivation, and social learning. In S. Koch (Ed.), *Psychology: A study of a science (Vol. 2). General systematic formulations, learning, and special processes* (pp. 196–292). New York: McGraw–Hill.

Moretti, M. M., & Higgins, E. T. (1989). The development of self-system vulnerabilities: Social and cognitive factors in developmental psychopathology. In R. J. Sternberg & J. Kolligan (Eds.), *Perceptions of competence and incompetence across the lifespan.* New Haven, CT: Yale University Press.

Moretti, M. M., & Higgins, E. T. (in press). Relating self-discrepancy to self-esteem: The contribution of discrepancy beyond actual-self ratings. *Journal of Experimental Social Psychology.*

Olson, J. M., & Ross, M. (1984). Perceived qualifications, resource abundance, and resentment about deprivation. *Journal of Experimental Social Psychology, 20,* 425–444.

Olweus, D. (1980). Familial and temperamental determinants of aggression behavior in adolescents—A causal analysis. *Developmental Psychology, 16,* 644–660.

Parke, R. D., & Slaby, R. G. (1983). The development of aggression. In P. H. Mussen, (Ed.)., *Handbook of child psychology, Vol. 4: Socialization, personality, and social development* (pp. 547–641). New York: Wiley.

Piaget, J. (1951). *Play, dreams and imitation in childhood.* New York: Norton.

Piaget, J. (1965). *The moral judgment of the child.* New York: Free Press. (Original trans. 1932)

Piaget, J. (1970). Piaget's theory. In P. H. Mussen (Ed.), *Carmichael's manual of child psychology* (Vol. 1, 3rd ed., pp. 703–732). New York: Wiley.

Radke–Yarrow, M., Zahn–Waxler, C., & Chapman, M. (1983). Children's prosocial dispositions and behavior. In P. H. Mussen (Ed.), *Handbook of child psychology, Vol. 4: Socialization, personality, and social development* (pp. 643–691). New York: Wiley.

Rosenberg, M. (1979). *Conceiving the self.* Malabar, FL: Robert E. Krieger.

Ruble, D. N., & Rholes, W. S. (1981). The development of children's perceptions and attributions about their social world. In J. D. Harvey, W. Ickes, R. F. Kidd (Eds.), *New directions in attribution research* (Vol. 3, pp. 3–36). Hillsdale, NJ: Lawrence Erlbaum Associates.

Selman, R. L. (1980). *The growth of interpersonal understanding: Developmental and clinical analyses.* New York: Academic Press.

Selman, R. L., & Byrne, D. F. (1974). A structural-developmental analysis of levels of role-taking in middle childhood. *Child Development, 45,* 803–806.

Shantz, C. U. (1983). Social cognition. In J. H. Flavell & E. M. Markman (Eds.), *Cognitive Development* (Vol. 3). In *Carmichael's manual of child psychology,* (4th ed., pp. 495–555). New York: Wiley.

Shapiro, D. (1965). *Neurotic styles.* New York: Basic Books.

Sroufe, L. A. (1984). The organization of emotional development. In K. R. Scherer & P. Ekman (Eds.), *Approaches to emotion* (pp. 109–128). Hillsdale, NJ: Lawrence Erlbaum Associates.

Strauman, T. J. (1988). Self-discrepancies in clinical depression and social phobia: Cognitive structures that underlie affective disorders? *Journal of Abnormal Psychology.*

Strauman, T. J., & Higgins, E. T. (1987). Automatic activation of self-discrepancies and emotional syndromes: When cognitive structures influence affect. *Journal of Personality and Social Psychology, 53,* 1004–1014.

Thomas, W. I., & Thomas, D. S. (1928). *The child in America.* New York: Knopf.

Trevarthen, C. (1984). Emotions in infancy: Regulators of contact and relationships with persons. In K. R. Scherer & P. Ekman (Eds.), *Approaches to emotion* (pp. 129–157). Hillsdale, NJ: Lawrence Erlbaum Associates.

Van Hook, E., & Higgins, E. T. (1988). Self-related problems beyond the self-concept: The motivational consequences of discrepant self-guides. *Journal of Personality and Social Psychology, 55,* 625–633.

Werner, H. (1957). *Comparative psychology of mental development.* New York: International Universities Press.

Werner, H., & Kaplan, B. (1963). *Symbol formation.* New York: Wiley.

9 The Self and Interpersonal Relations

C. Douglas McCann
Department of Psychology, York University

INTRODUCTION

It is becoming increasingly clear that the study of the self and self-relevant processes is considered central to the study of social psychology. This is equally true of social psychology approached from the psychological and the sociological perspective. However, as Berkowitz (1988b) points out, the notion of the centrality of the self is a more recent addition for the psychological version of social psychology. The general increase in interest in the self is reflected in the large number of published papers, books, and edited volumes that have appeared on the topic in the last few years in the psychological literature (e.g., Berkowitz, 1988a; Schlenker, 1985; Suls, 1982; Suls & Greenwald, 1983, 1986; Wegner & Vallacher, 1980; Yardley & Honess, 1987).

Although the reasons for this increased attention to the self on the part of social psychologists are numerous, a couple of these are worthy of mention because of their relevance to the concerns of this chapter. First, in its initial stages, general psychology was concerned with the nature of the self and with exploring means through which to capture it empirically (e.g., James, 1890). However, difficulties with the latter combined with a general emphasis on observables resulted in a temporary (albeit lengthy) abandonment of the topic as the subject of legitimate scientific inquiry. New and more sophisticated techniques and theories derived from the social cognitive approach (e.g., Markus, 1977; Rogers, Kuiper, & Kirker, 1977) have created a context in which the self is more accessible to systematic investigation.

More central to the concerns of this chapter, however, has been the renewed interest on the part of social psychologists and others in the nature of interpersonal interaction. In their attempts to explicate the nature of important processes in this area, they have recently found it necessary to consider the important role played by the self and self-relevant processes (see McCann & Higgins, in press, for a review). More recently, these two lines of investigation have tended to converge and have led to a more specific focus on the interpersonal effects of the self-concept and self-inference processes. This research indicates that the self is critically implicated in interpersonal relations through its impact on such things as behavioral strategies, interpersonal expectancies and the perception of others (see Markus & Wurf, 1987, for a review). It is this focus that will be most closely examined in the present chapter.

This chapter is divided into two major sections. In the first, I briefly review some of the work examining the effects of social processes on the emergence, maintenance and change of self. In the second section, I consider the interpersonal effects of the self and self-relevant processes by reviewing both the work of others and some recent research conducted in my own laboratory.

SOCIAL PROCESS AND THE SELF

Symbolic Interactionism and the Constructivist Perspective

Traditionally, the self has been linked with interpersonal relations and social processes in several ways. Some of the earliest treatments of the self considered it to be situated in social relations and to emerge from such processes. This general orientation toward considering the emergent properties of the self as tied to social process is most evident in the writings of the early symbolic interactionists.

According to sociologists such as Mead (1934) and Cooley (1902), the young child's conception of self and personal action is closely tied to views communicated to him or her by parents and other significant caregivers. In this context, the child becomes the target of both overt action and the more subtle reactions carried by nonverbal means. Children are assumed to adopt these evaluations and to apply them to their own developing view of self. Children acquire a conception of self from the regularity of reactions they elicit from others (Shibutani, 1961). Thus, the differentiation between the self and others and the development of self-concept is assumed to be closely tied to social process.

One aspect of this traditional symbolic interactionist perspective that is worthy of note is its implications for views of the relative stability or malleability of an individual's self-concept. If carried to the extreme, this view would suggest that there is no self-knowledge outside of social opinion and that as social context changes, so does an individual's self-concept (e.g., Gergen, 1987). Resolution of this issue has been the subject of much current work. The nature of these attempts at resolving this issue will be dealt with later in this section. Suffice it to say at this point that early work on the self emphasized the important role played by social process in the development of an individual's sense of self.

A second orientation focusing on the effects of social context on the self is broadly referred to as the social constructivist or contextual position (e.g., Gergen, 1987; Harré, 1987; Markova, 1987; McGuire & McGuire, 1982). In its extreme form, the constructivist position asserts that the self is an artifact of local social conventions that result from the imposition of specific grammatical forms. Thus, "there is no entity at the centre of our experience of ourselves. But there are standard ways in which we express our comments upon our own mentation" (Harré, 1987, pp. 41). In fact, the self exists only as a concept, a central concept in a theory used by individuals to impose a system on their thoughts and action. As such, what individuals refer to as the self is open to variation due to local differences in the theories used to impose order. A related point is made by Gergen and Gergen (1988) in their discussion of the self as narrative.

The impact of variation in immediate social context has been most systematically examined in the work on distinctiveness by McGuire and his colleagues (e.g., McGuire & Padawer–Singer, 1976). This work has focused on the impact of social context on identity and suggests that individuals' spontaneous self-concepts reflect a tendency to view the self as unique. For example, the study by McGuire and Padawer–Singer (1976) presented children with the simple task of telling the researchers about themselves. The results indicated that children's spontaneous self-descriptions tended to include unique or distinctive attributes. For example, redheads were more likely than black- and brown-haired children to mention their hair color; thin and heavy children were more likely to mention body weight, and so on. One implication of this research, similar to what we have discussed, is that spontaneous self-descriptions and/or identities may vary from context to context. This and similar views regarding the malleability of the self stand in contrast to the traditional view of stability of the self-concept expressed in other work (e.g., Allport, 1937; Greenwald, 1982; Markus, 1977; Swann, 1987). This raises the issue of how the self-concept can, at the same time, be both malleable and stable. Although several possible solutions have been offered (e.g., Gergen, 1982), one of the most interesting recent formulations is that proposed by Markus and her colleagues (e.g., Markus & Kunda, 1986; Markus & Nurius, 1986; Markus & Wurf, 1987).

In the context of her work on possible selves (Markus & Nurius, 1986), Markus has suggested the notion of the working self-concept. The working self-concept refers to "that set of self-conceptions that are presently accessible in thought and memory" (pp. 163). The self-concept proper refers to the total set of information about the self that is represented in memory. It is assumed that only a small part of this information is accessible at any point in time (e.g., Higgins & Bargh, 1987). Following earlier work on construct accessibility (Higgins & King, 1981), it is assumed that what is accessible is a function of several factors (e.g., salience, recency, frequency) that can be affected by features of the imme-diate social context. Thus, while malleability may be characteristic of the *accessible* working self-concept, relative stability characterizes the self-relevant information *available* to the individual. This potential variation in working self-concept is important in terms of its impact on such things as personal motivations and goals that may be reflected in interpersonal behavior.

The formulations that have been reviewed present a picture of the self that retains stability while emphasizing the extent to which the self is open to substan-tial influence from various factors and processes located in the interpersonal context. These effects on identity and self-concept are important in terms of their potential implications for subsequent interpersonal behavior. In the next section, we examine more systematically the impact of the self on social processes and interpersonal relations.

THE INTERPERSONAL EFFECTS OF THE SELF

In the preceding section, theory and research examining some of the ways in which the self is influenced by aspects of social context and process was re-viewed. This type of orientation has been a traditional one (see McCann & Higgins, in press) and continues to be a major interest area. Other recent for-mulations have evidenced a complementary interest in examining the ways in which the self, in turn, impacts on various aspects of the social environment and interpersonal behavior. The remainder of this chapter is devoted to a considera-tion of this work.

In a recent review of work on the self, Markus and Wurf (1987) distinguished between two broad categories of effects that have been linked to the self. The first general category of effects is referred to as "intrapersonal effects." Included here is the influence of the self on such things as information processing, person-al affect regulation, and the motivational consequences of the self.

The second broad category of effects is what Markus and Wurf (1987) term the "interpersonal effects of the self." Included in this category are such things as the effects of the self on social perception, social comparison processes, and the nature of self-generated interaction strategies. In the remainder of the present chapter, I focus on past work examining these and other interpersonal effects of the self. In the context of this review, I present some of the recent research conducted by my colleagues and me that address related concerns. More specifi-cally, our recent research has examined: (a) the effects of self-relevant processes in depression on memory for information received about other people; (b) the relations between self-concept in depressives and interactional expectancies; and (c) the role played by the self in producing specific affective experiences in close relationships. Although this work was conducted to examine the implications of current models of depression, it has more general implications for considerations of the interpersonal effects of the self and self-relevant processes.

The Self and Social Perception

Recent research in social cognition has examined the information processing consequences of the self-schema (e.g., Markus, 1977; Rogers, Kuiper & Kirker, 1977). In this work, the self is conceptualized as a cognitive structure or set of structures (e.g., Epstein, 1973) that is assumed to have the same types of information-processing consequences as any other type of cognitive structure (e.g., Bartlett, 1932; Neisser, 1967). Information about the self is organized within the self-schema which impacts on the encoding, representation, and retrieval of self-relevant information. These information-processing effects have been well documented in the literature (e.g., Fiske & Taylor, 1984). One of the most productive approaches has been that of Rogers, Kuiper, and colleagues on the self-reference effect.

In this research, the investigators employ a modified version of Craik and Tulving's (1975) method for examining the effects of encoding orientation on incidental recall. Craik and Tulving had subjects make a variety of types of judgments about adjectives presented to them (i.e., structural, phonemic, and semantic judgments) and then tested subjects for incidental recall of the adjectives. The results provided support for a depth of processing interpretation in that encoding orientations producing deeper encoding (i.e., semantic judgments) facilitated memory. Rogers et al. (1977) added a self-reference condition in which subjects were asked to decide whether the adjectives presented to them describe them or not. They found that this latter condition led to the best recall (see Higgins & Bargh, 1987, for a review and critique). Other paradigms were also developed to demonstrate the important implications that the self-structure can have for the processing of self-relevant information (e.g., Markus, 1977).

This type of research was subsequently extended to consider the impact of the self-schema on the processing of information about others (e.g., Fong & Markus, 1982; Lewicki, 1983; Markus & Smith, 1981; Markus, Smith, & Moreland, 1985). Various explanations have been offered for the demonstrated impact of the self-structure on social perception. For example, Markus and Smith (1981) assume, given the centrality of the self in the social environment, that all incoming stimuli are initially evaluated with respect to their relevance to the self and, if high relevance is confirmed, that the self-structure is activated and used to process features of the incoming information. Since it is usually the case that others in the social environment are relevant to concerns about the self then the self-structure will be implicated in processing information about those others. The research by Markus and others has provided strong support for the relevance of self-relevant structures on the processing of information about others (see also

Dornbusch, Hastorf, Richardson, Muzzy, & Vreeland, 1965; Higgins & King, 1981).

The type of effect described is often taken as evidence of the status of self as a unique, special cognitive structure (e.g., Rogers, et al., 1977) that serves as a reference point for social evaluation. Another proposal, however, suggests that these effects are also compatible with a "construct accessibility" interpretation (Higgins & Bargh, 1987). According to this view, the observed similarity between self and other judgments may reflect the fact that individuals differ in the accessibility of cognitive constructs in general, and that those constructs that are most accessible for a specific individual will be used in processing information both about the *self* and *others*. This model does not necessarily ascribe a special status to representations about the self in assuming that the self exists as a *unique* cognitive structure. This notion is relevant to some of the research recently conducted by my colleagues and me in which we examined the implications of construct accessibility differences associated with depression for the perception of others.

Accessibility and Social Perception in Depression

Recent social-cognitive models of depression have accorded a primary role to schema-based processing and the self in the etiology and maintenance of depression (e.g., Beck, 1967, 1976; Gotlib & McCann, 1984; Ingram, 1984; Kuiper & Derry, 1982; McCann, in press). Pre-eminent among these is the model proposed by Beck (1967). Beck suggests that depressives are characterized by a negative cognitive triad which consists of a negative view of the self, the world, and the future. This negative cognitive triad is supported by a set of negative cognitive distortions or inferential errors (e.g., selective abstraction or the tendency to focus attention on negative events) that reflect the operation of negative schemata that are assumed to form the basis for the vulnerability of the individual to depression. According to Beck, the schemata used by depressives are negative in nature, leading the depressive to attend selectively to negative information at the expense of positive information and to perceive ambiguous information to be more negative than it actually is. This dysfunctional style is seen to lead depressives to develop self-conceptions that are extremely negative in nature reflecting themes of worthlessness, self-blame, personal deficiency, hopelessness, and rejection.

These negative schemata are assumed to be latent before the onset of a depressive episode, leading the individual to be vulnerable to depression when confronted with experiences that activate the schema. The predictions of this model have received generally strong support in the literature (but see Coyne & Gotlib, 1983).

The role of the self in depression has been emphasized in these models (e.g., Greenberg, Vazquez, & Alloy, 1988). This view follows Beck's (1967) suggestion that the dysfunctional cognitions of the depressive are primarily *biased against the self*. For example, one of the best known programs of research examining self-schemata and depression is the work of Kuiper and his colleagues (e.g., Kuiper & Derry, 1982; see Kuiper, Olinger, & MacDonald, 1988, for a review) examining self-reference processes in depressed and normal individuals. They have shown that incidental recall of negative content adjectives receiving a prior self-reference judgment (e.g., it describes me) increases with increasing levels of depression. This suggests, in part, that the self-schemata of depressives are increasingly characterized by negative content with heightened depression. These negative self-schemata are assumed to be critically involved in the onset of depressive episodes.

Along with other researchers, my colleagues and I have been interested in extending these self-relevant effects to the processing of information about others. Relevant here is the contrast between the predictions of the traditional cognitive models of depression and those of recent self-schema work and accessibility models of depressive cognitions. According to the formulation proposed by Beck (1967), the negatively biased information processing style characteristic of depressives is *restricted* to information about the *self*. This prediction, however, is in contrast to that derived from other, more recent work.

Two social-cognitive models converge in suggesting that the negatively biased information processing characteristic of depressives when dealing with information about the self should also be evident in the processing of information about others. This proposal is clearly compatible with the self-schema work we have discussed (e.g., Fong & Markus, 1982). In addition, this other-relevant processing prediction is compatible with the construct accessibility model of depression proposed by McCann, Higgins, and their colleagues (e.g., Higgins & King, 1981; Gotlib & McCann, 1984; McCann & Higgins, 1984; see also the work of Spielman & Bargh, in press). In this latter model, it is assumed that the cognitive effects associated with depression reflect chronic differences in construct accessibility (e.g., McCann & Higgins, 1984). If this formulation is accurate, then there is no basis upon which to assume that the negative information processing associated with depression should be restricted to information about the self. While it is beyond the purposes of the present chapter, it is interesting to note here that these latter two models, while *agreeing* on this aspect of self-relevant information processing in depression, *disagree* in terms of their conceptualization of the nature of the self. In the accessibility formulation, individual differences in self-concept are assumed to reflect differences in *chronically* accessible cognitive constructs. Little emphasis is given in these models with respect to the *interconnectedness* between these accessible constructs. The nature of the interconnectedness is, however, a primary focus of current self-schema models (see Spielman & Bargh, in press). The present research was derived from an accessibility perspective and was designed to test various aspects of the implications of this view for the nature of depressive information processing (i.e., other-relevant processing effects). It was not designed to examine the relative viability of the accessibility versus self-schema formulations concerning the nature of the self.

Ian Gotlib and I were initially interested in deriving some preliminary support for a construct accessibility interpretation of depressive information processing. In our first study, we attempted to provide evidence to support the assumption that negative cognitive constructs would tend to be more accessible for depressed subjects, and that this would not be characteristic of nondepressed individuals. It was our view that these differences in construct accessibility were the basis of many of the cognitive effects associated with depression.

In that study (Gotlib & McCann, 1984), we presented mildly depressed and nondepressed university students with a modified version of the Stroop color word task (Stroop, 1935). Subjects were presented with depressed-content, neutral-content, and manic-content words printed in different color and were required to name the colors of the word as quickly as they could. The latency of response to the color-naming task constituted the primary dependent measure. We suggested that if depressives were indeed characterized by more accessible negative cognitive constructs then their color-naming latency for depressed or negative-content adjectives should be significantly longer than for the other word types. No such differences were expected for nondepressed subjects. The results of that study strongly confirmed these predictions. In addition, the results of a second study (Gotlib & McCann, 1984, Study 2) suggested that these effects were not due to temporary mood differences but were instead, due to chronic differences in construct accessibility.

In the second study, we manipulated the mood of a group of nondepressed subjects through elation and depression mood induction procedures. We then presented these two groups of subjects with the same color-naming task as was performed by subjects in Study 1. The results revealed no parallel differences in color-naming latencies for the three word types as a function of temporary mood differences. Although not definitive, this suggested to us that the observed effects in Study 1 were more likely due to chronic differences in construct accessibility than to mood differences between depressed and nondepressed subjects. These results suggest that many of the information-processing effects characteristic of depression may be due to increased accessibility of negative cognition constructs for depression. These accessible constructs are seen to underlie the negative self-concepts and other biased information-processing effects associated with depression.

Based on the supportive nature of our initial findings and our understanding of the nature of accessibility effects (e.g., Higgins & King, 1981; McCann & Higgins, 1984; Wyer & Srull, 1981), we conducted a subsequent study to examine the implications of accessibility differences between depressed and nondepressed subjects for the processing of information about other people.

Social Perception and Depression

This study (McCann & Gotlib, 1988) was designed to examine the effects of chronic differences in construct accessibility that were assumed to underlie the dysfunctional self-concept associated with depression on the perception of others. We intended to extend past work on the social cognitive bases of depression in three ways. First, as was discussed, traditional social cognitive models (e.g., Beck, 1967) have suggested that the cognitive deficits characteristic of depression were primarily associated with biased information processing related to the self. In this study, we examined the implications of the dysfunctional cognitive style typical of depressives for social perception. Second, most past work examining the cognitive correlates of depression have focused on indexes of *amount* of recall, for example, the tendency of depressives to recall more negative than positive content stimuli (e.g., Kuiper & Derry, 1982). In this study, we examined the effects of the hypothesized differences in construct accessibility on the *distortion* of information in recall. This focus is consistent with the results of previous social cognitive research on the effects of construct accessibility (e.g., Higgins, Rholes, & Jones, 1977). Finally, we extended past work by considering individual differences in types of vulnerability for depression (e.g., Beck, 1983).

In a recent paper, Beck (1983) presented an extension of his earlier theory of cognitive vulnerability for depression (e.g., Beck, 1967). In this extension, Beck distinguished between sociotropic and autonomous depression. He suggested that the premorbid personalities of depressives would tend to show a predominance of one of these two types.

Sociotropic and autonomous individuals were viewed as differing in terms of orientation, cognitive sensitivities, precipitating factors for depression, and depressive symptoms. The sociotropic or dependent type is primarily oriented toward social relations and is particularly vulnerable to disturbances in this area. The autonomous individual is primarily oriented toward independence and achievement and is sensitive and vulnerable to disturbances in this area. Our research was designed in part as an initial examination of the utility of this distinction. We assumed that both types of individuals would be characterized by chronically accessible negative cognitive constructs but that the nature of these accessible constructs would differ between them and would be related to the types of concerns outlined by Beck (1983). In addition, we assumed the chronically accessible constructs characteristic of depressives would lead them to recall the social information they were presented in a more negatively distorted fashion and that this distortion would be more evident with increasing temporal delay due to the increasing impact of reconstructive memory effects (see Higgins et al., 1977).

A group of 107 undergraduate psychology students was recruited for this study and were requested to complete Beck's (1983) Sociotropic-Autonomy

Scale. This scale consists of two subscales and subjects receive scale scores for both Sociotropy and Autonomy. According to Beck (1983), although it is theoretically possible that subjects can evidence characteristics of both person types, the majority show a predominance of one or the other. Subjects were also presented with a prose description of a target person that contained 12 behavioral exemplars (see McCann & Hancock, 1983, for a description of this material) that focuses primarily on individual, achievement-type items. Since this material was assumed to be more clearly related to the sensitivities characteristic of autonomous individuals, it was expected that analyses based on classification of subjects as high or low autonomous would evidence support for the accessibility formulations presented herein. That is, high autonomous subjects should demonstrate increased negative distortion of stimulus information with increased temporal delay. The primary analysis, therefore, classified subjects into person types based on their responses to the autonomy subscale (i.e., high and low autonomous individuals).[1]

After being exposed to the information describing the target person, subjects were asked, after either a brief (20 minutes) or long delay (7–10 days later), to recall the stimulus information they read "word for word." Subjects had not been previously informed about the recall task. Two judges scored the recall protocols (interrater agreement, $r = .92$) for the number of positive and negative distortions of the original information contained in the recall protocols. As an example of the distortion index, consider the item presented to subjects stating that "Donald (the stimulus person) was well aware of his ability to do many things well." Pilot testing had indicated that subjects, in general, were equally likely to view this item as referring to a positive (i.e., confident) or negative trait (i.e., conceit). A subject's reproduction of this item as "Donald kept going around and telling people how good he was" would be scored as a negative distortion of the originally ambiguous item. The number of positive and negative distortions constituted the primary dependent measure.

The numbers of distortions of the original stimulus information were analyzed by means of a 2 (Person Type–High Autonomous, Low Autonomous) × 2 (Temporal Delay–Brief or Long) × 2 (Distortion Type–Positive or Negative) mixed analysis of variance. For this analysis, subjects were classified by means of a median split on the Autonomy Scale. This analysis revealed several significant main and interaction effects: Distortion Type, $F(1,100) = 5.74$, $p < .02$; Person Type × Delay, $F(1,100) = 4.12$, $p < .05$; Person Type × Distortion Type, $F(1,100) = 3.86$, $p < .05$; Distortion Type × Delay, $F(1,100) = 6.73$, p

---

[1]We subsequently reanalyzed the data classifying subjects according to their responses to the Sociotropy subscale. This analysis revealed no interactions between Subject Type, Temporal Delay, and Distortion Type ($F < 1$), which would have been expected had the information items presented to subjects been related to the sensitivities characteristic of high-sociotropic individuals.

TABLE 9.1
Reproduction Distortion as a Function of Autonomous Personality Type
and Temporal Delay

	Low Autonomous		High Autonomous	
	Brief Delay	Long Delay	Brief Delay	Long Delay
Positve distortions	.52	.47	.53	.25
Negative distortions	.57	.56	.43	1.75

$< .01$. All of these effects, however, were qualified by the presence of the predicted three-way interaction, Person Type × Distortion Type × Delay, $F(1,100) = 5.94$, $p < .02$). As expected, it was only the reproductions of the High Autonomous subjects (see Table 9.1) that became increasingly negative over time. No such effect was observed for the Low Autonomous subjects.

The results of this study were taken as strong support for our assumptions regarding the effects of differences in chronic construct accessibility for social perception. Subjects presented with information concerning another person that was related to their own presumably accessible constructs (sensitivities in Beck's terms) showed a tendency to recall that information in a negatively distorted fashion with increased temporal delay. This pattern of results is consistent with those found in other research examining the effects of more temporary activation (i.e., increased accessibility) of cognitive constructs produced by various priming techniques (e.g., Higgins et al., 1977). In the present research, however, we are dealing with the effects of more chronically accessible constructs relative to personality type (McCann & Higgins, 1984). Although not examined in the present research, we assume that presenting Sociotropic individuals with information about others specifically related to sociotropic-type sensitivities or accessible constructs would produce a similar pattern of results (i.e., increased negative distortion over time of sociotropic-relevant items). This assumption is the focus of some of our current research efforts.

This research has clear implications for current social-cognitive models of depression and suggests that construct accessibility differences associated with the negative self-views of depressives may have implications that go beyond "self-bias." More generally, however, this research parallels previous work with normal individuals in demonstrating the effects of self-relevant processes on the perception of others in individuals' social environments. To the extent that individuals develop biased views of their interaction partners, it can be assumed that their relations with those others will be less than maximally effective. In the next section, we examine another way in which the self may potentially impact on social relations.

The Self and Interpersonal Expectancies

One of the ways in which the self can impact on social relations is through its influence on social perception. To the extent that the self and self-relevant processes influence the impressions we form of others, they may elicit specific patterns of interaction based on those impressions. A number of other formulations have also been developed that demonstrate the potential effects of the self on social process. For example, Secord and Backman (1961, 1964, 1965; see Backman, 1988, for a review and extension) have written extensively about the impact of self-relevant congruency processes on interpersonal relations and partner choice.

According to congruency theory, individuals are hypothesized to attempt to achieve a state of consistency between three types of cognitive elements: (a) a characteristic attributed to the self; (b) the individuals' interpretation of their behavior relevant to that characteristic; and (c) their representation of the behavior, perceptions, and feelings of some other person in their social environment relevant to that attribute. Incongruency was assumed to be threatening to the individual since it entails a lack of predictability in the social environment. When faced with incongruency, Secord and Backman (1965) suggested that the individual would tend to engage in several types of processes in an attempt to restore congruency. Several of these strategies have direct implications for interpersonal relations.

For example, when faced with incongruency, individuals may engage in the strategies of selective interaction and response evocation. Individuals may select as partners individuals who hold perceptions of them that are similar to their own. In addition, individuals might pursue particular interaction strategies in their encounters with others that would tend to elicit from those others congruent responses. This aim can be achieved through altercasting in which an individual succeeds in casting the interaction partner into a role that calls for the desired congruent response. Another related strategy is that of self-presentation.

Following the early work of Goffman (1959) on self-presentation and impression management, several recent formulations have systematically explored the strategies used by individuals in their attempts to mold a particular identity of themselves in the eyes of others (e.g., Arkin, 1980; Baumeister, 1982; Jones & Pittman, 1982). Individuals are assumed to engage in such pursuits in an attempt to gain approval as well as because of the instrumental value attached to created identities (see also Baumeister, this volume).

Although primarily designed to create desired images of self in the minds of others (Jones, this volume) in order to impact positively on self-gain, these self-presentational strategies have been shown to have (presumably) unintended personal consequences in some circumstances (e.g., Jones, Rhodewalt, Berglas, & Skelton, 1981; McCann & Hancock, 1983; McCann & Higgins, 1984). Jones et al. (1981), for example, have conducted research demonstrating that behavior enacted in pursuit of self-presentational concerns may influence self-concept change through the related processes of dissonance reduction and biased-scanning or self-perception (see Fazio, Zanna, & Cooper, 1977).

One recent formulation focusing on personal strategies that are engaged in when self-presentation has been less than maximally effective is Swann's work on self-verification. Swann's (1983, 1987) self-verification theory describes the cognitive and behavioral processes engaged in by individuals in order to confirm their own self-conception especially in the face of disconfirming feedback from others (e.g., Swann & Ely, 1984; Swann & Hill, 1982; Swann & Read, 1981a, 1981b). Of particular interest in this program of research is the finding that the motivation to engage in self-verification may at times override the desire for self-enhancement in terms of individuals' cognitive reactions to confirming but *negative* feedback (e.g., Swann, Griffin, Predmore, & Gaines, 1987).

The research reviewed herein has detailed some of the ways in which the self and self-relevant processes can influence the nature of ongoing social interaction. Most of this research, however, has focused on the role of the self in directing and shaping the interaction once it has been set in motion (Markus & Wurf, 1987). Another important role played by the self is in terms of its effects on the personal and interactional expectancies that individuals carry with them into such interactions. Some of our more recent research has focused on this issue in the context of depression (McCann, in press; Moretti & McCann, 1986).

Social Expectancies in Depression

Past research has documented the important role played by expectancies in shaping the nature of our interpersonal interactions (e.g., Athay & Darley, 1981; Darley & Fazio, 1980; Miller & Turnbull, 1986). Critical here are the personal expectancies we have both for ourselves and the nature of the upcoming interaction. In a recent study, Marlene Moretti and I examined these factors in light of what we know about the differences in self-views held by depressed and nondepressed individuals. Depressives characteristically view themselves as being, among other things, worthless, personally deficient, unlikable, and socially unskillful. It can be assumed that these types of self-attributions would lead to general expectations of failure and rejection.

In our research, we attempted to examine more systematically the extent to which the negative self-views associated with depression were manifested in differences between depressed and nondepressed individuals in terms of their personal and interactional expectancies. To this end, we examined the nature of assumed similarity judgments on the part of depressives relative to nondepressed individuals and the types of interpersonal expectancies each type of individual generated when they were asked to imagine a forthcoming interaction with a specific type of individual with whom they were as of yet unacquainted. Our interest in assumed similarity was based on our assumption that an individual's judgments with regard to his or her relative similarity to specific types of persons is one basis upon which personal expectancies are generated. The differences between the assumed similarity judgments of depressed and nondepressed individuals were previously examined by Tabachnik, Crocker, and Alloy (1983).

In their study, Tabachnik et al. (1983) asked depressed and nondepressed college students to rate the extent to which a series of depression-relevant and depression-irrelevant attributes were true of themselves and true of the average college student. The authors then constructed and analyzed an assumed similarity score by computing the absolute difference between ratings of self and ratings of average other for each attribute (see Marks & Miller, 1987). The results indicated that depressives tended to show less assumed similarity than did nondepressed subjects and tended to show less self-enhancement than did the nondepressed subjects (see McCauley, 1985; Crocker, Kayne, & Alloy, 1985; Suls & Wan, 1987). Thus, depressed subjects were found to view themselves as less similar to the average college student than did nondepressed subjects. In our research, we decided to re-examine this issue, using a modified version of previous methods as well as examining our related concern with interactional expectancies.

We recruited 70 York University psychology students to participate in our research and these subjects were classified as depressed or nondepressed, based on their responses to the Beck Depression Inventory (Beck, Ward, Mendelsohn, Mock, & Erbaugh, 1961). We first asked our subjects to complete self-evaluations by completing the Multiple Affect Adjective Checklist (MAACL—Today Form, Zuckerman & Lubin, 1965) and then to imagine *either* an average York University student or a depressed student and to complete another MAACL by marking those adjectives that they believed would be most descriptive of that person. Our interest here centered on responses to the Depression subscale of the MAACL. The absolute discrepancy between self- and target-evaluation was computed for each subject and used as our index of assumed similarity for depressed and nondepressed subjects.

These assumed similarity scores were analyzed by means of a 2 (Subject Type–Depressed or Nondepressed) $\times$ 2 (Target Type–Average or Depressed student) analysis of variance. The results revealed significant main effects for Subject Type, $F(1,66) = 4.62$, $p < .04$, Target Type, $F(1,66) = 89.16$, $p < .0001$, as well as a significant interaction between these two factors, $F(1,66) = 6.11$, $p < .02$. The means associated with these effects (see Table 9.2) revealed that while both depressed and nondepressed subjects tended to see themselves as more similar to the average university student, depressed subjects showed less discrepancy between themselves and a depressed target person than did nondepressed subjects. Subsequent analyses indicated that these differences were attributable to differences in subjects' ratings of themselves, rather than to differences in how they perceived the target individuals. In addition, there was little evidence that depressed and nondepressed subjects differed in their assumed

TABLE 9.2
Absolute Difference Between Self-
and Target-ratings on the Depression
Subscale of the MAACL

Subject Type	Target Type	
	Average	Depressed
Nondepressed	5.50	24.63
Depressed	6.00	17.19

similarity judgments with respect to average university students, an effect contrary to that found by Tabachnick et al. (1983).

In addition to this assumed similarity measure, we elicited interactional expectancies by employing a modified version of Cacioppo and Petty's cognitive response analysis technique (e.g., Cacioppo, Glass, & Merluzzi, 1979). We asked our subjects to imagine interacting with the target person they had been thinking about and to list all the thoughts that came into their mind about that interaction. Two judges then rated these expectations and categorized them as positive or negative expectancies. We then analyzed the proportion of positive expectancies by means of a 2 (Subject Type) $\times$ 2 (Target Type) analysis of variance (see Table 9.3). The results revealed significant main effects for Subject Type, $F(1,66) = 4.10$, $p < .05$, Target Type, $F(1,66) = 5.54$, $p < .02$, and a significant interaction between these two factors, $F(1,66) = 4.00$, $p < .05$. These results indicated that while the interaction expectancies of nondepressed subjects tended to be *target-based,* those of the depressed subjects were *perceiver-based.* That is, whereas nondepressed subjects varied the nature of their expectancies, depending on target type, depressed subjects generated more negative expectancies, regardless of what type of person they anticipated interacting with.

These two sets of results combine nicely in demonstrating the important impact that the negative self-concept associated with depression can have on

TABLE 9.3
Mean Percentage of Positive
Interaction Expectancy

Subject Type	Target Type	
	Average	Depressed
Nondepressed	71	42
Depressed	40	40

interpersonal expectancies. Depressed subjects showed a greater tendency to position (i.e., assume greater similarity) themselves next to a stigmatized other (i.e., the depressed target). It is possible that this tendency could lead them to anticipate rejection and to generate the type of negative interactional expectancies displayed by them in this study. More generally, these results combine with those that have been discussed to suggest the important potential role that the self and self-relevant processes can play in shaping our interactions with others. In the next section, we consider a final interpersonal effect of the self in terms of its impact on affective reactions in interpersonal relationships.

The Self and Affect in Relationships

Thus far, we have discussed the potential effects of the self and self-relevant processes on social perception and their role in shaping interpersonal interaction. As is clear from this discussion, each of these areas have received considerable empirical and theoretical attention. One final concern relates to the role of the self in generating affective experience in the context of ongoing personal relationships (see McCann & Higgins, 1988, for a review). This area has received much less attention to date. Although the self has frequently been implicated in the experience of affect and emotion more generally (e.g., James, 1890), its role in interpersonal affective experience has been examined only more recently.

One link between self and affect in the context of social relations has been provided by the work of Tesser and his colleagues (e.g., Tesser & Campbell, 1983; Tesser, Millar, & Moore, 1988) in their examination of the Self-evaluation Model. This model is based on the assumption that individuals are motivated to maintain a positive self-evaluation in terms of their personal competence. Self-inference with respect to competence is often influenced by the performance of those with whom one shares a relationship. Especially important are situations in which the other clearly outperforms the self. Tesser has extended the reasoning of Festinger's (1954) social comparison theory and the work on "basking in reflected glory" (e.g., Cialdini & Richardson, 1980) in order to delineate the conditions under which high achievement by comparison with others leads to positive or negative self-evaluation and affect.

According to the model, two processes are implicated in self-evaluation under these conditions. A "reflective" process occurs when one basks in the reflected glory of another's high performance. A "comparison process" occurs when self-inferences and affect are based upon an individual's view of his or her relative competence with respect to the other. On the surface, these two processes would seem to lead to contradictory predictions with regard to the effects of better performance by someone else. Tesser suggests that a consideration of three additional variables allows for a specification of conditions under which one or the other of the two processes will dominate. Positive or negative self-inference and affect can result from identical performance on the part of the other. Which type of reaction eventuates depends critically on the quality of the performance of the other, the personal relevance of the action, and the psychological closeness of the other. Pride of reflection tends to occur when the person is close to you, his or her performance is good, and the particular attribute involved is of low relevance to your own self-concept. On the other hand, if the personal relevance of the attribute is high, negative self-evaluation will result. If the other's performance is poor, relevance is high and the individual is close, then positive self-evaluation and accompanying affect would be expected. Clearly, the relevance of the attribute to one's self-concept is a critical determinant of whether reflection or comparison processes are operative.

This formulation also has relevance to some of the issues discussed earlier in that a condition of high relevance and good performance on the part of the other may lead an individual to redefine the relationship as less close or important in an attempt to maintain positive self-evaluation (e.g., Tesser & Campbell, 1983). In our own work (McCann & Higgins, 1988), we have also been interested in examining the implications of the self for affective experience in relationships. We have, however, approached this issue from a different perspective and have based our research on the implications of Higgins's (1987) self-discrepancy theory.

Self-discrepancy and Affect in Relationships

In self-discrepancy theory (Higgins, 1987), the self is conceptualized as a multi-faceted entity composed of several discrete self-states (Higgins, Tykocinski, & Vookles, this volume). According to Higgins, it is important to distinguish between these self-states along two cognitive dimensions: domains and standpoints on the self. Integrating previous formulations (e.g., Colby, 1968; Freud, 1923; James, 1890; Rogers, 1961), the theory posits the existence of three discriminable domains of the self. The "actual self" includes an individual's representation of the attributes that someone (self or another) believes the individual actually possesses. The "ought self" includes an individual's representation of the attributes that someone (self or another) believes the person ought to possess (i.e., beliefs about the duties, responsibilities, and obligations for the person). The "ideal self" consists of an individual's representation of the attributes that someone (self or another) would like the individual ideally to possess (i.e., hopes, goals, or wishes for the person). According to the theory, it is also necessary to distinguish between self-states according to standpoint on the self, where standpoint refers to a point of view from which the self can be judged. There are two basic standpoints: a person's own standpoint and the standpoint of a significant other, such as mother or close friend.

The most basic proposition included in the model is that these self-states may be discrepant from one another and that the type and degree of discrepancy is related to different intensities and qualities of experienced affect. Research to date has most systematically considered the affective implications of four types of discrepancies: actual/own versus ideal/own, actual/own versus ought/own, actual/own versus ideal/other, and actual/own versus ought/other.

All actual–ideal discrepancies involve the absence of positive outcomes and are assumed to be associated with the experience of "dejection" or depression-related affect. All actual–ought discrepancies involve the perceived presence of negative outcomes and are predicted to be associated with "agitation" or anxiety-related affect. Research to date has provided strong support for these predictions (see Higgins et al., this volume).

Most of the research that has been conducted to examine this model has focused primarily on discrepancies involving "own" standpoint as related to general affective vulnerability. In a recent study (McCann & Higgins, 1988), we sought to extend this work by considering the implications of self-discrepancies involving own and other standpoints for affective experience in the context of relationships with the significant other implicated in the self-discrepancy.

Ideal and ought self-states are conceptualized by Higgins to be standards against which the actual self can be compared. We assumed that to the extent an individual believes that he or she is not living up to the standards set for them by significant others (i.e., actual/own–ideal/other and actual/own–ought/other discrepancies) that individual should experience negative emotions in the context of that relationship. More specifically, we expected that actual/own–ideal/other discrepancies would be associated with experienced dejection and that actual/own–ought/other discrepancies would be associated with experienced agitation. In addition, we assumed that the affect would be specific to the relationship with the significant other implicated in the self-discrepancy. We examined these predictions in the context of parent–child relationships.

Ninety-four undergraduate students at York University were asked to complete a version of Higgins's Selves Questionnaire. On this questionnaire, subjects are first asked to list the attributes associated with each domain of self from each of the three standpoints (i.e., own, mother, and father). Additionally, subjects were asked to rate the extent to which the standpoint individual (e.g., self or parent) either believed they actually possessed, or ought to possess, or wanted them to ideally possess each attribute listed. This four-point extent rating scale ranged from slightly (1) to extremely (4). Responses to this questionnaire were used to calculate the following discrepancy scores for use in our analyses: actual/own–ideal/own, actual/own–ideal/mother, actual/own–ideal/father, actual/own–ought/own, actual/own–ought/mother, and actual/own–ought/father. These discrepancy scores were calculated following the procedures outlined by Higgins (1987). For each self-discrepancy, the attributes in one self-state were compared with the attributes listed for the other self-state in order to determine the number of attributes that *matched* (i.e., the attributes listed were the same or were synonymous, and the extent rating varied by no more than 1 scale point), were examples of what Higgins refers to as *Type 1 mismatches* (i.e., the attributes listed were the same or synonymous but the extent rating varied by 2 or more), or were examples of *Type 2 mismatches* (i.e., an attribute in one self-state was an antonym of an attribute in the other self-state). The final discrepancy score for any specific combination of self-states was calculated by subtracting the number of matches from the sum of Type 1 and Type 2 (weighted double) mismatches. Thus, higher numbers indicated greater discrepancy.

We also asked our subjects to complete two modified versions of Higgins's Emotions Questionnaire (see Higgins, 1987) in which they reported on the amount of dejection and agitation they experienced (separately) in the context of their relationships with their mother and their father. We then conducted a series of correlational analyses to examine our assumptions.

The initial correlational analysis provided strong support for our expectations concerning the relationship between specific discrepancies and affective experience. Actual/own–ideal/mother and actual/own–ideal/father discrepancy scores were significantly related to reported dejection in each of those relationships (r's = .31, $p < .02$, and .41, $p < .0001$, respectively). In addition, actual/own–ought/mother and actual/own–ought/father scores were significantly related to experienced agitation in each relationship (r's = .36, $p < .0001$ and .39, $p < .0001$, respectively).

We also conducted several other correlational analyses in order to provide stronger support for our assumptions regarding both affective and relationship (target) specificity in terms of the link between discrepancies and affect (see Table 9.4).

TABLE 9.4
Correlations Between Self-discrepancies and Affect

Target Specificity	Affect Specificity
Actual/own–Ideal/mother (Actual/own–Ideal/father)[a] with mother dejection (father dejection) $r = .21**$	Actual/own–Ideal/mother (Actual/own–Ought/mother) with mother dejection (mother agitation) $r = .22**$
Actual/own–Ought/mother (Actual/own–Ought/father) with mother agitation (father agitation) $r = .20**$	Actual/own–Ought/mother (Actual/own–Ideal/mother) with mother agitation (mother dejection) $r = .27**$
Actual/own–Ideal/father (Actual/own–Ideal/mother) with father dejection (mother dejection) $r = .30***$	Actual/own–Ideal/father (Actual/own–Ought/father) with father dejection (father agitation) $r = .24**$
Actual/own–Ought/father (Actual/own–Ought/mother) with father agitation (mother agitation) $r = .22**$	Actual/own–Ought/father (Actual/own–Ideal/father) with father agitation (father dejection) $r = .17*$

$* = p < .10$, $** = p < .05$, $*** = p < .01$.
[a]Terms in parentheses indicate what has been partialed out of the preceding concept.

In these analyses, we semipartialed out of the predicted relationship several indexes in order to examine more systematically our assumptions. In examining Target Specificity, we semipartialed out (see the left-hand column of Table 9.4) of the predicted relationship (e.g., actual/own–ideal/mother with reported dejection in relations with mother) the contribution of the same type of discrepancy from the other parent's standpoint (e.g., actual/own–ideal/father) and we semipartialed out of the theoretically related affect (e.g., dejection in mother relationship) the same type of affect reported in relations with the other parent (e.g., dejection in father relationship). In examining Affective Specificity (see the right-hand column of Table 9.4), we semipartialed out of the predicted relationship (e.g., actual/own–ideal/mother with dejection in relations with mother) the contribution of the other discrepancy involving the same standpoint (e.g., actual/own–ought/mother) and from the theoretically related affect (i.e., dejection in relations with mother) we semipartialed out the other affect (e.g., agitation in relations with mother). As is clear from the results of this analysis presented in Table 9.4, the results provide strong support for our assumptions.

We consider this research to be a preliminary examination of these issues but the potential implications are clear in terms of linking the self to interpersonal relations in yet another way. It would appear that perceived failure to live up to the standard that individuals believe significant others set for them makes those individuals vulnerable to the experience of specific types of affect in the context of those relationships. It would be expected that the affect would be experienced whenever the discrepancies become accessible for the individuals. This would most clearly be the case during face-to-face interaction when these discrepancies could be assumed to be highly activated.

SUMMARY AND IMPLICATIONS

Psychologists have evidenced a continuing interest in examining the nature and implications of the self and self-relevant processes. This interest has been maintained in the face of many paradigmatic shifts which suggest the fundamental nature of the self regarding issues of importance to psychologists in many different areas. Although those working in different areas of psychology have tended to approach the study of the self in slightly different ways, they have tended to converge in terms of their assumptions regarding the social nature of the self. This chapter has been concerned with an examination of the ways in which the self is linked with social process both as a causal and consequent factor.

Research to date has focused on examining the impact of self-relevant processes on several aspects of interpersonal events, including the perception of others, expectancies generated in anticipation of interaction, and affective experience in the context of specific relationships. As such, it has been focused on processes implicated in interpersonal interaction. The self and self-relevant processes have clear relevance to the nature of our relations with others. To date, however, only limited attention has been given to more direct effects of the self on interpersonal interaction. In the future, more attention needs to be directed at examining the effects of the self on the form and structure of *ongoing* interpersonal interaction. One of the ways in which the self may influence the nature of the actions engaged in by partners in an interaction is through its potential links to the interactants' social goals or personal motivations.

Most students of social interaction have emphasized its strategic nature and have assumed that interpersonal interaction is enacted in pursuit of specific personal goals (e.g., Athay & Darley, 1981). Personal goal orientations are seen by some to give concrete form to features of the self (e.g., Markus & Nurius, 1986) and, thus, may provide a link between the self-concept and the nature of behavior enacted in interpersonal contexts (McCann & Higgins, 1988). This general view is clearly reflected in some of the current work on impression management goals (e.g., Jones, this volume). Future work in this area may allow us to integrate more systematically current work on the self with the processes of ongoing interaction that are clearly implicated in some of the work reviewed herein.

ACKNOWLEDGMENT

Preparation of this article, and the research reported in it, was partly supported by a Social Sciences and Humanities Research Council of Canada Grant (No. 410–87–0099) and a National Sciences and Engineering Research Council of Canada Grant (OPG0002016) awarded to the author. I would like to thank Alexander Mackenzie, Jim Olson, and Mark Zanna for their insightful comments on an earlier draft. I would also like to express my appreciation to the participants in the first Ontario Symposium held in 1978 at the University of Western Ontario. I attended that conference as a graduate student and have not forgotten the excitement it generated for me.

REFERENCES

Allport, G. W. (1937). *Personality: A psychological interpretation*. New York: Holt.
Arkin, R. M. (1980). Self-presentation. In D. M. Wegner & R. R. Vallacher (Eds.), *The self in social psychology* (pp. 158–182). Oxford, England: Oxford University Press.
Athay, M., & Darley, J. M. (1981). Toward an interaction-centered theory of personality. In N. Cantor & J. F. Kihlstrom (Eds.), *Personality, cognition and social interaction* (pp. 281–308). Hillsdale, NJ: Lawrence Erlbaum Associates.
Backman, C. W. (1988). The self: A dialectical approach. In L. Berkowitz (Ed.), *Advances in experimental social psychology* (pp. 72–93). New York: Academic Press.
Bartlett, F. C. (1932). *Remembering*. Cambridge, England: Cambridge University Press.

Baumeister, R. F. (1982). A self-presentational view of social phenomena. *Psychological Bulletin, 91*, 405–417.

Beck, A. T. (1967). *Depression: Causes and treatments*. Philadelphia: University of Pennsylvania Press.

Beck, A. T. (1976). *Cognitive therapy and the emotional disorders*. New York: International Universities Press.

Beck, A. T. (1983). Cognitive therapy of depression: New perspectives. In P. J. Clayton & J. E. Barrett (Eds.), *Treatment of depression: Old Controversies and new approaches* (pp. 265–290). New York: Raven Press.

Beck, A. T., Ward, C. H., Mendelsohn, M., Mock, J., & Erbaugh, J. (1961). An inventory for measuring depression. *Archives of General Psychiatry, 4*, 53–63.

Berkowitz, L. (1988a). (Ed.). *Advances in experimental social psychology* (Vol. 21). New York: Academic Press.

Berkowitz, L. (1988b). Introduction. In L. Berkowitz (Ed.), *Advances in experimental social psychology* (Vol. 21, pp. 1–14). New York: Academic Press.

Cacioppo, J. T., Glass, C. R., & Merluzzi, T. V. (1979). Self-statements and self-evaluation: A cognitive-response analysis of heterosexual anxiety. *Cognitive Therapy and Research, 3*, 249–262.

Cialdini, R. B., & Richardson, K. D. (1986). Two indirect tactics of image management: Basking and blasting. *Journal of Personality and Social Psychology, 39*, 406–415.

Colby, K. M. (1968). A programmable theory of cognition and affect in individual personal belief systems. In R. P. Abelson, E. Aronson, W. J. McGuire, T. M. Newcomb, M. J. Rosenberg, & P. H. Tannenbaum (Eds.), *Theories of cognitive consistency: A source book* (pp. 520–575). Chicago: Rand McNally.

Cooley, C. H. (1902). *Human nature and the social order*. New York: Schocken Books.

Coyne, J. C., & Gotlib, I. H. (1983). The role of cognition in depression. *Psychological Bulletin, 94*, 472–505.

Craik, F. I. M., & Tulving, E. (1975). Depth of processing and the retention of words in episodic memory. *Journal of Experimental Psychology: General, 104*, 268–294.

Crocker, J., Kayne, N., & Alloy, L. (1985). Comparing the self with others in depressed and nondepressed college students: Reply to McCauley. *Journal of Personality and Social Psychology, 48*, 1579–1583.

Darley, J. M., & Fazio, R. H. (1980). Expectancy confirmation processes arising in the social interaction sequence. *American Psychologist, 35*, 867–881.

Dornbusch, S., Hastorf, A., Richardson, S. A., Muzzy, R., & Vreeland, R. S. (1965). The perceiver and the perceived: Their relative influence on the categories of interpersonal perception. *Journal of Personality and Social Psychology, 1*, 434–440.

Epstein, S. (1973). The self-concept revisited, or a theory of a theory. *American Psychologist, 28*, 404–416.

Fazio, R. H., Zanna, M. P., & Cooper, J. (1977). Dissonance versus self-perception: An integrative view of each theory's proper domain of application. *Journal of Experimental Social Psychology, 13*, 464–479.

Festinger, L. (1954). A theory of social comparison processes. *Human Relations, 7*, 117–140.

Fiske, S. T., & Taylor, S. E. (1984). *Social cognition*. Reading MA: Addison–Wesley.

Fong, G. T., & Markus, H. (1982). Self-schema and judgments about others. *Social Cognition, 1*, 171–204.

Freud, S. (1923). The ego and the id. In J. Strachey (Ed. & Trans.), *The standard edition of the complete psychological works of Sigmund Freud* (Vol. 19, pp. 3–66). London: Hogarth Press.

Gergen, K. J. (1982). From self to science: What is there to know? In J. Suls (Ed.), *Psychological perspectives on the self* (Vol. 1, pp. 129–149). Hillsdale, NJ: Lawrence Erlbaum Associates.

Gergen, K. J. (1987). Toward self as a relationship: In K. Yardley & T. Honess (Eds.), *Self and identity: Psychosocial perspectives* (pp. 53–63). New York: Wiley.

Gergen, K. J., & Gergen, M. M. (1988). Narrative and the self as relationship. In L. Berkowitz (Ed.), *Advances in experimental social psychology* (Vol. 21, pp. 17–55). New York: Academic Press.

Goffman, E. (1959). *The presentation of self in everyday life.* Garden City, NY: Doubleday.

Gotlib, I. H., & McCann, C. D. (1984). Construct accessibility and depression: An examination of cognitive and affective factors. *Journal of Personality and Social Psychology, 47,* 427–439.

Greenberg, M. S., Vazquez, C. V., & Alloy, L. B. (1988). Depression versus anxiety: Differences in self- and other-schemata. In L. B. Alloy (Ed.), *Cognitive processes in depression* (pp. 109–142). New York: Guilford Press.

Greenwald, A. G. (1982). Ego task analysis: An integration of research on ego involvement and self-awareness. In A. H. Hastorf & A. M. Isen (Eds.), *Cognitive social psychology* (pp. 109–148). New York: Elsevier.

Harré, R. (1987). The social construction of self. In K. Yardley & T. Honess (Eds.), *Self and identity: Psychosocial perspectives* (pp. 41–52). New York: Wiley.

Higgins, E. T. (1987). Self-discrepancy: A theory relating self and affect. *Psychological Review, 94,* 319–340.

Higgins, E. T., & Bargh, J. A. (1987). Social cognition and social perception. *Annual Review of Psychology, 38,* 369–425.

Higgins, E. T., & King, G. A. (1981). Accessibility of social constructs: Information processing consequences of individual and contextual variation. In N. Cantor & J. F. Kihlstrom (Eds.), *Personality, cognition, and social interaction* (pp. 69–122). Hillsdale, NJ: Lawrence Erlbaum Associates.

Higgins, E. T., Rholes, W. S., & Jones, C. R. (1977). Category accessibility and impression formation. *Journal of Experimental Social Psychology, 13,* 141–154.

Ingram, R. E. (1984). Toward an information processing analysis of depression. *Cognitive Therapy and Research, 8,* 443–478.

James, W. (1890). *Psychology.* New York: World Publishing Co.

Jones, E. E., & Pittman, T. S. (1982). Toward a general theory of strategic self-presentation. In J. Suls (Ed.), *Psychological perspectives on the self* (Vol. 1, pp. 231–261). Hillsdale, NJ: Lawrence Erlbaum Associates.

Jones, E. E., Rhodewalt, F., Berglas, S., & Skelton, J. A. (1981). Effects of strategic self-presentation on subsequent self-esteem. *Journal of Personality and Social Psychology, 41,* 407–421.

Kuiper, N. A., & Derry, P. A. (1982). Depressed and nondepressed content self-reference in mild depressives. *Journal of Personality, 50,* 67–79.

Kuiper, N. A., Olinger, L. J., & MacDonald, M. R. (1988). Vulnerability and episodic cognitions in a self-worth contingency Model of depression. In L. B. Alloy (Ed.), *Cognitive processes in depression* (pp. 289–309). New York: Guilford Press.

Lewicki, P. (1984). Self-schema and social information processing. *Journal of Personality and Social Psychology, 47,* 1177–1190.

Markova, I. (1987). Knowledge of the self through interaction. In K. Yardley & T. Honess (Eds.), *Self and identity: Psychosocial perspectives* (pp. 65–80). New York: Wiley.

Marks, G., & Miller, N. (1987). Ten years of research on the false-consensus effect: An empirical and theoretical review. *Psychological Bulletin, 102,* 72–90.

Markus, H. (1977). Self-schemata and processing information about the self. *Journal of Personality and Social Psychology, 35,* 63–78.

Markus, H., & Kunda, Z. (1986). Stability and malleability of the self-concept. *Journal of Personality and Social Psychology, 51,* 858–866.

Markus, H., & Nurius, P. (1986). Possible selves. *American Psychologist, 41,* 954–969.

Markus, H., & Smith, J. (1981). The influence of self-schema on the perception of others. In N. Cantor & J. F. Kihlstrom (Eds.), *Personality, cognition and social interaction* (pp. 233–262). Hillsdale, NJ: Lawrence Erlbaum Associates.

Markus, H., Smith, J., & Moreland, R. L. (1985). Role of the self-concept in the perception of others. *Journal of Personality and Social Psychology, 49,* 1494–1512.

Markus, H., & Wurf, E. (1987). The dynamic self-concept: A social psychological perspective. *Annual Review of Psychology, 38,* 299–337.

McCann, C. D. (in press). Interpersonal factors in depression. In C. D. McCann & N. S. Endler (Eds.), *Depression: New directions in research, theory and practice.* Toronto: Wall & Thompson.

McCann, C. D., & Gotlib, I. H. (1988). *Individual differences in social perception: An examination of depressive subtypes.* Unpublished manuscript, York University, Toronto.

McCann, C. D., & Hancock, R. D. (1983). Self-monitoring in communicative interactions: Social cognitive consequences of goal-directed message modification. *Journal of Experimental Social Psychology, 19,* 109–121.

McCann, C. D., & Higgins, E. T. (in press). Social cognition and communication. In H. Giles & W. P. Robinson (Eds.), *Handbook of language and social psychology.* Chichester, England, & New York: Wiley.

McCann, C. D., & Higgins, E. T. (1984). Individual differences in communication: Social cognitive determinants and consequences. In H. E. Sypher & J. L. Applegate (Eds.), *Understanding interpersonal communication: Social cognitive and strategic processes in children and adults* (pp. 172–210). Beverly Hills, CA: Sage.

McCann, C. D., & Higgins, E. T. (1988). Motivation and affect in interpersonal relations: The role of personal orientations and discrepancies. In L. Donohew, H. E. Sypher & E. T. Higgins (Eds.), *Communication, social cognition and affect* (pp. 53–79). Hillsdale, NJ: Lawrence Erlbaum Associates.

McCauley, C. (1985). Depression and the false consensus effect: A note concerning the study by Tabachnik, Crocker & Alloy. *Journal of Personality and Social Psychology, 48,* 1576–1578.

McGuire, W. J., & McGuire, C. V. (1982). Significant others in self-space: Sex differences and developmental trends in the social self: In J. Suls (Ed.), *Psychological perspectives on the self* (Vol. 1, pp. 71–96). Hillsdale, NJ: Lawrence Erlbaum Associates.

McGuire, W. J., & Padawer–Singer, A. (1976). Trait-salience in the spontaneous self-concept. *Journal of Personality and Social Psychology, 33,* 743–754.

Mead, G. H. (1934). *Mind, self and society.* Chicago: University of Chicago Press.

Miller, D. T., & Turnbull, W. (1986). Expectancies and interpersonal processes. *Annual Review of Psychology, 37,* 233–256.

Moretti, M. M., & McCann, C. D. (1986). *Interpersonal beliefs and expectancies in depression.* Paper presented at the 47th annual convention of the Canadian Psychological Association, Toronto.

Neisser, U. (1967). *Cognitive psychology.* New York: Appleton-Century-Crofts.

Rogers, C. R. (1961). *On becoming a person.* Boston: Houghton Mifflin.

Rogers, T. B., Kuiper, N. A., & Kirker, W. S. (1977). Self-reference and the encoding of personal information. *Journal of Personality and Social Psychology, 35,* 677–788.

Schlenker, B. R. (1985). (Ed.). *The self and social life.* New York: McGraw-Hill.

Secord, P. F., & Backman, C. W. (1961). Personality theory and the problem of stability and change in individual behavior: An interpersonal approach. *Psychological Review, 68,* 21–32.

Secord, P. F., & Backman, C. W. (1964). Interpersonal congruency, perceived similarity and friendship. *Sociometry, 27,* 115–127.

Secord, P. F., & Backman, C. W. (1965). Interpersonal approach to personality. In B. H. Mahler (Ed.), *Progress in experimental personality research* (Vol. 2, pp. 91–125). New York: Academic Press.

Shibutani, T. (1961). *Society and personality: An interactionist approach to social psychology*. Englewood Cliffs, NJ: Prentice–Hall.

Spielman, L. A., & Bargh, J. A. (in press). Does the depressive self-schema really exist? In C. D. McCann & N. S. Endler (Eds.), *Depression: New direction in research, theory and practice*. Toronto: Wall & Thompson.

Stroop, J. R. (1935). Studies of interference in serial verbal reactions. *Journal of Experimental Psychology, 18,* 643–662.

Suls, J. (1982). (Ed.). *Psychological perspectives on the self* (Vol. 1). Hillsdale, NJ: Lawrence Erlbaum Associates.

Suls, J., & Greenwald, A. G. (1983). *Psychological perspectives on the self* (Vol. 2). Hillsdale, NJ: Lawrence Erlbaum Associates.

Suls, J., & Greenwald, A. G. (1986). *Psychological perspectives on the self* (Vol. 3). Hillsdale, NJ: Lawrence Erlbaum Associates.

Suls, J., & Wan, C. K. (1987). In search of the false-uniqueness phenomenon: Fear and estimates of social consensus. *Journal of Personality and Social Psychology, 52,* 211–217.

Swann, Jr., W. B. (1983). Self-verification: Bringing social reality into harmony with the self. In J. Suls & A. G. Greenwald (Eds.), *Psychological perspectives on the self* (Vol. 2, pp. 33–66). Hillsdale, NJ: Lawrence Erlbaum Associates.

Swann, Jr., W. B. (1987). Identity negotiation: Where two roads meet. *Journal of Personality and Social Psychology, 53,* 1038–1051.

Swann, Jr., W. B., & Ely, R. J. (1984). A battle of wills: Self-verification versus behavioral confirmation. *Journal of Personality and Social Psychology, 46,* 1287–1302.

Swann, Jr., W. B., Griffin, Jr., J. J., Predmore, S. C., & Gaines, B. (1987). The cognitive-affective crossfire: When self-consistency confronts self-enhancement. *Journal of Personality and Social Psychology, 52,* 881–889.

Swann, Jr., W. B., & Hill, C. A. (1982). When our identities are mistaken: Reaffirming self-conceptions through social interaction. *Journal of Personality and Social Psychology, 43,* 59–66.

Swann, Jr., W. B., & Read, S. J. (1981a). Acquiring self-knowledge: The search for feedback that fits. *Journal of Personality and Social Psychology, 49,* 1609–1617.

Swann, Jr., W. B., & Read, S. J. (1981b). Self-verification processes: How we sustain our self-conceptions. *Journal of Experimental Social Psychology, 17,* 351–372.

Tabachnik, N., Crocker, J., & Alloy, L. B. (1983). Depression, social comparison and the false consensus effect. *Journal of Personality and Social Psychology, 45,* 688–699.

Tesser, A., & Campbell, J. (1983). Self-definition and self-evaluation maintenance. In J. Suls & A. G. Greenwald (Eds.), *Psychological perspectives on the self* (Vol. 2, pp. 1–31). Hillsdale, NJ: Lawrence Erlbaum Associates.

Tesser, A., Millar, M., & Moore, J. (1988). Some affective consequences of social comparison and reflection processes: The pain and pleasure of being close. *Journal of Personality and Social Psychology, 54,* 49–61.

Wegner, D. M., & Vallacher, R. R. (1980). (Eds.). *The self in social psychology*. Oxford, England: Oxford University Press.

Wyer, R. S., & Srull, T. K. (1981). Category accessibility: Some theoretical and empirical issues concerning the processing of social stimulus information. In E. T. Higgins, C. P. Herman, & M. P. Zanna (Eds.), *Social cognition: The Ontario symposium* (Vol. 1). Hillsdale, NJ: Lawrence Erlbaum Associates.

Yardley, K., & Honess, T. (1987). (Eds.). *Self and identity: Psychosocial perspectives*. New York: Wiley.

Zuckerman, M., & Lubin, B. (1965). *Manual for the multiple affect adjective checklist*. San Diego: Educational Testing Service.

10

Self-Perception and Social-Perception Processes in Tutoring: Subtle Social Control Strategies of Expert Tutors

Mark R. Lepper
Lisa G. Aspinwall
Donna L. Mumme
Stanford University

Ruth W. Chabay
Carnegie–Mellon University

"I think I can. I think I can. I think I can." "I'm not very big, but I think I can. I think I can. I think I can." With this onomatopoetic refrain, in Mabel Bragg's 1928 story, *The Little Engine That Could* pushes itself to its limit and manages to pull the abandoned cars full of toys and circus folk and good things to eat across the mountain to the eagerly awaiting boys and girls on the other side.

"I think I can. I think I can. I think I can." Embodied in this children's classic, as many have noted, are those fundamental American ideals of individual initiative and self-reliance, of personal effort and resulting accomplishment, and of persistence in the face of seemingly overwhelming odds (e.g., Kramnick, 1980; McClelland, 1961). Several of the bigger, newer, and stronger engines had already said that *they* couldn't do it, or at least that *they* couldn't be bothered. No cooperative or social solution is considered in this story; no compromise is suggested. Instead, by dint of its sheer effort and its dogged persistence, the little engine accomplishes this difficult task all on its own.

Beneath this central ideological theme that undoubtedly accounts for much of the popularity of this perenniel best-seller, however, lies a second social-psychological message. By repeating over and over to itself, "I think I can. I think I can. I think I can," the little engine seems able to harness its full energies, to draw on its last reserves, to accomplish what has to be done. The story of the little engine is written *as if* its very repetition of this simple catechism helped it to scale the mountain despite its heavy burden.

Could this be so? With the hindsight of 60 years, such a hypothesis may seem to us unexceptional. Certainly, one could take it as one of the central, and most significant, findings of the last two decades of research in social cognition that what we say to ourselves may have motive power. Whether in the domains of attribution theory and the study of causal reasoning (e.g., Kelley, 1967, 1973), the use of self-reinforcement and self-instructional techniques (e.g., Bandura, 1977; Mahoney & Thoreson, 1974), or the efficacy of cognitive-behavioral therapies (e.g., Mahoney, 1974; Meichenbaum, 1977), psychologists have increasingly arrived at the view that the thoughts we voice, even if only to ourselves, may determine the actions we take.

In achievement situations, students who "think they can" are more likely to succeed than those who remain unconfident about their abilities (e.g., Bandura, 1986). They are also more likely to persist in the face of difficulties than those who have attributed their prior performance outcomes to external causal factors (e.g., Weiner, 1974) and are less likely to respond to failure with subsequent helplessness than those with theories that lead them to interpret failure as indicative of an immutable lack of capability (e.g., Dweck, 1986). Thus, instead of merely reflecting its determination, the little engine's affirmative self-statements might actually have helped it to succeed in its quest to conquer the mountain.

ATTRIBUTION PROCESSES IN THE CLASSROOM

Perhaps the area in which such attribution processes figure most prominently, and certainly the area in which they have been studied most extensively, is the domain of motivation and achievement in school. This is not accidental. By its very nature, any institution designed to provide universal compulsory group education will necessarily involve children in at least two significant attributional problems—assessing their own reasons for engaging in various classroom activities and determining the causes of their successes and failures at those activities.

Although these two types of questions are often closely related, they remain conceptually distinct. In the first case, the appropriate question is one concerning the *reasons* underlying the individual's *voluntary actions* (Deci, 1975, 1981; Lepper, 1981, 1983; Lepper & Greene, 1978). Did I undertake that activity or choose that task because I expected to enjoy the satisfactions inherent in my engagement in that activity, or did I do so only in order to obtain some extrinsic incentive or meet some externally imposed contingency or constraint? In the second case, the relevant issue is one of discerning the *causes* of the individual's *performance outcomes,* his or her successes and failures in a given domain (e.g., Dweck, 1975, 1986; Weiner, 1974, 1985). Was my success, or failure, due to something about me, the task, the situation, or my competition?[1]

---

[1]A detailed analysis of the ways in which these two issues overlap each other is beyond the scope of the present chapter (see Lepper, 1988, for a more extended consideration of these issues). The primary area of joint concern, however, involves students' perceptions of self-efficacy and competence at the activity. Such perceptions, on the one hand, clearly depend on the causal attributions that

The answers students give to both sorts of questions have important implications for their eventual classroom motivation, their subsequent persistence in the face of difficulties, and their learning and retention of the material presented in school (Lepper, 1988; Nicholls, 1989). Students who see themselves as extrinsically, rather than intrinsically, motivated may learn less effectively and may avoid similar activities in the future (Deci & Ryan, 1985; Lepper & Hodell, 1989). Pupils who see their academic successes and failures as beyond their control may prove unwilling to persist when tasks prove difficult or demanding.

These attribution and social-perception processes in the student are closely tied, as well, to teachers' goals. In describing their objectives, teachers characteristically give as much weight to motivational and affective, as to purely cognitive and informational, outcomes (e.g., Prawat, 1985; Prawat & Nickerson, 1985). Paramount among teachers' motivational goals, moreover, are two objectives corresponding to the two attribution processes that we have described: first, to sustain and enhance their students' motivation and interest in learning, even in the face of prominent extrinsic incentives and constraints, and second, to maintain their pupils' feelings of self-esteem and self-efficacy, even in the face of difficult or impossible problems.

STUDIES OF EXPERT HUMAN TUTORS

How might teachers best achieve these objectives? What sorts of instructional strategies are most likely to enhance students' persistence at educational activities, to maintain or increase their intrinsic interest in the topics studied, or to bolster their self-confidence and self-esteem, while simultaneously providing effective instruction to those students? Over the past 15 years, a relatively large experimental literature has developed that addresses questions regarding both the conditions that appear to produce desirable attributional patterns concerning the causes of one's successes and failures (e.g., Dweck, 1986; Dweck & Elliott, 1983; Dweck & Leggett, 1988; Foersterling, 1985; Weiner, 1974, 1980) and the conditions that appear to produce high levels of intrinsic motivation toward the material (e.g., Deci, 1975, 1981; Lepper, 1988; Lepper & Greene, 1978; Malone & Lepper, 1987).

In this chapter, we take a second look at some of the conclusions to which this previous experimental work has led, in light of a series of current studies trying to examine the methods that expert human tutors use, in one-to-one tutoring situations, to instruct and to interest students in some subject matter. In particu-

---

children make concerning the causes of their successes and failures (e.g., Dweck & Leggett, 1988; Weiner, 1980). These same beliefs, however, also provide one important source of intrinsic motivation (e.g., Bandura & Schunk, 1981; Deci, 1975; Harter, 1978; Lepper & Greene, 1978; Schunk, 1985).

lar, as part of a larger research project (Lepper, Gurtner, Mumme, Woolverton, Chabay, & Larkin, in preparation), we have recently been involved in a detailed analysis of the strategies and techniques employed by experienced human tutors working individually with primary school students in arithmetic.

The general procedure of these studies has involved the recruitment of practiced tutors with experience in the domain of elementary-level mathematics and the subsequent observation of these tutors as they work with students in individual tutorial sessions. In these studies, students have ranged from the second through the fifth grade, depending on the educational activity involved. Topics of instruction have included addition with regrouping, the representation of fractions on number lines, and the use of Cartesian coordinates. All of these cases, therefore, have involved work with generally concrete-operational children on mathematical tasks involving primarily the acquisition of procedural skills and their conceptual underpinnings. Each tutoring session was videotaped, transcribed, and examined in detail from a number of perspectives, although here we will focus exclusively on the two attributional questions that we have outlined.[2]

ATTRIBUTIONAL STRATEGIES OF EXPERT TUTORS

What is it, then, that experienced tutors do, both to instruct and to interest children in the subject matter they present? Are they even successful in accomplishing these two goals simultaneously? Our preliminary observations of effective tutors have led us to be quite optimistic. What really good tutors can accomplish in a limited amount of time, in both motivational and cognitive terms, can be extremely impressive. In the best cases, one can observe initially unconfident and inept pupils at least temporarily transformed into highly confident, and highly competent, students within the course of a single 1-hour session. A self-effacing student unable to add two two-digit numbers correctly at the outset of a session can be seen successfully solving problems involving five-digit numbers, with multiple zeroes in the middle and multiple carries, and then asking the tutor if he or she can't provide some more difficult and challenging problems for the next time. Hence, it has seemed to us both interesting and important to analyze the strategies that such highly effective tutors use.

To do so, obviously, requires a sample of effective tutors. Our attempts to obtain such a sample have involved a series of steps. We began by seeking out individuals who had both had extensive experience working with students in grades one through six on grade-appropriate topics in mathematics and had been

---

[2]In one case, these protocols were videotaped, transcribed, and initially discussed by Putnam (1985, 1987). In the other cases, the tutoring sessions were conducted in our own laboratories. In these latter instances, the protocols themselves were supplemented by stimulated-recall interviews conducted with the tutors as they observed replays of segments of their own tutoring sessions.

recommended to us by one or more outside sources. We then observed these experienced tutors working with individual students in the laboratory and made judgments regarding their level of effectiveness on the basis of their performance in these tutorial sessions. For this purpose, parallel ratings of the success of these tutors—in both motivational and intellectual domains—were obtained from other experienced math tutors, to ensure that these judgments would be independent of any subsequent analyses we performed.

This procedure permits us both to examine the commonalities that characterize the techniques of experienced tutors in these areas and to investigate the factors that distinguish more from less effective tutors in this domain. As will become apparent later in this chapter, for the questions that we address here, these two issues appear closely related. Strategies generally characteristic of experienced tutors also seem more prominent and more systematic in the protocols of those tutors who proved most effective in the laboratory.

Tutors' Strategies and Students' Achievement Attributions

Consider the techniques that experienced tutors employ to leave their students with a feeling of personal competence and self-efficacy. Here two questions arise: First, how do these tutors respond to the actual or anticipated successes and failures of their pupils? Second, what social and motivational consequences are these techniques likely to produce?

Tutors' Strategies.   How do effective tutors encourage the development of functional achievement attributions in their pupils? Our data suggest two complementary ways of addressing this initial question. The first approach is to consider what experienced human tutors do *not* seem to do in working with students; the second approach is to examine what they actually do seem to do.

The literature on student attributions for achievement outcomes is, of course, quite extensive (e.g., Dweck, 1986; Dweck & Elliott, 1983; Weiner, 1974, 1980). Most of the research in this tradition begins with a conceptual analysis of performance attributions, in terms of the two orthogonal dimensions of internality and stability. This analysis, presented in the form of a familiar 2×2 matrix of possible causal attributions for success and failure displayed in Fig. 10.1, was initially proposed by Weiner and his colleagues (Weiner, Kukla, Frieze, Reed, Rest, & Rosenbaum, 1971).[3] The research literature from which

---

[3]Over time, a number of more complex variations on this basic table, usually adding factors such as "controllability," "globality," and the like, have been presented (e.g., Abramson, Seligman, & Teasdale, 1978; Weiner, 1979). For purposes of the present discussion, however, these additional complexities of the analysis are moot. We have, however, added to Weiner et al.'s (1971) original formulation the category of "strategy" as an alternative or supplement to "mere effort" as a prototypical example of an internal, yet unstable, causal factor (e.g., Anderson & Jennings, 1980).

LOCUS OF CONTROL

	INTERNAL	EXTERNAL
STABLE	Ability	Task Difficulty
UNSTABLE	Effort Strategy	Luck

FIG.10.1.   A taxonomy of different types of performance attributions.
Adapted from Weiner et al. (1971).

this figure derives suggests that attributions of student performance to internal, unstable, and controllable factors such as effort and strategy appear to have beneficial motivational consequences, whereas attributions of student performance to either external (e.g., task difficulty or luck) or immutable internal (e.g., ability) factors appear to have relatively detrimental motivational consequences for the student.

As research in this area progressed, a number of researchers sought to determine how dysfunctional attributional patterns in students might be modified or supplanted by more effective attributional orientations. Beginning with Dweck's (1975) study of procedures for overcoming feelings of helplessness among remedial students, a considerable literature examining this question has developed. This literature, on the problem of "attributional retraining," has recently been reviewed by Foersterling (1985). The design of a typical study in this tradition is quite straightforward. In order to induce children initially identified as "helpless" to attribute their own failures to internal and controllable factors such as effort or strategy, students were exposed to adult models who themselves displayed this more functional attributional style in commenting on students' successes and failures. Subsequently, corresponding shifts in students' effort and strategy attributions, increased persistence in the face of difficulties, and decreased disruption of performance following failure are commonly observed (Foersterling, 1985).

A first interesting feature of the performance attributions of practiced tutors, therefore, is that they do not at all follow the script suggested by this prior experimental research. Attributions of student successes to effort or to an effective strategy or attributions of student failures to a lack of effort or to an ineffective strategy are relatively rare in the protocols of our experienced tutors, as can be seen in Figs. 10.2 and 10.3. Both effects, moreover, are more pronounced when we examine separately the data from the very best of the tutors we have studied.

PERFORMANCE ATTRIBUTIONS OF "ADDITION" TUTORS

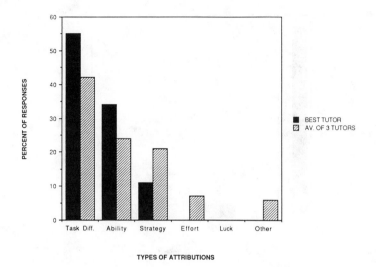

FIG.10.2.   Performance attributions of experienced addition tutors, by type.

Figs. 10.2 and 10.3 catalog the entire corpus of performance attributions displayed by six highly experienced tutors. In Fig. 10.2 are the data from three tutors studied by Putnam (1985) working with remedial second graders on basic addition with regrouping. Comparable findings for the best individual tutor at this task are presented separately in darker bars of this figure. Likewise, Fig. 10.3 displays the data from three experienced tutors working with fourth graders on the use of number lines to represent fractions and mixed numbers; again, the black bars present analogous data from the single best tutor observed in this second situation.

The second interesting feature of these data, of course, concerns what these tutors actually do instead of offering effort and strategy attributions. Here the answer can also be seen clearly in Figs. 10.2 and 10.3. They focus primarily on highlighting the high difficulty of the task, and secondarily on noting the considerable ability of the student. Such potentially dysfunctional attributions, however, are delivered in a quite strategic fashion. The majority of these attributions concerning task difficulty, for example, are offered in the form of forewarnings about the difficulty of the upcoming task (even in some cases in which the objective difficulty of the task can be shown not to have changed), and not as responses to failure. The result of these anticipatory mentions of task difficulty, on the one hand, is that if students fail at this "difficult" task, they have an obvious "excuse" for poor performance, without inferring either a lack of ability

PERFORMANCE ATTRIBUTIONS OF "FRACTIONS" TUTORS

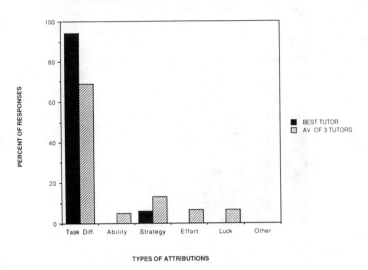

FIG.10.3.   Performance attributions of experienced fractions tutors, by type.

or a lack of effort. On the other hand, if students succeed, despite the obstacle of a difficult task, it must mean that they are actually reasonably capable.

Interestingly, our best tutors most often leave the attributional implications of these forewarnings about task difficulty unstated. Occasionally, they may offer explicit commiseration on the difficulty of the task to students who are having major problems. Similarly, they may sometimes make overt ability attributions following success in order to compliment students explicitly on their ability to succeed despite the difficulty of the problem. More frequently, however, the expert tutor will find ways of emphasizing these social messages indirectly. The most effective of the arithmetic tutors, for instance, would often respond to the student's successful completion of one difficult problem with a statement that "I guess we'll have to try to find an even harder one for you," a quite indirect and subtle compliment. Nonetheless, it appears from their responses to such comments that even young children clearly understand the underlying messages that the tutors are seeking to convey.

Strategy Effectiveness.   In their behavior in actual tutoring sessions and in their stimulated-recall interviews afterwards, our experienced tutors voiced their shared belief in the effectiveness of this indirect attributional strategy as a means of enhancing persistence and increasing feelings of competence—especially among students who are having great difficulty with the subject matter. To what extent are their beliefs justified?

To examine this question experimentally, we created a controlled tutoring situation in which we could observe undergraduate volunteers trained to employ different attribution strategies with students in different conditions. The basic design included two experimental groups and one control condition. In addition, because previous research on attribution retraining had focused on populations diagnosed as having difficulties in school, an attempt was made to include as many such problematic cases as possible. Thus, in the end, approximately one-third of the students in each condition were drawn from the school's remedial program; the remainder were enrolled in the regular program.

In the two experimental conditions, tutors were trained to add to a baseline control procedure one of two sets of overt performance attributions. In the "task attribution" condition, the tutors' responses were patterned after those just described as characteristic of our experienced tutors. In this group, new levels of difficulty were introduced to students with some explicit comment that the new problems were likely to prove more difficult, student errors were met with comments on the difficulty of the problem being attempted, and their successes were followed by praise for solving a difficult problem. The "effort attribution" condition, on the other hand, was derived from the procedures previously investigated in the attribution-retraining literature. In this condition, new levels of difficulty were introduced with the comment that the student might have to work even harder to succeed, student errors were followed by a suggestion that trying harder or using a different strategy might produce success, and successes were met with praise and a comment noting that the student seemed to have worked hard on that problem.

Subsequently, an array of motivational and cognitive measures was administered. A first such measure assessed students' persistence at a novel, and insoluble, task. The results from this measure appear in Fig. 10.4. There is only one significant finding in these results: Remedial students in the task attribution condition showed significantly increased persistence in the face of failure, compared with their counterparts in the effort attribution and the control conditions. Persistence at this new task showed no significant differences across conditions for nonremedial students.

Later, students were given a questionnaire that examined their perceptions of competence at, and their liking for, mathematics. The findings for these two measures are presented in Figs. 10.5 and 10.6. In both cases, the two experimental attribution conditions had statistically equivalent and significant positive effects for remedial students, compared with students in the control group. Once again, however, no significant effects were found for their nonremedial counterparts. Finally, student learning in the various conditions was assessed by a written posttest on the material. All groups performed near the maximum on this test, and no significant differences across conditions were obtained.

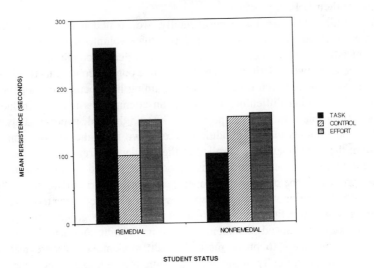

FIG. 10.4.   Mean persistence at a subsequent novel insoluble task, by student status and experimental condition, Experiment 1.

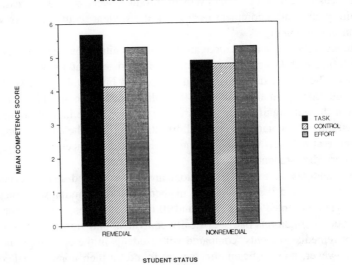

FIG. 10.5.   Mean perceived competence in mathematics, by student status and experimental condition, Experiment 1.

ATTITUDES TOWARD MATH

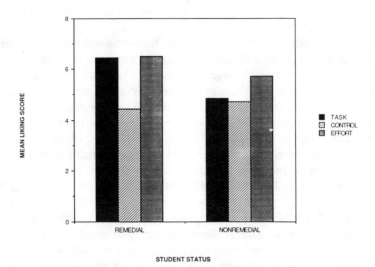

FIG. 10.6. Mean reported attitudes toward mathematics, by student status and experimental condition, Experiment 1.

In short, for the remedial students—those pupils likely to have already developed a dysfunctional attributional style—the strategy employed by our expert tutors proved more effective in producing subsequent persistence at a new task than a strategy derived from the existing literature and equally effective as this more traditional strategy in producing increases in liking for, and feelings of competence in, mathematics. For nonremedial students, however, none of the benefits of either attributional strategy proved significant.

Tutors' Strategies and Students' Self-perceptions of Intrinsic Motivation

In the preceding section, we examined the performance attributions of expert tutors; in this section, we turn our attention to the strategies that expert tutors employ to maintain and increase students' feelings of personal control and intrinsic motivation. That is, tutors not only want their students to feel competent in a subject area; they also want their students to feel motivated to engage in the activity and to be interested in the subject matter even when the tutor, or other authority figure, is no longer around. How, then, do they seek to accomplish this second motivational objective?

Tutors' Strategies.   As with the study of performance attributions, it is possible to examine the strategies that effective tutors use to enhance students' intrinsic motivation from two complementary perspectives. Let us consider first what these tutors do *not* do, but might have been expected to do. Then let us examine what they appear to do instead.

Within the field of instructional design, there is a great deal of traditional wisdom concerning the techniques that should promote the reinforcement of learning and performance. Although one can find discussions of these traditional instructional issues in a wide array of sources (e.g., Bower & Hilgard, 1985; Gagné, 1975), these issues have recently come to the fore once again in domain of educational computing. Because the computerization of instruction requires a precise and complete specification of one's model of teaching, designers of computer-based educational programs must consider explicitly a variety of pedagogical questions that often remain implicit in regular classroom instruction (Bork, 1985; Lepper & Chabay, 1985, 1988; Steinberg, 1984; Walker & Hess, 1984).

Consider, from this perspective, some of the central questions that any instructional model must address: How, for example, should the tutor respond when the student has failed? Early computer-assisted instruction often tended to employ what one might call a straightforward "corrective feedback" model. In this tradition, when students have made a mistake, the first important consideration is that they be informed of that error. They then may, or may not, be given another chance to answer. If they continue to fail, however, they need to be given the correct answer. Then, a decision must be made as to whether additional instruction is required before the student is allowed to proceed to the next problem. Such procedures are common in traditional educational computing activities, and the theoretical justification for such procedures has been spelled out by a number of authors (e.g., Gagné & Briggs, 1974; Skinner, 1968; Walker & Hess, 1984).

As computers have become more powerful and more sophisticated in recent years, of course, a number of other instructional models have been examined. Of these, one of the most popular and potentially powerful approaches involves what are known as intelligent tutoring systems (e.g., Anderson, Boyle, & Reiser, 1985; Dede, 1986; Sleeman & Brown, 1982). In these more complex teaching systems, the basic idea is to make use of the computational power of the machine to perform a precise and detailed diagnosis of what individual students do and do not understand about a given domain of knowledge. Once this is done, it is possible for a tutorial program to inform students of their misconceptions and to contrast their ideas and procedures with the correct approach.

In this context, the first thing that we can say about our experienced tutors is that they generally provide students with extremely little in the way of overt diagnoses concerning their errors or explicit corrective feedback. As is evident in Fig. 10.7, these human tutors rarely provide overt corrective feedback following student errors. In fact, 95% of the time they do not even explicitly label the student's mistake as incorrect or as an error. Nor do they provide direct help or

TUTOR RESPONSES TO STUDENT ERRORS

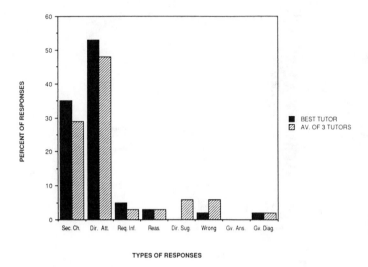

FIG.10.7   Responses to student errors by experienced addition tutors, by types.

give the student the answer to the problem, except as a last resort after all other techniques have failed. Similarly, although the best tutors are actually very effective in diagnosing the problems that a student is experiencing, they almost never inform the student directly of their diagnoses.

What these tutors do instead is also illustrated in Fig. 10.7, which displays the responses of our three arithmetic tutors to all situations in which their students have made an error, are thought to be about to make an error, or have said they are stuck or confused. Instead of providing explicit corrective feedback, these tutors rely on a much more subtle and indirect strategy. They offer students *hints*—questions or remarks that indirectly imply the inaccuracy of their prior response, suggest the direction in which they might proceed, or highlight the section of the problem that appears to be causing them difficulty. The two most common types of responses by our tutors, represented by the left-most bars in Fig. 10.7, were to direct the child's attention to the source of difficulty and to offer the child a second chance. Once again, this general pattern holds even more strongly when we examine separately the responses of the best of these tutors, displayed in the darker bars in the figure.

Additionally, one can see further evidence of the indirectness of the feedback strategies that good tutors employ in the *form* of their responses to student errors and confusions. As shown in Fig. 10.8, two thirds of these tutors' responses to student difficulties are presented in the form of questions, rather than statements

CLASSIFICATION OF TUTOR RESPONSES

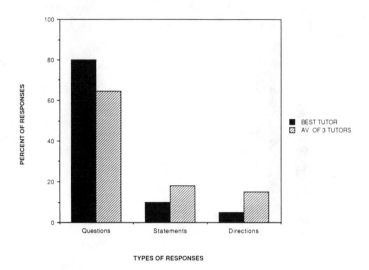

FIG. 10.8.   Forms of all responses to students by experienced addition tutors.

or directions. For the best tutor alone, the ratio of questions to directions is more than 16 : 1. Thus, when faced with a pupil who has added 36 and 36 to get 126 (rather than 72), this tutor asks the student simply, "Now how did you get that 6?" Then, when this hint proved insufficient, the tutor continued with a long series of increasingly specific questions such as, "Which column do we start in?" and "Where is the one's column?" until they eventually reached a question that the student could answer correctly.

Strategy Effectiveness.   As in the earlier case, it is clear that our tutors have strong beliefs in the efficacy of their techniques in this area. In their responses to students within tutoring sessions, they frequently persist in their use of indirect instructional methods, even in the face of long strings of student errors, when a more direct approach would have saved them considerable time and effort. In their interviews, they also justify their efforts on both cognitive and motivational grounds. They suggest that students will remember and employ the information more effectively, to the extent that more of the information can be drawn from the students themselves. Similarly, they propose that students will remain more interested and excited if they are encouraged to respond actively, rather than passively, to the demands of the situation.

To investigate these possibilities, we conducted a second experimental study, in which undergraduate volunteers were again taught to use different tutoring styles with students in different conditions. Three procedures, derived from this second set of observations, were compared. In the two experimental conditions, "normal" fourth-grade students were tutored on a series of problems modeled after Raven's (1965) progressive matrices. In the "indirect style" condition, patterned after the strategies employed by the experts, our undergraduate tutors were taught to respond to student errors or confusions with a graded series of prompts or hints, ordered from the most general to the most specific. Once the children succeeded, in this condition, the tutor then asked them to articulate and to name the rule they had used to obtain their answer. In the "direct style" condition, by contrast, identical information was conveyed to students in a more highly didactic fashion. Thus, when students erred, the tutor provided them with increasingly specific directions for solving the problem; once they succeeded, the tutor articulated and named the rule used for them. In the control condition, the tutors worked with students in an informal fashion on a completely unrelated task (i.e., crossword puzzles).

Following these individual tutoring sessions, a number of measures were obtained from each student. First, each student was asked to select a further problem to work on, sight unseen, from packages designated as appropriate for four different grade levels: the student's own grade, one grade below, and one or two grades above. On this measure of preference for challenge, students in the indirect style condition selected significantly more difficult problems to attempt, as shown in the results presented in Fig. 10.9.

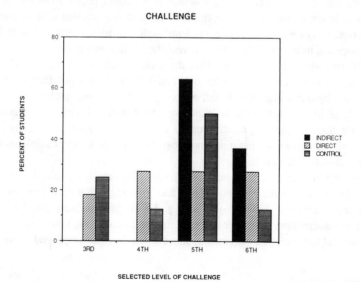

FIG. 10.9. Levels of challenge selected by students, by experimental condition, Experiment 2.

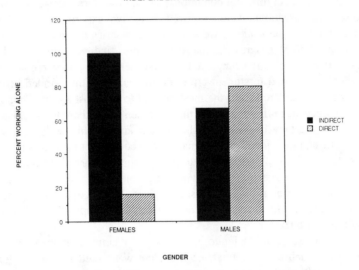

FIG. 10.10. Reported preference for undertaking a subsequent task either alone or together with the tutor, by student gender and experimental condition, Experiment 2.

Next, the students were asked whether they would prefer to work on this further problem alone, or with the tutor, in order to see whether a more indirect instructional style might increase students' self-confidence and enhance their desire to work independently in the future. The results on this measure appear in Fig. 10.10, where it is apparent that the effects differed for boys and girls, producing a significant interaction between condition and gender.[4] Girls, as anticipated by our initial hypothesis, were significantly more likely to choose to work alone in the indirect-style condition than in the direct-style condition. Boys, by contrast, showed no difference. They chose to work alone even in the direct-style condition, so that it was not possible to observe any possible increase in the indirect-style condition.

Some further light is shed on these gender differences by additional unexpected differences in the reports of boys and girls regarding their enjoyment of the tutoring sessions. As displayed in Fig. 10.11, this measure also yielded a significant interaction of gender and experimental condition. Thus, boys tended to report that they enjoyed the sessions more when the tutor employed an indirect

---

[4]Students in the control condition in this study are not included in Figs. 10.10 and 10.11, because these students had not worked on the same task as those in the experimental conditions.

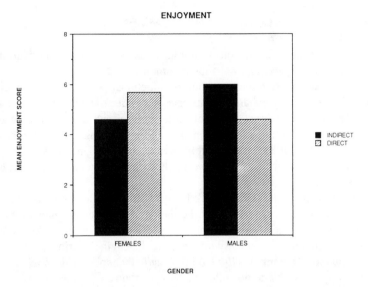

FIG. 10.11.   Mean reported enjoyment of the tutoring session, by student gender and experimental condition, Experiment 2.

style, whereas girls tended to report that they enjoyed the sessions more when the tutor employed a direct style. One possibility, therefore, is that our measure of "independent mastery" may have had a different meaning for boys and girls. For boys, their overall preference for working alone is paralleled by their preference for an indirect tutoring strategy; for girls, the choice of whether to work alone or together more closely parallels the differences in their liking for the tutor in the two experimental conditions.

Two final measures yielded no significant effects. First, students' persistence on a last problem of nearly impossible difficulty was also assessed. Here, although the means for both sexes again favored subjects in the indirect conditions, there were no significant differences among groups. Second, this study also failed to show significant differences in learning as a function of experimental condition. Again, however, high levels of overall learning (i.e., posttest means of over 4.5 out of a maximum score of 5) may have precluded the observation of group differences on this measure.

Overall, in these results, we see once again some evidence of the potential wisdom of expert practice. In fact, even the "direct" style in this experiment involved a procedure much less overt and didactic than those in widespread use in educational computing today. Nonetheless, although they seem to vary somewhat for boys and girls, there appear to be significant motivational advantages to the use of a more subtle and indirect instructional style.

CONCLUDING COMMENTS

How, then, do expert human tutors simultaneously instruct and motivate their pupils? The most general answer—the common thread that unites our observations of these tutors' strategies for eliciting functional performance attributions and their techniques for enhancing intrinsic motivation—involves a reliance on relatively subtle and indirect forms of social control and a disavowal of more obvious and direct methods for influencing and controlling students' behaviors (cf. Lepper, 1981, 1983). These tutors persist in these methods, moreover, despite their belief that more directive methods may sometimes have clear instructional benefits for students.

"I think I can. I think I can. I think I can," said the little engine out loud for all to hear—making clear and salient the theme of achievement motivation and the dependence of one's strivings on one's perceptions of the likelihood of success. Less obvious, but equally important to the engine's actions, however, is a second theme: "I think I *will*. I think I *will*. I choose to do so." That is, perceptions of capability do not automatically guarantee relevant actions. All the bigger and stronger and newer engines certainly knew that they could pull the little train over the mountain, but they chose not to do so. What was needed was a little engine that believed that it could *and* that wanted to do so.

If, in our schools, we seek to produce students who will pursue learning for its own sake, who will seek out challenging problems to conquer, and who will persist in the face of difficulties—even when there is no immediate extrinsic payoff in sight—we will need to pay attention to both their feelings of competence and their feelings of constraint. As George Bernard Shaw suggested about our Western educational system some years ago: "What we want is to see the child in pursuit of knowledge, and not knowledge in pursuit of the child."

ACKNOWLEDGMENTS

The research reported in this chapter and the preparation of this report were supported, in part, by Research Grant HD–MH–09814 from the National Institute of Child Health and Human Development to Mark R. Lepper and a grant from the Undergraduate Research Opportunities Office at Stanford University to Lisa Aspinwall. Lisa Aspinwall is now at the University of California, Los Angeles. Donna Mumme was supported in this work, in addition, by graduate fellowships from Phi Kappa Phi and the National Science Foundation. Requests for reprints may be sent to Mark R. Lepper, Department of Psychology, Jordan Hall—Building 420, Stanford University, Stanford, CA 94305–2130.

The authors would like to express their appreciation to the principals, Sister Mary Howard, Ms. Lois Bauer, and Ms. Kathy Machado, their staffs, and the children of St. Elizabeth Seton School in Palo Alto, St. Nicholas School in Los

Altos Hills, and the St. Williams School in Los Altos, California. Without their kind help and cooperation, these studies could not have been conducted. We are indebted, as well, to Mary Hartsuch, Maria Krysan, Shelley Lawrence, Margaret Mutch, Monique Prado, Dianne Scott, Aimée Vosti, and Lori Woskow who served as research assistants and tutors in the experimental studies. We are also extremely grateful to Ralph Putnam for his willingness to share with us the transcripts of his tutoring protocols (Putnam, 1985) and to Jean–Luc Gurtner and Maria Woolverton for their assistance in the analysis of the tutoring protocols.

REFERENCES

Abramson, L. Y., Seligman, M. E. P., & Teasdale, J. D. (1978). Learned helplessness in humans: Critique and reformulation. *Journal of Abnormal Psychology, 87,* 49–74.

Anderson, C. A., & Jennings, D. L. (1980). When experiences of failure promote expectations of success: The impact of attributing failure to ineffective strategies. *Journal of Personality, 48,* 393–407.

Anderson, J. R., Boyle, C. F., & Reiser, B. (1985). Intelligent tutoring systems. *Science, 228,* 456–468.

Bandura, A. (1977). Self-efficacy: Toward a unifying theory of behavioral change. *Psychological Review, 84,* 191–215.

Bandura, A. (1986). *Social foundations of thought and action.* Englewood Cliffs, NJ: Prentice–Hall.

Bandura, A., & Schunk, D. H. (1981). Cultivating competence, self-efficacy, and intrinsic interest through proximal self-instruction. *Journal of Personality and Social Psychology, 41,* 486–598.

Bork, A. (1985). *Personal computers for education.* New York: Harper & Row.

Bower, G. H., & Hilgard, E. R. (1985). *Theories of learning.* Englewood Cliffs, N.J.: Prentice–Hall.

Deci, E. L. (1975). *Intrinsic motivation.* New York: Plenum.

Deci, E. L. (1981). *The psychology of self-determination.* Lexington, MA: Heath.

Deci, E. L., & Ryan, R. M. (1985). *Intrinsic motivation and self-determination in human behavior.* New York: Plenum Press.

Dede, C. J. (1986). A review and synthesis of recent research in intelligent computer-assisted instruction. *International Journal of Man-Machine Studies, 24,* 329–353.

Dweck, C. S. (1975). The role of expectations and attributions in the alleviation of learned helplessness. *Journal of Personality and Social Psychology, 31,* 674–685.

Dweck, C. S. (1986). Motivational processes affecting learning. *American Psychologist, 41,* 1040–1048.

Dweck, C. S., & Elliott, E. S. (1983). Achievement motivation. In E. M. Hetherington (Ed.), *Socialization, personality, and social development* (pp. 643–681). New York: Wiley.

Dweck, C. S., & Leggett, E. L. (1988). A social-cognitive approach to motivation and personality. *Psychological Review, 95,* 256–273.

Foersterling, F. (1985). Attributional retraining: A review. *Psychological Bulletin, 98,* 495–512.

Gagné, R. M. (1975). *Essentials of learning for instruction.* New York: Holt, Rinehart, & Winston.

Gagné, R. M., & Briggs, L. J. (1974). *Principles of instructional design.* New York: Holt, Rinehart, & Winston.

Harter, S. (1978). Effectance motivation reconsidered: Toward a developmental model. *Human Development, 1,* 34–64.

Kelley, H. H. (1967). Attribution theory in social psychology. In D. Levine (Ed.), *Nebraska symposium on motivation*. (Vol. 15, pp. 192–240). Lincoln: University of Nebraska Press.

Kelley, H. H. (1973). The processes of causal attribution. *American Psychologist, 28*, 107–128.

Kramnick, I. (1980). Children's literature and bourgeois ideology: Observations on culture and industrial capitalism in the later eighteenth century. In P. Zagorin (Ed.), *Culture and politics from puritanism to the enlightenment*. Berkeley: University of California Press.

Lepper, M. R. (1981). Intrinsic and extrinsic motivation in children: Detrimental effects of superfluous social controls. In W. A. Collins (Ed.), *Minnesota symposium on child psychology* (Vol. 14, pp. 155–214). Hillsdale, NJ: Lawrence Erlbaum Associates.

Lepper, M. R. (1983). Extrinsic reward and intrinsic motivation: Implications for the classroom. In J. M. Levine, & M. C. Wang (Eds.), *Teacher and student perceptions: Implications for learning* (pp. 281–317). Hillsdale, NJ: Lawrence Erlbaum Associates.

Lepper, M. R. (1988). Motivational considerations in the study of instruction. *Cognition and Instruction, 5*, 289–309.

Lepper, M. R., & Chabay, R. W. (1985). Intrinsic motivation and instruction: Conflicting views on the role of motivational processes in computer-based education. *Educational Psychologist, 20*, 217–230.

Lepper, M. R., & Greene, D. (Eds.). (1978). *The hidden costs of reward*. Hillsdale, NJ: Lawrence Erlbaum Associates.

Lepper, M. R., Gurtner, J., Mumme, D. M., Woolverton, M., Chabay, R. W., & Larkin, J. H. (in preparation). Expertise in tutoring: Motivational and informational considerations in successful tutorial interactions.

Lepper, M. R., & Hodell, M. (1989). Intrinsic motivation in the classroom. In C. Ames & R. Ames (Eds.), *Research on motivation in education* (Vol. 3, pp. 73–105). New York: Academic Press.

Mahoney, M. J. (1974). *Cognition and behavior modification*. Cambridge, MA: Ballinger.

Mahoney, M. J., & Thoreson, C. E. (Eds.). (1974). *Self-control: Power to the person*. Monterey, CA: Brooks–Cole.

Malone, T. W., & Lepper, M. R. (1987). Making learning fun: A taxonomy of intrinsic motivations for learning. In R. E. Snow, & M. J. Farr (Eds.), *Aptitude, learning, and instruction: III. Conative and affective process analyses* (pp. 223–253). Hillsdale, NJ: Lawrence Erlbaum Associates.

McClelland, D. C. (1961). *The achieving society*. Princeton, NJ: Van Nostrand.

Meichenbaum, D. H. (1977). *Cognitive behavior modification: An integrative approach*. New York: Plenum.

Nicholls, J. G. (1989). *The competitive ethos and democratic education*. Cambridge, MA: Harvard University Press.

Prawat, R. S. (1985). Affective versus cognitive goal orientations in elementary teachers. *American Educational Research Journal, 22*, 587–604.

Prawat, R. S., & Nickerson, J. R. (1985). The relationship between teacher thought and action and student affective outcomes. *Elementary School Journal, 85*, 529–540.

Putnam, R. T. (1985). Teacher thoughts and actions in live and simulated tutoring of addition. *Dissertation Abstracts International, 46*, 933A–934A.

Putnam, R. T. (1987). Structuring and adjusting content for students: A study of live and simulated tutoring of addition. *American Educational Research Journal, 24*, 13–48.

Raven, J. C. (1965). *Advanced progressive matrices, Sets I and II*. London: H. K. Lewis.

Schunk, D. H. (1985). Self-efficacy and classroom learning. *Psychology in the Schools, 22*, 208–223.

Skinner, B. F. (1968). *The technology of teaching*. New York: Appleton–Century–Crofts.

Sleeman, D., & Brown, J. S. (Eds.). (1982). *Intelligent tutoring systems*. New York: Academic Press.

Steinberg, E. (1984). *Teaching computers to teach*. Hillsdale, NJ: Lawrence Erlbaum Associates.

Walker, D. F., & Hess, R. D. (Eds.). (1984). *Instructional software: Principles and perspectives for design and use.* Belmont, CA: Wadsworth.

Weiner, B. (Ed.). (1974). *Achievement motivation and attribution theory.* Morristown, NJ: General Learning Press.

Weiner, B. (1979). A theory of motivation for some classroom experiences. *Journal of Educational Psychology, 71,* 3–25.

Weiner, B. (1980). *Human motivation.* New York: Holt, Rinehart, & Winston.

Weiner, B. (1985). An attributional theory of achievement motivation and emotion. *Psychological Review, 92,* 102–107.

Weiner, B., Frieze, I., Kukla, A., Reed, L., Rest, R., & Rosenbaum, R. M. (1971). Perceiving the causes of success and failure. In E. E. Jones, D. E. Kanouse, H. H. Kelley, R. E. Nisbett, S. Valins, & B. Weiner (Eds.), *Attribution: Perceiving the causes of behavior.* Morristown, NJ: General Learning Press.

11 Uncertainty Orientation: Individual Differences in the Self-Inference Process

Richard M. Sorrentino
Christopher J. R. Roney
University of Western Ontario

The last Ontario Symposium was on social influence (see Zanna, Olson, & Herman, 1986). At that symposium, we suggested that many of the contributors should consider individual differences, particularly individual differences in uncertainty orientation (cf. Sorrentino & Short, 1986), when constructing their theories. For example, presenters such as Shelley Chaiken, Alice Eagly, Russel Fazio, Richard Petty, and John Cacioppo were theorizing that as the content of the message becomes more personally or self-relevant, people move from more automatic forms of information processing to more controlled forms. That is, as the message becomes more relevant to the self, people will become less reliant on such heuristic devices as source expertise, attractiveness of the source, and sheer frequency of arguments, and more reliant on the actual content of the message in forming their opinions.

We argued that although this might be true for persons we call uncertainty-oriented, certainty-oriented persons will actually move from controlled processing of information to more automatic forms. That is, as we strengthen the relevance of the information to the self, certainty-oriented persons will pay even less attention to the message, and rely more on heuristic devices to form their attitudes (the possible explanations for this paradoxical effect will be articulated later in this chapter).

Although we had little data at the time, we recently have published two studies (Sorrentino, Bobocel, Gitta, Olson, & Hewitt, 1988) that support our hypothesis. In the first study, we predicted that when personal relevance was high, uncertainty-oriented persons would be even more persuaded by a two-sided communication (conducive to systematic processing of information) and less persuaded by a one-sided communication (conducive to heuristic processing)

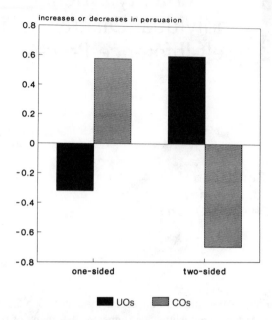

FIG. 11.1.   Mean attitude change difference from low to high personal
relevance for uncertainty-oriented (UOs) and certainty-oriented (COs)
persons as a function of argument sides. (Based on data from "Uncertainty Orientation and Persuasion: Individual Differences in the Effects
of Personal Relevance on Social Judgements," by R. M. Sorrentino, D.
R. Bobocel, M. Z. Gitta, J. M. Olson, & E. C. Hewitt, 1988, *Journal of
Personality and Social Psychology, 55,* p. 362. Copyright 1988 by the
American Psychological Association. Reprinted by permission.)

than when personal relevance was low. Certainty-oriented persons, however,
should actually show the reverse pattern of interaction, being more persuaded by
a one-sided and less persuaded by a two-sided communication under high than
low personal relevance. Fig. 11.1 illustrates the results of this study by showing
increases or decreases in persuasion (concerning the desirability of a comprehensive examination requirement for graduation) from low to high personal relevance for uncertainty-oriented versus certainty-oriented persons. (Subjects in the
high personal relevance condition were led to believe that they were likely to
have to meet this requirement; subjects in the low personal relevance condition
were led to believe that they were not likely to have to meet this requirement.)

As can be seen in Fig. 11.1, our hypothesis was supported. Persuasiveness of
the message decreased from low to high personal relevance with a one-sided
communication, and increased with a two-sided communication, for uncertainty-
oriented persons. Note, however, that precisely the reverse occurred for certainty-oriented persons. These people were more persuaded by a one-sided commu-

nication and less persuaded by a two-sided communication as personal relevance increased.

In the second study, we manipulated variables thought to be more directly related to systematic versus heuristic information processing; that is, strength of arguments (strong vs. weak) and source expertise (expert vs. nonexpert). Here, as well, we found evidence in support of our hypothesis. For both source expertise and argument strength, Fig. 11.2 shows the change in impact from the low personal relevance condition to the high personal relevance condition.

As can be seen, high personal relevance increased the influence of argument strength and decreased the influence of source expertise, as various theorists would predict (e.g., Chaiken, 1980; Fazio, 1986; Petty, Cacioppo, & Goldman, 1981), but *only* for uncertainty-oriented persons. Certainty-oriented persons again showed the reverse pattern of interaction. These persons were actually more influenced by source expertise and less influenced by argument strength in

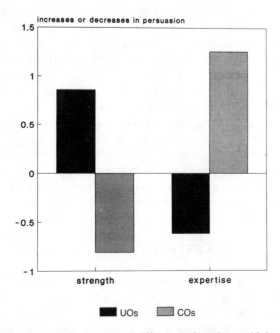

FIG. 11.2. Mean attitude change differences from low to high personal relevance for uncertainty-oriented (UOs) and certainty-oriented (COs) persons as a function of argument strength and source expertise. (Based on data from "Uncertainty Orientation and Persuasion: Individual Differences in the Effects of Personal Relevance on Social Judgements," by R. M. Sorrentino, D. R. Bobocel, M. Z. Gitta, J. M. Olson, & E. C. Hewitt, 1988, *Journal of Personality and Social Psychology, 55,* pp. 365–366. Copyright 1988 by the American Psychological Association. Reprinted by permission.)

high rather than low personal relevance. None of the above theorists would predict this pattern.

These data become even more compelling when one considers that, in both studies, subjects were telephoned 2 weeks later under the guise of an independent survey. Results from these telephone surveys showed that the initial findings not only held up over time, but actually became somewhat stronger. Thus, for the certainty-oriented group, we obtained reliable and persistent effects in two studies that are exactly opposite to expectations derived from previous theories. It appears that those theorists were really talking about uncertainty-oriented persons and not certainty-oriented persons.

In this chapter, we began with the findings from Sorrentino et al. (1988), not only because the findings sprung directly from thoughts and ideas concerning the last Ontario Symposium (see Sorrentino & Hancock, 1986), for which we are grateful, but also because they have implications for this symposium as well. In these studies (i.e., Sorrentino et al., 1988), our uncertainty-oriented persons did the "natural" thing. When attention was drawn to the self (i.e., personal relevance was high), they began paying close attention to the message. Our certainty-oriented persons, however, did quite the opposite. They became more reliant on heuristics (one-sided messages, source expertise), appearing to ignore rather than employ controlled processing of information.

This research, emphasizing the role of self-relevance, has led us to focus increasingly on the importance of the self in understanding individual differences in uncertainty orientation. Indeed, we now have reason to believe that many theories of self-inference are concerned mainly with the behavior of the uncertainty-oriented person, whereas the behavior of certainty-oriented persons is relatively neglected. This may be of major importance, as we also have reason to believe that the majority of the lay population in our culture is certainty-oriented and not uncertainty-oriented (see Sorrentino, Short, & Raynor, 1984).

UNCERTAINTY ORIENTATION

For those of you unaware of our previous research (see Sorrentino & Hancock, 1986; Sorrentino & Short, 1986), you might be wondering, "Who are these certainty-oriented persons?" We are still learning about them ourselves, but let us tell you some of the things we know so far, beginning with the uncertainty-oriented end of the dimension.

An uncertainty-oriented person is one who scores high on our projective measure of the need to resolve uncertainty, or *n* Uncertainty (Frederick, Sorrentino, & Hewitt, 1987), and low on a measure of authoritarianism (Byrne & Lamberth, 1971). He or she is thought to be primarily concerned with, and interested in, finding out new things about the self or the environment. He or she is the "need to know" type. The consequences of self-discovery are not important; it is the resolution of uncertainty that is important.[1]

A certainty-oriented person is thought to be primarily concerned with maintaining clarity about what is already known. He or she is not interested in discovering new information about the self or the environment, as such activities could be harmful.[2] Thus, curiosity is not their forte. They score relatively low on our measure of *n* uncertainty and high on our measure of authoritarianism.

We originally devised our measure of uncertainty orientation in order to consider its influence on achievement behavior (see Sorrentino & Hewitt, 1984; Sorrentino & Roney, 1986; Sorrentino, Short, & Raynor, 1984). We felt that an important dimension, heretofore neglected, was the uncertainty of the outcome. In several studies, we predicted and found that expected differences in performance as a function of achievement-related motives were moderated by uncertainty-orientation and the uncertainty of the outcome (e.g., Sorrentino et al., 1984). These findings led to the conclusion that relevant sources of motivation are engaged primarily in situations consistent with one's uncertainty orientation. Uncertainty-oriented persons are motivated by situations where the outcome is uncertain. Certainty-oriented persons are motivated by situations where the outcome is relatively certain. This, in turn, led to a number of interesting conclusions, subsuming both cognitive and affective theories of achievement motivation within a more integrative approach (see Sorrentino & Short, 1986).

UNCERTAINTY ORIENTATION AND THE SELF

Although our primary concern was with achievement behavior, we couldn't help but notice that one of the primary sources of uncertainty is uncertainty about the self. Many of our earlier studies could, in fact, be reinterpreted in terms of manipulating the extent to which the situation resolves uncertainty about the self. In our grades study (Study 3 of Sorrentino et al., 1984), for example, we found that arousal of achievement-related motives (as judged by performance on midterm and final exams) was greatest for uncertainty-oriented persons in courses perceived as relevant to future goals and careers. For certainty-oriented persons, arousal of achievement-related motives was greatest in courses perceived as

---

[1]Indeed, in her recent M.A. thesis, Maria Gitta (1988) found on the Teledominance Scale (Murgatroyd, Rushton, Apter, & Ray, 1978), that whereas certainty-oriented persons are goal or end-state-oriented, uncertainty-oriented persons are process-oriented (i.e., they care as much or more about engaging in the activity than in the actual outcome).

[2]Using a subscale of the Teledominance Scale, Ms. Gitta also found that certainty-oriented persons were significantly more arousal avoidant than uncertainty-oriented persons, suggesting that they choose to avoid the arousal associated with a process orientation.

irrelevant to future goals or careers. So when the course offered self-assessment of important abilities, uncertainty-oriented students were motivated; when it did not, certainty-oriented students were motivated.

Given this reinterpretation, we set out to show that uncertainty-oriented persons would be more motivated by situations where the self was an important factor, whereas certainty-oriented persons would be less motivated by self-relevant situations. Our key study in this respect, Sorrentino and Hewitt (1984), was a replication of an earlier one by Yaacov Trope (1979). Trope showed that people are motivated to engage in activity that will resolve uncertainty about their ability, regardless of whether the resolution will lead to positive or negative consequences (i.e., to the conclusion that they are good or bad at that ability). We showed that this was true only for uncertainty-oriented persons. Certainty-oriented persons actually chose to engage in activities that would tell them nothing new about the self, regardless of whether the new information was likely to be good news or bad news.

These results, although predicted a priori, were sufficiently controversial that we wanted to confirm them in a conceptual replication and extension. In a study by Sorrentino and Roney (1986), we demonstrated that expected differences in performance due to achievement-related motives were greatest in situations that were perceived as diagnostic of one's ability, but only if people were uncertainty-oriented. These performance differences were greatest in nondiagnostic situations for certainty-oriented persons. Again, whereas uncertainty-oriented persons appeared to be motivated by self-relevant situations, certainty-oriented persons seemed to be motivated by situations that were not self-relevant.

Social Comparison and Values

In our next step, we investigated implications for social comparison theory (Roney & Sorrentino, 1988, Study 1). Some of these data are presented in Figs. 11.3 and 11.4. In this study, conducted entirely on a microcomputer, subjects first rated themselves on the Allport and Vernon (1931) human values scale. This scale provides scores for six different types of human values: theoretical, economic, political, aesthetic, social, and religious. Immediately upon completion of the scale, subjects received feedback about their scores on each of the six values. After seeing their own scores, subjects had the opportunity to access six "files" on the computer, one for each value type, which contained scores from other people on these values. Subjects were told either that the scores were those of other students (similar others) or nonstudents from the community (dissimilar others). At this point, subjects were free to view as many of the scores in the files as they wished (up to 20 scores). This measure is conceptually similar to that used by Brickman and Berman (1977).

An ANOVA was computed on the number of comparison scores examined, with uncertainty orientation (uncertainty-oriented, certainty-oriented) and sim-

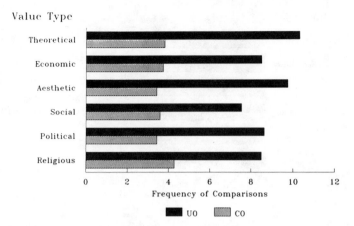

FIG. 11.3. Mean comparison scores viewed by uncertainty-oriented (UO) and certainty-oriented (CO) persons as a function of value type.

ilarity of the comparison group (similar, dissimilar) as between groups factors and type of value (theoretical, economic, aesthetic, social, political, religious) as a within-subjects factor. A significant main effect for uncertainty orientation was found on the number of comparisons made, $F(1,56) = 5.76, p < .05$.

It can be seen in Fig. 11.3 that, for all six values, uncertainty-oriented persons chose to view more scores than certainty-oriented persons. This supports the hypothesis that uncertainty-oriented people are more interested in seeking out new information about how they compare with others than are certainty-oriented people.

Also of interest from this study were differences on people's actual scores on the value survey. As can be seen in Fig. 11.4, uncertainty-oriented persons scored higher than certainty-oriented persons on theoretical and aesthetic values, but lower on all others, including religious values. This produced a significant uncertainty orientation by values interaction, $F(5,290) = 2.56, p < .05$. Individual comparisons revealed that significant differences occurred on theoretical values, $t(307) = 2.93, p < .01$, aesthetic values, $t(307) = 3.00, p < .01)$, and religious values, $t(307) = 2.96, p < .01$. Theoretical values, as defined by Spranger (1928, cited in Allport & Vernon, 1931), relate to the discovery of truth. The interests of the "theoretical man" are empirical, critical, and rational. This fits nicely with our conception of uncertainty-oriented persons as valuing scientific reasoning (see Sorrentino & Short, 1986). In terms of aesthetic values, Spranger suggests that aesthetic individuals judge their experiences in terms of "grace, symmetry, or fitness." Again, this seems compatible with our notion that uncertainty-oriented persons are akin to Rokeach's (1960) open-minded persons, who like to synthesize new or novel information (see Sorrentino & Short, 1986). Such an "artistic" orientation may also involve understanding oneself and one's

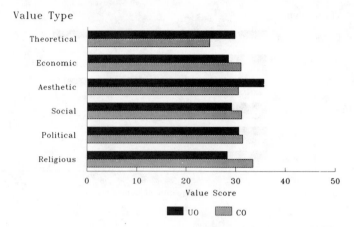

FIG. 11.4. Mean value scores for uncertainty-oriented (UO) and certainty-oriented (CO) persons as a function of value type.

environment, only in a different manner than that implied in a theoretical orientation (cf. Berlyne's, 1960, work on aesthetics and curiosity). In terms of religious values, one would expect certainty-oriented persons to be higher than uncertainty-oriented persons, since religiosity is highly correlated with our component measure of authoritarianism (see Sorrentino, 1981).

Finally, it is interesting to note that uncertainty-oriented persons are more interested in comparing themselves on *all* values, even on those that certainty-oriented persons appear to value more. Hence, uncertainty-oriented persons are more interested in comparing the self with others than certainty-oriented persons, regardless of the importance of the value to the self.

Self-discrepancy Theory

Perhaps our most exciting new development comes from recent findings on self-discrepancy theory (Higgins, Strauman, & Klein, 1986). This theory predicts that perceived discrepancies between the way people believe they are (their actual selves) and their different abstract selves will result in different types of negative affect. Emotions related to dejection (e.g., unhappy, dissatisfied) are predicted to result if a discrepancy is perceived from one's actual self and one's ideal self (hopes, goals, and aspirations), either as the person holds it for himself or herself (own standpoint) or as some significant other holds it for that person (other standpoint). Agitation-related emotions (e.g., anxiety, fear) are predicted if a discrepancy is perceived between one's actual self and one's ought self (sense of duty, expectation, and obligation) from an own or other standpoint.

These authors (Higgins et al., 1986) go on to argue that differences in behavior as a function of achievement-related motives may be a function of differences in types of self-discrepancies for success-oriented and failure-threatened persons. They speculate that success-oriented persons have ideal–own discrepancies with their actual selves, and therefore work hard at achievement-oriented activity in order to reduce this discrepancy. Failure-threatened persons, however, have ought–other discrepancies with their actual selves, and therefore their performance is inhibited by fear and anxiety.

Our argument would be that self-discrepancy theory, as currently formulated, applies mainly to uncertainty-oriented people, but not to certainty-oriented people, because comparing oneself with abstract standards involves self-evaluation. We believe that, given the choice, certainty-oriented people will not even attend to self-discrepant information. Second, we would argue that the foregoing speculation concerning differences in behavior as a function of achievement-related motives will be subsumed by an interaction with uncertainty orientation. Consistent with our findings from previous research (Sorrentino & Roney, 1986; Sorrentino et al., 1984), we would expect that whereas uncertainty-oriented persons will show the greatest differences in performance as a function of achievement-related motives when there is a self-discrepancy, certainty-oriented persons will show the greatest differences in performance as a function of achievement-related motives when there is no self-discrepancy.

Study 1. In our initial foray into this area (Roney & Sorrentino, 1988, Study 2), we replicated a correlational investigation by Higgins, Klein, and Strauman (1985) that examined self-discrepancies and affect. As in the original study, subjects were given a questionnaire designed to assess their self-discrepancies and four different depression and general affect scales. The self-discrepancy questionnaire asked subjects to list the traits that described their "actual selves" (the way they think they actually are), their "ideal selves" (the way they would like to be), and their "ought selves" (the way they feel they "ought" to be, or are obliged to be). All of these were asked both from their own perspective (own standpoint) and as they thought an important other viewed them (other standpoint).

As described previously, self-discrepancy theory maintains that negative affect results from discrepancies between our actual selves and either of the two abstract selves (ideal or ought). In addition, the nature of the affect experienced is argued to depend on the nature of the discrepancy, with actual–ideal discrepancies leading mainly to "dejection-related" emotion, and actual–ought discrepancies leading mainly to "agitation-related" emotion (see Higgins et al., 1985).

The replication of this study differed only in the addition of a measure of subjects' uncertainty orientation. Of primary interest here were comparisons of the self-discrepancies and self-reported affects for uncertainty-oriented and certainty-oriented subjects. First, as presented in Fig. 11.5, it can be seen that uncertainty-oriented people had greater discrepancies in general than did certainty-oriented subjects. This was the only significant effect in a gender × uncertainty orientation × type of discrepancy split-plot analysis of variance, $F(1,58) =$

Discrepancy Type

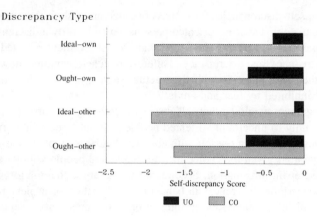

FIG. 11.5. Mean self-discrepancy scores for uncertainty-oriented (UO) and certainty-oriented (CO) persons as a function of discrepancy type. Negative scores represent less discrepancy from the standard.

5.52, $p < .03$. It thus appears that uncertainty-oriented people view themselves as being further from their abstract "selves" than do certainty-oriented people, as we would predict.

When it comes to affect, uncertainty-oriented subjects generally indicated more negative affect. For example, uncertainty-oriented subjects scored significantly higher than certainty-oriented subjects in helplessness, $t(62) = 2.57$, $p < .05$; guilt, $t(62) = 2.75$, $p < .01$; discontent, $t(62) = 3.09$, $p < .01$); and loneliness, $t(62) = 2.22$, $p < .05$. They also reported feeling less peaceful, $t(62) = 2.55$, $p < .01$; calm, $t(62) = 2.60$), $p < .02$; and pleasant, $t(62) = 2.50$, $p < .02$. The means for these affects are presented in Table 11.1.

We analyzed these data several different ways (see Roney & Sorrentino, 1988), with all analyses leading to the conclusion that uncertainty-oriented sub-

TABLE 11.1
Mean Affect Scores as a Function of Uncertainty Orientation

| | Uncertainty Orientation | | | |
	Uncertainty-oriented	Certainty-oriented	t-value	p
Helpless	4.50	3.37	2.57	<.05
Guilty	4.00	2.87	2.57	<.01
Discontent	3.38	2.37	3.09	<.01
Pleasant	4.15	4.73	2.50	<.05
Peaceful	3.12	3.93	2.55	<.05
Calm	3.15	3.93	2.60	<.05
Lonely	1.97	1.33	2.22	<.05

Note: Higher scores indicate greater affect.

jects reported greater discrepancies and greater negative affect than did certainty-oriented subjects. Indeed, the only items we found to be somewhat positive for uncertainty-oriented people were having a better appetite, ($t(62) = 2.21$, $p < .05$) and a greater interest in sex, ($t(62) = 2.14$, $p < .05$) than certainty-oriented people. So, there may be some consolation for readers who view themselves as uncertainty-oriented.

These data thus offer initial evidence that uncertainty-oriented people may be particularly likely to experience self-discrepancies and several types of negative affect. Because the present study is correlational, it is not clear why these differences exist. Perhaps uncertainty-oriented people are more likely to find themselves wanting relative to their self-concepts because they are more likely to seek out self-relevant information. Another possibility is that certainty-oriented people do not have well elaborated self-concepts and therefore simply use their actual selves when asked to describe their ideal and ought selves. Either of these would be consistent with the current view of uncertainty orientation.

Study 2.   Having had some success with our initial research, we moved on to studies that were interactive in nature. We present herein the preliminary results from an experiment and a field study conducted to examine self-discrepancies in relation to motivation (Roney & Sorrentino, 1989).

Early in a Fall term, we held mass testing sessions, where we assessed individual differences in uncertainty orientation and achievement-related motives. At this time, we also gave out a questionnaire designed to get at subjects' self-discrepancies concerning their expected performance in their introductory psychology course. Subjects were asked to estimate what grade they thought they would receive in the course, what grade they ideally would like to get, what grade significant others ideally would like them to get, and what grade they ought to get from their own and the other's standpoint. Four months later, we called subjects back for the experimental study, where we tested performance predictions from Higgins et al. (1986). Recall that these authors predict that an ideal–own discrepancy should lead to higher performance than no discrepancy, and an ought–other discrepancy should lead to lower performance, because ". . . failure relative to an ideal/own guide produces dissatisfaction that could spur the individual to try harder, whereas failure relative to an ought/other guide produces fear of punishment and anxiety that could paralyze the individual" (Higgins et al., 1986, p. 49).

Upon their arrival, subjects received either no prime, an ideal/own prime, or an ought/other prime following procedures by Higgins, Bond, Strauman, and Klein (1986). The primes required subjects to think and write about the standards they or others had for achievement, career, and general competence. For example, the ideal/own prime asked subjects to describe their ideal self including their ideal achievement standards (i.e., academic, career, and general competence) and to discuss whether there had been any changes in their hopes and ideals.

Following the primes, subjects received a complex arithmetic-ability test, which ostensibly was a test of general mental ability. We then compared their performance in the three experimental conditions as a function of their total self-discrepancy scores (i.e., collapsed across kinds of discrepancies) obtained 4 months earlier (i.e., between each of their standards and the grade they actually expected to get in introductory psychology). A median split divided subjects into having high or low self-discrepancies.

Table 11.2 shows the performance on the arithmetic test of uncertainty-oriented and certainty-oriented subjects with high or low total self-discrepancies in the two prime and the control conditions. The pattern of interaction shown in Table 11.2 is significant at the .03 level. Note that for the uncertainty-oriented group, differences between subjects with high and low total discrepancies seem to follow the predictions from Higgins, Strauman, and Klein (1986). That is, high total discrepancies were associated with better performance than low total discrepancies in the ideal/own prime condition, and this difference was greater than in the control group. Also, high total discrepancies in the ought/other prime condition were associated with worse performance than low total discrepancies, and this difference was also greater than in the control condition.

Now note the certainty-oriented group. These subjects behaved quite differently, with the ideal/own prime having a negative effect (i.e., high total self-

TABLE 11.2
Mean Performance as a Function of Uncertainty-orientation,
Priming Condition, and Combined Self-discrepancy

	Uncertainty-oriented		
	Ideal/Own Prime	Ought/Other Prime	Control (No Prime)
High total discrepancy	12.55	10.53	11.93
	(11)	(15)	(15)
Low total discrepancy	11.38	15.29	11.85
	(16)	(7)	(13)
Difference (high–low)	+1.17	−4.76	0.08
	Certainty-oriented		
	Ideal/Own Prime	Ought/Other Prime	Control (No Prime)
High total discrepancy	10.70	11.20	11.95
	(10)	(15)	(19)
Low total discrepancy	15.23	10.25	14.14
	(13)	(8)	(14)
Difference (high–low)	−4.53	0.95	−2.19

discrepancy subjects performed worse than low total self-discrepancy subjects, and this difference was greater than in the control condition). The ought/other prime produced little difference between those with high and low total self-discrepancies, leading to a smaller difference in performance relative to the control condition.[3]

Although we cannot easily explain the data for certainty-oriented subjects without further research, it seems clear that predictions derived from self-discrepancy theory were confirmed only for uncertainty-oriented subjects. Thus, the consequences of self-discrepancies appear to be very different for certainty-oriented and uncertainty-oriented subjects.

Study 3. The next study was a field study examining the interaction of achievement-related motives and uncertainty orientation. Based on our past research, we predicted that uncertainty-oriented subjects would show the greatest characteristic differences in performance due to achievement-related motives (i.e., success-oriented subjects would perform better than failure-threatened subjects) when there was a self-concept discrepancy, but that the certainty-oriented subjects would show the greatest differences when there was no discrepancy. These predictions were based on the logic that whereas uncertainty-oriented people will attempt to deal with self-discrepancies because they want to resolve uncertainty about the self, certainty-oriented people will basically tune out from or ignore situations where there is a self-concept discrepancy. Thus, for these latter individuals, achievement-related motives will be engaged when there is no uncertainty about the self.

The results provided qualified support both for Higgins et al. (1986) and for our predictions. Seven months following a statement of their discrepancies, students received higher grades if they had a large ideal–own-actual discrepancy than if they did not ($F(1,80) = 3.12, p < .08$), and received lower grades if they had a large ought–other-actual discrepancy than if they did not ($F(1,80) = 16.10, p < .001$).

We obtained no evidence, however, that these discrepancies were systematically related to achievement-related motives as these authors predict. Rather, differences in performance as a function of achievement-related motives were subsumed, at least for one type of discrepancy, by an interaction with uncertainty orientation. These findings are shown in Fig. 11.6.

This figure presents the mean scores on final examinations for uncertainty-oriented and certainty-oriented students as a function of their achievement-related motives and their ought–other discrepancies measured 7 months earlier. The pattern of interaction is significant ($F(1,180) = 4.82, p < .03$) and exactly as predicted by Sorrentino and Short (1986). For the uncertainty-oriented group,

---

[3]A similar pattern of interaction was found using either ideal/own discrepancies or ought–other discrepancies in the place of total self-discrepancies.

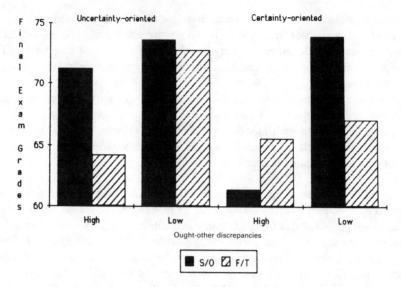

FIG. 11.6. Mean final exam grades for success-oriented (S/O) and failure-threatened (F/T) persons as a function of uncertainty orientation and magnitude of ought–other discrepancies.

success-oriented persons had higher examination scores and failure-threatened persons lower scores when they had a large ought–other discrepancy, and this difference disappeared where they had no discrepancy. For the certainty-oriented group, it was when the discrepancy was small that the greatest difference between success-oriented and failure-threatened persons occurred, with little difference when there was a large ought–other discrepancy.[4] Hence, 7 months following a statement of their ought–other standard and their actual-own standard, students were affected by this discrepancy, but only in interaction with uncertainty orientation and achievement-related motives.

As this chapter goes to press, we are still attempting to discern why we didn't get similar effects on the other standards. Nevertheless, taken together with the results of the previous study, these data indicate that not all persons handle self-concept discrepancies the same way, and existing theories must address individual differences not only in a more or less fashion, but in an interactive fashion. We have found actual reversals of effects in different groups of persons, based on the same type of self-discrepancy or its absence.

---

[4]Interestingly, results were quite similar and significant when we substituted students' actual midterm examination scores for their estimates of their actual performance in calculating discrepancies from standards.

UNCERTAINTY ORIENTATION AND OTHER THEORIES

Although we have directed our attention to self-discrepancy theory, we believe that individual differences in uncertainty-orientation may have considerable relevance for other theories of self-inference as well. A few examples from other contributors to this book are presented in this concluding section.

Self-inferences in Emotionality

Underlying Jim Olson's (Chapter 2, this volume) theoretical approach is the assumption that people make conscious and deliberate inferences about the causes of their feelings and behaviors. We wonder whether this is really true for certainty-oriented persons; perhaps such individuals do not engage in causal attribution to the same extent as uncertainty-oriented persons. If this is the case, one might not expect them to follow the model set forth by Ross and Olson (1981), which identifies the preconditions for misattribution and expectancy effects. We might also expect that in the "real world" where cues facilitating both self-inference processes (i.e., misattribution) and preparatory information exist, uncertainty-oriented persons would be more affected by the former, but certainty-oriented persons would be more affected by the latter. It may be, then, that Olson could expect an interaction between uncertainty orientation and the two complementary processes of self-inference and accurate information.

The Multifaceted Self

Gerald Sande states that "people perceive themselves as having a rich and multifaceted nature that allows them to act flexibly and adaptively in various situations," (Sande, Chapter 1, this volume). We believe that this is more likely to be true for uncertainty-oriented persons than for certainty-oriented persons. Indeed, Roney and Sorrentino (1987) found that when it came to evaluating occupational categories, certainty-oriented persons perceived fewer dimensions within categories (i.e., less variability of traits within occupational groups), and less overlap of dimensions across categories (i.e., fewer traits appearing across categories) than uncertainty-oriented persons. This pattern may hold for self-perception as well.

We would also suggest that whereas uncertainty-oriented persons may see themselves as more flexible and having more traits than others, certainty-oriented persons may see themselves as being less flexible and having fewer traits than others. In other words, certainty-oriented persons might take pride in being consistent and straightforward, as opposed to those complex and "wishy washy liberals."[5]

---

[5]We suspect that it is the certainty-oriented person who would embrace conservative philosophy and accept the fact that the "L" word (i.e., liberal) is evil.

Constrained Behavior and Self-concept Change

Ned Jones (Chapter 4, this volume), states that constrained laboratory situations can produce changes in self-concept. We would predict that certainty-oriented people will be more resistant to any change in the self-concept than will uncertainty-oriented people, and that the former group will not succumb to such manipulations as described by Jones. Note that at the core of Jones's analysis is the idea that information within one's latitude of acceptance will be internalized to the extent that there is less biased scanning of such information. Conversely, information within one's latitude of rejection will be internalized (given the illusion of choice) from dissonance reduction.

From our research on attitudes and personal relevance (Sorrentino et al., 1988), we know that uncertainty-oriented people are more likely to process information when it is personally relevant than are certainty-oriented people. This leads to the possibility that in the situations that should lead to changes in the self-concept as described by Jones, uncertainty-oriented persons will show the greatest change in self-concept. Because uncertainty-oriented persons are more likely to process information when it is self-relevant, they will be more likely than certainty-oriented persons to internalize within the latitude of acceptance, as systematic processing of information should lead to an unbiased scanning of information. Similarly, uncertainty-oriented people will be more likely than certainty-oriented persons to internalize within the latitude of rejection, given the illusion of choice, as they will be more likely to experience cognitive dissonance. This is because, with increased processing of self-relevant information, they should paradoxically be more affected by discrepant and dissonant information.

Self-persuasion via Self-perception

Given our speculations about Jones's research, Tim Wilson's research on self-persuasion via self-reflection (Chapter 3, this volume) would appear to be open to a similar analysis. Wilson notes that self-reflection can lead people to adopt a new attitude and make decisions that they will later regret. Since we believe that it is uncertainty-oriented people who follow Socrates's dictum that an unexamined life is not worth living, it is they who should be advised to, "Answer just what your heart prompts you."

Specifically, given that self-relevant information leads to systematic information processing for uncertainty-oriented people, they should be less likely to "follow the heart" than certainty-oriented people and more likely to make decisions they will later regret. Here, again, the uncertainty-oriented person's search for consistent and logical arguments for self-relevant information should lead to greater change and persistence in a belief that is detached from their emotions, compared with certainty-oriented people. On the other hand, if the situation is dissonance-inducing (see *supra*), then they may in fact bring their emotions into line with their new position. Interestingly, our position dictates that whether self-reflection leads to regret or dissonance reduction, it is the "wishy-washy" uncertainty-oriented person who will be most affected.

Self-perception and Social Perception Processes

Mark Lepper's research (Chapter 10, this volume) brings to mind our ongoing research on uncertainty orientation and teaching techniques, where we hope to show that "discovery learning" techniques may work best for uncertainty-oriented children, who like to figure things out for themselves, whereas certainty-oriented children may do poorly unless they receive directions and correct answers. That is, the latter group may work best under more traditional teaching styles. Again, these predictions follow from our work on persuasion and personal relevance (Sorrentino et al., 1988), in that certainty-oriented people seem to prefer to be told what to do when issues are personally relevant. Of course, an interesting question is whether Lepper's training of intrinsic motivation can actually change and benefit certainty-oriented people, or is it too late?

Escaping the Self: Avoidance of Self-awareness

Finally, Roy Baumeister's work on avoidance of self-awareness (Chapter 12, this volume), is an interesting lesson in what can happen when one gets too wound up in the self. If we are correct that uncertainty-oriented individuals are more likely to focus on the self, then they may also be the people who end up in freakish and bizarre behaviors designed to tune out self-awareness when it becomes aversive. Perhaps this explains why the majority of people may tend to steer away from self-inferences and self-analysis in the first place.

Conclusion

Although much of what we have said in this last section is speculation, it is based on several published studies indicating that as situations become relevant to the self, not everyone acts the same way. When theorists talk about self-inference, they may often be thinking of a particular type of person, the uncertainty-oriented individual—someone like most academics. Unfortunately (for the theories), most people outside of academia aren't like academics, and their self-inferences may be quite different. More, in fact, like those of the certainty-oriented person.

ACKNOWLEDGMENTS

The research reported in this chapter was supported by various grants from the Social Sciences and Humanities Research Council to the first author. Our thanks to James Olson for his helpful comments concerning this manuscript.

REFERENCES

Allport, G. W., & Vernon, P. E. (1931). *A study of values.* Cambridge, MA: Houghton Mifflin.

Berlyne, D. E. (1960). *Conflict, arousal, and curiosity.* New York: McGraw–Hill.

Brickman, P., & Berman, J. J. (1971). Effects of performance expectancy and outcome certainty on interest in social comparison. *Journal of Experimental Social Psychology, 7,* 600–609.

Byrne, D., & Lamberth, J. (1971). The effect of erotic stimuli on sex arousal, evaluative responses, and subsequent behavior. *Technical Reports of the Commission on Obscenity and Pornography* (Vol. 8). Washington, DC: U.S. Government Printing Office.

Chaiken, S. (1980). Heuristic versus systematic information processing and the use of source versus message cues in persuasion. *Journal of Personality and Social Psychology, 39,* 752–766.

Fazio, R. H. (1986). How do attitudes guide behavior? In R. M. Sorrentino & E. T. Higgins (Eds.), *Handbook of motivation and cognition: Foundations of social behavior* (pp. 204–243). New York: Guilford Press.

Frederick, J. E., Sorrentino, R. M., & Hewitt, E. C. (1987). *A scoring manual for the motive to master uncertainty.* Research Bulletin No. 618, University of Western Ontario, Ontario.

Gitta, M. Z. (1988). *Uncertainty orientation and balance theory.* Unpublished master's thesis, University of Western Ontario, London, Ontario.

Higgins, E. T., Bond, R. N., Klein, R., & Strauman, T. (1986). Self-discrepancies and emotional vulnerability: How magnitude, accessibility, and type of discrepancy influence affect. *Journal of Personality and Social Psychology, 51,* 5–15.

Higgins, E. T., Klein, R., & Strauman, T. (1985). Self-concept discrepancy theory: A psychological model for distinguishing among different aspects of depression and anxiety. *Social Cognition, 3,* 51–76.

Higgins, E. T., Strauman, T., & Klein, R. (1986). Standards and the process of self-evaluation: Multiple affects from multiple stages. In R. M. Sorrentino & E. T. Higgins (Eds.), *Handbook of motivation and cognition: Foundations of social behavior* (pp. 23–63). New York: Guilford Press.

Murgatroyd, S., Rushton, C., Apter, M. J., & Ray, C. (1978). The development of the Telic Dominance Scale. *Journal of Personality Assessment, 42,* 519–528.

Petty, R. E., Cacioppo, J. T., & Goldman, R. (1981). Personal involvement as a determinant of argument-based persuasion. *Journal of Personality and Social Psychology, 41,* 847–855.

Rokeach, M. (1960). *The open and closed mind: Investigations into the nature of belief systems and personality systems.* New York: Basic Books.

Roney, C. J. R., & Sorrentino, R. M. (1987). Uncertainty orientation and person perception: Individual differences in categorization. *Social Cognition, 5,* 369–382.

Roney, C. J. R., & Sorrentino, R. M. (1988). *Self-evaluation and its affective consequences: Social comparison, self-concept discrepancies, and affect as a function of uncertainty orientation.* Unpublished manuscript.

Roney, C. J. R., & Sorrentino, R. M. (1989). *The motivating properties of self-discrepancies as a function of uncertainty orientation and achievement-related motives.* Unpublished manuscript.

Ross, M., & Olson, J. M. (1981). An expectancy-attribution model of the effects of placebos. *Psychological Review, 88,* 408–437.

Sorrentino, R. M. (1981). Derogation of an innocently suffering victim: So who's the "good guy"? In J. P. Rushton & R. M. Sorrentino (Eds.), *Altruism and helping behavior: Social, personality, and developmental perspectives* (pp. 267–283). Hillsdale, NJ: Lawrence Erlbaum Associates.

Sorrentino, R. M., Bobocel, R., Gitta, M. Z., Olson, J. M., & Hewitt, E. C. (1988). Uncertainty orientation and persuasion: Individual differences in the effects of personal relevance on social judgments. *Journal of Personality and Social Psychology, 55,* 357–371.

Sorrentino, R. M., & Hancock, R. D. (1986). The role of information and affective value for social influence: A case for the study of individual differences. In M. P. Zanna, J. M. Olson, & C. P.

Herman (Eds.), *Social influence: The Ontario Symposium* (Vol. 5, pp. 244–268). Hillsdale, NJ: Lawrence Erlbaum Associates.

Sorrentino, R. M., & Hewitt, E. C. (1984). The uncertainty reducing properties of achievement tasks revisited. *Journal of Personality and Social Psychology, 47,* 884–899.

Sorrentino, R. M., & Roney, C. J. R. (1986). Uncertainty orientation, achievement-related motivation, and task diagnosticity as determinants of task performance. *Social Cognition, 4,* 420–436.

Sorrentino, R. M., & Short, J. C. (1986). Uncertainty, motivation, and cognition. In R. M. Sorrentino & E. T. Higgins (Eds.), *The handbook of motivation and cognition: Foundations of social behavior* (pp. 379–403). New York: Guilford Press.

Sorrentino, R. M., Short, J. C., & Raynor, J. O. (1984). Uncertainty orientation: Implications for affective and cognitive views of achievement behavior. *Journal of Personality and Social Psychology, 46,* 189–206.

Trope, Y. (1979). Uncertainty-reducing properties of achievement tasks. *Journal of Personality and Social Psychology, 37,* 1505–1518.

Zanna, M. P., Olson, J. M., & Herman, C. P. (Eds.). (1987). *Social influence: The Ontario Symposium* (Vol. 5). Hillsdale, NJ: Lawrence Erlbaum Associates.

12 Anxiety and Deconstruction: On Escaping the Self

Roy F. Baumeister
Case Western Reserve University

The fascination with self[1] pervades modern society, from the popular media to the research journals (Baumeister, 1987). Seeking, learning about, asserting, cultivating, repairing, fulfilling, and otherwise tending the self seems a national preoccupation. The colloquial metaphors for this inner search, such as identity crises and finding oneself, are so familiar that they have become almost clichés.

Yet this relentless interest in self is not unproblematical. The demands and expectations surrounding the self have become inflated. The cultivation and exploration of self have become a central and powerful aspect of the meaning of many people's lives. As a result, self can become burdensome, especially when some threat or failure is encountered. If maintaining a proper, desirable self is an important aspect of the meaning of one's life, then having a failed or inadequate self is an existential catastrophe. And to the extent that self is a vital part of human functioning, failures of self may bring anxiety. The individual may often find that these aversive states can best be escaped by forgetting the self.

The desire to escape from awareness of self is much older than identity crises or the modern "culture of narcissism" (Lasch, 1978). Ancient religious mysticisms were centrally concerned with achieving a dissolution of self. Early and

---

[1]Although the term "self" defies easy definition, some effort to explain the concept is necessary. The term is used here roughly corresponding to its usage in everyday speech, which (like its technical usages in psychology) combines two aspects. First, self refers to the subjective experience of reflexivity: Self is the entity that decides, chooses, thinks, feels, and acts. Second, the agentic aspect of self is overlaid with cognitive structures which define it, assign attributes to it, and so forth. These cognitive structures are not merely added on to the agentic core, however, for they often form the basis for thoughts, feelings, and behavioral choices.

medieval Christianity focused on self as the source of much evil, such as in greed, selfishness, pride, and other self-based sins. More recently, the problematical aspect of the concern with self has been implicated as a central and causal aspect of several dysfunctional behavior patterns, such as shyness (Schlenker & Leary, 1982), alcohol abuse (Jones & Berglas, 1978), text anxiety (Wine, 1971), "choking" under pressure (Baumeister, 1984), and sexual inadequacy (Masters & Johnson, 1970).

Earlier this century, the seeming ambivalence about self led a number of prominent psychological thinkers to propose that people are deeply motivated by hostility toward themselves. Some concluded that innate human nature contains a substantial dose of self-destructiveness. Thus, Freud (1920, 1930) concluded that people are motivated in part by a "death instinct," which causes people to desire destruction and death. Originally he seems to have used this term to refer simply to an aggressive instinct, which might easily be directed outward, but in his later thinking he came to emphasize the inward direction of the instinct—that is, the motivation to seek one's own destruction and death. Menninger (1938) epitomized this view in his work *Man Against Himself*, in which he discussed suicide, masochism, alcoholism, and other patterns as indicative of broad human tendencies of self-hatred and self-destruction.

The majority of psychologists remained skeptical of the death instinct and of similar hypotheses about deeply rooted self-destructive tendencies. Suicide, which might seem to be the ultimate in self-destruction, is quite rare among human beings and even rarer among other species, which makes instinctual arguments doubtful. Masochism, often understood as a motivated pattern of self-defeating behavior, has been a perennial source of conflict and controversy. Some have held that the existence of masochism is strong evidence that at least some people are motivated by self-hatred and self-destructiveness (e.g., Stekel, 1953; see Glick & Meyers, 1988, for recent review). Others have disputed the evidence, claiming that all these behaviors have been misinterpreted (e.g., Caplan, 1984; Franklin, 1987).

Recently, Steve Scher and I searched the social psychology research literature for evidence of self-destructive behavior among normal (nonclinical) individuals. There was ample evidence that people do sometimes sabotage their efforts and defeat themselves. There was no evidence, however, that people ever deliberately or primarily desire harm to self. Self-defeating behavior occurs as a result of judgment errors, and it occurs as the result of tradeoffs between conflicting, incompatible goals, but it does not appear that normal behavior is ever guided by any motivation to harm or sabotage oneself (Baumeister & Scher, 1988).

Of particular interest was the repeated implication that harm to self is caused by efforts to forget the self. Unpleasant awareness of self was an apparent cause of many of the self-defeating patterns, and it appeared that people will often accept risks and costs in order to escape from this awareness of self. Alcohol abuse is prototypical. There is little doubt that alcohol use can lead to physical and social harm to the user. But users are rarely if ever motivated by the desire to harm themselves. Rather, the appeal of alcohol rests in part on its capacity to help the individual lose self-awareness (Hull, 1981; Hull, Levenson, Young, & Sher, 1983), including helping the person shed inhibitions and internal conflicts and forget recent failures (Hull & Young, 1983; Steele & Southwick, 1985; Steele, Southwick, & Critchlow, 1981). Thus, to understand this important category of self-destructive behavior, one must study the motive to escape from self rather than a putative motive to harm the self.

The purpose of this chapter is to provide theoretical development for two important causal factors in the process of escape from self. First, anxiety will be examined as one common cause of the desire to escape. When self-awareness causes anxiety, people often desire to escape from awareness of self. Second, the process of cognitive deconstruction will be examined as a common means of escaping the self. Forgetting the self is not easy, for one cannot force oneself *not* to think about oneself. Instead of attempting to direct the mind away from the self, people may tend to use a more general technique of avoiding meaningful thought, by deconstructing their actions and experiences (i.e., removing awareness of their meanings and implications). To the extent that the person succeeds in avoiding meaningful thought, the idea of self will vanish from the mind, and people can enjoy whatever relief or other benefits are associated with the form of escape they have chosen.

EXCLUSION THEORY OF ANXIETY

There are multiple usages of the term anxiety. Some researchers appear to use the word as a generic description for almost any unpleasant affect. Others use it in a variety of more specific ways. Still others doubt that anxiety exists at all and regard it as merely a reified metaphor (Sarbin, 1968).

For present purposes, anxiety can be defined as an acute, unpleasant affective state, akin to panic and fear except that it is not necessarily as intense as those states and it occurs without any apparent physical threat. ("A splendid cure for anxiety is being chased by a lion. Fear takes precedence over anxiety," Goodwin, 1986, p. 9.) Anxiety has both a strong physiological aspect (which, again, is difficult to distinguish from panic and fear) and strong subjective, experiential aspect. The physical dimension of anxiety is compatible with an argument that the capacity for anxiety is to some extent innate. The hypothesis of an innate basis is likewise supported by cross-cultural evidence that anxiety is extremely widespread.

It seems rather clear that anxiety occurs and that a variety of behaviors are motivated by the need to prevent or escape anxiety. Indeed, anxiety may be more prevalent than one might assume, for people may prefer to forget experiences of anxiety (e.g., Sullivan, 1953). Many theorists have followed the progression in

Freud's thinking, in which each reconceptualization assigned anxiety a more prominent causal role (e.g., Freud, 1965/1933; May, 1977).

The association of anxiety with fear and panic has led some theorists to link it to the fear of physical harm or death. Becker (1973) elaborated this view from an existential perspective. He asserted that human beings are unique among living species in realizing their own mortality, and this realization is so upsetting and threatening that they have created culture to protect themselves against it. Becker's ideas have recently been revived by Greenberg, Pyszczynski, and Solomon (1986), who argue that self-esteem is essentially a protection against anxiety, which is at bottom fear of death. Their provocative and insightful work is especially relevant to the present arguments, for it links self and anxiety. If the self is essentially a defense against anxiety, then when the self fails (such as when self-esteem is lost), anxiety could result. Threats to self could elicit anticipatory anxiety, which might then be escaped by forgetting the self.

I wish to propose an alternative view of anxiety, however. Rather than fear of death, anxiety may be fundamentally a fear of social exclusion—that is, fear of being rejected, ostracized, abandoned, or refused by desirable social groups. More precisely, there may be an innate preparedness to learn to feel a panic reaction in response to being actively separated from important social groups. This view of anxiety is hardly revolutionary, for several past theorists have emphasized the interpersonal causes of anxiety (e.g., Sullivan, 1953), even especially the threat of losing a particular relationship (e.g., Bowlby, 1969, 1973). Still, these past theorists have disagreed among themselves (for example, Bowlby was quite critical of Sullivan; e.g., Bowlby, 1973, pp. 395–396), and the lack of acceptance of past formulations of this view (plus the recent accumulation of empirical evidence) has rendered it desirable and feasible to attempt a reformulation.

My views are perhaps most similar to those proposed by Bowlby, so some discussion of continuities and differences is needed. Bowlby explicitly disclaimed any intention of offering a general theory of anxiety (e.g., 1973 p. 30), and even his discussion of separation anxiety focused very heavily on the bond between infant and mother. When he did discuss anxiety in other contexts, he tended to treat it as derivative of the mother–infant separation anxiety. This was a very reasonable extension of current psychodynamic thinking. In that way, anxiety can be discussed in many relationship contexts by seeing various relationship partners as substitutes for the mother. Attachment to political or ethnic groups, and attachment to employment institutions, are more difficult to explain as substitutes for mother, but Bowlby suggested that often the attachment is to the group or institution leader (or other authority figure), who was symbolically equivalent to a parent (1969, p. 207). It would be unfair to portray Bowlby as advocating the reduction of all such relationships to filial symbolism; he merely suggested that such symbolism could operate in many cases, thereby offering a basis for explaining anxiety in many contexts as derivative of the infant's anxiety over separation from mother.

The present view differs from Bowlby's approach by offering a broader view of the motive for social exclusion. Instead of focusing narrowly on the mother–infant attachment as the causal prototype for separation anxiety, exclusion theory (i.e., the theory to be presented here) holds that a wide number and variety of groups and relationships hold the potential for causing anxiety by excluding the individual. Any important group or relationship can produce anxiety by excluding the individual. Bowlby's analyses and insights about the anxiety of maternal separation are quite correct, but they may be regarded as an especially vivid and important instance of the more general pattern of social exclusion. The undeniably special power of the child's fear of maternal separation may be attributed in part to the fact that the child has few alternative relationships and is so multiply dependent on that particular one.

Thus, the exclusion theory of anxiety is a more general and flexible formulation than Bowlby attempted with his work on separation anxiety. This breadth and generality offers several advantages. First, anxiety resulting from exclusion from work groups or ideological groups can be understood without postulating a symbolic parent, for these groups are legitimate and important, so loss of membership could easily cause anxiety. Second, exclusion theory seems quite compatible with the many observations indicating that anxiety is often reduced by the presence of a familiar companion, not merely the mother—which was apparent in Bowlby's own observations (1973, p. 201; also Friedman, 1981). Again, from the perspective of exclusion theory, it is not necessary to regard these familiar companions as symbolic mothers. Observations of agoraphobics have long noted that the anxiety associated with public places is reduced if a trusted companion is present (e.g., Goodwin, 1986, p. 148).

Indeed, Bowlby found that even separation from the child's mother produced less distress if the child had alternative companions (1973, p. 16). It seems doubtful that children are sufficiently gullible, consciously or unconsciously, that they could be consoled by symbolic substitutes for mother when it is precisely the *real* mother's departure that is producing the anxiety. A more plausible explanation for all these effects is that being included in a salient social group or relationship reduces anxiety, and that this capability resides in a variety of groups and relationships.

Death Anxiety, Exclusion Anxiety

If it is possible to find one general cause to encompass all (or even most) instances of anxiety, then death and social exclusion would seem to be the most likely candidates. It is difficult to find episodes of anxiety that have neither any threat of death (or at least physical harm) nor any threat of social exclusion. A well-known study of the specific thoughts and fears in anxiety neuroses found essentially two groups of contents: physical harm or death, and social exclusion (Beck, Laude, & Bohnert, 1974). These were about equal in frequency, and there was almost nothing else.

It is also apparent that the threats of death and exclusion are not entirely distinct, especially from an evolutionary perspective. Under primitive conditions, staying with one's social group was probably vital for survival, from infancy throughout life (see Bowlby, 1969, 1973). The link between social exclusion and death was retained in many cultural forms. In many primitive and early civilized societies, exclusion was equated with death, and the two punishments were regarded as almost interchangeable. Sometimes the choice was left up to the individual, as if it were all the same to the society whether the person died or merely departed from the group permanently. It appears that Socrates was offered that choice, and he chose death, which suggests that even he perceived his life as inextricably linked to inclusion in his social groups.

The overlap between the threat of death and the threat of social exclusion makes it somewhat difficult to treat the two theories as rivals. Instead, it may be a matter of emphasis whether one treats social exclusion or death as the fundamental cause of anxiety. From the present perspective, there are four theoretical advantages to be gained by emphasizing social exclusion rather than death, as follows:

First, developmental observations suggest that children fear separation from mother long before they can be said to have knowledge of their eventual death. Already during the first year of life, the child cries when the mother leaves the room (Bowlby, 1973). Soon thereafter the child learns to anticipate the mother's departure and begins crying before she leaves (Bowlby, 1973), which incidentally indicates the great potential power of anxiety for learning and association. In short, the link between anxiety and abandonment is readily apparent and observable very early in life, whereas postulating that anxiety is based on fear of death at that age requires some very doubtful and empirically weak assumptions about the child's self-awareness, understanding of mortality, and so forth.

Second (and related to the first advantage), exclusion anxiety could more plausibly have an innate basis than death anxiety. Becker's (1973) analysis explicitly described fear of death as based on the human existential recognition of one's own mortality, which requires abstraction and inference—which are hardly innate. Becker is careful to point out that only human beings know that they will die, because of the ability to reason and to extrapolate from the observed deaths of others. Thus, Becker's formulation seemingly precludes any argument about an innate basis for anxiety.

In contrast, most if not all animal species are sensitive to the presence of conspecifics (e.g., Zajonc, Heingartner, & Herman, 1969, on cockroaches). One may follow Hogan's (1982) socioanalytical theory or any of the recent sociobiological theories that postulate humans are biologically adapted to the conditions of group (social) life. If there is any truth to socioanalytic or socio-biological theories, then there must be some innate motivation to be included in the social group. One very plausible mechanism for this motivational pattern would be a panic reaction that causes acute distress whenever the individual's membership in the group is jeopardized. Such an alarm would help keep hunting and fighting groups together, would help prevent babies from being lost or abandoned, would keep mates together, and so forth, all of which would facilitate survival and reproduction.

The third advantage pertains directly to Greenberg et al.'s (1986) insightful analyses of culture and self. Elaborating Becker's suggestions, these authors propose that culture and self are defenses against anxiety (which, in Becker's view, is the existential fear of death). In my view, culture and self are more plausible as defenses against social exclusion than as defenses against death. If culture is designed to protect the individual from death, then in the final analysis it is an exercise in futility based on self-deception, for everyone dies, culture notwithstanding. Likewise, in that view, self is merely a role player in the theater of the absurd that is culture, for self participates in the culture without solving the problem of mortality.

But although culture and self fail to protect people from death, they often succeed at preventing social exclusion. Culture provides means and frameworks that allow people to live together and belong to groups, relationships, and communities. Thus, culture greatly increases the possibility and feasibility of social inclusion. And the interpersonal aspects of self (cf. Baumeister, 1982, 1986a, 1986b; Schlenker, 1985) make it seem very likely that the self is partly a means of relating to other people, which is essential for social inclusion. In short, culture and self appear as doomed quixotic undertakings as protection against death, but from the perspective of exclusion theory they are effective adaptations.

The fourth advantage of exclusion theory is that the threat of social exclusion is a much more common and pervasive threat than the threat of death. Very few modern North Americans confront the threat of death on a daily basis. But the struggle to maintain and enhance one's standing in important social groups is a regular feature of daily life. Saying the wrong thing, shirking an obligation, performing inadequately—these are typical of the familiar concerns of everyday life, and they reflect the pervasive risk of social exclusion but not any danger of death. People worry about losing their romantic relationships, alienating their kin, or losing their jobs, all of which involve social exclusion. Being jilted does not lead to death, but it always involves social exclusion, and so it produces anxiety.

Empirical support for the exclusion view would be furnished if social exclusion could generate anxiety in the absence of any fear of death. One strategy would be to give subjects feedback, possibly based on bogus statistical tables, that they would probably live very long lives but be unable to find a marriage partner or other intimate relationship. Unfortunately, it seems impossible to create the opposite manipulation, that is, death that does not break social bonds. It is noteworthy, however, that one of the most comforting messages in the face of death is the prospect of reunion with loved ones in the afterlife (e.g., Graham, 1987), which suggests that the fear of death is at least partly caused by fear of social separation.

In conclusion: It would be foolish to deny that people fear harm, pain, and death. Furthermore, there is substantial and important common ground between the respective views of anxiety based on death and based on social exclusion. The question is merely whether death or social exclusion deserves emphasis as the most pervasive and immediate cause of anxiety. Although further research is needed, it does appear at present that there are empirical and conceptual grounds for emphasizing social exclusion.

Function of Anxiety

According to the exclusion theory, anxiety operates as an alarm signal that alerts the individual to the danger of social exclusion. It is worth considering whether this hypothesized function is compatible with the effects of anxiety.

To be sure, it is difficult to make functional arguments about anxiety (at least, beyond the minimal need to avoid whatever causes anxiety), because its effects are primarily negative. Anxiety impairs a broad variety of behaviors, including manual task performance, problem solving, speech, and social interaction. What are the potential benefits of impairment? It seems plausible that if the individual is engaged in some activity that might lead to exclusion from the group, then it would be optimal to disrupt performance of that activity.

Simon's (1967) classic discussion of interrupt systems provides a useful context for examining the function of anxiety. Simon undertook to provide a conceptual model for the cognitive control of behavior. Consistent with much other work, he described how a goal-directed feedback system seemed essential to such control; but Simon also perceived the inadequacy of a goal-directed feedback system to account for all the complexities of human behavior. In particular, he argued that such a model must contain *interrupt systems,* that is, mechanisms for interrupting a goal-directed sequence without reaching either a success or failure outcome. Circumstances change and people re-evaluate their ongoing projects, reorder their priorities, and make decisions to abandon behavioral responses that are intrinsically succeeding but whose goals have come to seem undesirable.

Simon suggested vaguely that emotions may be involved in the interrupt systems. He paid scant attention to differentiation among the emotions and ignored questions such as whether (and how) joy might cause people to reorder priorities or abandon their projects. Still, his arguments seem especially well suited to apply to anxiety. The apparent fact that anxiety disrupts the execution of nearly any sort of activity, from playing sports to speaking in public to taking

exams to having sexual intercourse, makes anxiety seem to be an ideal inter-
rupter. Thus, anxiety seems capable of overriding nearly any feedback system or
behavioral sequence, which may often cause the individual to re-evaluate the
desirability of any particular course of action.

It seems reasonable to propose three main reasons that groups exclude individuals. Individuals are excluded for breaking the group's norms and rules,
thereby violating the structure of assumptions that makes group interaction possible; they are excluded for failing to make adequate contributions to the group's
success or survival, thereby constituting a net unproductive drain on the group's
resources; and they are excluded if they are personally unattractive to the group,
which makes their companionship unpleasant. In short, immortality, incompetence, and unattractiveness represent the major threats to one's inclusion in the
group. These reasons correspond to three major manifestations of anxiety, namely guilt, performance anxiety, and social anxiety.

To follow Simon's (1967) model, then, one would suggest that anxiety operates to cause the individual to attempt to control his or her behavior so as to avoid
those three classes of behavior that risk exclusion. Upon realizing that one is
breaking the group's rules, the person feels anxiety (guilt) which interrupts the
unacceptable behavior and thus helps prevent the transgression. If one realizes
that one is not contributing enough to the group, one may try harder or even
replace one's activities with more productive ones. And if one is acting in a way
that may alienate others, anxiety will interrupt one's behavior, even impairing
one's very speech (e.g., Leary, Knight, & Johnson, 1987), thus helping prevent
the unattractive behavior from occurring.

It is obvious that anxiety is at best a crude mechanism for helping the individual. By impairing task performance or social interaction, anxiety often makes
the problem worse, not better. But it is hardly surprising that broad, natural
mechanisms are often ill-suited to the complexities of human social life. As
Simon indicated, it is necessary that a model of the human control system include
some mechanism for interrupting behavioral sequences that are underway, and
anxiety does seem to be a prime candidate for serving this function.

Empirical Evidence

The purpose of this section is to provide a partial review of empirical findings
relevant to the exclusion hypothesis. The empirical literature on anxiety is much
too vast to permit a comprehensive review, at least in the space allotted here, but
some consideration of relevant findings is necessary.

There seems to be little doubt but that social rejection causes anxiety. For
example, when laboratory subjects are induced to imagine scenes of social rejection, they experience anxiety (Craighead, Kimball, & Rehak, 1979). Neurotic
anxiety is often explicitly focused on the fear of social rejection (Beck et al.,
1974).

It is noteworthy that anxiety generally seems to focus on fear of a specific rejection rather than on blanket ostracism by everyone (Beck et al., 1974, p. 323). This seems consistent with the argument that the anxiety mechanism is deeply rooted and possibly innate, for it does not require abstract inference or generalization but responds to immediately apparent threats of exclusion. It is also interesting that although anxiety often involves fear of being left alone, the fear arises on occasions of social contact, such as parties or weddings. This is consistent with the view that anxiety is a fear of the event of being excluded, not fear of the state of being alone. Anxiety is a response to a change in circumstances, not a response to chronic circumstances. This too fits the hypothesis that the anxiety mechanism is deeply rooted or innate, because such mechanisms can respond more easily to changing circumstances than to stable conditions. Moreover, it would also be more adaptive for anxiety to occur in response to the event of exclusion, while there may still be something that can be done to prevent it, rather than to the condition of being chronically alone.

Evaluation is a major cause of anxiety (e.g., Kendall, 1978). Smith, Ingram and Brehm (1983) showed that when anxiety-prone people encounter an evaluative situation, they are more likely than others to respond with increased cognitive activity focusing on how other people are regarding them. Thus, anxiety has the empirical result of making one think about social inclusion and exclusion, which seems most consistent with the exclusion theory. Moreover, the link between evaluation and social exclusion was quite explicit in the fantasies of Beck et al.'s (1974) anxiety neurotics. These fantasies often began with failure or negative evaluation and ended with being socially rejected and ostracized.

Although most studies of evaluation anxiety focus on fear of failure, a few have addressed the possibility that success could cause anxiety. Horner's (1972) construct of the "fear of success" was important in this regard. It is noteworthy that Horner's evidence generally rested on explicit links between success and social exclusion. In her view, some women believed that occupational success would make them unattractive to men, and they began to fear success because of the anticipated social exclusion that would accompany it. More recent analyses of success anxiety have invoked the notion of a "burden of expectations" (e.g., Baumeister, Hamilton, & Tice, 1985; Baumgardner & Brownlee, 1987; Berglas, 1986; Jones & Berglas, 1978). Baumgardner and Brownlee showed that highly anxious people will even avoid successes that might foster such a burden of expectations. The anxious person feels that to succeed is to cause others to expect continued or greater successes in the future, which he or she feels incapable of achieving, and which therefore will eventually cause the person to let others down, which in turn may cause them to reject the individual. Thus, the negative consequences of success, especially including the self-destructive responses to success, appear to depend on a perceived link between success and social exclusion.

Ingraham and Wright (1987) found that each individual tends to experience different levels of anxiety in different relationships, which they interpreted as consistent with Sullivan's (1953) hypothesis of the interpersonal nature of anxiety. Thus, although some individuals are more prone to anxiety than others, anxiety is not simply a product of the person but rather of the interaction between person and social context. This pattern seems to fit an explanation of anxiety as fear of social exclusion better than it fits anxiety as the result of intrapsychic repression, castration fear, death anxiety, or maternal separation. Exclusion theory makes the further prediction that the degree of anxiety an individual experiences in a given relationship is a product of the subjective importance of that relationship to the individual and the degree of perceived threat (i.e., the subjective probability of being excluded from it). Future research may test this prediction.

If anxiety arises from social exclusion, then salient inclusion in an important social group should reduce it. Evidence does suggest that social support helps reduce anxiety. Sarason (1986) reports several studies in which a supportive intervention by the researcher improved the performance of highly anxious subjects but had no effect on the performance of low-anxious subjects. Parallel effects were found for subjects with low vs. high social support networks. That is, supportive intervention helped people whose normal support networks were relatively deficient. Thus, assurance of social inclusion reduces anxiety and removes its harmful effects on task performance.

Research on agoraphobia makes a similar point. Agoraphobics suffer from debilitating anxiety attacks in connection with being outdoors. But these attacks are reduced or even prevented by companionship, especially that of someone close and trusted (e.g., Goodwin, 1986; Hallam, 1985; indeed, this was observed in the first publication on anxiety, by the German researcher Westphal in 1871).

The power of social bonds for mitigating agoraphobia has led some researchers to propose that agoraphobia itself arises in part from misattributing the causes of interpersonal conflict and distress. Goldstein and Chambless (1978) suggest that these individuals often are upset about their relationships, but they relabel this aversive arousal as fear of being on the street alone (see also Hallam, 1985). Although further research is needed, the exclusion theory is greatly enhanced by the suggestion that issues of social exclusion cause this major category of pathological anxiety. A similar and less controversial conclusion has arisen from studies of "school phobia," that is, children's apparent fear of attending school. It appears that such fears can be understood as fear of leaving home, that is, of separation from the family (see Bowlby, 1973). The evidence for this conclusion is sufficiently compelling that DSM–III renamed school phobia as "separation anxiety disorder" (see Goodwin, 1986, for discussion). Thus, again, fear of exclusion from important social groups apparently causes a major pattern of anxiety.

Several studies of interpersonal interaction have provided relevant evidence. Ickes (1984) found that anxiety was increased by problematical interracial interactions; specifically, racially prejudiced whites who interacted with blacks tended to act in a somewhat aloof fashion, which was accompanied by an increase in anxiety in both persons. A general formulation by Stephan and Stephan (1985) holds that people experience *intergroup anxiety* when interacting with someone from a different social or ethnic group. Their work provides an important contribution to the exclusion view, for it indicates that the anxiety is caused by encountering people from whose social group one is excluded.

Before closing, it is worth looking for contradictory evidence, that is, evidence indicating that social exclusion might reduce anxiety rather than increase it. The closest thing to such evidence would appear to be in shyness. The shy person experiences anxiety upon contact with others and therefore remains socially isolated to avoid anxiety.

To be sure, shyness is only a borderline phenomenon with respect to the exclusion theory. Shy people are reluctant to approach strangers more than they shun contact with people they know well. Shyness thus represents a reluctance to form new social bonds rather than a tendency to break existing bonds.

Recent work on shyness suggests that it does not contradict the exclusion hypothesis. It appears that shy people avoid others because they fear being rejected. They dislike the state of loneliness and isolation, but they fear to approach others and be rejected. The shy person strongly desires to make contact with others and form social bonds with them, but he or she fears the negative consequences of attempting and failing to present a socially desirable image of self (e.g., Arkin, 1981; Schlenker & Leary, 1982). Rather than risk making a bad impression, the shy person avoids making any impression at all, such as by avoiding social encounters altogether.

Thus, the anxiety in shyness is focused precisely on the fear of being rejected by others. The state of isolation is experienced as painful, but it is preferred over the acute pain of rejection. The event of social exclusion is the ultimate threat, and the shy person tries to avoid it at all costs. This is entirely consistent with the exclusion theory of anxiety. As noted earlier, anxiety appears to be a response to the process of being excluded more than to the chronic state of aloneness. The evidence about shyness indicates that many individuals choose the latter over the former, which shows how acutely unpleasant the experience of exclusion can be.

In short, the exclusion hypothesis is consistent with a substantial amount of empirical evidence about the causes and effects of anxiety. A comprehensive review is beyond the scope of this chapter. For the present, it suffices to conclude that the exclusion theory appears to be viable and to be capable of explaining a broad assortment of empirical findings.

Self and Anxiety

A wide variety of empirical approaches have led researchers to conclude that anxiety is often characterized by a high degree of attention to self (e.g., Friedman, 1981; Schlenker & Leary, 1982; Wine, 1971). Other theorists have gone so far as to portray the self as a structure that is developed explicitly to prevent anxiety (e.g., Becker, 1973; Greenberg et al., 1986; Sullivan, 1953). For present purposes, the important point is that failures or inadequacies of the self[2] are likely to *cause* anxiety.

The social, communicative aspect of the self is centrally important (e.g., Baumeister, 1982, 1986a, 1986b; Schlenker, 1980, 1985), which is consistent with the view that one of the self's main functions is to facilitate interaction and coexistence with others. Societies require and consist of identities, and individuals are located within social structures by their selves. But if selves are defined by membership in social groups, they can also entail exclusion from groups. A particular race or heritage may mean belonging to one ethnic group, but it then also denotes exclusion from other groups (cf. Stephan & Stephan, 1985).

Exclusion from one's primary social groups may often be accompanied by redefinition of self. To use extreme examples, societies exclude individuals categorically when these individuals are redefined from being citizens to being traitors or murderers. At a more individual level, getting a divorce, changing job, or leaving home all involve redefinition of self (e.g., Ebaugh, 1988).

Of particular interest are cases in which the self is redefined as unattractive, immoral (guilty), or incompetent, causing the social group to exclude him or her. Such exclusions would presumably cause acute anxiety, and it seems likely that people would learn to anticipate such judgments well in advance, in order to prevent them. As a result, individuals presumably become very sensitive to any implication about themselves that might potentially lead to social exclusion. Any event that might imply that oneself is unattractive, immoral, or incompetent could cause anticipatory anxiety, long before the threat of exclusion is imminent.

As suggested earlier, anxiety may have evolved originally as an interrupt mechanism. The function of anxiety is thus to stop people from carrying out actions that might cause them to be excluded from the group—in this case by defining them as unattractive, immoral, or incompetent. Unfortunately, anxiety is not a finely tuned mechanism sensitive to nuances of meaning and probability, but a broad and crude mechanism whose response may often be disproportionate to the threat. As a result, the anxiety may become the problem rather than being merely a signal that a problem exists. From a functional perspective, presumably, when a person experiences anxiety in connection with some implication about the self, he or she should change behaviors so as to ensure continued inclusion in the group (possibly by countering the dangerous implication). But in practice the threat to social inclusion may be merely symbolic or possible, and a pragmatic

---

[2]In terms of the two aspects of self suggested previously, it is primarily the meaningful aspect of self (rather than the agentic) that is a source of anxiety. Definitions of, or implications about, the self are associated with potential threats of social exclusion, so awareness of the self in these respects may cause anxiety.

behavioral response is neither necessary nor available. In such a case, the aversiveness of the anxious state may become paramount, and the person becomes concerned with ending the anxiety. Removing the threatening aspect of self from awareness may be sufficient. Instead of changing the self—which may have been the purpose of anxiety from a functional perspective—the person may simply try to forget the self.

Inferences about the self, then, may be among the most common precipitating causes of anxiety. Although the fear of social exclusion may be the underlying cause of the anxiety, subjectively the *self* will be experienced as the immediate cause of anxiety. In order to terminate this aversive state, therefore, people may often concentrate their efforts on escaping from awareness of the self, particularly of the self's failures or inadequacies.

COGNITIVE DECONSTRUCTION

The preceding section articulated a theory about anxiety and described how anxiety may motivate individuals to desire to escape from awareness of self. Reducing self-awareness is not easy, however, for it cannot be simply switched off like a lamp (see Wicklund, 1975, for an early discussion of the problems of reducing self-focused attention). Attempts to suppress any thought are at best only partly successful, sometimes producing a latent tendency to dwell on the forbidden thought (Wegner, Schneider, Carter, & White, 1987), and attempting to suppress thoughts of the self may be especially difficult. Indeed, the attempt to be unaware of self may be a paradoxical undertaking, for any effort to monitor the success of one's attempt would bring attention back to self, thus undermining the attempt. Instead of turning off self-awareness by sheer cognitive effort, then, people may be required to find alternate means. This section will focus on the process of cognition deconstruction as a viable means of escaping self-awareness.

Cognitive deconstruction may be defined as the attempted refusal of meaningful thought, particularly with reference to integrative, interpretive mental acts. Instead of controlling the focus of attention, the person limits the degree of cognitive elaboration that he or she performs. Normally, the individual may understand the world (and one's own experiences) in relatively complex, sophisticated, integrative terms, often involving interpretations (such as attributions) and analyses and evaluations. Cognitive deconstruction entails forsaking this normal mode of understanding and encountering the world merely as a set of stimuli, simple associations, and immediate responses.

Before proceeding to a description of the process and effects of deconstruction, it is useful to review the derivation of the concept. The notion of deconstruction has been widely discussed in the humanities and has recently attracted some attention in the social sciences.

Deconstruction in the Humanities

The term deconstruction is borrowed from the humanities. It became fashionable there in connection with recent developments in literary criticism, although its usages may not be uniform. Recent, influential works on deconstruction include those by Culler (1982) and Johnson (1980). The following discussion relies substantially on these sources.

The French critic Derrida is generally regarded as the seminal thinker in critical uses of deconstruction; his work drew heavily on Heidegger and other phenomenologists (e.g., Merleau-Ponty). Heidegger's approach to art began with his general principle that every experience is capable of supporting more than one interpretation. The act of thinking, in Heidegger's view, was a matter of moving among these possible interpretations (1968/1954). Interpretation can thus be understood as taking the sensory input of immediate events and elaborating them with meaning, which would include associating them with other events, placing them in contexts, making attributions about them, evaluating them against general attitudes, comparing them against standards, and otherwise analyzing them.

The potential impact of these ideas on the practice of literary criticism can readily be seen. In past centuries, literary interpretation was regarded as a matter of determining what the author had intended to express. It soon became obvious, however, that the appeal and importance of many great works went beyond the specific messages planned by the author. Critics began to feel that many interpretations of works were legitimate and acceptable even if the author had not necessarily intended them. Thus, literary critics came to accept the possibility that many works could support multiple interpretations.

In Heidegger's influential view, one interpretation is merely a construct that more or less clumsily attempts to make sense of an experience, and it is not to be expected that any particular general interpretation will perfectly and exhaustively fit all potentially relevant data. As critics began to explore multiple meanings, some began to suspect that no great and complex work—and perhaps not any work—would fit neatly and entirely into a single integrative interpretation. Inevitably, some features or connotations or implications would run counter to it. As a result, deconstructionists have become fascinated with how broad interpretations are contradicted by various features of the text. For example, Johnson's (1980) treatment of Melville's short novel *Billy Budd, Foretopman* points out that Billy, despite his goodness and innocence, commits murder and dies a criminal's death; while Claggart, the sinister villain, dies a helpless victim; and the wise-old-man figure of Captain Vere, despite his wisdom and morality, ends up having to insist on the death of a virtuous and innocent man.

If each text can support more than one legitimate interpretation (and no single interpretation is fully and thoroughly correct), it becomes difficult to decide whether any possible interpretation is wrong. The very occupation of literary criticism can begin to seem a kind of endless, pointless proliferation of multiple interpretations. Structuralism, a movement closely related to deconstructionism, responded to this seeming anarchy of interpretation by focusing narrowly on the surface structure (see Culler, 1975). Instead of aiming to decipher the one ultimate deep meaning of a text, or (indeed) instead of adding one more to the accumulation of legitimate interpretations, structuralists focused on the question of *how* does the text express meaning. Deconstructionism inherited this fascination with surface structure. In a sense, this movement was an effort to return attention to the work itself, rather than attending to the critic's ingenuity at spinning elaborate webs of meaning around the work. Deeper meanings, elaborate interpretations, and the author's original intentions were downplayed or even abandoned, while instead the text itself was to be the central focus.

Poststructuralism (including deconstructionism) differed from structuralism in that it rejected the possibility of comprehensive, structural, systematic knowledge of the text. Structuralism was a kind of last-ditch effort to find a basis for dealing with texts in a reliable, verifiable way, one that could reach *correct* conclusions and arrive at a valid understanding of the text. The author's intention was discarded as a valid basis for that effort and was replaced with surface structure. Deconstructionists rejected even that basis, for they concluded that an unequivocal and consistent interpretation of a text's surface structure was not possible. They retained the interest in surface structure, but they gave up on the idealized fantasy of coming up with a definitive account of it.

Needless to say, these views do not suggest a very optimistic or flattering view of the activity of literary criticism, and deconstructionists have not been universally popular among their colleagues. Indeed, deconstruction is often perceived and criticized as being nihilistic, especially by literally critics who believe in the possibility of valid and correct interpretation.

Ultimately, the term deconstruction seems to have acquired two related meanings. On the one hand, it refers to the failure and collapse of integrative constructions (such as unifying interpretive syntheses, hierarchical distinctions, and deeper meanings). In the example given, the general view of Billy Budd as an innocent, virtuous hero is deconstructed by his commission of murder. On the other hand, the term is sometimes used to refer to the activities of the critic or thinker who approaches texts in this way. For present purposes, the first of these meanings is much more important than the second.

One last point deserves mention. In literary criticism, deconstruction is very concerned with marginal events and with indeterminacy. Deconstructive criticism often focuses on how details or peripheral factors contradict the broad meanings. The most general message of deconstructionism may be described as the failure or inadequacy of general interpretations, and this is often revealed by marginal events or characters that constitute "data" which do not fit the broad meanings. In addition, the rejection of integrative syntheses and all-encompassing interpretations tends to have the result that ". . . deconstructive readings show scant respect for the wholeness or integrity of individual works. They concentrate on parts . . ." (Culler, 1982, p. 220). The focus on parts and processes, rather than on integrative wholes, is particularly important for present purposes, for the self is generally regarded as an integrated whole, and it is escaped by attending only to bits and pieces.

Deconstruction in the Social Sciences

Several lines of inquiry in the social sciences are relevant to the concept of deconstruction. The notion of a *construct* is widely familiar. A construct may be defined as an entity consisting entirely of meaning, often made by linking several meanings together. A schema, for example, is a construct, in the sense that it is a concept that is an organized network of related concepts (cf. Fiske & Taylor, 1984).

Berger and Luckmann's (1966) classic work *The Social Construction of Reality* argued forcefully that people's understanding of their worlds depends heavily on collective meanings and interpretive processes, despite the common illusion that one simply see things as they are. Berger and Luckmann emphasized that meaning is fundamentally social, because language and culture are social—that is, held by the social group collectively. Human experience is thus constructed in the sense of being a product of interpretations that filter sensory events through broad associative frameworks of ideas shared by many members of the culture. Without such construction, daily life would be a disconnected, fragmented, incoherent chaos of sensations and movements. Cognitive *deconstruction* aims at bringing one's experience into something approaching that state.

Recently, social psychologists have used ideas like these in examining the control of behavior. A first step was the recognition that behaviors can be understood and directed at different levels of meaning. Carver and Scheier (1981, 1982) adapted a cybernetic model from Powers (1973), describing how people can seek to control their actions at different levels, ranging from broad abstract principles to narrow, mechanical processes. Carver and Scheier elaborated the feedback-loop aspect of the theoretical model. When outcomes fail to measure up to internal standards, people shift to lower levels of meaning, that is, to more concrete, immediate, mechanistic levels. In other words, unsuccessful behaviors cause the person to focus on how he or she is pursuing the desired result, presumably in the hope of discovering some procedural flaw that can be corrected.

Vallacher and Wegner's (1985, 1987) theory of action identification is at present probably the most elaborate and sophisticated treatment of these issues. These authors began with the philosophical insight that each behavior can be identified at different levels. Thus, the same behavior can be described as moving one's arm or as participating in the political history of the 20th century, as well as many intermediate levels. Vallacher and Wegner abandoned Carver and Scheier's attempt to delineate a fixed number of levels and concentrated instead on move-ment among the levels. They elaborated Carver and Scheier's suggestion that failures and setbacks move people to lower levels and provided empirical evi-dence that this shift may be a vital step in forming new, more successful higher-level meanings. To reinterpret one's actions, it is apparently necessary first to deconstruct the old meanings (that is, to strip them away by focusing awareness on the mechanical, procedural aspects, such as muscle movements). Once the old meanings are deconstructed, they can be replaced by elaborating new meanings.

It is tempting to retain the "high-" and "low-level" terminology as used by Vallacher and Wegner (and by Carver and Scheier). Unfortunately, these terms contain some misleading connotations, especially if one seeks to use them more broadly than referring only to action. Spatial metaphors for quantity of mean-ingful elaboration have been used commonly in both directions. Thus, more elaborate, sophisticated, abstract, or contextualized meanings are sometimes described as "higher" and other times as "deeper," so an upward movement could imply either increments or decrements in meaningful elaboration. Accord-ingly, the present discussion will use the more precise term "deconstruction."

How Deconstruction Works

Cognitive deconstruction has been defined here as the attempted rejection of meaningful, integrative thought. This may often occur as an attempt to escape from troubling thoughts or implications. A person may feel anxiety because some recent event implies certain inadequacies or shortcomings about him or her, and these implications may carry the threat of possible exclusion from desired social groups and relationships. To stop the anxiety, the person must somehow cease to think about those implications. By ceasing meaningful thought al-together, those particular and troublesome meanings can be avoided.

To understand how deconstruction works, it is necessary to appreciate the nature of meaning. Without meaning, awareness is confined to the sensations and movements that occur in the immediate present. The awareness of pain, warmth, running, and so forth does not require language or interpretation. Mean-ingless awareness permits only a disjointed series of sensory events. Meaning links these events, beginning with associations and distinctions. A concept, for example, unites many individual entities or events, and a sentence describes relationships among several different kinds of concepts. Thus, meaning is funda-mentally relational.

Furthermore, meaning does not come in isolated pieces but rather in broader, organized structures. Thus, for example, the system of numbers has to stand as a system; a single number, such as 44, would be meaningless if there were no other numbers, for its meaning depends on its place in relation to all other numbers.

When people use meaning, then, they link their immediately present events, experiences, and concerns across space and time to other events, experiences, and concerns, as well as to broad abstract contextual structures (such as religious beliefs). Interpretation is a matter of taking the immediate event and integrating it into a broader structure, such as placing it in a context, relating it to general principles, evaluating it against general attitudes, inferring the existence of stable traits and tendencies, and so forth. In social psychology, the two most widely studied interpretive activities are attitudinal evaluation and attributional inference; both of these typically take the single, distinct event (or stimulus) and relate it to stable, enduring dispositions or principles.

The rejection of meaning is a matter of breaking these conceptual links. The interpretive activity that relates present, immediate events to other times, places, events, and concepts is suspended. Broad, general contexts are avoided, as are general principles, inferences about stable properties, invocation of general attitudes, and the like. Attributions are not made, and general attitudes are not accessed. The present is cut off from other events and times. Experience is left uninterpreted and unelaborated.

Time perspective appears to be highly correlated with level of meaning, which greatly facilitates operationalization (cf. Vallacher & Wegner, 1985). Broadly meaningful thought typically invokes categories that encompass a long time period, whereas less meaningful thought tends to use briefer, more immediate time frames. Thus, for example, in the interpersonal realm one would probably tend to describe a "meaningful relationship" as one that lasts a relatively long time, whereas a "meaningless relationship" would tend to be typically a brief encounter with no lasting importance or value. Likewise, a meaningful life would tend to be one that has some continuity across the life span, in which many discrete life events fit together into some broad themes, and which may perhaps even relate to categories that transcend the temporal limits of the individual life (such as relating to long-term religious, political, or historical factors). The meaningless life, in contrast, is a series of events that do not fit together into such a pattern; instead, the person may live from day to day, without much sense of continuity or of broader context.

These distinctions among levels of meaning may be applied to the self. The self can be constructed in a very meaningful fashion, in terms of identity and personality, which by definition describe the individual on the basis of continuity across long periods of time. In contrast, someone can be aware of self in a relatively meaningless, deconstructed fashion. The deconstructed self may be merely the physical body, or a motley collection of impulses and behaviors. The constructed self exists at a long-term level, maintaining some continuity across years and even decades. The deconstructed self exists in the immediate present. To deconstruct the self, then, one may shift the temporal frame of self-awareness from the long range to the immediate present, or one may shrink one's phenomenal self-concept from the stable identity to the body.

Attributions, in particular, are increments in meaning, for they take single events and draw broad, stable inferences from them, such as traits or attitudes.

Attribution thus often expands the time frame in which an event is understood—moving from the momentary observation to the enduring disposition. Consequently, cognitive deconstruction will tend to reject attributional thinking, preferring to think only in terms of isolated, discrete events rather than lasting traits, patterns, or inferences.

Escape from self through deconstruction, then, can be understood as a psychological effort to confine awareness to the immediate present as a way of avoiding integrative, meaningful thought. Instead of exploring and elaborating the pathways by which one can interpret immediate events, linking them to past and future events, invoking broad principles and general attitudes, and so forth, one experiences only the immediate present in conceptual isolation. Instead of meaningful action and meaningful experience, one is aware only of movement and sensation. Instead of being aware of self as an integrated entity symbolically constructed as part of an ongoing network of relationships, commitments, institutional ties, ambitions, projects, and enduring traits, one is aware of self only as a physical thing (a body) or as a jumble of short-term feelings, desires, and behaviors.

The Deconstructed State

This section will examine the characteristics and consequences of the state achieved by cognitive deconstruction. It is important to keep in mind that efforts at deconstruction are unlikely to be entirely successful. Probably in most cases the resultant state is relatively but not absolutely devoid of meaning. It may be impossible for a fully socialized adult human being to achieve a state of complete meaninglessness, perhaps except under extraordinary situations (e.g., in extreme pain, or after several years of meditating alone in a cave), but one can certainly achieve a state of mind that is relatively impoverished with respect of meaning. In other words, it is feasible to avoid much meaning, but it may not be possible to avoid all meaning.

Cognitive Immediacy. A first characteristic of the deconstructed state is a narrow focus of awareness on the immediate present. The person attends to goals, projects, and events that occur here and now. Past and future events recede from awareness. This short-term focus may also cause some alteration in the subjective sense of the passage of time. Time may seem to pass more slowly, in the sense that relatively brief intervals seem to take a long time. This might be compared with the time sense of young children, heroin users, or depressives, for whom each day may seem interminable.

Procedure Orientation. Means are more proximal than ends, by definition, so the deconstructed state tends to focus on means—that is, on processes, techniques, procedures. Ends invoke broader contexts, such as moral evaluations, comparisons against performance standards, and relations to even broader endeavors. Processes have only their immediate goal as context. To avoid meaningful thought, therefore, one may tend to focus on procedures and techniques. In literary deconstruction, this corresponds to the fascination with surface structure and with stylistic technicalities. In behavior, this may take the form of fascination with procedural details when broader meanings would be threatening. Thus, evidence suggests that the Nazi mass murderers focused their attention narrowly on technical aspects and procedures rather than moral issues (e.g., Arendt, 1977; Lifton, 1986). Likewise, criminals appear to focus on procedures and technicalities rather than on the broader meanings of their acts (e.g., Wegner & Vallacher, 1986). Suicide attempts also tend to be characterized by an intense, narrow focus on procedures rather than on broader meanings or philosophical issues (e.g., Baumeister, in press; Savage, 1979; see also Henken, 1976).

Passivity and Impulsivity.   Actively taking initiative often involves the use of meaning. Planning, deciding, accepting responsibility, evaluating possible consequences and implications, and other aspects of action are all essentially matters of meaning. The attempt to avoid meaningful thought is therefore often incompatible with the active role.

To the extent that action involves meaning, then, people may become passive when they try to reject meaning. Passivity may be particularly important for escaping the self. The self's actions define and express it in meaningful ways, but passivity is noncommittal. By remaining passive, the person can often preserve the self from commitment, responsibility, and other possible implications of action. Passivity is thus supremely consistent with cognitive deconstruction.

On the other hand, it may be possible to act in some ways without invoking meaning. Such deconstructed actions, by definition, would not express stable commitments or articulated intentions, would not be based on long-range plans or distal goals, and would not be considered in connection with the person's enduring values, attitudes, or beliefs. In short, such actions would tend to be impulsive. Action identification research has already established the link between impulsive action and low levels of thinking, which correspond directly to deconstruction (Vallacher & Wegner, 1985, 1987; also Wegner & Vallacher, 1986).

Low-level action identification terms may even facilitate the rejection of meaning (Vallacher & Wegner, 1985). By engaging in activities that are experienced only in very short-term, low-level, immediate fashion, the person may help distract himself or herself from broader issues of meaning.

Compulsive actions may represent one sort of extreme case of deconstructed action. By definition, the person who engages in compulsive behavior is not fully aware of the meanings of his or her actions. A therapist or analyst may be able to discern the meanings in these acts, but the person who engages in them is oblivious to them. The appeal of such deconstructed actions may be that they enable the person to address some personal conflict symbolically while avoiding awareness of the troublesome meanings.

Cognitive deconstruction thus promotes passivity at high levels of action identification, but the person may become active at low levels. Meaningful action is avoided, but impulsive action may increase.

Close-mindedness. Cognitive deconstruction has strong and direct effects on the thinking processes. When necessary, the person can draw on knowledge and experience. The rejection of meaningful thought entails, however, that thinking may tend to follow narrow, rigid, or stereotyped patterns.

In particular, the person may tend to avoid any sort of creative or divergent thinking. Applying rules and solving linear problems would be easier for someone in a deconstructed state than would learning, or revising rules, or solving complex, ambiguous, or open-ended problems. Openness to new ideas would tend to be minimal, for that requires some flexibility. Integrating new ideas into one's belief system may often require rethinking one's assumptions about self and world, which is a highly meaningful activity. Playing with ideas, shifting contexts, and seeking insight would all be contrary to the main thrust of deconstruction. Also, in general, meaning involves abstractions, so the deconstructed state would favor highly concrete and specific thinking over broad and abstract thinking.

Thus, the thought processes during deconstruction will tend to be rigid, concrete, linear, and uncreative. Fiske and Taylor (1984) used the term "cognitive miser" to refer to broad tendencies to resist new ideas, to minimize effortful thought, and to avoid revising one's beliefs. This model of social cognition may be particularly applicable to the deconstructed state.

Inconsistencies. Social psychologists have long been fascinated with the effects of regarding one's own behavior as inconsistent (e.g., Festinger & Carlsmith, 1959). To be aware of such inconsistencies, however, requires a fairly sophisticated cognitive operation. The person must attend to two different aspects of his behavior (or to behaviors occurring at different times), elaborate and compare them, and ascertain that they are inconsistent. In other words, awareness of inconsistency requires cognitive synthesis and elaboration, or at least a failed attempt at meaningful integration of diverse acts.

The deconstructed state would tend to preclude such cognitive operations. The person avoids meaningful elaboration of all actions and focuses narrowly on the immediate present. Thus, he or she will tend not to reflect on how present actions and their implications might contradict broad principles or the implications of past actions. In literary criticism, deconstruction emphasizes the conflicts, inconsistencies, and contradictions in the surface structure of a text. In psychology, a deconstructed state means that the person may be prone (and yet oblivious) to inconsistency and contradiction.

Thus, deconstruction may tend to make people more likely to behave in an inconsistent fashion, because they are less likely to be aware of these inconsistencies. Many of the normal tendencies toward cognitive and behavioral consistency would be reduced or eliminated, partly because the person simply will not recognize inconsistencies.

Disinhibition. Just as recognizing inconsistency requires meaningful, integrative thought, inhibitions rely on comparing possible behaviors against abstract standards. Most people have internalized a substantial number of norms, rules, moral principles, and restrictions, and these may prevent the individual from engaging in certain possible acts. Inhibitions are commonly connected with the act's meaning, not the muscle movements it involves; thus, for example, a person will object to shoplifting, rather than objecting to putting one's hand in one's pocket.

Cognitive deconstruction reduces meaningful awareness of one's actions, so the individual is less likely to weigh possible actions against abstract standards, such as moral prohibitions. Inhibitions against certain actions are thus disconnected, for they are only activated by meaningful thought. As a result, the person may shed many inhibitions in the deconstructed state.

Describing the deconstructed state as a disinhibited one is not the same as saying that such individuals are open to new experiences or seeking to broaden their horizons. On the contrary, their closemindedness (cited *supra*) entails that they would tend to avoid new experiences and the like. But if the opportunity arises for doing something that violates the person's normal inner standards, the person may be more likely to engage in that action in a deconstructed state than in a normal state.

Emotion. Emotion typically involves meaningful evaluation of circumstances. Meanings cause emotions, which are themselves meaningful (e.g., Baumeister & Tice, 1987; Schachter & Singer, 1962; Solomon, 1976). Indeed, Averill's (1980) "constructivist" theory of emotion emphasizes the social construction involved in emotion, as does Hochschild's (1983) research on "feeling rules." Emotions tend to be based on evaluations of circumstances in relation to the self's ongoing projects, in the context of culturally taught guidelines that prescribe evaluative standards and associate emotional responses (and expressions) to them.

The rejection of meaning must therefore reduce emotional responses substantially. By not thinking in terms of abstract standards, the self's goals and projects, and cultural guidelines, the basis for emotional response is undermined. Some evidence is consistent with the view that deconstructed mental processes are characterized by the lack of emotion. Pennebaker (in press) reviews evidence indicating that thoughtful, introspective people have greater frequencies and intensities of emotion (especially negative affect) and that people sometimes avoid thinking about traumatic or stressful events by focusing their minds intently on trivial, immediate, or relatively meaningless issues.

Indeed, escaping from emotion may often be one of the motivations behind deconstruction. Negative emotions are generally aversive, but they may be difficult to shut off. To eliminate and prevent such emotions, the person may resort to deconstruction. The present argument has emphasized deconstruction as a means of removing awareness of the self's inadequacies in order to escape the anxiety associated with that awareness. It must be emphasized, however, that deconstruction does not only remove anxiety; rather, it will tend to remove all emotions.

Cognitive Vulnerability.   Lastly, the person who successfully achieves a deconstructed state may have certain vulnerabilities that deserve to be noted. The removal of the broad meanings that shape one's interpretation of self and world may create a vacuum, and it is possible that other meanings may sometimes enter in to fill this vacuum.

One may speculate, therefore, that deconstruction may leave the individual vulnerable to irrational thinking, to fantasy, and to external influence. Irrational thought patterns might easily occur, because the person would tend not to recognize their irrationality (for the same reason that he or she would tend not to notice inconsistency). Fantasy requires positive, cognitive elaboration, but once the person has removed from awareness all the troublesome meanings that caused anxiety, he or she may be receptive to elaborating new meanings that offer more benign, pleasant, and controllable implications. Obviously, fantasy is constructive and thus moves beyond deconstruction per se, but it is at least plausible that deconstruction may often be a first step in the development of fantasied or irrational beliefs. Lastly, people without a coherent interpretive structure for integrating their experiences may sometimes be receptive to an external agent who provides a new, appealing structure. A religious cult or political sect that offers a radically new interpretation of events may be able to attract some people who have succeeded in deconstructing the world-view they were originally taught.

CONCLUSION: ESCAPE ROUTES

This chapter has argued that anxiety will be most commonly caused by the threat of social exclusion. When current events imply something about the self that might potentially cause others to reject, exclude, or ostracize the individual, that individual will tend to feel anxiety. To escape from this aversive state, the person needs to cease being aware of this problematical aspect of self. Controlling self-awareness is not easy, however, and often the most effective response will be the broad attempt to prevent meaningful thought in general. This response of cognitive deconstruction will remove the meaningful bases and causes of unpleasant affect, as well as having a variety of secondary effects (such as disinhibition).

The variety of effects of the deconstructed state entails that it may appeal to individuals for reasons other than the reduction of anxiety. Indeed, *ecstasy* is defined partly as a loss of self-awareness, and so the deconstruction of self may be an intrinsically pleasant, desirable state. Although escapes from self may generally share the process of deconstruction, therefore, they may not all be uniformly motivated by anxiety.

Before closing, it may be worth briefly mentioning several categories of behavior that can be understood as escapes from self. One may hypothesize that these will all tend to follow the process of deconstruction, and that many of them will also show evidence of anxiety resulting from the threat of social exclusion.

Alcohol use is one form of escape, and considerable evidence shows that it is an (apparently effective) response to aversive self-awareness (e.g., Hull, 1981). People drink more alcohol when under self-evaluative stress, although other forms of stress do not increase drinking (Hull, 1981). People drink more to cope with anxiety (Hallam, 1985; Hull, Young, & Jouriles, 1986). Alcohol's physiological effects enforce deconstruction, for they impair higher-level, abstract thinking, focusing the person instead on immediate sensations; an important aspect of this process is the removal or reduction of self-awareness (Hull, 1981; Hull et al., 1983). People drink to escape the implications of failure (Hull & Young, 1983) or in response to negative life events that are attributed to the self (Hull et al., 1986). Research findings are also consistent with several other features of the deconstructed state, such as reduction of inhibitions (e.g., Steele & Southwick, 1985). In our society, most people consume some alcohol, and it may be the most common way of achieving the benefits of escape, including reduction of inhibitions, removal of anxieties and worries, focus on sensations, and so forth.

Masochism can be understood as a systematic set of techniques for removing awareness of self (Baumeister, 1988a, 1988b, 1989). Pain has a powerful deconstructive effect, for pain makes abstract and systematic thought difficult and removes broader concerns from awareness, focusing the person instead on immediate sensations (Scarry, 1985). There is no systematic evidence for the causal role of anxiety, although this may be due to the difficulty of obtaining etiological or causal data about masochism. The anxiety hypothesis is thus still plausible; alternatively, it may be that masochists are attracted to the deconstructed state for reasons other than the reduction of anxiety. Various features of the deconstructed state are amply indicated in masochism, such as reduction of inhibitions, passivity, cognitive immediacy, and construction of fantasied meanings to replace normal everyday meanings (Baumeister, 1988a, 1988b, 1989).

Other possible escapes may be suggested. Immersing oneself in strenuous physical activity or sensation may deconstruct one's ordinary self and thus remove its cares and anxieties. Jogging, racquetball, dancing, and playing music may often appeal to individuals because of such effects. Of course, not everyone who plays racquetball does so for the sake of escape, but this may be one important aspect of its appeal to some people. In particular, intensive or excessive immersion in such activities—running marathons, playing music loudly, dancing for hours—may indicate that the activity is desired as an escape.

Meditative exercises may often have a similar function. Most meditative regimens begin with a strong effort to cultivate the deconstructed state, usually by forcing the individual to focus attention narrowly on some immediate stimulus (such as one's breathing). In religious mysticism, meditation is part of the broader effort to break down the person's ways of thinking about the world and achieve a loss of sense of self (sometimes called "ego dissolution"). Deconstruction is thus a means to an end.

At a more pathological extreme, it is plausible that the pathological eating patterns seen in bulimia involve cognitive deconstruction aimed at escaping anxiety. According to this analysis, which needs to be tested, the bulimic feels anxious about social inclusion because of some negative perception of self, and the binge eating is an attempt to forget these anxieties by focusing attention narrowly on the immediate sensations of eating.

To provide a more thorough account of one escape mechanism, I shall focus on suicide, which clearly is the most pathological and maladaptive form of escape imaginable.

Abundant evidence is consistent with an analysis of the presuicidal process as an attempt at escaping the self (see Baumeister, in press, for review). Anxiety-prone people are more likely than others to attempt suicide (e.g., Bhagat, 1976; Mehrabian & Weinstein, 1976), and abundant evidence indicates that experiences of social exclusion (especially romantic breakup and loss of employment) increase suicide risks.

Moreover, these anxieties appear to be linked to the self. Guilt and self-blame have been implicated as central factors in many studies of suicide (e.g., Hendin, 1982; Maris, 1981; Miller & Chabrier, 1987; Palmer, 1971). Shame over personal failure (Breed, 1972) and insecurity about one's capabilities (Harris, 1979) have also been implicated. More generally, many studies have documented that suicidal individuals feel worthless, and some longitudinal data indicate that drops in self-esteem are followed by increases in suicidal tendencies (Kaplan & Pokorny, 1976).

As a result, these individuals are not merely experiencing anxiety (and other negative affect), but the aversive states are focused on the self. Suicidals see themselves, as individuals, in especially negative terms compared with others (Neuringer, 1974). Careful, quantitative studies of suicide notes have revealed an extremely high proportion of first-person references and pronouns (Henken, 1976; Ogilvie, Stone, & Shneidman, 1983), which are generally interpreted as evidence of high self-awareness (e.g., Davis & Brock, 1975; Wegner & Guilano, 1980). Other evidence indicates that groups known for high levels of aversive self-awareness, such as adolescents, alcoholics, depressives, and individualistic cultures, have the highest suicide rates (Baumeister, in press).

Thus, a major causal pathway leading to suicide features anxiety associated with negative views of self. According to escape theory, the common response should involve the attempt to remove the self from awareness by cognitive deconstruction. Is there any evidence of this response?

A variety of evidence confirms the deconstructive process in the presuicidal state (Baumeister, in press). Sense of time is drastically limited to the present (e.g., Brockopp & Lester, 1970; Greaves, 1971; Hendin, 1982; Neuringer & Harris, 1974; Yufit & Benzies, 1973). Thinking becomes extremely concrete (Henken, 1976; Ogilvie et al., 1983) and rigid (see Arffa, 1983, for partial review). Thought processes become inflexible, one-sided, prone to fixed patterns, and the emotional range is severely curtailed (Ringel, 1976). Creative problem-solving capabilities diminish drastically (Asarnow, Carson, & Guthrie, 1987; Schotte & Clum, 1987), although other cognitive capabilities are unimpaired. Goals become extremely short-term, and behavior is often impulsive or otherwise characterized by the lack of anticipated consequences (Bhagat, 1976; Breed, 1972; Cantor, 1976; Weiss, 1957).

Although these individuals may exhibit deconstructed, impulsive actions (even including the suicide attempt itself), they show an aversion to meaningful action, and this is reflected in some forms of passivity. The tendency to deny responsibility for one's actions was demonstrated in a careful study by Gerber, Nehemkis, Farberow, and Williams (1981). Passivity is apparent in the grammar and syntax of suicide notes (Henken, 1976), as well as in suicidal individuals' responses to temperament assessment devices (Mehrabian & Weinstein, 1985). Their coping strategies tend to be more passive than those of other people (Linehan, Camper, Chiles, Strosahl, & Shearin, 1987; Spirito, Stark, Williams, & Guevremont, 1987). Significantly, although the act of suicide combines the roles of murderer and victim, the weight of evidence suggests that the suicidal individuals identify mainly with the role of victim (Baumeister, in press; Hendin, 1982), which is the passive role.

Cognitive deconstruction was presented here as primarily a means of escaping from aversive emotion. An important study by Williams and Broadbent (1986) portrays the presuicidal state in this light. Subjects were presented with emotional cues and asked to recount autobiographical memories embodying the cued emotions. Contrary to the researchers' predictions, suicidals were not quicker than controls to respond to negative emotional cues. Rather, the main difference was that suicidals were slower to respond to all emotional cues (especially the positive ones), and they were more likely to refuse the cue or to give irrelevant, inappropriate responses. These results portray suicidal individuals as people struggling to shut down their emotional systems.

Lastly, reduction of inhibitions was proposed as a consequence of deconstruction. Although suicidal individuals do not appear to be chronically, dispositionally impulsive individuals, their suicide attempts are usually described in terms that clearly reflect impulsive action (Patsiokas, Clum, & Luscomb, 1979). Likewise, although they are not chronic risk takers, suicidal individuals in the suicidal state are more prone to behavioral risks (Adams, Giffen, & Garfield, 1973; Silberfeld, Streiner, & Ciampi, 1985). This apparent reduction in normal caution, leading to increased willingness to take risks, may often be a causal factor leading to the suicide attempt itself.

Thus, cognitive deconstruction does appear to be an important link in the causal chain leading to a suicide attempt. Several of its major features have been documented, and often there is evidence indicating that these features reflect temporary states rather than chronic dispositions (e.g., Perrah & Wichman, 1987). This evidence is most consistent with the view of escape theory that deconstruction is part of a response to an immediate crisis, rather than a stable trait or predisposing factor.

When personal crises occur and generate considerable anxiety that is linked to self-awareness, the natural response may be to try to deconstruct the meanings that produce the aversive state. Once these meanings are deconstructed, the individual may then reinterpret events by constructing new, more benign illusions to integrate them (e.g., Taylor, 1983), which ultimately will enable the person to resume normal life. Suicide appears to result when the coping process breaks down in the middle, that is, when the construction of new meanings is unsuccessful. The individual is thus left trapped in the immediate present, which is experienced as meaningless and constricted yet threatened by anxiety if meaningful action or thought is attempted. The emotional emptiness, dislike of self, and disinhibition remove the usual barriers against taking one's own life, and oblivion may seem appealing as a relief from anxiety and threat. Suicide thus emerges as an escalation of the attempt to deconstruct the self.

Fortunately, most people manage to cope with anxiety without resorting to such drastic measures as suicide. Still, anxiety can be regarded as a highly unpleasant experience whenever social exclusion is threatened or implied. When anxiety occurs, the best escape from the aversive state may be to stop the meaningful thought and self-awareness that is associated with the anxiety, and cognitive deconstruction may often be the best available means of accomplishing this.

REFERENCES

Adams, R. L., Giffen, M. B., & Garfield, F. (1973). Risk-taking among suicide attempters. *Journal of Abnormal Psychology, 82*, 262–267.

Arendt, H. (1977). *Eichmann in Jerusalem: A report on the banality of evil.* New York: Penguin (Original work published 1963)

Arffa, S. (1983). Cognition and suicide: A methodological review. *Suicide and Life-Threatening Behavior, 13*, 109–122.

Arkin, R. M. (1981). Self-presentation styles. In J. T. Tedeschi (Ed.), *Impression management theory in social psychological research.* (pp. 311–333). New York: Academic Press.

Asarnow, J. R., Carson, G. A., & Guthrie, D. (1987). Coping strategies, self-perceptions, hopelessness, and perceived family environments in depressed and suicidal children. *Journal of Consulting and Clinical Psychology, 55,* 361–366.

Averill, J. (1980). A constructivist view of emotion. In R. Plutchik & H. Kellerman (Eds.), *Theories of emotion* (pp. 305–339). Orlando, FL: Academic Press.

Baumeister, R. F. (1982). A self-presentational view of social phenomena. *Psychological Bulletin, 91,* 3–26.

Baumeister, R. F. (1984). Choking under pressure: Self-consciousness and paradoxical effects of incentives on skillful performance. *Journal of Personality and Social Psychology, 46,* 610–620.

Baumeister, R. F. (1986a). *Identity: Cultural change and the struggle for self.* New York: Oxford University Press.

Baumeister, R. F. (1986b). *Public self and private self.* New York: Springer–Verlag.

Baumeister, R. F. (1987). How the self became a problem: A psychological review of historical research. *Journal of Personality and Social Psychology, 52,* 163–176.

Baumeister, R. F. (1988a). Masochism as escape from self. *Journal of Sex Research, 25,* 28–59.

Baumeister, R. F. (1988b). Gender differences in masochistic scripts. *Journal of Sex Research, 25,* 478–499.

Baumeister, R. F. (in press). Suicide as escape from self. *Psychological Review.*

Baumeister, R. F. (1989). *Masochism and self.* Hillsdale, NJ: Lawrence Erlbaum Associates.

Baumeister, R. F., Hamilton, J. C., & Tice, D. M. (1985). Public versus private expectancy of success: Confidence booster or performance pressure? *Journal of Personality and Social Psychology, 48,* 1447–1457.

Baumeister, R. F., & Scher, S. J. (1988). Self-defeating behavior patterns among normal individuals: Review and analysis of common self-destructive tendencies. *Psychological Bulletin, 104,* 3–22.

Baumeister, R. F., & Tice, D. M. (1987). Emotion and self-presentation. In R. Hogan & W. H. Jones (Eds.), *Perspectives in personality: Theory, measurement, and interpersonal dynamics* (Vol. 2, pp. 181–199). Greenwich, CT: JAI Press.

Baumgardner, A. H., & Brownlee, E. A. (1987). Strategic failure in social interaction: Evidence for expectancy disconfirmation processes. *Journal of Personality and Social Psychology, 52,* 525–535.

Beck, A. T., Laude, R., & Bohnert, M. (1974). Ideational components of anxiety neurosis. *Archives of General Psychiatry, 31,* 319–325.

Becker, E. (1973). *The denial of death.* New York: Free Press.

Berger, P., & Luckmann, T. (1966). *The social construction of reality.* Garden City, NY: Doubleday.

Berglas, S. C. (1986). *The success syndrome.* New York: Plenum.

Bhagat, M. (1976). The spouses of attempted suicides: A personality study. *British Journal of Psychiatry, 128,* 44–46.

Bowlby, J. (1969). *Attachment and loss. Vol. 1: Attachment.* New York: Basic Books.

Bowlby, J. (1973). *Attachment and loss. Vol. 2: Separation anxiety and anger.* New York: Basic Books.

Breed, W. (1972). Five components of a basic suicide syndrome. *Life-Threatening Behavior, 2,* 3–18.

Brockopp, G. W., & Lester, D. (1970). Time perception in suicidal and nonsuicidal individuals. *Crisis Intervention, 2,* 98–100.

Cantor, P. C. (1976). Personality characteristics found among youthful female suicide attempters. *Journal of Abnormal Psychology, 85,* 324–329.

Caplan, P. (1984). The myth of women's masochism. *American Psychologist, 39,* 130–139.

Carver, C. S., & Scheier, M. F. (1981). *Attention and self-regulation: A control-theory approach to human behavior.* New York: Springer–Verlag.

Carver, C. S., & Scheier, M. F. (1982). Control theory: A useful conceptual framework for personality-social, clinical, and health psychology. *Psychological Bulletin, 92,* 111–135.

Craighead, W. E., Kimball, W. H., & Rehak, P. J. (1979). Mood changes, physiological responses, and self-statements during social rejection imagery. *Journal of Consulting and Clinical Psychology, 47,* 385–396.

Culler, J. (1975). *Structuralist poetics.* Ithaca, NY: Cornell University Press.

Culler, J. (1982). *On deconstruction: Theory and criticism after structuralism.* Ithaca, NY: Cornell University Press.

Davis, D., & Brock, T. C. (1975). Use of first person pronouns as a function of increased objective self-awareness and prior feedback. *Journal of Experimental Social Psychology, 11,* 381–388.

Ebaugh, H. R. F. (1988). *Becoming an ex: The process of role exit.* Chicago: University of Chicago Press.

Festinger, L., & Carlsmith, L. (1959). Cognitive consequences of forced compliance. *Journal of Abnormal and Social Psychology, 58,* 203–211.

Fiske, S. T., & Taylor, S. E. (1984). *Social cognition.* Reading, MA: Addison–Wesley.

Franklin, D. (1987). The politics of masochism. *Psychology Today, 21*(No. 1), 52–57.

Freud, S. (1920). *Beyond the pleasure principle* (J. Strachey, trans.). New York: Norton.

Freud, S. (1930). *Civilization and its discontents.* (J. Strachey, trans.). New York: Norton.

Freud, S. (1965). *New introductory lectures on psychoanalysis* (J. Strachey, trans.). New York: Norton. (Original work published 1933)

Friedman, L. (1981). How affiliation affects stress in fear and anxiety situations. *Journal of Personality and Social Psychology, 40,* 1102–1117.

Gerber, K. E., Nehemkis, A. M., Farberow, N. L., & Williams, J. (1981). Indirect self-destructive behavior in chronic hemodialysis patients. *Suicide and Life-Threatening Behavior, 11,* 31–42.

Glick, R. A., & Meyers, D. I. (1988). *Masochism: Current psychoanalytic perspectives.* Hillsdale, NJ: Analytic Press.

Goldstein, A. J., & Chambless, D. L. (1978). A reanalysis of agoraphobia. *Behavior Therapy, 9,* 47–59.

Goodwin, D. W. (1986). *Anxiety.* New York: Oxford University Press.

Graham, B. (1987). *Facing death.* Waco, TX: Word Books.

Greaves, G. (1971). Temporal orientation in suicidals. *Perceptual and Motor Skills, 33,* 1020.

Greenberg, J., Pyszczynski, T., & Solomon, S. (1986). The causes and consequences of self-esteem: A terror management theory. In R. Baumeister (Ed.), *Public and Private Self.* New York: Springer–Verlag.

Hallam, R. S. (1985). *Anxiety: Psychological perspectives on panic and agoraphobia.* London, England: Academic Press.

Harris, R. (1979). Suicide attempts among drug abusers. *Suicide and Life-Threatening Behavior, 9,* 15–23.

Heidegger, M. (1968). *What is called thinking?* (J. G. Gray, trans.) New York: Harper & Row. (Original work published 1954)

Hendin, H. (1982). *Suicide in America.* New York: Norton.

Henken, V. J. (1976). Banality reinvestigated: A computer-based content analysis of suicidal and forced-death documents. *Suicide and Life-Threatening Behavior, 6,* 36–43.

Hochschild, A. (1983). *The managed heart: Commercialization of human feeling.* Berkeley: University of California Press.

Hogan, R. (1982). A socioanalytic theory of personality. In M. Page & R. Dienstbier (Eds.), *Nebraska Symposium on Motivation* (pp. 55–89). Lincoln, NE: University of Nebraska Press.

Horner, M. (1972). Toward an understanding of achievement-related conflicts in women. *Journal of Social Issues, 28,* 157–176.

Hull, J. G. (1981). A self-awareness model of the causes and effects of alcohol consumption. *Journal of Abnormal Psychology, 90,* 586–600.

Hull, J. G., Levenson, R. W., Young, R. D., & Sher, K. J. (1983). Self-awareness-reducing effects of alcohol consumption. *Journal of Personality and Social Psychology, 44,* 461–473.

Hull, J. G., & Young, R. D. (1983). Self-consciousness, self-esteem, and success-failure as determinants of alcohol consumption in male social drinkers. *Journal of Personality and Social Psychology, 44,* 1097–1109.

Hull, J. G., Young, R. D., & Jouriles, E. (1986). Applications of the self-awareness model of alcohol consumption: Predicting patterns of use and abuse. *Journal of Personality and Social Psychology, 51,* 790–796.

Ickes, W. (1984). Compositions in black and white: Determinants of interaction in interracial dyads. *Journal of Personality and Social Psychology, 47,* 330–344.

Ingraham, L. J., & Wright, T. L. (1987). A social relations model test of Sullivan's anxiety hypothesis. *Journal of Personality and Social Psychology, 52,* 1212–1218.

Johnson, B. (1980). *The critical difference: Essays in the contemporary rhetoric of reading.* Baltimore: Johns Hopkins University Press.

Jones, E. E., & Berglas, S. C. (1978). Control of attributions about the self through self-handicapping strategies: The appeal of alcohol and the role of underachievement. *Personality and Social Psychology Bulletin, 4,* 200–206.

Kaplan, H. B., & Pokorny, A. D. (1976). Self-attitudes and suicidal behavior. *Suicide and Life-Threatening Behavior, 6,* 23–35.

Kendall, P. C. (1978). Anxiety: States, traits—situations? *Journal of Consulting and Clinical Psychology, 46,* 280–287.

Lasch, C. (1978). *The culture of narcissism.* New York: Norton.

Leary, M. R., Knight, P. D., & Johnson, K. A. (1987). Social anxiety and dyadic conversation: A verbal response analysis. *Journal of Social and Clinical Psychology, 5,* 34–50.

Lifton, R. J. (1986). *The Nazi doctors: Medical killing and the psychology of genocide.* New York: Basic Books.

Linehan, M. M., Camper, P., Chiles, J. A., Strosahl, K., & Shearin, E. (1987). Interpersonal problem solving and parasuicide. *Cognitive Therapy and Research, 11,* 1–12.

Maris, R. (1981). *Pathways to suicide: A survey of self-destructive behaviors.* Baltimore: Johns Hopkins University Press.

Maris, R. (1985). The adolescent suicide problem. *Suicide and Life-Threatening Behavior, 15,* 91–100.

Masters, W. H., & Johnson, V. E. (1970). *Human sexual inadequacy.* Boston: Little, Brown.

May, R. (1977). *The meaning of anxiety.* New York: Norton.

Mehrabian, A., & Weinstein, L. (1985). Temperament characteristics and suicide attempters. *Journal of Consulting and Clinical Psychology, 53,* 544–546.

Menninger, K. (1966/1938). *Man against himself.* New York: Harcourt, Brace, & World.

Miller, F., & Chabrier, L. A. (1987). The relation of delusional content in psychotic depression to life-threatening behavior. *Suicide and Life-Threatening Behavior, 17,* 13–17.

Neuringer, C. (1974). Attitudes toward self in suicidal individuals. *Life-Threatening Behavior, 4,* 96–106.

Neuringer, C., & Harris, R. M. (1974). The perception of the passage of time among death-involved hospital patients. *Life-Threatening Behavior, 4,* 240–254.

Ogilvie, D. M., Stone, P. J., & Shneidman, E. S. (1983). A computer analysis of suicide notes. In E. Shneidman, N. Farberow & R. Litman (Eds.), *The psychology of suicide.* (pp. 249–256). New York: Aronson.

Palmer, S. (1971). Characteristics of suicide in 54 nonliterate societies. *Life-Threatening Behavior, 1*, 178–183.

Patsiokas, A., Clum, G., & Luscomb, R. (1979). Cognitive characteristics of suicide attempters. *Journal of Consulting and Clinical Psychology, 47*, 478–484.

Pennebaker, J. W. (in press). Stream of consciousness and stress: Levels of thinking. In J. S. Uleman & J. A. Bargh (Eds.), *The direction of thought: Limits of awareness, intention, and control.*

Perrah, M., & Wichman, H. (1987). Cognitive rigidity in suicide attempters. *Suicide and Life-Threatening Behavior, 17*, 251–262.

Powers, W. T. (1973). *Behavior: The control of perception.* Chicago: Aldine.

Ringel, E. (1976). The presuicidal syndrome. *Suicide and Life-Threatening Behavior, 6*, 131–149.

Sarason, B. (1986). Social support, social behavior, and cognitive processes. In R. Schwarzer (Ed.), *Self-related cognitions in anxiety and motivation* (pp. 77–85). Hillsdale, NJ: Lawrence Erlbaum Associates.

Sarbin, T. R. (1968). Ontology recapitulates philosophy: The mythic nature of anxiety. *American Psychologist, 23*, 411–418.

Savage, M. (1979). *Addicted to suicide.* Cambridge, MA: Schenkman.

Scarry, E. (1985). *The body in pain: The making and unmaking of the world.* New York: Oxford University Press.

Schachter, S., & Singer, J. (1962). Cognitive, social, and physiological determinants of emotional state. *Psychological Review, 69*, 378–399.

Schlenker, B. R. (1980). *Impression management: The self-concept, social identity, and interpersonal relations.* Monterey, CA: Brooks/Cole.

Schlenker, B. R. (1985). *The self and social life.* New York: McGraw–Hill.

Schlenker, B. R., & Leary, M. R. (1982). Social anxiety and self-presentation. *Psychological Bulletin, 92*, 641–669.

Schotte, D. E., & Clum, G. A. (1987). Problem-solving skills in suicidal psychiatric patients. *Journal of Consulting and Clinical Psychology, 55*, 49–54.

Silberfeld, M., Streiner, B., & Ciampi, A. (1985). Suicide attempters, ideators, and risk-taking propensity. *Canadian Journal of Psychiatry, 30*, 274–277.

Simon, H. A. (1967). Motivational and emotional controls of cognition. *Psychological Review, 74*, 29–39.

Smith, T. W., Ingram, R. E., & Brehm, S. S. (1983). Social anxiety, anxious self-preoccupation, and recall of self-relevant information. *JPSP, 44*, 1276–1283.

Solomon, R. C. (1976). *The passions.* Garden City, NY: Doubleday Anchor.

Spirito, A., Stark, L. J., Williams, C. A., & Guevremont, D. C. (1987, November). *Common problems and coping strategies reported by normal adolescents and adolescent suicide attempters.* Paper presented to the Association for the Advancement of Behavior Therapy, Boston.

Steele, C. M., & Southwick, L. (1985). Alcohol and social behavior I: The psychology of drunken excess. *Journal of Personality and Social Psychology, 48*, 18–34.

Steele, C. M., Southwick, L. L., & Critchlow, B. (1981). Dissonance and alcohol: Drinking your troubles away. *Journal of Personality and Social Psychology, 41*, 831–846.

Stekel, W. (1953). *Sadism and masochism: The psychology of hatred and cruelty* (trans. E. Gutheil). Vol. 1. New York: Liveright. (Original work published 1929)

Stephan, W. G., & Stephan, C. W. (1985). Intergroup anxiety. *Journal of Social Issues, 41*, 157–175.

Sullivan, H. S. (1953). *The interpersonal theory of psychiatry.* New York: Norton.

Taylor, S. E. (1983). Adjustment to threatening events: A theory of cognitive adaptation. *American Psychologist, 38*, 1161–1173.

Vallacher, R. R., & Wegner, D. M. (1985). *A theory of action identification.* Hillsdale, NJ: Lawrence Erlbaum Associates.

Vallacher, R. R., & Wegner, D. M. (1987). What do people think they're doing: Action identification and human behavior. *Psychological Review, 94*, 3–15.

Wegner, D. M., & Guilano, T. (1980). Arousal-induced attention to self. *Journal of Personality and Social Psychology, 38*, 719–726.

Wegner, D. M., Schneider, D. J., Carter, S. R., & White, T. L. (1987). Paradoxical effects of thought suppression. *Journal of Personality and Social Psychology, 53*, 5–13.

Wegner, D. M., & Vallacher, R. R. (1986). Action identification. In R. M. Sorrentino & E. T. Higgins (Eds.), *Handbook of cognition and motivation* (pp. 550–582). New York: Guilford Press.

Weiss, J. M. A. (1957). The gamble with death in attempted suicide. *Psychiatry, 20*, 17–25.

Wicklund, R. A. (1975). Objective self-awareness. In L. Berkowitz (Ed.), *Advances in experimental social psychology* (Vol. 8, pp. 233–275). New York: Academic Press.

Williams, J. M., & Broadbent, K. (1986). Autobiographical memory in suicide attempters. *Journal of Abnormal Psychology, 95*, 144–149.

Wine, J. (1971). Test anxiety and direction of attention. *Psychological Bulletin, 76*, 92–104.

Yufit, R. I., & Benzies, B. (1973). Assessing suicidal potential by time perspective. *Life-Threatening Behavior, 3*, 270–282.

Zajonc, R. B., Heingartner, A., & Herman, E. M. (1969). Social enhancement and impairment of performance in the cockroach. *Journal of Personality and Social Psychology, 13*, 83–92.

13 Self-Inference Processes: Looking Back and Ahead

James M. Olson
Carolyn L. Hafer
University of Western Ontario

The chapters in the present volume address self-inference processes—the ways that individuals make judgments about themselves. Some authors discuss the antecedents of self-inference (e.g., the conditions that are necessary for valid self-perception; see Wilson's chapter), some discuss the self-inference process itself (e.g., how people infer emotions from internal sensations and external cues; see Olson's chapter), and some discuss the consequences of self-inferences (e.g., the effects of self-judgments on depression and interpersonal behavior; see McCann's chapter). The targets of the self-inferences (the aspects of the self that are inferred) also are diverse in the various chapters, encompassing physical characteristics, personality traits, standards and goals, self-esteem, attributes in the self-image, and previous events in one's past (see, respectively, the chapters by Polivy, Herman, & Pliner; Sande; Higgins, Tykocinski, & Vookles; Jones; Turnbull, Miller, & McFarland; and Ross & Holmberg).

The breadth of topics addressed in this volume underscores the importance of self-inference processes as an area of study. Judgments about the self can influence stable conceptions of the self (identity), salient or accessible aspects of the self-image (termed the phenomenal self by Jones & Gerard, 1967, and the working self-concept by Markus & Nurius, 1986), attitudes toward the self (self-esteem), causal inferences about the self (self-attributions), and plans for the future (e.g., goals, intentions, and expectations). Although the effects of self-inference processes are undoubtedly stronger and more immediate on the phenomenal self than on stable identity, temporary changes in self-image can sometimes become permanent (as several authors in the current volume document).

Self-inference processes have been studied in social psychology and sociology for many years, although a distinct, identifiable literature on this topic has not emerged, probably because of the diversity of relevant issues, as has been indicated. The foundation for the current volume was provided by such well-known theories as symbolic interactionism (Mead, 1934), dissonance (Festinger, 1957), dramaturgy (Goffman, 1959), and self-perception (Bem, 1972). More recent developments, such as self-handicapping (e.g., Jones & Berglas, 1978) and self-schemata (e.g., Markus & Sentis, 1982), also provided important building blocks for the research programs reported in this book.

In this concluding chapter, we have two goals. First, we will look back on some of the contributions that set the stage for the present volume. Our review of past research will necessarily be selective, focusing on those contributions that were important for the particular issues addressed in this volume. Second, we will look ahead at some broad themes or issues that seem likely to receive attention in future research and theory on self-inference processes. Again, these speculations will focus on trends that extend the present volume.

LOOKING BACK

Many different aspects of the "self" relevant to self-inference processes have been addressed in past research. In this section, we briefly review seven areas of research that provided important foundations for chapters in the present volume.

1. The Looking Glass Self

It may seem paradoxical that social psychologists and sociologists have been at the forefront of the study of the self, a potentially private and nonsocial topic. Yet, self-conceptions and self-images arise largely from social interactions. Families, peers, and reference groups provide feedback about our distinctive qualities and help to define the central aspects of our identities.

This social aspect of the self has been recognized from the very start of the scientific study of the self. Cooley (1902) argued that our identities develop from imagining how we appear to others and how they evaluate us, a subjective process he referred to as "the looking glass self." Mead (1934) emphasized a more objective impact of others' evaluations on self-conceptions. He proposed that children observe and imitate the behavior of important others in their social environment (e.g., parents) and eventually internalize the attitudes implied by those behaviors. This role taking extends to behavior directed at the children themselves. Thus, being treated as shy or outgoing by significant others will lead to a matching self-conception. Of course, this should not be taken to mean that self-conceptions are necessarily inaccurate or the result of arbitrary treatment by others; presumably, people will often behave toward us in ways that reflect, at least in part, our actual attributes. (In a recent paper, Felson, 1989, presents interesting longitudinal data on the interrelations among self-conceptions, actual appraisals from others, and "reflected appraisals," i.e., perceptions of others' appraisals.)

Given the intuitive plausibility of the hypothesis that feedback from others will affect self-evaluations, it is not surprising that there are supportive experimental data. For example, Videbeck (1960) showed that students' self-ratings of their speech skills changed after receiving a (randomly assigned) positive or negative appraisal from an alleged expert. Of course, we do not always accept appraisals from others uncritically (see Gergen, 1971, pp. 43–49, for a discussion of some factors that influence the acceptance of appraisals). In fact, as will be discussed in more detail in the section on "self-assessment versus self-enhancement versus self-verification," individuals may strenuously resist information that is discrepant with a pre-existing view of self.

Another important theory in the tradition of the "looking glass self" is social comparison theory (Festinger, 1954). This theory provided a careful analysis of when and why our self-conceptions will be affected by other people. Building on previous work on reference groups (e.g., Merton & Kitt, 1950), Festinger proposed that humans have an innate drive to evaluate their opinions and abilities. When possible, people will use physical reality to make these evaluations, but comparisons with others (social reality) may often constitute the only available manner of assessment. In such circumstances, people will compare themselves with others who are similar on relevant dimensions (see Goethals & Darley, 1977; Zanna, Goethals, & Hill, 1975). Thus, people make judgments about the correctness of their attitudes or the level of their abilities by comparing their own opinions and performances with those of similar others. For recent reviews of the social comparison literature, see Goethals (1986), Olson and Hazlewood (1986), and Wood (in press).

The final research program to be mentioned in this section is the work by McGuire and his colleagues (for a review, see McGuire & McGuire, 1982) on "self-spaces," defined as the content that comes to mind when people are asked to reflect about themselves. McGuire's data show the impact of the social environment on self-conceptions. First, a surprisingly large proportion of spontaneous self-descriptions consist of references to other people; in of 560 schoolchildren in grades 1, 3, 7, and 11, 23% of all none produced when the children were asked to "Tell us about yourself tions of significant others (McGuire & McGuire, 1982). Second that an attribute will appear in the self-space is increased w highly distinctive in the individual's social environment. F are more likely to mention their gender to the extent that greater proportions of opposite-sexed siblings (McGu 1979). Presumably, gender should also be more salie setting in which people find themselves consist individuals.

All contributors to the present volume wo

appraisals from others, and "reflected appraisals," i.e., perceptions of others' appraisals.)

Given the intuitive plausibility of the hypothesis that feedback from others will affect self-evaluations, it is not surprising that there are supportive experimental data. For example, Videbeck (1960) showed that students' self-ratings of their speech skills changed after receiving a (randomly assigned) positive or negative appraisal from an alleged expert. Of course, we do not always accept appraisals from others uncritically (see Gergen, 1971, pp. 43–49, for a discussion of some factors that influence the acceptance of appraisals). In fact, as will be discussed in more detail in the section on "self-assessment versus self-enhancement versus self-verification," individuals may strenuously resist information that is discrepant with a pre-existing view of self.

Another important theory in the tradition of the "looking glass self" is social comparison theory (Festinger, 1954). This theory provided a careful analysis of when and why our self-conceptions will be affected by other people. Building on previous work on reference groups (e.g., Merton & Kitt, 1950), Festinger proposed that humans have an innate drive to evaluate their opinions and abilities. When possible, people will use physical reality to make these evaluations, but comparisons with others (social reality) may often constitute the only available manner of assessment. In such circumstances, people will compare themselves with others who are similar on relevant dimensions (see Goethals & Darley, 1977; Zanna, Goethals, & Hill, 1975). Thus, people make judgments about the correctness of their attitudes or the level of their abilities by comparing their own opinions and performances with those of similar others. For recent reviews of the social comparison literature, see Goethals (1986), Olson and Hazlewood (1986), and Wood (in press).

The final research program to be mentioned in this section is the work by McGuire and his colleagues (for a review, see McGuire & McGuire, 1982) on "self-spaces," defined as the content that comes to mind when people are asked to reflect about themselves. McGuire's data show the impact of the social environment on self-conceptions. First, a surprisingly large proportion of people's spontaneous self-descriptions consist of references to other people; in one survey of 560 schoolchildren in grades 1, 3, 7, and 11, 23% of all noun concepts produced when the children were asked to "Tell us about yourself" were mentions of significant others (McGuire & McGuire, 1982). Second, the likelihood that an attribute will appear in the self-space is increased when the attribute is highly distinctive in the individual's social environment. For example, children are more likely to mention their gender to the extent that their family consists of greater proportions of opposite-sexed siblings (McGuire, McGuire, & Winton, 1979). Presumably, gender should also be more salient when the particular social setting in which people find themselves consists primarily of opposite-sexed individuals.

All contributors to the present volume would agree that there is a significant social or "looking glass" component to the self. Perhaps the most direct descendant of this tradition is the chapter by Turnbull, Miller, and McFarland, who investigate some implications of McGuire's work on distinctiveness. Sorrentino and Roney propose in their chapter that there are individual differences in the extent to which people seek and use social comparison information.

2. Autobiographical Memory

A second area of research that provided an important foundation for the present volume is work on personal memories. A major theme in this literature has been that autobiographical memory is an active, (re)constructive process. That is, rather than necessarily reflecting the direct retrieval of information stored in memory, individuals' personal histories often represent inferences based on judgment cues and/or intuitive theories. Of course, such a view of autobiographical recall is consistent with work on other kinds of memory, where reconstructive, schema-driven effects have long been recognized (e.g., Bartlett, 1932; Bransford & Franks, 1971).

Reconstructive processes can sometimes produce inaccuracies, and theorists have offered both motivational and nonmotivational explanations for biases in autobiographical memory. For example, the Freudian (Freud, 1925) concept of repression is based on the notion that people are motivated to forget psychologically painful events and memories. Similarly, Greenwald (1980) has proposed the concept of the "totalitarian ego." Greenwald characterizes the ego as a personal historian, responsible for organizing knowledge about the self. He calls the ego "totalitarian" because it employs devices usually attributed only to dictators: "ego fabricates and revises history, thereby engaging in practices not ordinarily admired in historians" (p. 604). These revisions of personal memories presumably enhance one's apparent power, goodness, and stability. Greenwald proposes that such an ego structure has evolved because cognitive systems characterized by beliefs in personal efficacy are associated with effective functioning and adaptation (see also Taylor & Brown, 1988).

Biases in personal memories might also occur for nonmotivational reasons. For example, Hastie (1981) and Taylor and Crocker (1981) discuss several ways that individuals' cognitive structures, or schemata, can bias information processing and memory (including, presumably, autobiographical memory). Schemata can guide attention, facilitate storage, and serve as a cue in retrieval. Thus, personal memories will tend to be consistent with how one conceptualizes the world (e.g., with one's expectations, stereotypes, and goals).

Like schemata, moods can serve as associative cues that bias autobiographical memory. Research on the affect–memory relation has shown that mood-congruent information tends to be recalled better than mood-incongruent information, especially for positive but also for negative emotional states (e.g., Bower, 1981; Isen, Shalker, Clark, & Karp, 1978).

In a recent model of autobiographical memory, Ross (1989) has proposed that people possess implicit theories about the stability and instability of various characteristics. These implicit theories guide perceivers' recall of their own previous standings on the dimensions. For example, attitudes are generally assumed to be stable. If an experimental manipulation is used to change subjects' attitudes, they will overestimate the extent to which their previous attitudes and behaviors were consistent with their current views (e.g., Goethals & Reckman, 1973; Olson & Cal, 1984; Ross, McFarland, & Fletcher, 1981).

Another recent development in the literature on autobiographical memory is the concept of self-schemata. Building on social cognitive research on the information-processing effects of schemata (as described herein), some researchers began to address the structural nature of cognitive representations of the self. Self-schemata were proposed to be organizing constructs for information about the self.

Two influential studies in this area were conducted by Rogers, Kuiper, and Kirker (1977) and Markus (1977). The former authors found that self-reference tasks (judging the self-descriptiveness of trait adjectives) led to excellent recall of the stimuli. The latter author found that when an adjective conformed with subjects' self-conceptions, response latencies for self-descriptiveness ratings were very short.

These and other studies led Markus and Sentis (1982) to propose a schematic model of the self. Markus and Sentis argue that

> The self can be conceptualized as a system of *self-schemata*. These schemata are knowledge structures developed by individuals to understand and explain their own social experiences. They serve to integrate a wide range of stimulus information about the self. A schema integrates all the information known about the self in a given behavioral domain into a systematic framework used during processing. (p. 45)

We may see ourselves as shy or outgoing, slim or overweight, spontaneous or controlled (our self-schemata will presumably reflect, at least in part, others' reactions to us, as discussed in the previous section). Of course, some dimensions will not be relevant to particular individuals (e.g., some people never or rarely think about whether they are spontaneous or controlled); such individuals are labeled "aschematic" on the dimension. Markus and Sentis (1982) review evidence documenting a wide variety of effects of self-schemata on the processing of information, both about the self and about others. For example, compared with aschematics, individuals with self-schemata in a particular domain make self-judgments about the domain quickly, confidently, and consistently, and are sensitive to variations in the domain among other people.

Kuiper and his colleagues have proposed a self-schema model of depression (for reviews, see Kuiper, MacDonald, & Derry, 1983; Kuiper, Olinger, & Mac-

Donald, 1988). In this approach, which extends earlier work by Beck (1967), depressives are assumed to have a greater amount of negative, depressed content in their self-schemata than nondepressives. Consequently, the former individuals exhibit a negativity bias when processing information about themselves and their environment—a bias that predisposes them to depression and maintains depressed states.

Autobiographical memory and self-schemata are important elements of numerous chapters in the present volume. Perhaps not surprisingly given Ross's recent theory (described earlier), the chapter that deals most directly with autobiographical memory is the one by Ross and Holmberg, where possible gender differences in recall of events in close relationships are discussed. With respect to self-schemata, the roots of the research programs described in the chapters by McCann on the interpersonal consequences of the self and by Higgins, Tykocinski, and Vookles on self-beliefs can be traced to the self-schema literature.

3. Self-presentation

Goffman's (1959) dramaturgical account of social behavior recognized the ubiquity of self-presentation. Goffman pointed out that individuals' behaviors are often guided by situational and role-related demands. These demands produce behaviors that may not reflect actors' true feelings, but rather the normative requirements of their positions in the social system. Goffman used theatrical terms such as stages (and backstage), actors, roles, and performances to emphasize the intentional, controlled aspects of much self-presentation (Lauer & Handel, 1983).

Building on previous work including Goffman's (1959) theory and Jones's (1964) analysis of ingratiation, Jones and Pittman (1982) proposed a general theory of strategic self-presentation, which they defined as "those features of behavior affected by power augmentation motives designed to elicit or shape others' attributions of the actor's dispositions" (p. 233). In this theory, self-presentation consists of actions (whether consciously manipulative or not) that are motivated by a desire to create a certain impression of the actor; presumably, successful creation of the desired impression in the target's mind will have favorable consequences for the actor. Jones and Pittman also developed a taxonomy of self-presentation strategies, classified by the type of attribution sought by the actor. For example, intimidation is motivated by a desire to be seen as dangerous; exemplification is motivated by a desire to be seen as worthy; and supplication is motivated by a desire to be seen as helpless.

Self-presentation and impression management interpretations have been offered for many social behaviors (see Baumeister, 1982, for a review), including aggression (e.g., Borden, 1975), helping (e.g., Satow, 1975), distributing resources to others (e.g., Reis, 1981), reporting resentment about one's own outcomes (e.g., Olson, Hafer, Cousens, & Kramins, 1989), and expressing attitudes after induced compliance (e.g., Tedeschi, Schlenker, & Bonoma, 1971). Although the ability of researchers to distinguish unequivocally between impression management motives and other intrapsychic processes has been questioned (e.g., Tetlock & Manstead, 1985), self-presentation theories and research have continued to grow in number and stature (e.g., Arkin, 1980; Schlenker, 1980; Tedeschi, 1981).

There also appear to be stable individual differences in people's tendencies to engage in self-presentation. The most-researched dimension in this regard has been self-monitoring (Snyder, 1974). As Snyder and Gangestad (1986) put it,

> Individuals high in self-monitoring are thought to regulate their expressive self-presentation for the sake of desired public appearances, and thus be highly responsive to social and interpersonal cues of situationally appropriate performances. Individuals low in self-monitoring are thought to lack either the ability or the motivation to so regulate their expressive self-presentations. (p. 125)

Thus, the behaviors of high self-monitors are strongly affected by external cues such as situational and interpersonal norms, whereas the actions of low self-monitors are guided by internal standards and are relatively unaffected by self-presentational cues (for a review of supportive data, see Snyder, 1987).

In the present volume, the most thorough discussion of how self-presentation motives can affect self-inference processes is provided by Jones (whose previous contributions to the impression management literature have been noted). In his chapter, Jones presents data showing that successful self-presentation can cause changes in the self-concept, and he also examines the moderating role of self-monitoring in this phenomenon.

4. Self-attribution

Attribution theorists study the antecedents and consequences of individuals' causal judgments about observed events and behaviors. This topic has been one of the most heavily researched areas in social psychology (for reviews, see Harvey & Weary, 1984; Olson & Ross, 1985; Ross & Fletcher, 1985). Researchers have documented that perceivers make causal inferences not only about other people's actions, but also about their own behaviors and feelings. Self-attributions constitute one important type of self-inference.

In his analysis of commonsense causal reasoning, Heider (1958) set the stage for future self-attribution models. Heider proposed that people strive to understand the causes of events around them. To do so, perceivers note the covariation between effects and possible causes. Heider borrowed terms from Gestalt and Field theories, such as figure, ground, and field, to express the subjective, phenomenological nature of causal perception.

Although it was implicit in Heider's work that self-attributions followed similar principles to attributions about others, this assumption was not made explicit until Kelley (1967) published his extension of Heider's model. Kelley proposed that perceivers use three kinds of information (consensus, consistency, and distinctiveness) to determine the causes of their own and others' behaviors. Kelley also distinguished between three major categories of causal factors, namely person (internal), entity (external), and time (temporal) causes, which he viewed as being the possible "main effects" in an analysis of variance analogy.

Schachter (1964) proposed that attributional processes play a role in emotion. Specifically, he argued that the experience of emotion requires both physiological arousal and cognitive label with emotional relevance (i.e., the arousal must be attributed to an emotional cause). Schachter suggested that, under certain circumstances, arousal can be mislabelled, which will change the nature of the emotion.

Theorists also analyzed how people make attributions for achievement-related behaviors. Most notably, Weiner, Frieze, Kukla, Reed, Rest, and Rosenbaum (1971) proposed that two dimensions, internal-external and stable-unstable, underlie the four major attributions that can be made for success and failure: ability, task difficulty, effort, and luck. These authors argued that individuals' attributions for their own achievement outcomes will influence their affective reactions, expectations for the future, and subsequent actions (see Weiner, 1985, for a recent version of this theory).

The self-attribution models described above stimulated an enormous amount of research on a wide variety of issues. Some of the topics relevant to self-inference processes have included (1) differences between self-attributions by actors and other-attributions by observers (e.g., Jones & Nisbett, 1971; Jones, 1979), (2) misattribution effects in emotion (e.g., Fries & Frey, 1980; Olson, 1988), (3) the possible detrimental effects of external rewards on intrinsic motivation (e.g., Enzle, 1980; Lepper & Greene, 1978), (4) learned helplessness (e.g., Abramson, Seligman, & Teasdale, 1978; Dweck & Leggett, 1988), and (5) the accuracy of perceivers' awareness of their mental states (e.g., Nisbett & Wilson, 1977; Wilson, 1985).

Virtually every chapter in the present volume builds, in one way or another, on the self-attribution literature. The connections are clearest in the chapters by Sande (whose work extends Jones & Nisbett's reasoning about actor–observer differences), Olson (whose work on misattribution derives from Schachter's theory of emotion), and Lepper, Aspinwall, Mumme, and Chabay (whose analysis of strategies used by expert tutors relies, in part, on investigations of intrinsic motivation and learned helplessness).

5. Self-persusasion

Most research on attitude change has focused on persuasion that results from external sources, such as social influence and persuasive messages (see Olson & Zanna, in press). Yet, self-generated attitude change also occurs. In fact, social psychologists have identified numerous forms of self-persuasion.

Sometimes, self-persuasion results from the production of relevant thoughts and arguments. In an early study, King and Janis (1956) gave subjects a counterattitudinal message arguing that most university students would be drafted into the military. Some subjects simply read the message to themselves; other subjects read the message aloud; and subjects in a third condition were allowed to see the message but then had to put it away and give a spontaneous talk arguing for the same position. This last group of subjects manifested more attitude change in the direction of the message than did the first two groups of subjects. King and Janis suggested that these "improvisation" subjects expanded on the message content. That is, they generated additional arguments not in the original message and reorganized material from the message to make it more convincing, thereby persuading themselves that the position advocated in the message was valid.

More recently, Tesser (1978) identified another self-persuasion phenomenon that results from cognitive responses, which he calls "attitude polarization via mere thought." Tesser has shown that simply thinking about an issue often makes our attitudes more extreme, because we tend to generate thoughts that are consistent with our original position. For example, being asked to think for a few minutes about a likable or dislikable person leads to more extreme ratings than does a distraction-control condition (Sadler & Tesser, 1973).

Self-persuasion also can result from behavior that is inconsistent with existing opinions. Dissonance theory (Festinger, 1957) provides a motivational interpretation of the impact of behavior on attitudes; Festinger hypothesized that when people behave inconsistently with their opinions, they experience aversive arousal—"dissonance motivation"—which is reduced by changing their attitudes to be more consistent with the behavior. Revisions of dissonance theory (e.g., Cooper & Fazio, 1984) have clarified the prerequisites for such attitude change, including freedom of choice, negative consequences of the behavior, and feelings of responsibility for the consequences.

Bem's (1972) self-perception theory provides a nonmotivational interpretation of the impact of behavior on attitudes. Bem suggested that people's attitudes are often weak; consequently, when they are asked to express an attitude, people may have to infer an answer by reviewing their past behaviors (just as we infer other people's attitudes from their actions). If subjects have been induced to behave in a certain fashion by an experimenter, then "self-persuasion" will occur because this action will enter into the self-inference process (implying an attitude that corresponds to the behavior).

Recent work on self-persuasion indicates that dissonance and self-perception processes both occur, though under different circumstances (see Fazio, Zanna, & Cooper, 1977). Also, researchers are investigating the cognitive mechanisms that underlie self-persuasion. For example, Higgins (1981) has shown that modifying the public expression of one's attitudes (for strategical reasons) can alter memory for relevant information, thereby producing enduring attitude shifts.

The self-persuasion literature provided an important foundation for several chapters in the present volume. Wilson's analysis of how self-reflection can change attitudes represents an extension of previous research on cognitively mediated self-persuasion. In addition, some of the studies described in Jones's chapter on self-concept change and in Olson's chapter on emotion can be traced back to the dissonance and self-perception experiments on how behaviors affect attitudes.

6. Self-awareness

In the section on the "looking glass self," we noted that identity arises, at least in part, from taking other people's perspectives on the self (Cooley, 1902; Mead, 1934). Thus, viewing the self as an object that is evaluated by others plays a role in the development of self-conceptions.

Building on this early work (as well as more recent theorizing, e.g., Shibutani, 1961), Duvall and Wicklund (1972) proposed a theory of objective self-awareness. These authors suggested that individuals become self-aware or self-focused when "the self as an object of evaluation" is made salient. For example, an audience, a camera, or a mirror can produce a state of self-awareness (although the specific *aspects* of self that are made salient by these various situational factors may differ; see Froming, Walker, & Lopyan, 1982). In general, when people are self-aware, standards of conduct become salient, such as norms and ideals. Since we rarely match our ideals, the heightened salience of these standards will typically cause dissatisfaction. As a result, people may attempt to eliminate the negative affect associated with self-awareness by escaping from the self-focusing situation, either physically or psychologically (e.g., see Hull, 1981, for an analysis of alcohol consumption as a strategy for escaping self-awareness). When escape is impossible, Duvall and Wicklund (1972) suggested that people will attempt to reduce the discrepancy between themselves and the standards (i.e., they will attempt to match their ideals). For example, Diener and Wallbom (1976) found that a state of self-awareness, induced by working in front of a mirror while hearing one's own tape-recorded voice, significantly reduced the frequency with which subjects cheated in a situation where cheating was easy.

Deindividuation can be conceptualized as the opposite of self-awareness; the deindividuated state involves feelings of personal anonymity and/or group uniformity (see Diener, 1979). Zimbardo (1970) proposed a model of deindividuation that specified some of the antecedents and consequences of this state. For example, anonymity-producing clothing, large crowds, and alcohol were postulated to produce deindividuation. The consequences of deindividuation were hypothesized to include reductions in social inhibitions, strong attraction for the group, and more frequent counternormative behavior. Several studies have provided supportive evidence for this analysis of deindividuation (for reviews, see Diener, 1977; Prentice–Dunn & Rogers, 1983).

Stable individual differences in the degree of self-focused attention have been hypothesized (e.g., Buss, 1980; Carver & Scheier, 1981). Fenigstein, Scheier, and Buss (1975) developed the Self-consciousness Scale to measure the extent to which people are chronically self-aware. These authors distinguished between private self-consciousness, which involves awareness of one's internal states and feelings, and public self-consciousness, which involves awareness of one's external behaviors and impressions. Although the conceptual link between the Self-consciousness Scale and self-awareness has been questioned (e.g., Wicklund & Gollwitzer, 1987), the results of many studies have validated the differential consequences of private versus public self-consciousness (for reviews, see Carver & Scheier, 1987; Scheier & Carver, 1983). For example, Greenberg (1982) constructed an experimental situation where subjects allocated resources to two workers. Results showed that high private self-consciousness was associated with a tendency to use a distributive rule that conformed with subjects' own sense of what was fair, whereas high public self-consciousness was associated with a tendency to use a rule that would create a favorable public impression.

In the present volume, Baumeister's chapter is the most direct descendant of the self-awareness literature. Baumeister's analysis of deconstruction is predicated on the assumption that the state of self-awareness is often aversive.

7. Self-assessment Versus Self-enhancement Versus Self-verification

A continuing issue in the self-inferences literature has been the importance of different motives underlying self-relevant behavior. Some theorists have argued that individuals are primarily motivated to assess their attitudes and abilities in an objective fashion. Other theorists have argued that people are primarily motivated to enhance their self-image and self-esteem. Still others have argued that people's primary motivation is to verify or confirm the self-images that they have already formed. In this section, we will briefly describe a few examples of each of these perspectives.

Social comparison theory constitutes one example of the self-assessment position. Festinger (1954) argued that people are motivated to determine the correctness of their opinions and to achieve accurate appraisals of their abilities. Thus, as self-evaluators, Festinger conceptualized humans as rather open and rational information seekers. Attribution theorists also characterized perceivers in this manner, suggesting that naïve judges make inferences as if they were "lay scientists" (e.g., Heider, 1958; Kelley, 1967).

Another example of the self-assessment view comes from Trope's (1983, 1986) work on achievement behavior. Trope argues that "under specifiable conditions people are willing to assess themselves through task performance even when such assessment entails the risk of damage to one's self-esteem" (1983, p. 115). Trope agrees that self-enhancement and self-verification motives can operate, but he proposes that self-assessment is more fundamental, presumably because it is necessary for coping effectively with the environment. In numerous cleverly designed experiments, Trope has obtained evidence showing that subjects prefer "diagnostic" achievement tasks—tasks that will be informative about the subject's ability level. Thus, subjects act as if they are motivated to reduce uncertainty about their abilities and to achieve accurate self-assessments (see also Strube, Lott, Le–Xuan–Hy, Oxenberg, & Deichmann, 1986).

The self-enhancement perspective has been taken by researchers investigating many different phenomena, including affective reactions to interpersonal evaluations (e.g., S. C. Jones, 1973), self-handicapping (e.g., Jones & Berglas, 1978), self-serving biases in achievement attributions (e.g., Zuckerman, 1979), and the previously mentioned concept of the "totalitarian ego" (Greenwald, 1980). The social comparison literature has also generated considerable investigation of self-enhancement, despite Festinger's (1954) original self-assessment perspective (see Goethals, 1986; Olson & Hazlewood, 1986; Wood, in press). For example, Brickman and Bulman (1977) reviewed evidence concerning the social comparison of abilities which suggests that, for self-enhancement or self-protective reasons, people sometimes (a) avoid social comparisons, (b) prefer comparisons with dissimilar others, and (c) prefer comparisons with less fortunate others. The most explicit discussion of self-enhancement in social comparison comes from Wills (1981, 1986), who developed a theory of "downward comparisons" (comparisons with less fortunate others). Wills proposed that decreases in subjective well-being evoke downward comparisons, which serve to improve subjective well-being. He reviewed numerous phenomena that can be interpreted as manifestations of this process.

In another self-enhancement theory, Tesser and Campbell (1983) proposed the "self-evaluation maintenance" model of identity.

> [This model] is based on the assumption that persons are motivated to maintain a positive self-evaluation. They want to believe they are competent; they want others to believe they are competent; and they will behave so as to maintain a positive self-evaluation. (p. 5)

The basic purpose of the self-evaluation maintenance model is to explain the affective consequences of good and poor performances by other people. Tesser and Campbell distinguished between "reflection" processes, which involve affective reactions congruent with the other person's performance (e.g., pride in their good performance), and "comparison" processes, which involve affective reactions incongruent with the other's performance (e.g., lowered self-esteem caused by their good performance). Comparison processes are postulated to predominate when the performance occurs on a dimension that is central to the perceiver's identity, whereas reflection processes predominate when the performance dimension is low in personal relevance.

Finally, the self-verification perspective has also been taken by numerous theorists. Consistency models of attitudes, such as Heider's (1958) balance theory and Festinger's (1957) dissonance theory, assumed that people prefer consistency among their beliefs and behaviors. For example, Heider argued that "unbalanced" relationships (e.g., someone you like holds an attitude different from your own) are aversive and unstable. The perceiver will attempt to restore balance, either by changing their own attitude, by convincing the other person to change his or her attitude, or by coming to dislike the other. Thus, Heider conceptualized people as taking an active role in constructing a cognitively balanced environment.

Similarly, Secord and Backman (1965) proposed a congruency theory of interpersonal interaction. These authors suggested that when others' expectations are incongruent with an individual's self-concept, the individual will be motivated to restore congruency, either by misperceiving the others' expectations, by reinterpreting his or her own behaviors, or by restructuring the situation (e.g., by avoiding the other persons or by acting toward them in a manner that changes their perceptions to be consistent with the individual's self-concept). Like Heider, Secord and Backman saw humans as architects of congruent environments. For example, Backman and Secord (1968) found that people tend to select roles (occupations, college majors, etc.) that affirm their self-images. This is not surprising, of course; nor is it necessarily inappropriate—people's self-images are accurate, at least to some degree, and therefore should influence their selections of roles. Nevertheless, having selected roles that require behaviors congruent with self-images, people are (perhaps unintentionally) ensuring that their self-images will be sustained in future behavior and interactions.

Recently, Swann (1983, 1987) has also proposed a self-verification model of social interaction. Swann argues that once individuals have developed clear self-conceptions, they will work to confirm these views. Self-verification may reflect, in part, the assumption that confirmatory feedback is more accurate and diagnostic than disconfirmatory feedback. In addition, people may desire self-verification for reasons of predictability and stability. In a series of experiments, Swann has documented two kinds of self-verification strategies: People create social environments that confirm their self-views, and they process information in ways that make feedback from others seem more confirmatory than it really is.

In the present volume, several chapters deal with the motives underlying self-relevant behavior. The most explicit consideration of this issue occurs in the chapter by Sorrentino and Roney, who propose that different individuals are motivated by different concerns. Specifically, uncertainty-oriented individuals are hypothesized to have a predominant self-assessment motive, whereas certainty-oriented individuals are hypothesized to have a predominant self-verification motive. Self-assessment versus self-enhancement versus self-verification issues are also addressed in the chapters by McCann and by Turnbull, Miller, and McFarland.

Summary

We have reviewed seven areas of research that provided important foundations for the present volume. Although these seven areas have constituted distinct research topics in social psychology, all are relevant to our understanding of the ways that individuals make judgments about themselves, i.e., self-inference processes. For example, people develop a stable identity by attending to how others evaluate them (the "looking glass self"); people's judgments about what they were like in the past are affected by autobiographical memory; self-presentation concerns can change people's public behaviors, which, in turn, can sometimes alter their internalized views of themselves; people's inferences about the causes of their own actions are guided by self-attribution principles; self-persuasion processes can change people's judgments about their own attitudes; the state of self-awareness can change people's perceptions of the extent to which they have achieved their ideals; and the extent to which people will alter judgments about themselves following receipt of discrepant feedback may depend on whether they are motivated by self-assessment or self-enhancement or self-verification concerns.

These topics also have some important implications for one another. For instance, since self-persuasion can result from inferring one's attitudes from one's past behaviors (Bem, 1972), autobiographical memory can play a role in self-persuasion (e.g., see Salancik, 1974). Similarly, self-assessment, self-enhancement, and self-verification motives are interconnected with such topics as self-presentation (e.g., the desire to present oneself positively versus the desire to present oneself consistently with one's self-view) and self-attribution (e.g., the goal of achieving an accurate understanding of the causes of one's actions versus the goal of enhancing or defending one's ego). Thus, these topics are not independent, but rather comprise the foundation for an integrated, self-inferences literature. In the following section, we briefly identify some issues that are likely to receive attention in this literature over the next few years.

LOOKING AHEAD

The chapters in this volume describe some of the important recent research in the self-inferences literature. For example, the effects of self-reflection, the consequences of the patterns of individuals' self-beliefs, and the functions of deconstruction are three of the many topics in the book that represent exciting developments. Our goal in the remainder of this chapter is to look beyond the current volume and identify some general issues or themes (rather than specific topics) that we believe will receive attention from self-inference researchers over the next few years.

Of course, it is probable that some of the specific research areas reviewed earlier (which set the foundation for the current volume) will continue to flourish in the foreseeable future. For example, self-presentation, self-schemata, and self-consciousness appear to be enjoying ever-increasing popularity. It is also probable that certain methodological trends will become stronger in self-inferences research, such as greater use of natural settings and more heterogeneous samples. But we can also speculate about broader issues and themes. We will now identify five issues that we think qualify as both likely and worthy avenues for research in the self-inferences literature.

1. Stable Versus Malleable Self-conceptions

We begin with an issue that has been around for many years—the stability (or lack thereof) of the self-concept. Despite its age, this controversy continues, as researchers with different perspectives collect data to support their positions (in the present volume, see the chapters by Jones, by McCann, by Sande, by Sorrentino & Roney, and by Turnbull, Miller, & McFarland).

Among the most compelling data that imply malleability of the self-concept are findings by Allen and Potkay (1981) that individuals show little or no tendency to repeat words when they are asked to describe themselves on different occasions (at 1-week intervals), even when the instructions explicitly state "describe your true self, the real you, regardless of time, place or situations." McGuire's findings (e.g., McGuire & McGuire, 1982), described earlier in this chapter, also imply malleability of at least certain aspects of the self-concept. McGuire has shown that attributes are more likely to appear in individuals' spontaneous self-descriptions when those attributes differentiate the respondents from their social environment.

In contrast, Swann (1987) has argued cogently that the primary quality of the self-concept is stability. He cautions that laboratory investigations in which subjects are given self-discrepant feedback typically "place them in interpersonal strait-jackets," i.e., deprive subjects of opportunities to resist self-discrepant feedback, which they normally enjoy in nonlaboratory settings. In his research on self-verification, Swann has shown that "unconstrained" subjects do, indeed, act to stabilize their self-views after receiving discrepant feedback.

One plausible resolution to this controversy is that proponents of the two positions are focusing on different aspects of the self. In the opening section of this chapter, we distinguished between the concepts of "identity" (one's stable or chronically accessible self-conceptions) and "phenomenal self" (one's currently—and perhaps temporarily—salient self-conceptions). At times, individuals' phenomenal selves may correspond closely to their identities, but at other times, these concepts may have little overlap (see the discussion of the "working self-concept" by Markus & Kunda, 1986, and Markus & Nurius, 1986).

The concepts of identity and phenomenal self imply, respectively, that the self can be either stable or malleable. If one conceives of the self as a complex network of knowledge (Jones & Gerard, 1967; Markus & Kunda, 1986), then both positions can be seen to have validity. Indeed, Swann (1987) makes a similar point, arguing that "self-knowledge is organized hierarchically, with global abstractions about the self at the top and highly specific, temporarily or situationally bound information at the bottom" (p. 1044). Our global abstractions are probably quite stable, whereas our specific self-images are probably quite malleable.

Future research is likely to clarify the structure of self-knowledge and thereby address the stability versus malleability controversy. For example, Kunda and Sanitioso (1989) recently showed that increasing the social desirability of a trait increased the extent to which subjects rated it as self-descriptive. Thus, motivational forces can alter the phenomenal self. The impact of such manipulations on identity have yet to be investigated.

2. Self-environment Correspondence

An issue related to the preceding one is the manner in which the self impacts on the environment. That is, individuals do not respond passively to situational forces, but rather attempt actively to control and create desired environments. This idea is compatible with the previously described notion of a stable, self-verifying identity (e.g., Swann, 1987).

The hypothesis that individuals take an active role in creating environments that foster their identity is not new. Consistency theorists (e.g., Heider, 1958), symbolic interactionists (e.g., Secord & Backman, 1965), and functional theorists (e.g., Katz, 1960) all have argued that people behave in ways that express their values and evoke desired reactions from others. In the selective exposure literature (derived from dissonance theory), it has long been recognized that people's environments are structured—perhaps unintentionally—to provide consensus and support for their important attitudes (e.g., see Freedman & Sears, 1965; Frey, 1986).

Snyder (1981, 1984) has argued that when people test hypotheses, they tend to use information-gathering strategies that are more likely to produce confirmatory than disconfirmatory feedback. For example, if subjects are instructed to test whether a target person is introverted, they might ask the target person, "What do you dislike about loud parties?" This is a question that is biased toward obtaining information that implies introversion. Thus, Snyder's work characterizes people as unintentionally creating social environments that are consistent with their expectations (but see Skov & Sherman, 1986, and Trope & Bassok, 1983, for criticisms of Synder's methodology and data showing a "diagnosing" strategy).

These perspectives on human behavior recognize that personal and situational factors do not operate independently, nor even in the traditional "ANOVA" sense of an interaction (where, for example, a situational factor might affect some people more than others). Instead, there is a *dynamic* interdependence between personal and situational determinants of behavior, such that each category influences behavior but personal factors also influence the nature of the situation. Thus, self-conceptions and self-inferences affect both the behaviors that individuals manifest and the environments in which they operate (with the result that self-inferences exert a second, indirect effect on behavior via their effects on the environment).

An important direction for future research on self-inferences is to investigate the mechanisms that produce this "self-environment correspondence." A useful framework for such research has been provided by Buss (1987), who addressed the more general issue of how personality and social psychology can be integrated. Buss hypothesized that at least three mechanisms can produce person–environment correspondence: selection, evocation, and manipulation. Selection processes refer to the tendency for individuals to seek and avoid situations selectively. Evocation processes refer to the unintentional elicitation of responses from the environment (both the social environment—other people—and the physical environment). Manipulation processes refer to intentional alterations and manipulations of the environments individuals select to inhabit. Clearly, some of the studies we have described from the self-inferences literature fit nicely into this framework. We believe that future researchers should and will investigate additional aspects of self–environment correspondence.

3. Personality Moderators of Self-inferences

Another trend that seems likely to grow in the self-inferences literature is the investigation of personality factors. Given that the "self" is, obviously, an individual differences variable, it may seem paradoxical to talk about personality moderators of self-inferences. Yet, this issue has both a long history and a promising future.

For example, self-esteem is a variable that has been shown to have profound effects on self-inferences and the processing of self-relevant information. Self-esteem is usually conceptualized as a global evaluation of the self, or how favorably one regards oneself (e.g., Janis & Field, 1959; Wylie, 1974; see also Jones, this volume). Thus, self-esteem can be considered part of the self-inferences domain, since it consists of a judgment about the self (namely, an evaluative judgment). But self-esteem also has implications for other kinds of self-inferences. For example, on cognitive, affective, and behavioral measures, high self-esteem individuals have been shown to respond to performance feedback (success and failure) differently than low self-esteem individuals (e.g., Baumeister & Tice, 1985; Baumgardner, Kaufman, & Levy, 1989; Brockner & Hulton, 1978; Swann, Griffin, Predmore, & Gaines, 1987). Thus, the impact of performance feedback on self-conceptions is mediated by self-esteem. (There is also a substantial literature dealing with the effects of depression, which typically involves very low self-esteem, on self-inference processes; see McCann, this volume.)

Achievement motivation is another variable that has been shown to affect self-inferences. As conceptualized by Atkinson (1964; Atkinson & Raynor, 1974), achievement motivation refers to individuals' resultant tendencies either to approach success or to avoid failure. This personality factor has been shown to predict the kinds of settings that people enter, their interest in diagnostic information, their performance on achievement tasks, and their affective and behavioral reactions to success and failure (e.g., see Atkinson & Raynor, 1974; Trope, 1975).

In earlier sections of this chapter, we reviewed work on self-monitoring (Snyder, 1974) and self-consciousness (Fenigstein et al., 1975), two personality variables that are intimately related to self-inference processes. Specifically, these dimensions are associated with individual differences in self-presentational and self-awareness processes, respectively. Also, several contributors to this volume describe data illustrating the impact of other individual differences on self-inference processes, including self-monitoring and self-esteem (Jones), uncertainty orientation (Sorrentino & Roney), and sociotropy-autonomy (McCann).

These various investigations of personality moderators of self-inference processes reflect an increasing recognition of the complexity of the phenomena under study. Consistent with the preceding section, many researchers assume a dynamic interdependence between momentary intrapsychic processes (e.g., self-attributions), stable individual differences (e.g., self-esteem), and situational factors (e.g., failure on a task). We expect more researchers in the future to incorporate personality factors into their self-inference studies, not only the traits just listed but also dimensions that have not yet received any empirical attention.

4. Perceptions of Personal Agency

We borrow the term "personal agency" from Bandura (1982), who has provided a comprehensive analysis of the mechanisms by which people exert influence over what they perceive and do. In this section, however, we limit ourselves to *perceptions* of personal agency, i.e., *beliefs* that one can or does exert influence over one's perceptions and actions. We think that perceptions of personal agency will be a central theme in the self-inferences literature over the next few years.

Actually, perceptions of personal control and agency have interested social psychologists for a long time. Brehm's (1966) reactance theory was concerned with the attitudinal and behavioral consequences of restricting individuals' ability to behave in ways that they had previously considered to be among their "free acts" (i.e., behaviors over which they formerly had perceived agency). Rotter's (1966) locus of control scale was developed to differentiate between individuals who saw their outcomes as being determined primarily by internal factors and those who attributed their outcomes primarily to external forces (see also Lefcourt, 1976). Cognitive behavior modification techniques (e.g., Meichenbaum, 1977) have rested on the assumption that positive self-statements and optimistic thoughts concerning personal agency can have beneficial consequences.

Recently, though, perceived personal agency has really caught fire as a theoretical construct, appearing as a new element in a variety of theories in the self-inferences literature. The spark for this ignition was largely provided by Bandura's work on self-efficacy (e.g., Bandura, 1977, 1982). In a series of experiments, Bandura and his colleagues have documented the diverse effects of perceived self-efficacy (judgments about how well one can organize and execute courses of action). Self-efficacy affects, among other things, the selection of activities, the amount of effort exerted, and the attributions and emotions that occur prior to, during, and after behavior.

Let us provide a few examples of theories that have recently been expanded to include the concept of personal agency. Protection motivation theory (Rogers & Mewborn, 1976) was developed to account for the impact of fear-arousing messages on attitudes. Originally, the theory postulated that threatening messages will be effective to the extent that they convince the listeners of three things: The problem is serious, the listeners are susceptible to the problem, and the recommended actions will effectively avoid the problem. In 1983, Rogers added a fourth determinant of the impact of threatening messages: Listeners must feel personally capable of performing the recommended action (i.e., perceived self-efficacy must be high).

Fishbein and Ajzen's (1975) theory of reasoned action proposed that people's intentions to act in particular ways were determined by their attitudes toward the behavior (their positive or negative feelings about performing the behavior, based on their beliefs concerning the likely consequences of the act) and their subjective norms relevant to the behavior (their feelings of social pressure to perform or not perform the act). In 1985, Ajzen added another determinant of intentions: individuals' perceptions of personal control over the act (whether they feel capable of performing it). Ajzen termed his revised model the theory of planned behavior (see also Warshaw & Davis, 1985).

Weiner's theory of achievement attributions (Weiner et al., 1971) identified two dimensions that underlie attributions for success and failure, namely internal–external and stable–unstable. In a revision of this theory, Weiner (1985) added a third dimension: controllability. Whether individuals attribute their success/failure to a controllable or to an uncontrollable cause has important consequences for their emotional reactions, their expectations for the future, and their behavioral intentions.

We see no reason to believe that personal agency will not receive even more attention in the self-inferences literature over the next few years. Decisions about self-efficacy are fundamental to our motivation to undertake action; therefore, self-inferences often involve judgments about our ability to complete particular behaviors.

5. Adaptive and Maladaptive Self-inferences

Self-inferences can have important consequences for both subjective and objective well-being. For example, individuals' self-conceptions, self-attributions, and perceptions of personal agency can influence their perceived and actual ability to deal effectively with the environment. This assumption has been made in many previous self-inference studies. We have already mentioned in this chapter several investigations that examined the adaptive or maladaptive consequences of self-inferences. Among other things, researchers have studied how self-esteem influences whether people respond constructively to failure feedback (e.g., Brockner & Hulton, 1978), how attributions for success and failure can influence persistence at a task (e.g., Weiner et al., 1971), and how self-schemata may play a role in depression (e.g., Kuiper et al., 1983).

But, similar to perceptions of personal agency, the issue of adaptive versus maladaptive consequences of self-inferences has recently been receiving more attention than ever before. For example, in the present volume, Higgins, Tykocinski, and Vookles discuss the role of self-discrepancies in dejection and agitation, McCann discusses the role of self-inferences in depression and maladaptive interaction styles, and Baumeister discusses the roles of self-awareness and deconstruction in anxiety, masochism, suicide, and other maladaptive behaviors.

Other researchers are also investigating the consequences of self-inferences for coping and well-being. For example, Forsterling (1985, 1988) has written extensively about the implications of attribution processes for clinical psychology, including the role of attributions in loneliness, anxiety, marital distress, reactive depression, and other problems. Anderson and Arnoult (1985) have also focused on the role of attributions, proposing attributional models of depression, loneliness, and shyness. In a similar vein, Abramson, Metalsky, and Alloy (1989) have recently proposed the "hopelessness theory of depression," which hypothesizes that a subtype of reactive depression can result from certain patterns of causal attributions and/or from particular kinds of self-inferences (namely, negative self-deprecating judgments).

On the positive side, Taylor and Brown (1988) have identified several "cognitive illusions," such as exaggerated perceptions of control and undue optimism, that are associated with emotional well-being and productive performance. In action identification theory, Wegner and Vallacher (1986) hypothesized that there are "optimal" levels of identification for effective performance of various actions. For example, relatively easy behaviors are performed best when actors conceptualize the actions in "high-level" terms, such as their goals and implications.

Relatively difficult behaviors are performed best when actors conceptualize the actions in "low-level" terms, such as their molecular and mechanical details.

We suspect that the adaptive and maladaptive consequences of self-inferences will continue to grow in popularity as a research topic over the next few years. In part, expanded interest in this area seems likely because the findings from the self-inferences literature in social psychology are slowly making their way into related areas that involve explicit consideration of adjustment issues, such as clinical and developmental psychology.

Summary

We have identified five general themes or issues that, in our opinion, will receive increased attention in the self-inferences literature. Our predictions are admittedly speculative, and the trends we have described were chosen from a larger pool of possibilities. The most important point to be taken from our analysis is that self-inference processes constitute a vibrant research area, which seems destined to grow in the future.

CONCLUSIONS

Self-inference processes have a distinguished history and, we believe, a bright future in social psychology. Yet, there has not been a recognizable "literature" dealing with this topic. We hope that the present chapter has identified some of the common themes that run throughout self-inference studies. One goal of the symposium and of this book was to stimulate the building of theoretical and conceptual bridges among the diverse topics related to self-inferences. Although the chapters in this volume deal with many different issues, including self-conceptions, self-persuasion, emotional perception, identity, autobiographical memory, self-discrepancies, and self-awareness, all share some fundamental assumptions about self-perception. For example, the social environment is presumed to have a profound effect on self-conceptions, and there is presumed to be a dynamic relation between the self and the environment. These assumptions represent a uniquely social psychological perspective, which has much to contribute to the understanding of self-inferences. In fact, we believe that social psychologists can take the leading role in the study of self-inferences, but integrative models must be developed if this potential is to be realized.

ACKNOWLEDGMENTS

This chapter was prepared while the first author was supported by a research grant from the Social Sciences and Humanities Research Council of Canada and while the second author was supported by a doctoral fellowship from the same agency. We thank Mark P. Zanna for his comments on an earlier version of the chapter. Correspondence can be sent to James M. Olson, Department of Psychology, University of Western Ontario, London, Ontario, Canada N6A 5C2.

REFERENCES

Abramson, L. Y., Metalsky, G. I., & Alloy, L. B. (1989). Hopelessness depression: A theory-based subtype of depression. *Psychological Review, 96*, 358–372.

Abramson, L. Y., Seligman, M. E. P., & Teasdale, J. (1978). Learned helplessness in humans: Critique and reformulation. *Journal of Abnormal Psychology, 87*, 49–74.

Ajzen, I. (1985). From actions to intentions: A theory of planned behavior. In J. Kuhl & J. Beckmann (Eds.), *Action control: From cognition to behavior* (pp. 11–39). New York: Springer–Verlag.

Allen, B. P., & Potkay, C. R. (1981). On the arbitrary distinction between states and traits. *Journal of Personality and Social Psychology, 41*, 916–928.

Anderson, C. A., & Arnoult, L. H. (1985). Attributional models of depression, loneliness, and shyness. In J. H. Harvey & G. Weary (Eds.), *Attribution: Basic issues and applications* (pp. 235–279). New York: Academic Press.

Arkin, R. M. (1980). Self-presentation. In D. M. Wegner & R. R. Vallacher (Eds.), *The self in social psychology*. New York: Oxford University Press.

Atkinson, J. W. (1964). *An introduction to motivation*. Princeton, NJ: Van Nostrand.

Atkinson, J. W., & Raynor, J. O. (1974). *Motivation and achievement*. Washington, DC: Winston.

Backman, C. W., & Secord, P. F. (1968). The self and role selection. In C. Gordon & K. J. Gergen (Eds.), *The self in social interaction*. New York: Wiley.

Bandura, A. (1977). Self-efficacy: Toward a unifying theory of behavioral change. *Psychological Review, 84*, 191–215.

Bandura, A. (1982). The self and mechanisms of agency. In J. Suls (Ed.), *Psychological perspectives on the self* (Vol. 1, pp. 3–39). Hillsdale, NJ: Lawrence Erlbaum Associates.

Bartlett, F. C. (1932). *Remembering: A study in experimental and social psychology*. London: Cambridge University Press.

Baumeister, R. F. (1982). A self-presentational view of social phenomena. *Psychological Bulletin, 91*, 3–26.

Baumeister, R. F., & Tice, D. M. (1985). Self-esteem and responses to success and failure: Subsequent performance and intrinsic motivation. *Journal of Personality, 53*, 450–467.

Baumgardner, A. H., Kaufman, C. M., & Levy, P. E. (1989). Regulating affect interpersonally: When low esteem leads to greater enhancement. *Journal of Personality and Social Psychology, 56*, 907–921.

Beck, A. T. (1967). *Depression: Clinical, experimental, and theoretical aspects*. New York: Harper & Row.

Bem, D. J. (1972). Self-perception theory. In L. Berkowitz (Ed.), *Advances in experimental social psychology* (Vol. 6, pp. 1–62). New York: Academic Press.

Borden, R. J. (1975). Witnessed aggression: Influence of an observer's sex and values on aggressive responding. *Journal of Personality and Social Psychology, 31*, 567–573.

Bower, G. H. (1981). Mood and memory. *American Psychologist, 36*, 129–148.

Bransford, J. D., & Franks, J. J. (1971). The abstraction of linguistic ideas. *Cognitive Psychology, 2*, 331–350.

Brehm, J. W. (1966). *A theory of psychological reactance*. New York: Academic Press.

Brickman, P., & Bulman, R. J. (1977). Pleasure and pain in social comparison. In J. M. Suls & R.

L. Miller (Eds.), *Social comparison processes: Theoretical and empirical perspectives* (pp. 149–186). Washington, DC: Hemisphere.

Brockner, J., & Hulton, A. J. B. (1978). How to reverse the vicious cycle of low self-esteem: The importance of attentional focus. *Journal of Experimental Social Psychology, 14*, 564–578.

Buss, A. H. (1980). *Self-consciousness and social anxiety.* San Francisco: Freeman.

Buss, D. M. (1987). Selection, evocation, and manipulation. *Journal of Personality and Social Psychology, 53*, 1214–1221.

Carver, C. S., & Scheier, M. F. (1981). *Attention and self-regulation: A control-theory approach to human behavior.* New York: Springer–Verlag.

Carver, C. S., & Scheier, M. F. (1987). The blind men and the elephant: Selective examination of the public-private literature gives rise to a faulty perception. *Journal of Personality, 55*, 525–541.

Cooley, C. H. (1902). *Human nature and the social order.* New York: Scribners.

Cooper, J., & Fazio, R. H. (1984). A new look at dissonance theory: In L. Berkowitz (Ed.), *Advances in experimental social psychology* (Vol. 17, pp. 229–266). New York: Academic Press.

Diener, E. (1977). Deindividuation: Causes and consequences. *Social Behavior and Personality, 5*, 143–155.

Diener, E. (1979). Deindividuation, self-awareness, and disinhibition. *Journal of Personality and Social Psychology, 37*, 1160–1171.

Diener, E., & Wallbom, M. (1976). Effects of self-awareness on antinormative behavior. *Journal of Research in Personality, 10*, 107–111.

Duvall, S., & Wicklund, R. A. (1972). *A theory of objective self-awareness.* New York: Academic Press.

Dweck, C. S., & Leggett, E. L. (1988). A social-cognitive approach to motivation and personality. *Psychological Review, 95*, 256–273.

Enzle, M. E. (1980). Self-perception of motivation. In D. M. Wegner & R. R. Vallacher (Eds.), *The self in social psychology* (pp. 55–79). New York: Oxford University Press.

Fazio, R. H., Zanna, M. P., & Cooper, J. (1977). Dissonance and self-perception: An integrative view of each theory's proper domain of application. *Journal of Experimental Social Psychology, 13*, 464–479.

Felson, R. B. (1989). Parents and the reflected appraisal process: A longitudinal analysis. *Journal of Personality and Social Psychology, 56*, 965–971.

Fenigstein, A., Scheier, M. F., & Buss, A. H. (1975). Public and private self-consciousness: Assessment and theory. *Journal of Consulting and Clinical Psychology, 43*, 522–527.

Festinger, L. (1954). A theory of social comparison processes. *Human Relations, 7*, 117–140.

Festinger, L. (1957). *A theory of cognitive dissonance.* Stanford, CA: Stanford University Press.

Fishbein, M., & Ajzen, I. (1975). *Belief, attitude, intention, and behavior: An introduction to theory and research.* Reading, MA: Addison–Wesley.

Forsterling, F. (1985). Attributional retraining: A review. *Psychological Bulletin, 98*, 495–512.

Forsterling, F. (1988). *Attribution theory in clinical psychology.* New York: Wiley.

Freedman, J. L., & Sears, D. O. (1965). Selective exposure. In L. Berkowitz (Ed.), *Advances in experimental social psychology* (Vol. 2, pp. 57–97). New York: Academic Press.

Freud, S. (1925). Repression. In *Collected papers* (Vol. 4). London: Hogarth Press.

Frey, D. (1986). Recent research on selective exposure to information. In L. Berkowitz (Ed.), *Advances in experimental social psychology* (Vol. 19, pp. 41–80). New York: Academic Press.

Fries, A., & Frey, D. (1980). Misattribution of arousal and the effects of self-threatening information. *Journal of Experimental Social Psychology, 16*, 405–416.

Froming, W. J., Walker, G. R., & Lopyan, K. J. (1982). Public and private self-awareness: When personal attitudes conflict with societal expectations. *Journal of Experimental Social Psychology, 18*, 476–487.

Gergen, K. J. (1971). *The concept of self.* New York: Holt, Rinehart, & Winston.

Goethals, G. R. (1986). Social comparison theory: Psychology from the lost and found. *Personality and Social Psychology Bulletin, 12,* 261–278.

Goethals, G. R., & Darley, J. M. (1977). Social comparison theory: An attributional approach. In J. M. Suls & R. L. Miller (Eds.), *Social comparison processes: Theoretical and empirical perspectives* (pp. 259–278). Washington, DC: Hemisphere.

Goethals, G. R., & Reckman, R. F. (1973). The perception of consistency in attitudes. *Journal of Experimental Social Psychology, 9,* 491–501.

Goffman, E. (1959). *The presentation of self in everyday life.* Garden City, NY: Doubleday.

Greenberg, J. (1982). Self-image versus impression management in adherence to distributive justice standards: The influence of self-awareness and self-consciousness. *Journal of Personality and Social Psychology, 44,* 5–19.

Greenwald, A. G. (1980). The totalitarian ego: Fabrication and revision of personal history. *American Psychologist, 35,* 603–618.

Harvey, J. H., & Weary, G. (1984). Current issues in attribution theory and research. *Annual Review of Psychology, 35,* 427–459.

Hastie, R. (1981). Schematic principles in human memory. In E. T. Higgins, C. P. Herman, & M. P. Zanna (Eds.), *Social cognition: The Ontario symposium* (Vol. 1, pp. 39–88). Hillsdale, NJ: Lawrence Erlbaum Associates.

Heider, F. (1958). *The psychology of interpersonal relations.* New York: Wiley.

Higgins, E. T. (1981). The "communication game": Implications for social cognition and persuasion. In E. T. Higgins, C. P. Herman, & M. P. Zanna (Eds.), *Social cognition: The Ontario symposium* (Vol. 1, pp. 343–392). Hillsdale, NJ: Lawrence Erlbaum Associates.

Hull, J. G. (1981). A self-awareness model of the causes and effects of alcohol consumption. *Journal of Abnormal Psychology, 90,* 586–600.

Isen, A. M., Shalker, T. E., Clark, M. S., & Karp, L. (1978). Affect, accessibility of material in memory, and behavior: A cognitive loop? *Journal of Personality and Social Psychology, 36,* 1–12.

Janis, I. L., & Field, P. B. (1959). Sex differences and personality factors related to persuasibility. In C. I. Hovland & I. L. Janis (Eds.), *Personality and persuasibility.* New Haven, CT: Yale University Press.

Jones, E. E. (1964). *Ingratiation.* New York: Appleton–Century–Crofts.

Jones, E. E. (1979). The rocky road from acts to dispositions. *American Psychologist, 34,* 107–117.

Jones, E. E., & Berglas, S. C. (1978). Control of attributions about the self through self-handicapping strategies: The appeal of alcohol and the role of underachievement. *Personality and Social Psychology Bulletin, 4,* 200–206.

Jones, E. E., & Gerard, H. B. (1967). *Foundations of social psychology.* New York: Wiley.

Jones, E. E., & Nisbett, R. E. (1971). *The actor and the observer: Divergent perceptions of the causes of behavior.* Morristown, NJ: General Learning Press.

Jones, E. E., & Pittman, T. S. (1982). Toward a general theory of strategic self-presentation. In J. Suls (Ed.), *Psychological perspectives on the self* (Vol. 1, pp. 231–262). Hillsdale, NJ: Lawrence Erlbaum Associates.

Jones, S. C. (1973). Self- and interpersonal evaluations: Esteem theories versus consistency theories. *Psychological Bulletin, 79,* 185–199.

Katz, D. (1960). The functional approach to the study of attitudes. *Public Opinion Quarterly, 24,* 163–204.

Kelley, H. H. (1967). Attribution theory in social psychology. In D. Levine (Ed.), *Nebraska symposium on motivation* (pp. 192–240). Lincoln: University of Nebraska Press.

King, B. T., & Janis, I. L. (1956). Comparison of the effectiveness of improvised versus non-improvised role-playing in producing opinion change. *Human Relations, 9,* 177–186.

Kuiper, N. A., MacDonald, M. R., & Derry, P. A. (1983). Parameters of a depressive self-schema. In J. Suls & A. G. Greenwald (Eds.), *Psychological perspectives on the self* (Vol. 2, pp. 191–217). Hillsdale, NJ: Lawrence Erlbaum Associates.

Kuiper, N. A., Olinger, L. J., & MacDonald, M. R. (1988). Vulnerability and episodic cognitions in a self-worth contingency model of depression. In L. B. Alloy (Ed.), *Cognitive processes in depression* (pp. 289–309). New York: Guilford.

Kunda, Z., & Sanitioso, R. (1989). Motivated changes in the self-concept. *Journal of Experimental Social Psychology, 25,* 272–285.

Lauer, R. H., & Handel, W. H. (1983). *Social psychology: The theory and application of symbolic interactionism* (2nd ed.). Englewood Cliffs, NJ: Prentice–Hall.

Lefcourt, H. M. (1976). *Locus of control: Current trends in theory and research.* Hillsdale, NJ: Lawrence Erlbaum Associates.

Lepper, M. R., & Greene, D. (Eds.). (1978). *The hidden costs of reward: New perspectives on the psychology of human motivation.* Hillsdale, NJ: Lawrence Erlbaum Associates.

Markus, H. (1977). Self-schemata and processing information about the self. *Journal of Personality and Social Psychology, 35,* 63–78.

Markus, H., & Kunda, Z. (1986). Stability and malleability of the self-concept. *Journal of Personality and Social Psychology, 51,* 858–866.

Markus, H., & Nurius, P. (1986). Possible selves. *American Psychologist, 41,* 954–969.

Markus, H., & Sentis, K. (1982). The self in social information processing. In J. Suls (Ed.), *Psychological perspectives on the self* (Vol. 1, pp. 41–70). Hillsdale, NJ: Lawrence Erlbaum Associates.

McGuire, W. J., & McGuire, C. V. (1982). Significant others in self-space: Sex differences and developmental trends in the social self. In J. Suls (Ed.), *Psychological perspectives on the self* (Vol. 1, pp. 71–96). Hillsdale, NJ: Lawrence Erlbaum Associates.

McGuire, W. J., McGuire, C. V., & Winton, W. (1979). Effects of household sex composition on the salience of one's gender in the spontaneous self-concept. *Journal of Experimental Social Psychology, 15,* 77–90.

Mead, G. H. (1934). *Mind, self, and society.* Chicago: University of Chicago Press.

Meichenbaum, D. H. (1977). *Cognitive-behavior modification: An integrative approach.* New York: Plenum.

Merton, R. K., & Kitt, A. S. (1950). Contributions to the theory of reference group behavior. In R. K. Merton & P. F. Lazarsfeld (Eds.), *Continuities in social research: Studies in the scope and method of "The American Soldier"* (pp. 40–105). Glencoe, IL: Free Press.

Nisbett, R. E., & Wilson, T. D. (1977). Telling more than we can know: Verbal reports on mental processes. *Psychological Review, 84,* 231–259.

Olson, J. M. (1988). Misattribution, preparatory information, and speech anxiety. *Journal of Personality and Social Psychology, 54,* 758–767.

Olson, J. M., & Cal, A. V. (1984). Source credibility, attitude, and the recall of past behaviours. *European Journal of Social Psychology, 14,* 203–210.

Olson, J. M., Hafer, C. L., Cousens, A., & Kramins, I. S. (1989). *Self-presentation motives in reports of resentment about deprivation.* Unpublished manuscript, University of Western Ontario, London, Ontario.

Olson, J. M. & Hazlewood, J. D. (1986). Relative deprivation and social comparison: An integrative perspective. In J. M. Olson, C. P. Herman, & M. P. Zanna (Eds.), *Relative deprivation and social comparison: The Ontario symposium* (Vol. 4, pp. 1–15). Hillsdale, NJ: Lawrence Erlbaum Associates.

Olson, J. M., & Ross, M. (1985). Attribution research: Past contributions, current trends, and future prospects. In J. H. Harvey & G. Weary (Eds.), *Attribution: Basic issues and applications* (pp. 283–311). New York: Academic Press.

Olson, J. M., & Zanna, M. P. (in press). Attitude change and attitude-behavior consistency. In R. M. Baron & W. G. Graziano (Eds.), *Social psychology* (2nd ed.). New York: Holt, Rinehart, & Winston.

Prentice–Dunn, S., & Rogers, R. W. (1983). Deindividuation in aggression. In R. G. Geen & E. I. Donnerstein (Eds.), *Aggression: Theoretical and empirical reviews: Vol. 2. Issues in research* (pp. 155–171). New York: Academic Press.

Reis, H. T. (1981). Self-presentation and distributive justice. In J. T. Tedeschi (Ed.), *Impression management theory and social psychological research* (pp. 269–291). New York: Academic Press.

Rogers, R. W. (1983). Cognitive and physiological processes in fear appeals and attitude change: A revised theory of protection motivation. In J. T. Cacioppo & R. E. Petty (Eds.), *Social psychophysiology*. New York: Guilford.

Rogers, R. W., & Mewborn, C. R. (1976). Fear appeals and attitude change: Effects of a threat's noxiousness, probability of occurrence, and the efficacy of coping responses. *Journal of Personality and Social Psychology, 34,* 54–61.

Rogers, T. B., Kuiper, N. A., & Kirker, W. S. (1977). Self reference and the encoding of personal information. *Journal of Personality and Social Psychology, 35,* 677–688.

Ross, M. (1989). Relation of implicit theories to the construction of personal histories. *Psychological Review, 96,* 341–157.

Ross, M., & Fletcher, G. J. O. (1985). Attribution and social perception. In G. Lindzey & E. Aronson (Eds.), *The handbook of social psychology* (3rd ed., Vol. 2, pp. 73–122). New York: Random House.

Ross, M., McFarland, C., & Fletcher, G. J. O. (1981). The effect of attitude on the recall of personal histories. *Journal of Personality and Social Psychology, 10,* 627–634.

Rotter, J. B. (1966). Generalized expectancies for internal versus external control of reinforcement. *Psychological Monographs, 80*(Whole No. 609).

Sadler, O., & Tesser, A. (1973). Some effects of salience and time upon interpersonal hostility and attraction during social isolation. *Sociometry, 36,* 99–112.

Salancik, G. R. (1974). Inference of one's attitude from behavior recalled under linguistically manipulated cognitive sets. *Journal of Experimental Social Psychology, 10,* 415–427.

Satow, K. (1975). Social approval and helping. *Journal of Experimental Social Psychology, 11,* 501–509.

Schachter, S. (1964). The interaction of cognitive and physiological determinants of emotional state. In L. Berkowitz (Ed.), *Advances in experimental social psychology* (Vol. 1, pp. 48–81). New York: Academic Press.

Scheier, M. F., & Carver, C. S. (1983). Two sides of the self: One for you and one for me. In J. Suls & A. G. Greenwald (Eds.), *Psychological perspectives on the self* (Vol. 2, pp. 123–157). Hillsdale, NJ: Lawrence Erlbaum Associates.

Schlenker, B. R. (1980). *Impression management: The self-concept, social identity, and interpersonal relations*. Monterey, CA: Brooks–Cole.

Secord, P. F., & Backman, C. W. (1965). An interpersonal approach to personality. In B. A. Maher (Ed.), *Progress in experimental personality research* (Vol. 2, pp. 91–125). New York: Academic Press.

Shibutani, T. (1961). *Society and personality: An interactionist approach to social psychology*. Englewood Cliffs, NJ: Prentice-Hall.

Skov, R. B., & Sherman, S. J. (1986). Information-gathering processes: Diagnosticity, hypothesis-confirmatory strategies, and perceived hypothesis confirmation. *Journal of Experimental Social Psychology, 22,* 93–121.

Snyder, M. (1974). Self-monitoring of expressive behavior. *Journal of Personality and Social Psychology, 30,* 526–537.

Snyder, M. (1981). Seek, and ye shall find: Testing hypotheses about other people. In E. T. Higgins, C. P. Herman, & M. P. Zanna (Eds.), *Social cognition: The Ontario symposium* (Vol. 1, pp. 277–303). Hillsdale, NJ: Lawrence Erlbaum Associates.

Snyder, M. (1984). When belief creates reality. In L. Berkowitz (Ed.), *Advances in experimental social psychology* (Vol. 18, pp. 247–305). New York: Academic Press.

Snyder, M. (1987). *Public appearances/private realities: The psychology of self-monitoring.* New York: W. H. Freeman.

Snyder, M., & Gangestad, S. (1986). On the nature of self-monitoring: Matters of assessment, matters of validity. *Journal of Personality and Social Psychology, 51,* 125–139.

Strube, M. J., Lott, C. L., Le–Xuan–Hy, G. M., Oxenberg, J., & Deichmann, A. K. (1986). Self-evaluation of abilities: Accurate self-assessment versus biased self-enhancement. *Journal of Personality and Social Psychology, 51,* 16–25.

Swann, W. B., Jr. (1983). Self-verification: Bringing social reality into harmony with the self. In J. Suls & A. G. Greenwald (Eds.), *Psychological perspectives on the self* (Vol. 2, pp. 33–66). Hillsdale, NJ: Lawrence Erlbaum Associates.

Swann, W. B., Jr. (1987). Identity negotiation: Where two roads meet. *Journal of Personality and Social Psychology, 53,* 1038–1051.

Swann, W. B., Jr., Griffin, J. J., Jr., Predmore, S. C., & Gaines, B. (1987). The cognitive-affective crossfire: When self-consistency confronts self-enhancement. *Journal of Personality and Social Psychology, 52,* 881–889.

Taylor, S. E., & Brown, J. D. (1988). Illusion and well-being: A social psychological perspective on mental health. *Psychological Bulletin, 103,* 193–210.

Taylor, S. E., & Crocker, J. (1981). Schematic bases of social information processing. In E. T. Higgins, C. P. Herman, & M. P. Zanna (Eds.), *Social cognition: The Ontario symposium* (Vol. 1, pp. 89–134). Hillsdale, NJ: Lawrence Erlbaum Associates.

Tedeschi, J. T. (Ed.). (1981). *Impression management theory and social psychological research.* New York: Academic Press.

Tedeschi, J. T., Schlenker, B. R., & Bonoma, T. V. (1971). Cognitive dissonance: Private ratiocination or public spectacle? *American Psychologist, 26,* 685–695.

Tesser, A. (1978). Self-generated attitude change. In L. Berkowitz (Ed.), *Advances in experimental social psychology* (Vol. 11, pp. 289–338). New York: Academic Press.

Tesser, A., & Campbell, J. (1983). Self-definition and self-evaluation maintenance. In J. Suls & A. G. Greenwald (Eds.), *Psychological perspectives on the self* (Vol. 2, pp. 1–31). Hillsdale, NJ: Lawrence Erlbaum Associates.

Tetlock, P. E., & Manstead, A. S. R. (1985). Impression management versus intrapsychic explanations in social psychology: A useful dichotomy? *Psychological Review, 92,* 59–77.

Trope, Y. (1975). Seeking information about one's own ability as a determinant of choice among tasks. *Journal of Personality and Social Psychology, 32,* 1004–1013.

Trope, Y. (1983). Self-assessment in achievement behavior. In J. Suls & A. G. Greenwald (Eds.), *Psychological perspectives on the self* (Vol. 2, pp. 93–121). Hillsdale, NJ: Lawrence Erlbaum Associates.

Trope, Y. (1986). Self-enhancement and self-assessment in achievement behavior. In R. M. Sorrentino & E. T. Higgins (Eds.), *Handbook of motivation and cognition: Foundations of social behavior* (pp. 350–378). New York: Guilford.

Trope, Y., & Bassok, M. (1983). Information-gathering strategies in hypothesis-testing. *Journal of Experimental Social Psychology, 19,* 560–576.

Videbeck, R. (1960). Self-conception and the reaction of others. *Sociometry, 23,* 351–362.

Warshaw, P. R., & Davis, F. D. (1985). Disentangling behavioral intention and behavioral expectation. *Journal of Experimental Social Psychology, 21,* 213–228.

Wegner, D. M., & Vallacher, R. R. (1986). Action identification. In R. M. Sorrentino & E. T. Higgins (Eds.), *Handbook of motivation and cognition: Foundations of social behavior* (pp. 550–582). New York: Guilford.

Weiner, B. (1985). An attributional theory of achievement motivation and emotion. *Psychological Review, 92,* 548–573.

Weiner, B., Frieze, I. H., Kukla, A., Reed, L., Rest, S., & Rosenbaum, R. M. (1971). *Perceiving the causes of success and failure.* Morristown, NJ: General Learning Press.

Wicklund, R. A., & Gollwitzer, P. M. (1987). The fallacy of the public-private self-focus distinction. *Journal of Personality, 55,* 491–523.

Wills, T. A. (1981). Downward comparison principles in social psychology. *Psychological Bulletin, 90,* 245–271.

Wills, T. A. (1986). Downward comparison as a coping mechanism. In C. R. Snyder & C. Ford (Eds.), *Coping with negative life events: Clinical and social-psychological perspectives.* New York: Plenum.

Wilson, T. D. (1985). Strangers to ourselves: The origins and accuracy of beliefs about one's own mental states. In J. H. Harvey & G. Weary (Eds.), *Attribution: Basic issues and applications* (pp. 9–36). New York: Academic Press.

Wood, J. V. (in press). Theory and research concerning social comparisons of personal attributes. *Psychological Bulletin.*

Wylie, R. C. (1974). *The self concept: A review of methodological considerations and measuring instruments* (2nd ed., Vol. 1). Lincoln: University of Nebraska Press.

Zanna, M. P., Goethals, G. R., & Hill, J. F. (1975). Evaluating a sex-related ability: Social comparison with similar others and standard setters. *Journal of Experimental Social Psychology, 11,* 86–93.

Zimbardo, P. G. (1970). The human choice: Individuation, reason, and order versus deindividuation, impulse, and chaos. In W. J. Arnold & D. Levine (Eds.), *Nebraska symposium on motivation* (Vol. 17, pp. 237–307). Lincoln: University of Nebraska Press.

Zuckerman, M. (1979). Attribution of success and failure revisited, or: The motivational bias is alive and well in attribution theory. *Journal of Personality, 47,* 245–287.

Author Index

Subject Index